Goong

vol.1

Park SoHee

Yen Press

About the Creator

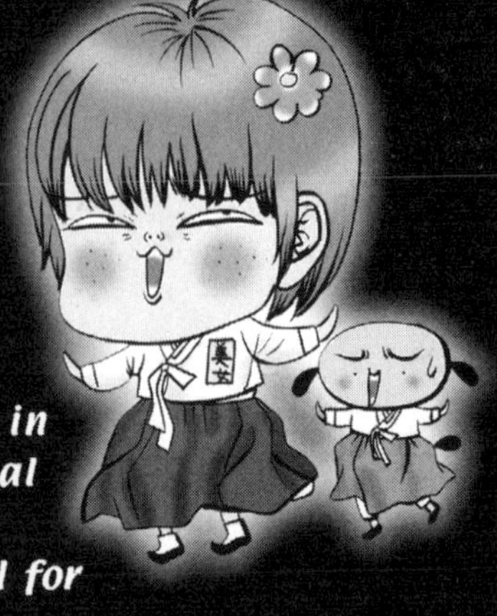

So-Hee Park

Birthday : March 24, 1978.

She graduated with a major in Manhwa from Gongjoo Cultural University.
She won Seoul Media's Silver Medal for "Best New Manhwa Creator" in 2000.

Major works : <Real Purple>, <Goong - The Royal Palace>

* Read more about the creator in the special interview at the end of the book!!

Words from the Creator

Oh my god... I wasn't very skillful when I first took out that blank paper and Chinese ink and began drawing <Goong - The Royal Palace> back in high school. My classmates were the only people to read it at the time. So, I never imagined that something I created when I was a high school student would make it into <WINK> magazine and be published as a manhwa book series. I guess my dream came true! Thank you so much to all the editors, especially editor Yoon (congratulations on the good news!). Also thanks to my friends who lifted my spirits when I was blue. Lastly, thank you, readers! (I'll stop here because II'll sound like Miss Korea giving a speech if I thank anymore people.)

So-Hee Park

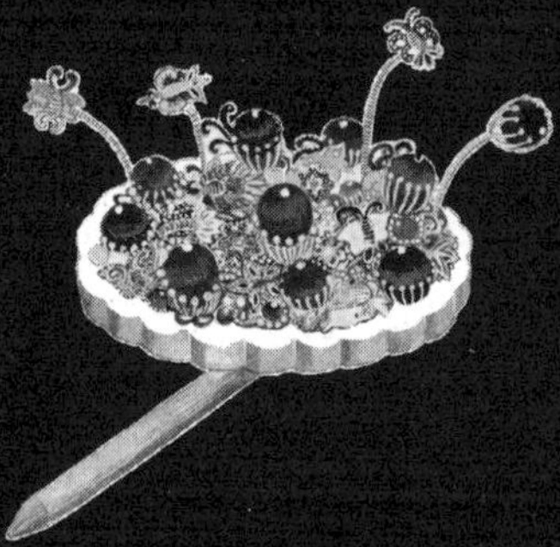

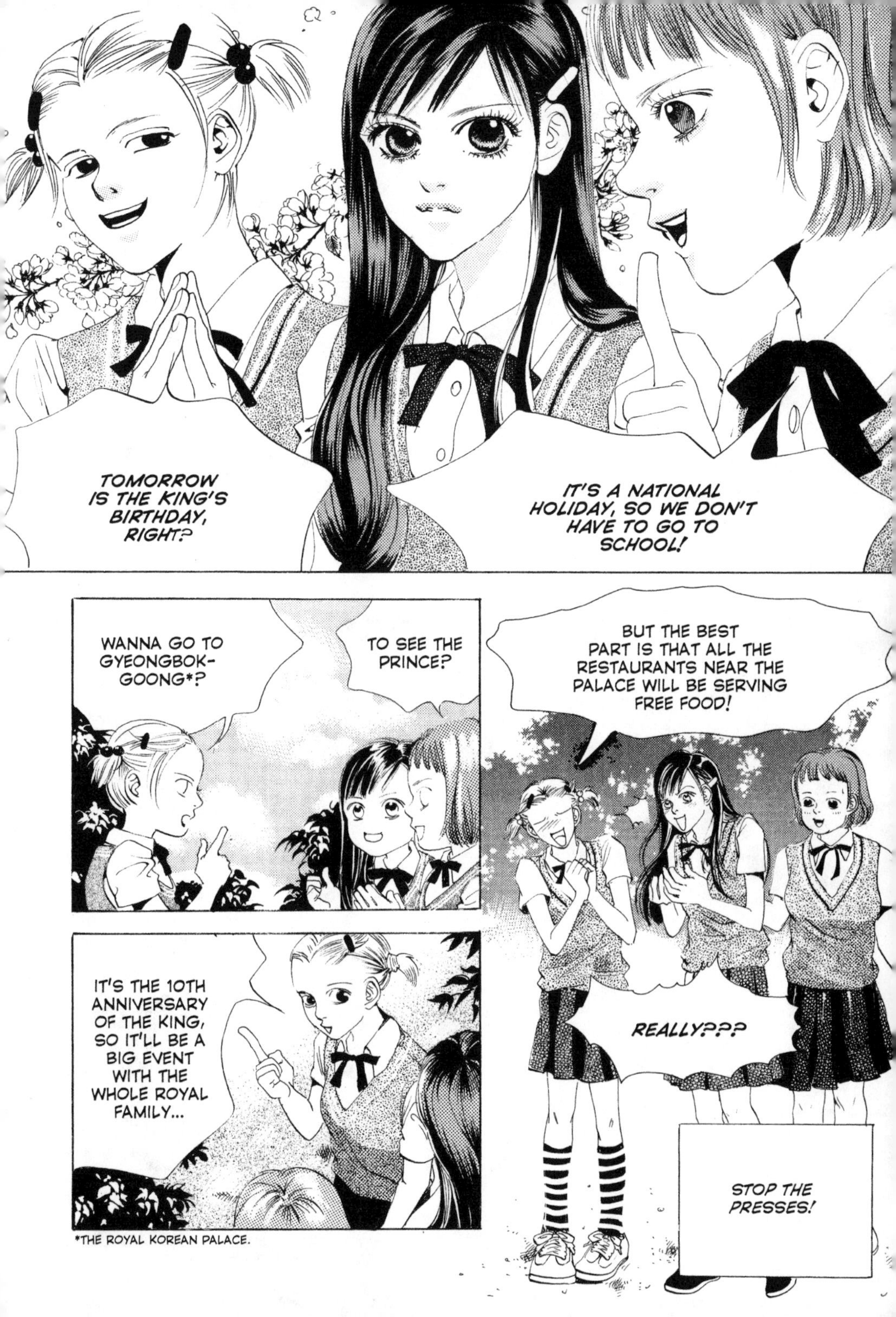
TOMORROW IS THE KING'S BIRTHDAY, RIGHT?
IT'S A NATIONAL HOLIDAY, SO WE DON'T HAVE TO GO TO SCHOOL!
WANNA GO TO GYEONGBOK-GOONG*?
TO SEE THE PRINCE?
IT'S THE 10TH ANNIVERSARY OF THE KING, SO IT'LL BE A BIG EVENT WITH THE WHOLE ROYAL FAMILY...
BUT THE BEST PART IS THAT ALL THE RESTAURANTS NEAR THE PALACE WILL BE SERVING FREE FOOD!
REALLY???
STOP THE PRESSES!

*THE ROYAL KOREAN PALACE.

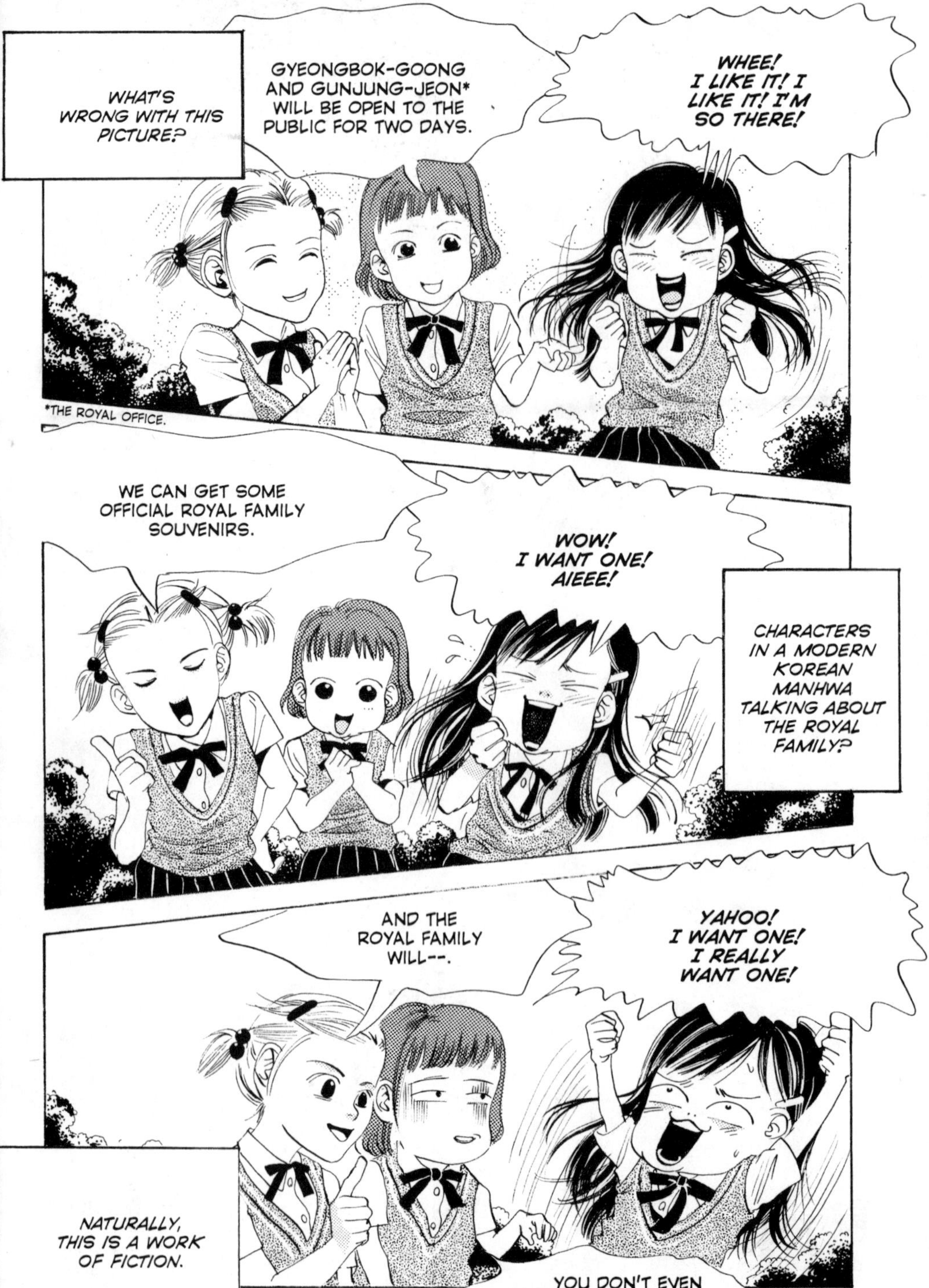
WHAT'S WRONG WITH THIS PICTURE?
GYEONGBOK-GOONG AND GUNJUNG-JEON* WILL BE OPEN TO THE PUBLIC FOR TWO DAYS.
WHEE! I LIKE IT! I LIKE IT! I'M SO THERE!
*THE ROYAL OFFICE.
WE CAN GET SOME OFFICIAL ROYAL FAMILY SOUVENIRS.
WOW! I WANT ONE! AIEEE!
CHARACTERS IN A MODERN KOREAN MANHWA TALKING ABOUT THE ROYAL FAMILY?
AND THE ROYAL FAMILY WILL--.
YAHOO! I WANT ONE! I REALLY WANT ONE!
NATURALLY, THIS IS A WORK OF FICTION.
YOU DON'T EVEN KNOW WHAT IT IS...

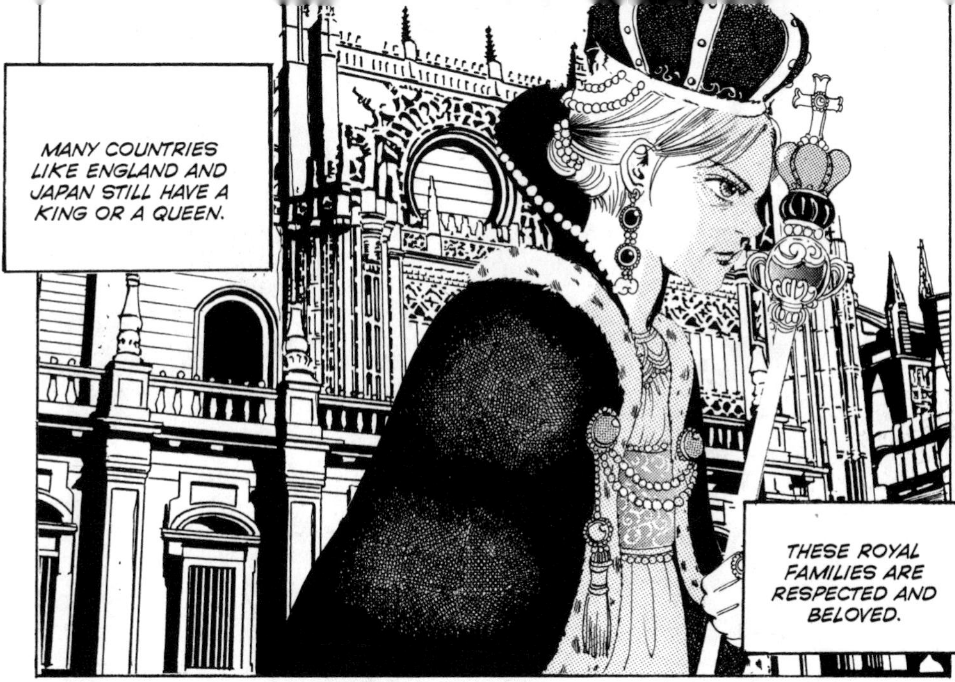
MANY COUNTRIES LIKE ENGLAND AND JAPAN STILL HAVE A KING OR A QUEEN.
THESE ROYAL FAMILIES ARE RESPECTED AND BELOVED.

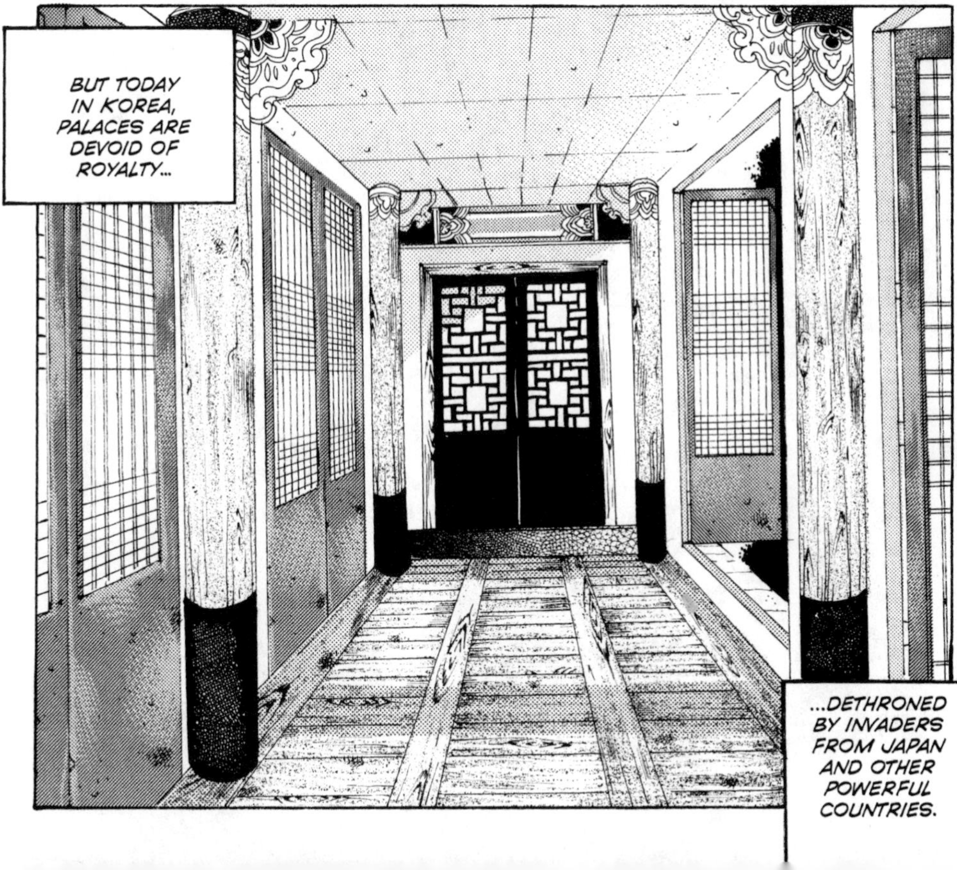
BUT TODAY IN KOREA, PALACES ARE DEVOID OF ROYALTY...
...DETHRONED BY INVADERS FROM JAPAN AND OTHER POWERFUL COUNTRIES.

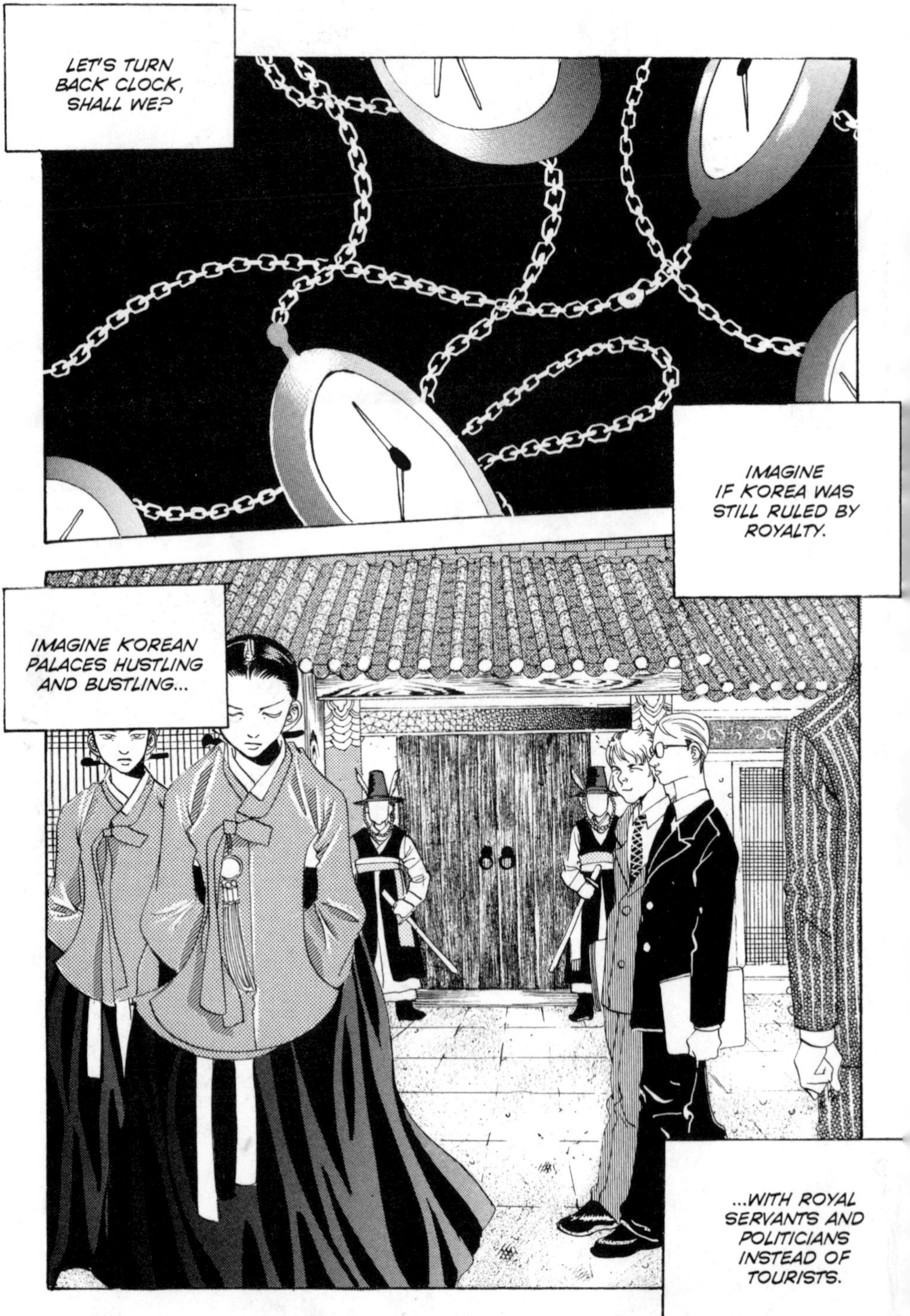
LET'S TURN BACK CLOCK, SHALL WE?
IMAGINE IF KOREA WAS STILL RULED BY ROYALTY.
IMAGINE KOREAN PALACES HUSTLING AND BUSTLING...
...WITH ROYAL SERVANTS AND POLITICIANS INSTEAD OF TOURISTS.

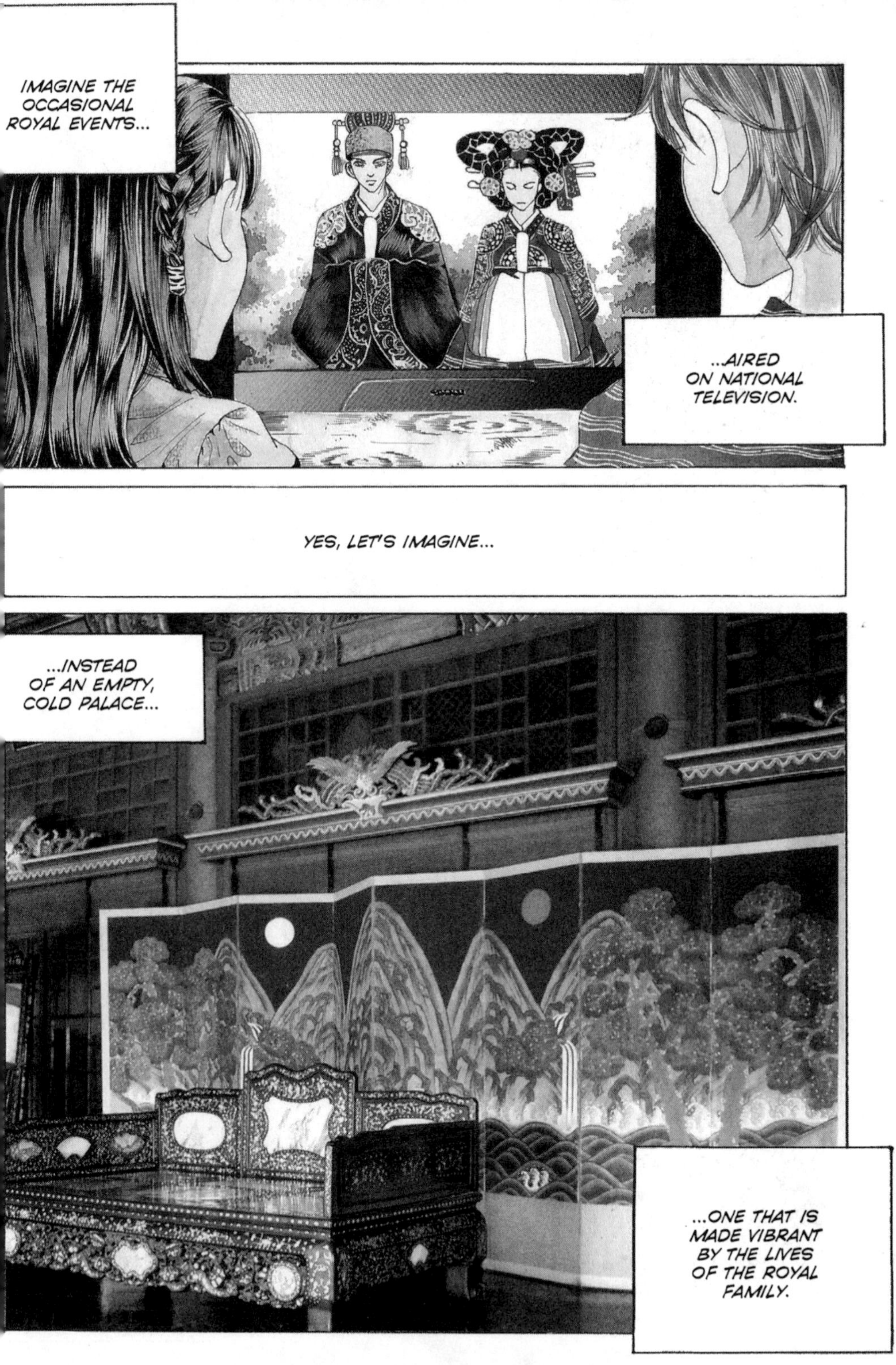
IMAGINE THE OCCASIONAL ROYAL EVENTS...
...AIRED ON NATIONAL TELEVISION.
YES, LET'S IMAGINE...
...INSTEAD OF AN EMPTY, COLD PALACE...
...ONE THAT IS MADE VIBRANT BY THE LIVES OF THE ROYAL FAMILY.

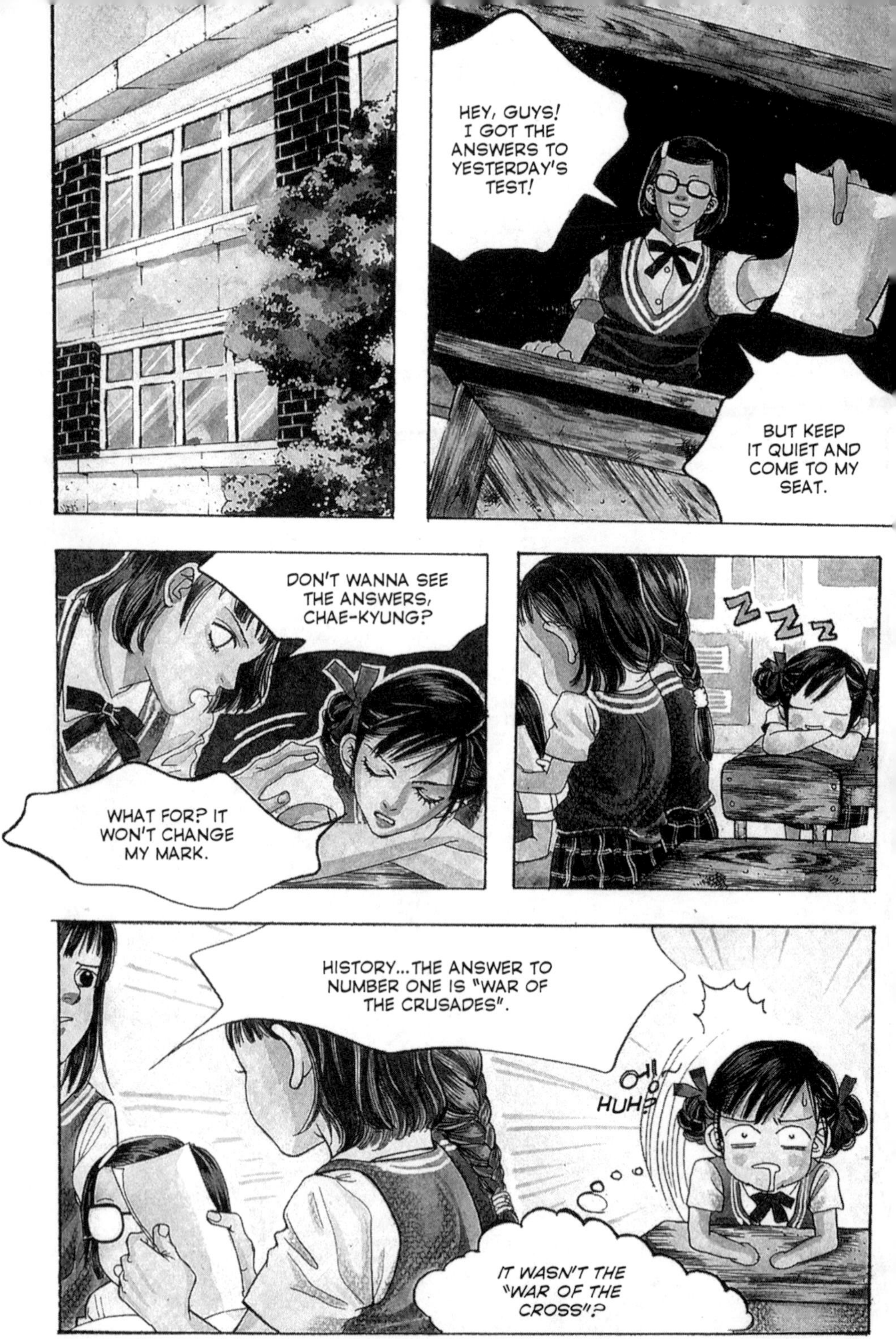
HEY, GUYS! I GOT THE ANSWERS TO YESTERDAY'S TEST!
BUT KEEP IT QUIET AND COME TO MY SEAT.
DON'T WANNA SEE THE ANSWERS, CHAE-KYUNG?
WHAT FOR? IT WON'T CHANGE MY MARK.
ZZZ
HISTORY...THE ANSWER TO NUMBER ONE IS "WAR OF THE CRUSADES".
HUH?
IT WASN'T THE "WAR OF THE CROSS"?

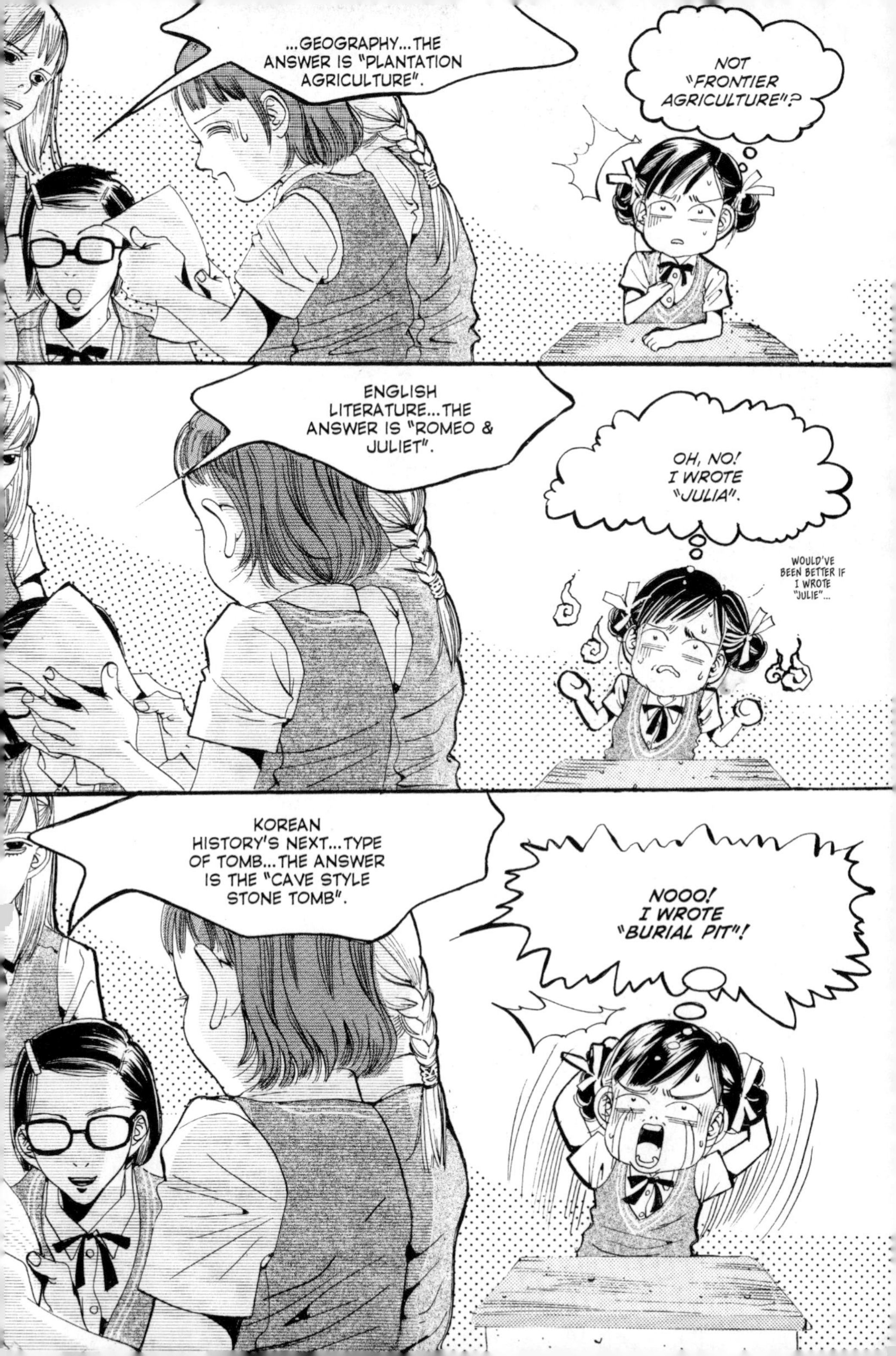
...GEOGRAPHY...THE ANSWER IS "PLANTATION AGRICULTURE".
NOT "FRONTIER AGRICULTURE"?
ENGLISH LITERATURE...THE ANSWER IS "ROMEO & JULIET".
OH, NO! I WROTE "JULIA".
WOULD'VE BEEN BETTER IF I WROTE "JULIE"...
KOREAN HISTORY'S NEXT...TYPE OF TOMB...THE ANSWER IS THE "CAVE STYLE STONE TOMB".
NOOO! I WROTE "BURIAL PIT"!

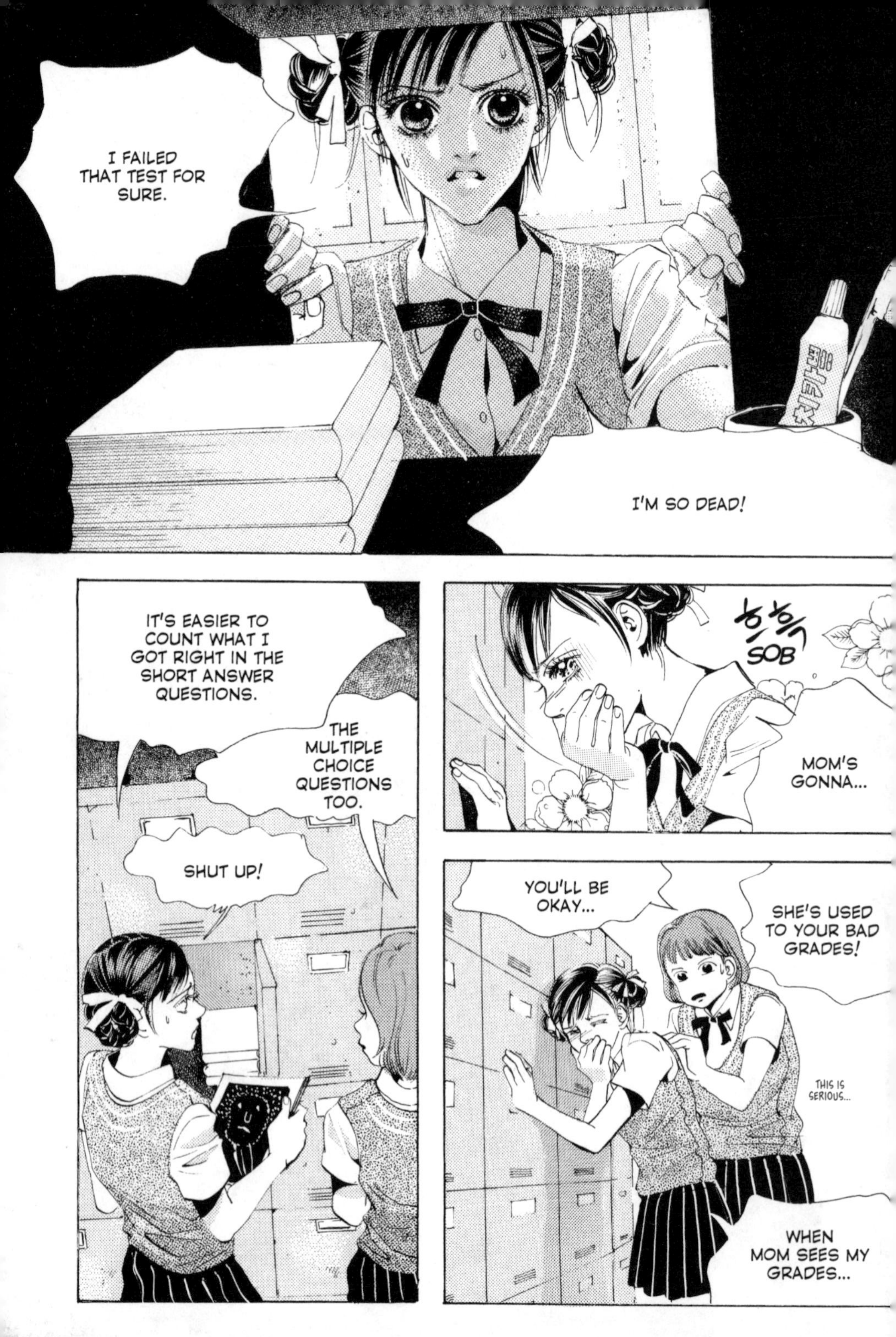
I FAILED THAT TEST FOR SURE.
I'M SO DEAD!
IT'S EASIER TO COUNT WHAT I GOT RIGHT IN THE SHORT ANSWER QUESTIONS.
THE MULTIPLE CHOICE QUESTIONS TOO.
SHUT UP!
SOB
MOM'S GONNA...
YOU'LL BE OKAY...
SHE'S USED TO YOUR BAD GRADES!
THIS IS SERIOUS...
WHEN MOM SEES MY GRADES...

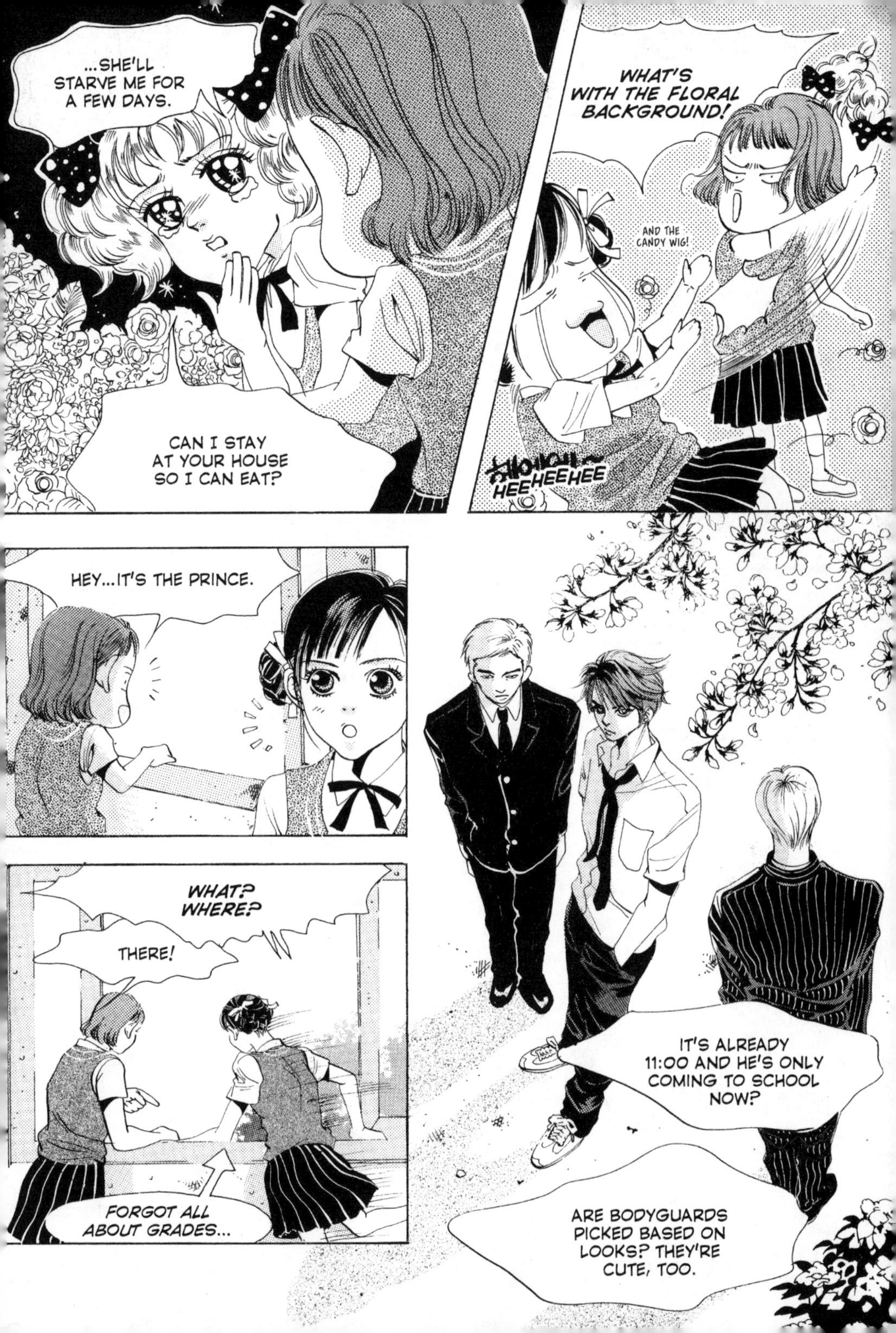
...SHE'LL STARVE ME FOR A FEW DAYS.
CAN I STAY AT YOUR HOUSE SO I CAN EAT?
WHAT'S WITH THE FLORAL BACKGROUND!
AND THE CANDY WIG!
HEEHEEHEE
HEY...IT'S THE PRINCE.
WHAT? WHERE?
THERE!
FORGOT ALL ABOUT GRADES...
IT'S ALREADY 11:00 AND HE'S ONLY COMING TO SCHOOL NOW?
ARE BODYGUARDS PICKED BASED ON LOOKS? THEY'RE CUTE, TOO.

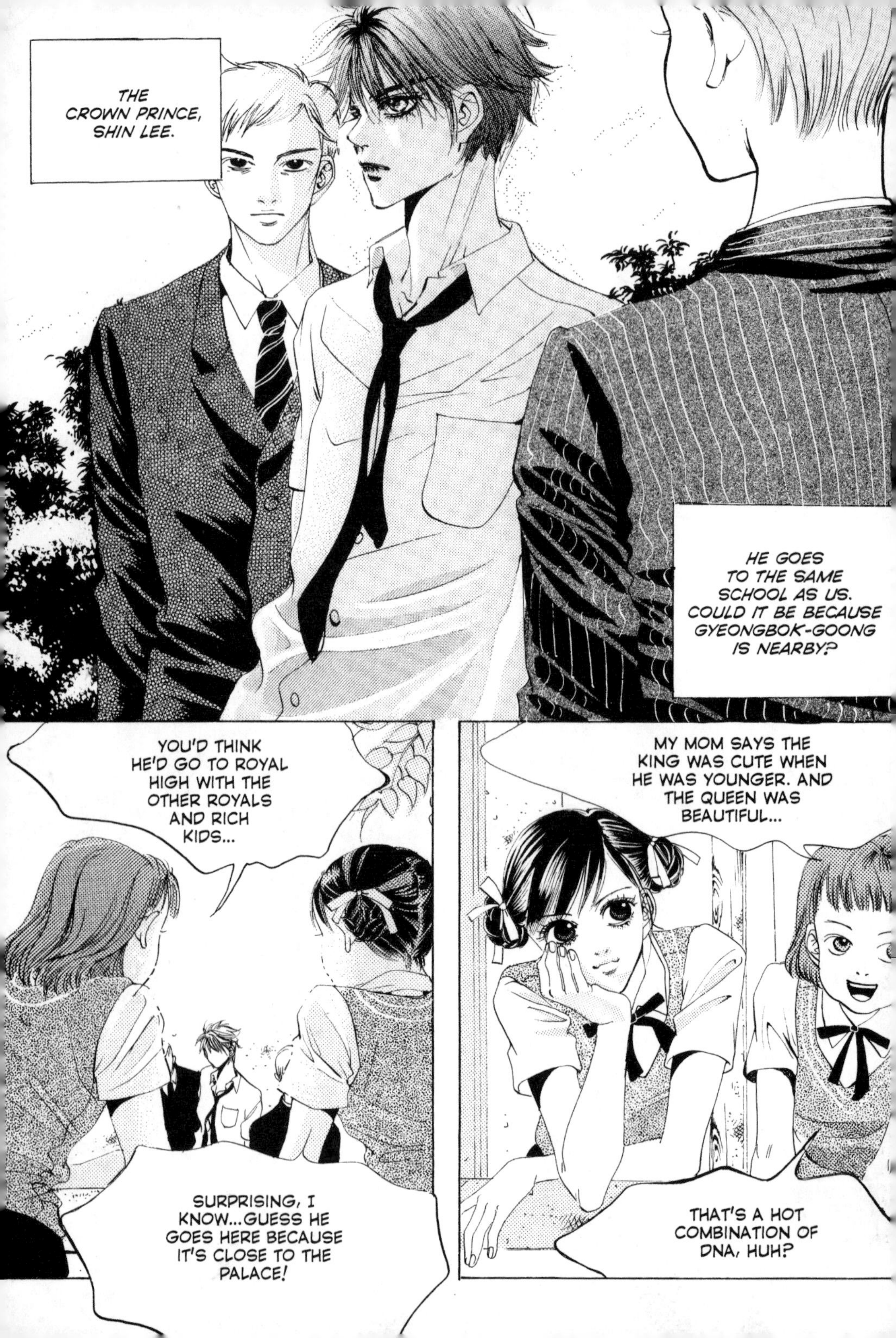
THE CROWN PRINCE, SHIN LEE.
HE GOES TO THE SAME SCHOOL AS US. COULD IT BE BECAUSE GYEONGBOK-GOONG IS NEARBY?
YOU'D THINK HE'D GO TO ROYAL HIGH WITH THE OTHER ROYALS AND RICH KIDS...
SURPRISING, I KNOW...GUESS HE GOES HERE BECAUSE IT'S CLOSE TO THE PALACE!
MY MOM SAYS THE KING WAS CUTE WHEN HE WAS YOUNGER. AND THE QUEEN WAS BEAUTIFUL...
THAT'S A HOT COMBINATION OF DNA, HUH?

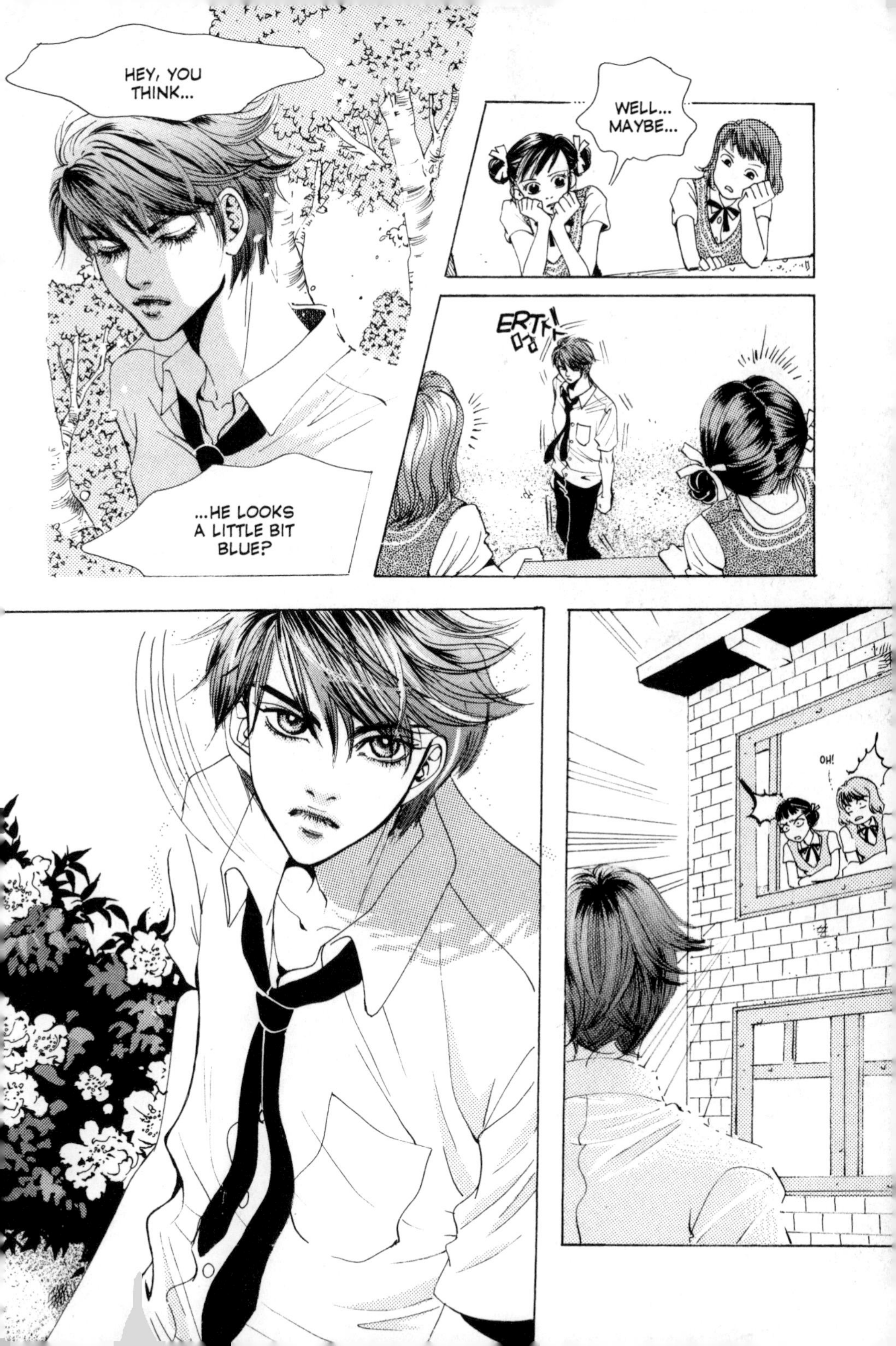
HEY, YOU THINK...
...HE LOOKS A LITTLE BIT BLUE?
WELL... MAYBE...
ERTK!
OH!

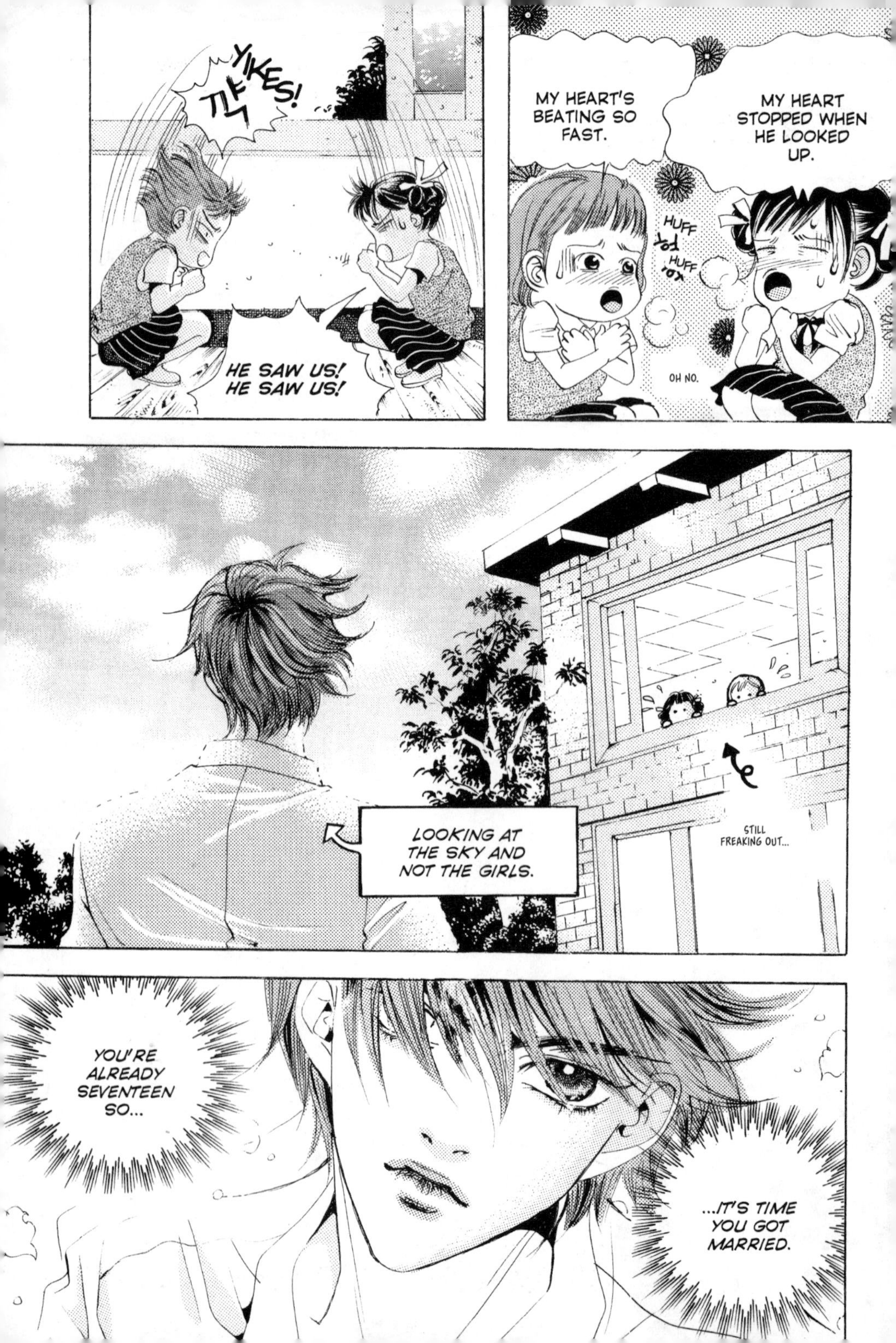
YIKES!
HE SAW US! HE SAW US!
MY HEART'S BEATING SO FAST.
MY HEART STOPPED WHEN HE LOOKED UP.
HUFF
HUFF
OH NO.
LOOKING AT THE SKY AND NOT THE GIRLS.
STILL FREAKING OUT...
YOU'RE ALREADY SEVENTEEN SO...
...IT'S TIME YOU GOT MARRIED.

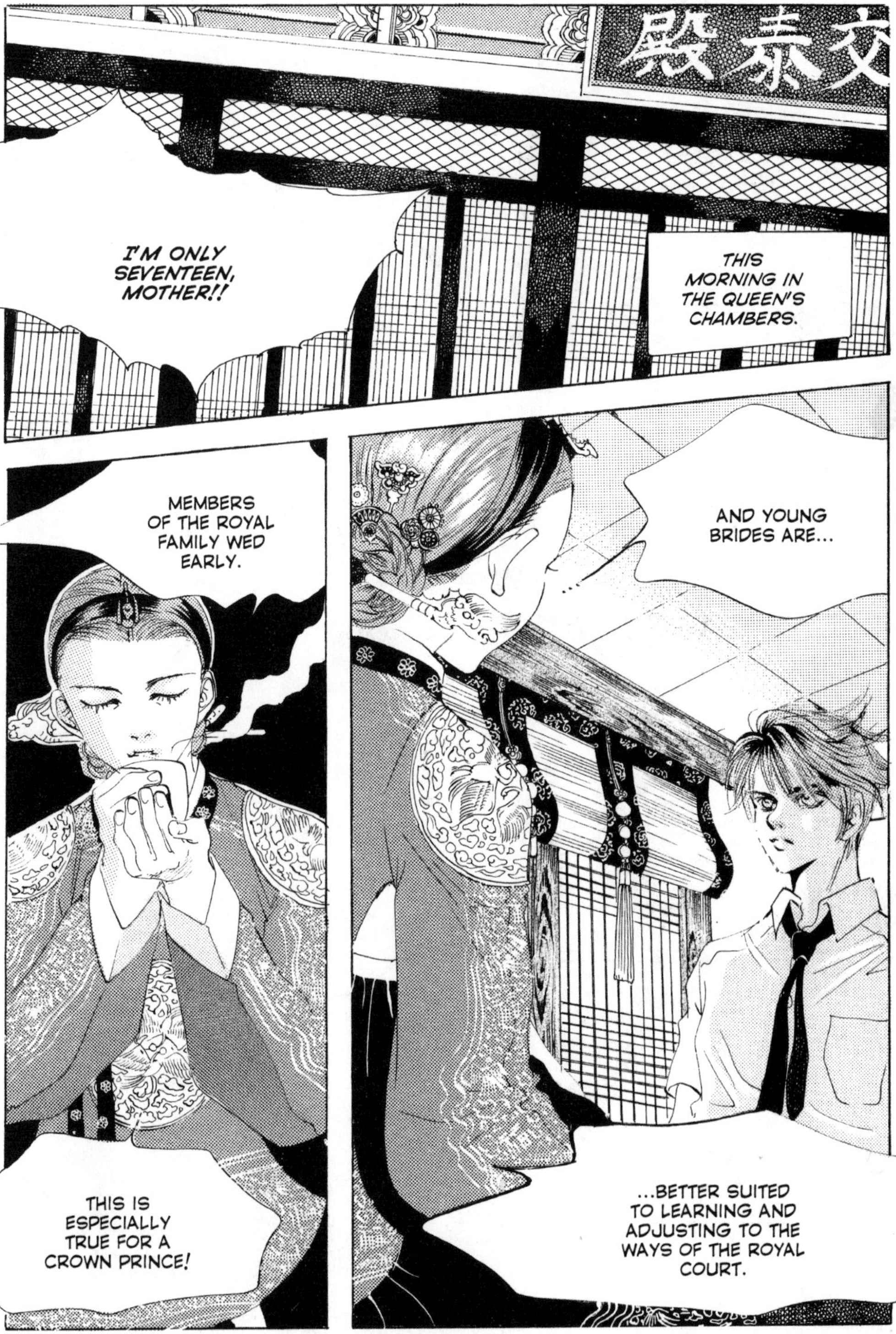
交泰殿
I'M ONLY SEVENTEEN, MOTHER!!
THIS MORNING IN THE QUEEN'S CHAMBERS.
MEMBERS OF THE ROYAL FAMILY WED EARLY.
THIS IS ESPECIALLY TRUE FOR A CROWN PRINCE!
AND YOUNG BRIDES ARE...
...BETTER SUITED TO LEARNING AND ADJUSTING TO THE WAYS OF THE ROYAL COURT.

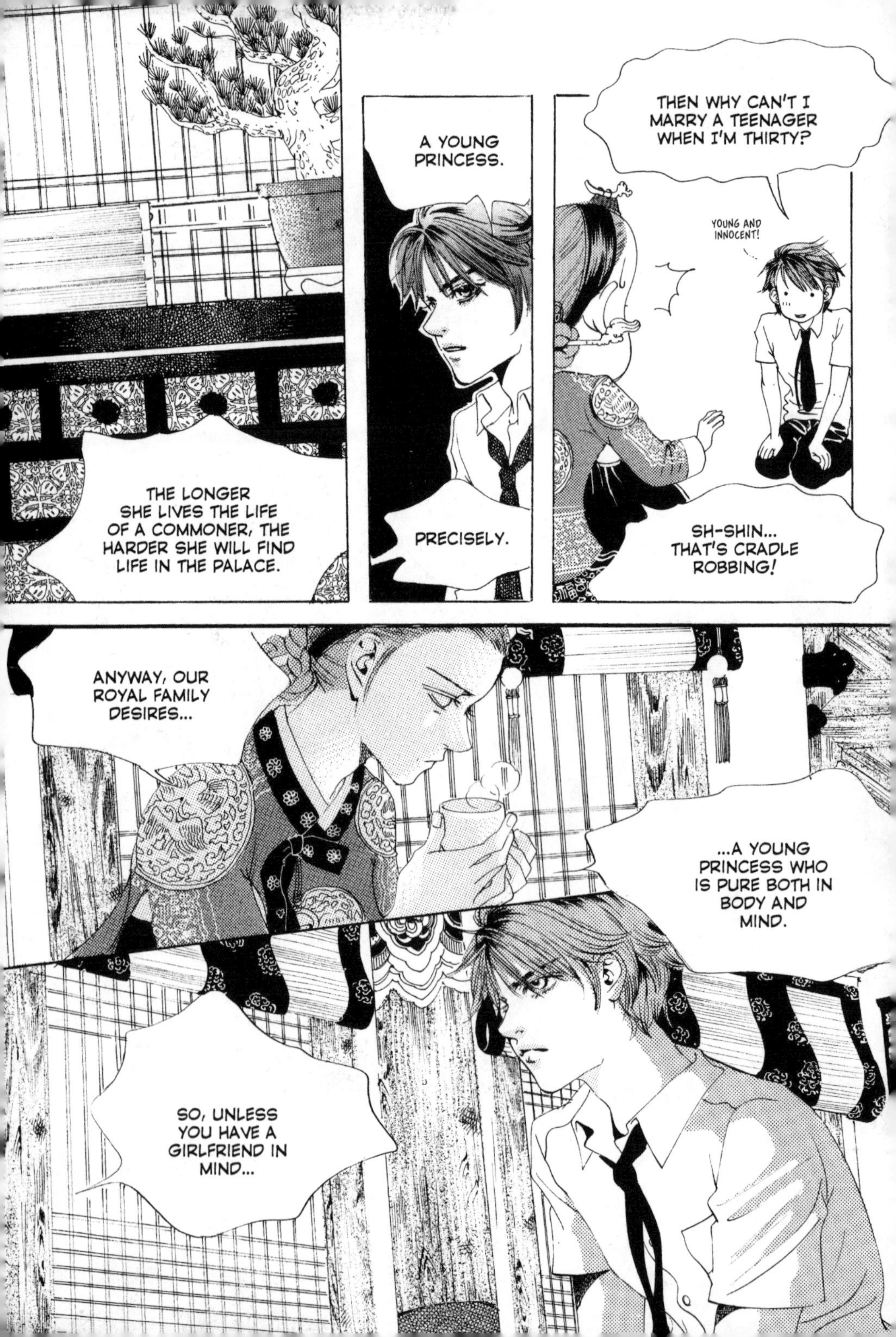
THE LONGER SHE LIVES THE LIFE OF A COMMONER, THE HARDER SHE WILL FIND LIFE IN THE PALACE.
A YOUNG PRINCESS.
PRECISELY.
THEN WHY CAN'T I MARRY A TEENAGER WHEN I'M THIRTY?
YOUNG AND INNOCENT!
SH-SHIN... THAT'S CRADLE ROBBING!
ANYWAY, OUR ROYAL FAMILY DESIRES...
...A YOUNG PRINCESS WHO IS PURE BOTH IN BODY AND MIND.
SO, UNLESS YOU HAVE A GIRLFRIEND IN MIND...

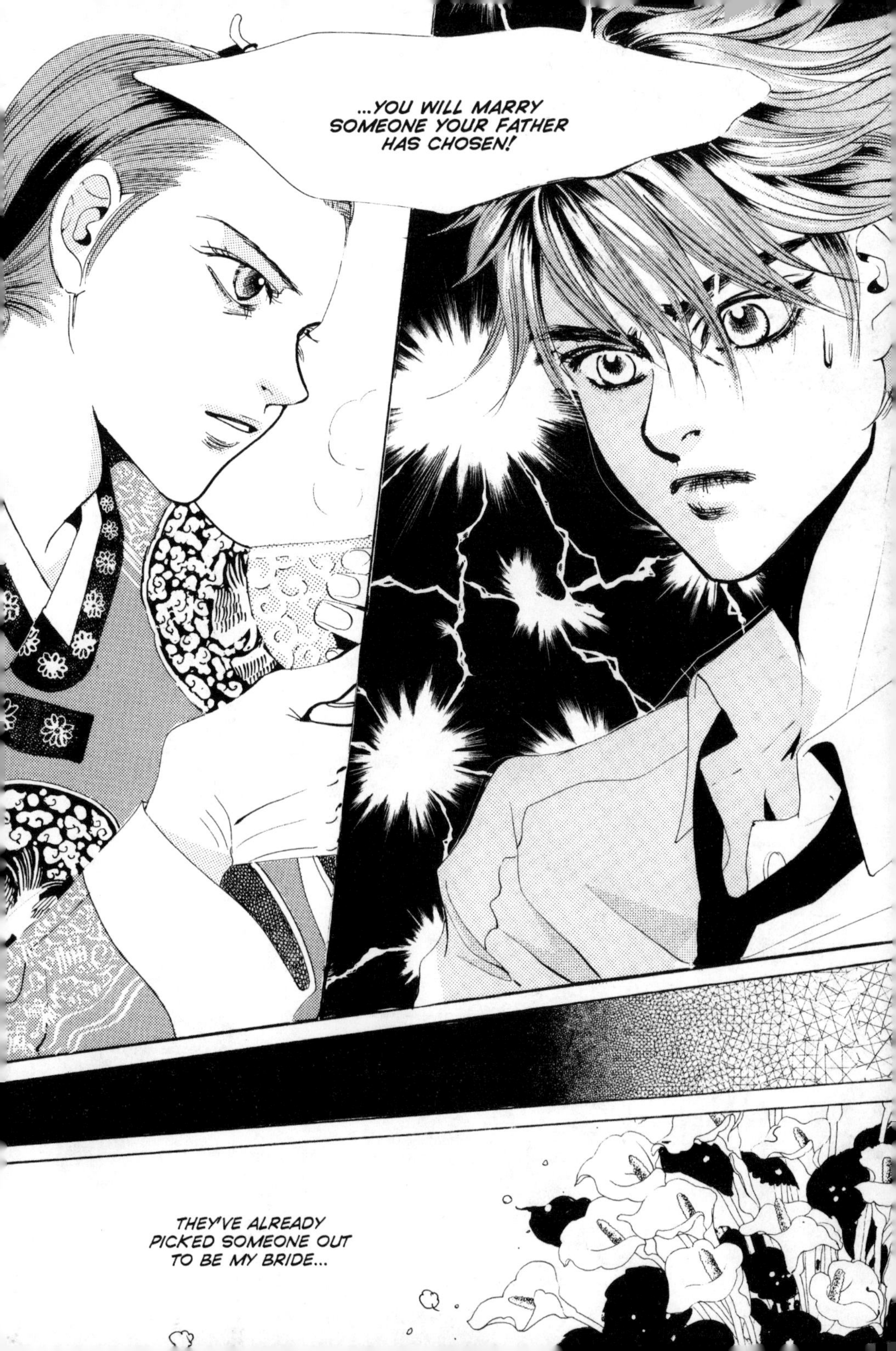
...YOU WILL MARRY SOMEONE YOUR FATHER HAS CHOSEN!
THEY'VE ALREADY PICKED SOMEONE OUT TO BE MY BRIDE...

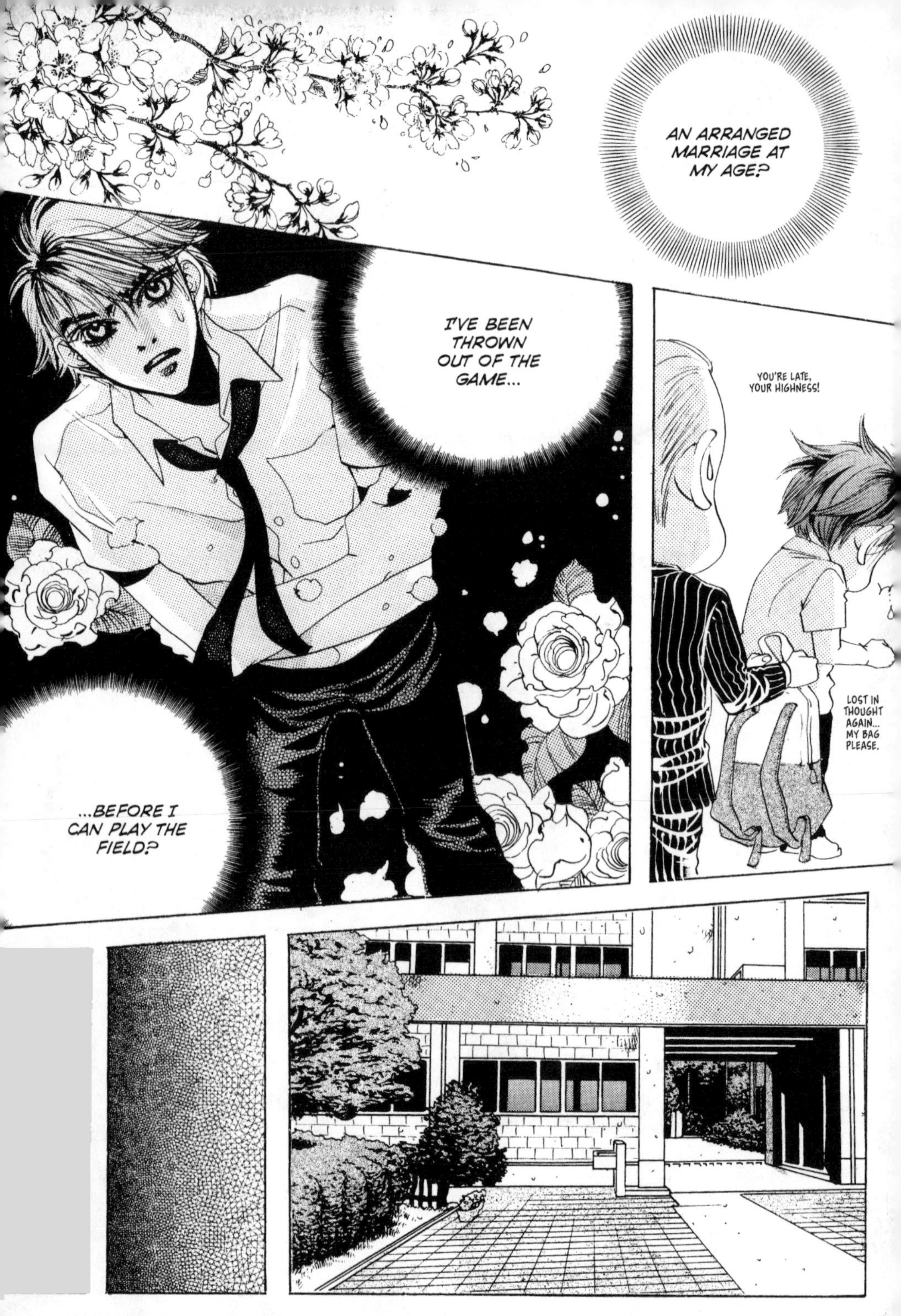
AN ARRANGED MARRIAGE AT MY AGE?
I'VE BEEN THROWN OUT OF THE GAME...
...BEFORE I CAN PLAY THE FIELD?
YOU'RE LATE, YOUR HIGHNESS!
LOST IN THOUGHT AGAIN... MY BAG PLEASE.

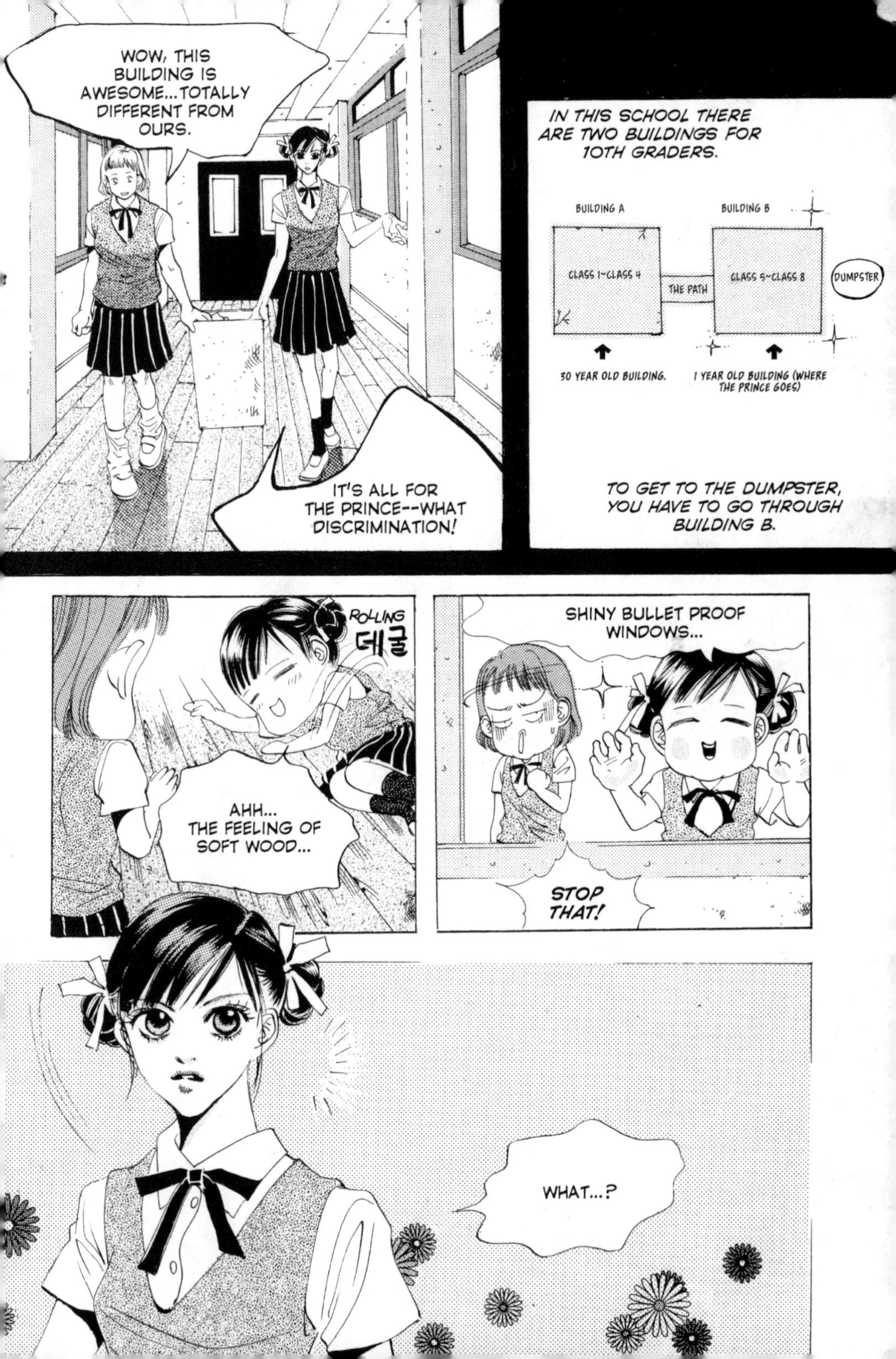

WOW, THIS BUILDING IS AWESOME...TOTALLY DIFFERENT FROM OURS.
IT'S ALL FOR THE PRINCE--WHAT DISCRIMINATION!
IN THIS SCHOOL THERE ARE TWO BUILDINGS FOR 10TH GRADERS.
BUILDING A
BUILDING B
CLASS 1~CLASS 4
THE PATH
CLASS 5~CLASS 8
DUMPSTER
30 YEAR OLD BUILDING.
1 YEAR OLD BUILDING (WHERE THE PRINCE GOES)
TO GET TO THE DUMPSTER, YOU HAVE TO GO THROUGH BUILDING B.
ROLLING
데굴
AHH... THE FEELING OF SOFT WOOD...
SHINY BULLET PROOF WINDOWS...
STOP THAT!
WHAT...?

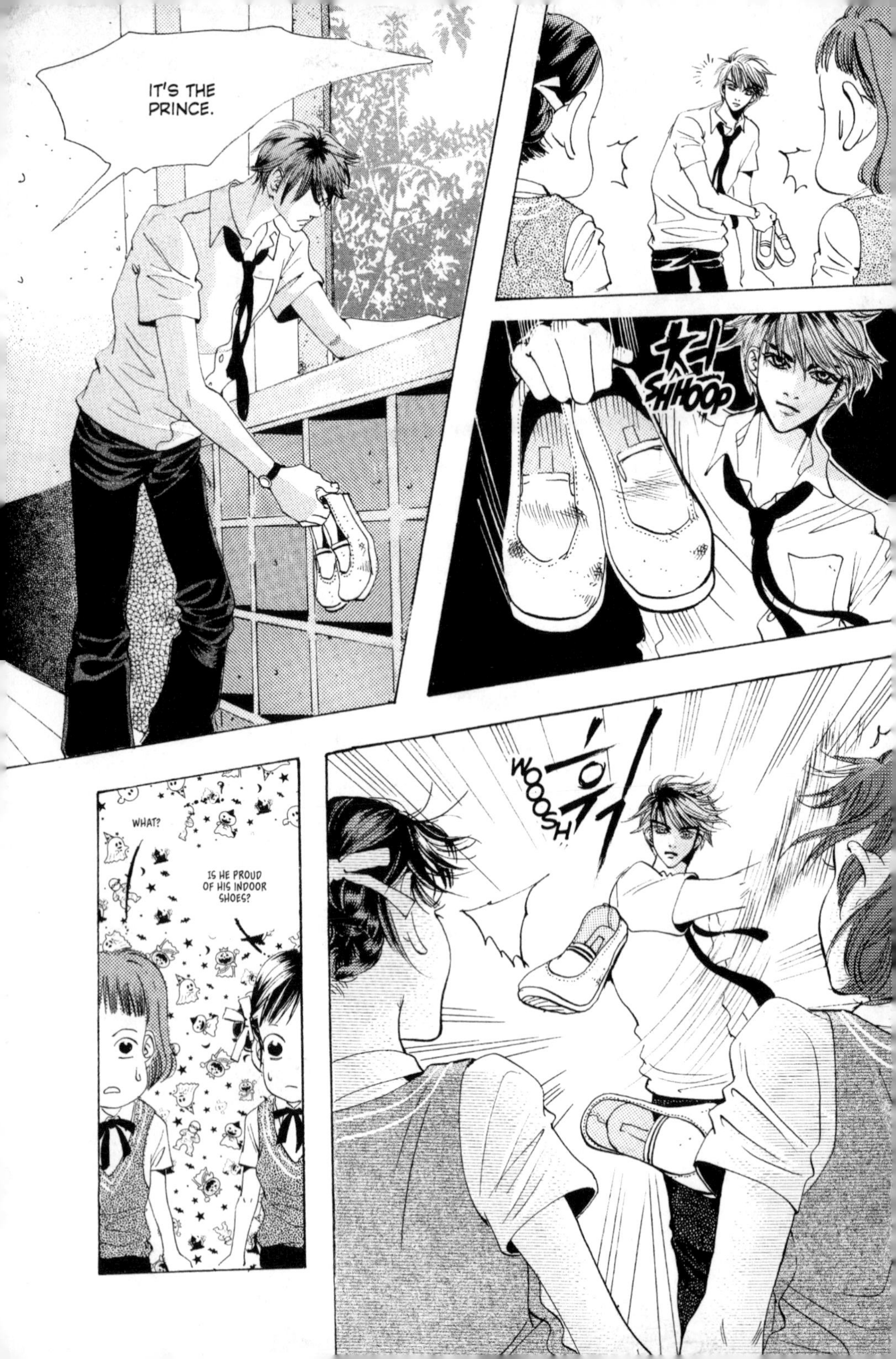
IT'S THE PRINCE.
SHHOOP
WHAT?
IS HE PROUD OF HIS INDOOR SHOES?
WOOOSH!

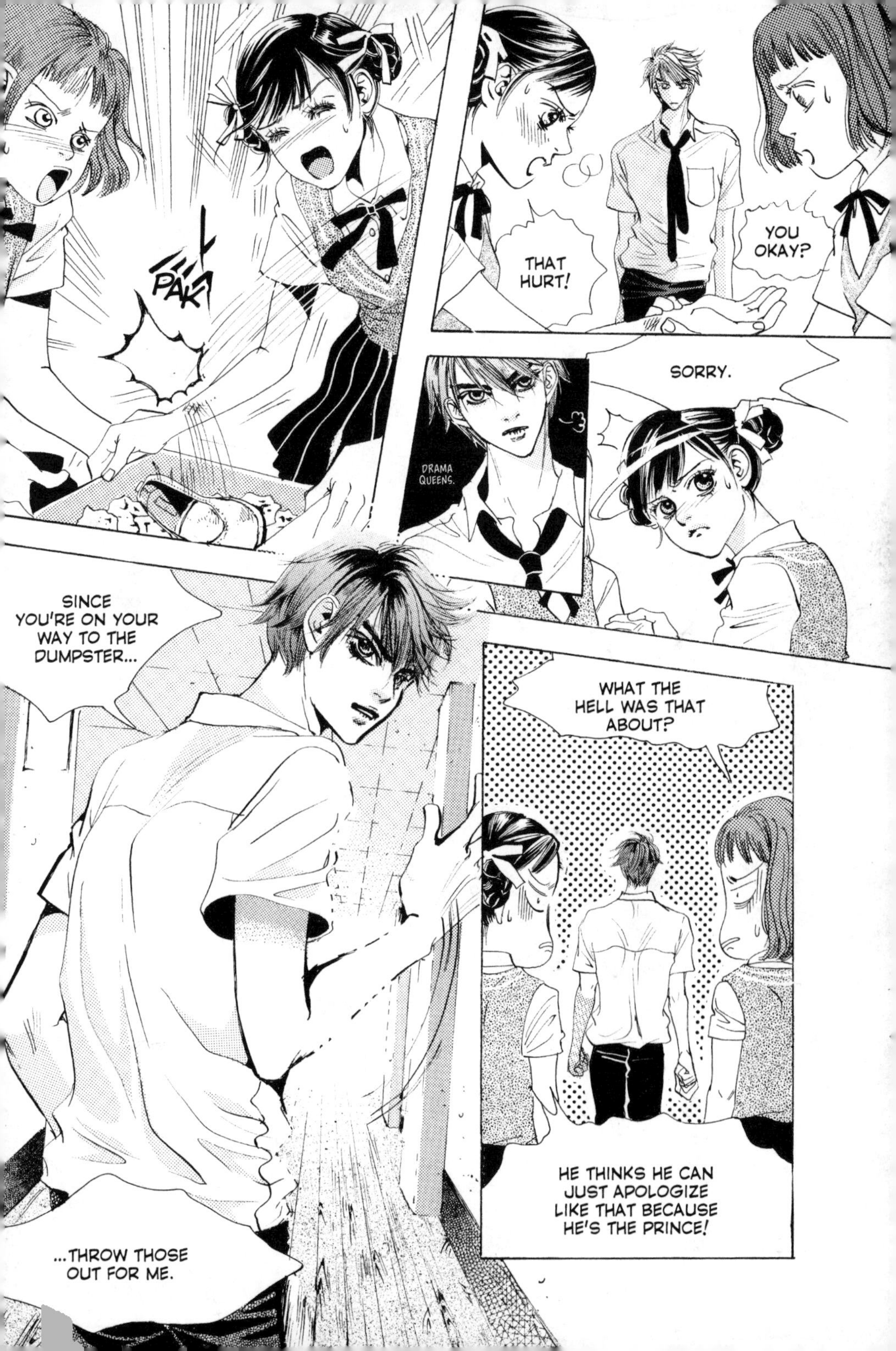
PAK!
THAT HURT!
YOU OKAY?
SORRY.
DRAMA QUEENS.
SINCE YOU'RE ON YOUR WAY TO THE DUMPSTER...
...THROW THOSE OUT FOR ME.
WHAT THE HELL WAS THAT ABOUT?
HE THINKS HE CAN JUST APOLOGIZE LIKE THAT BECAUSE HE'S THE PRINCE!

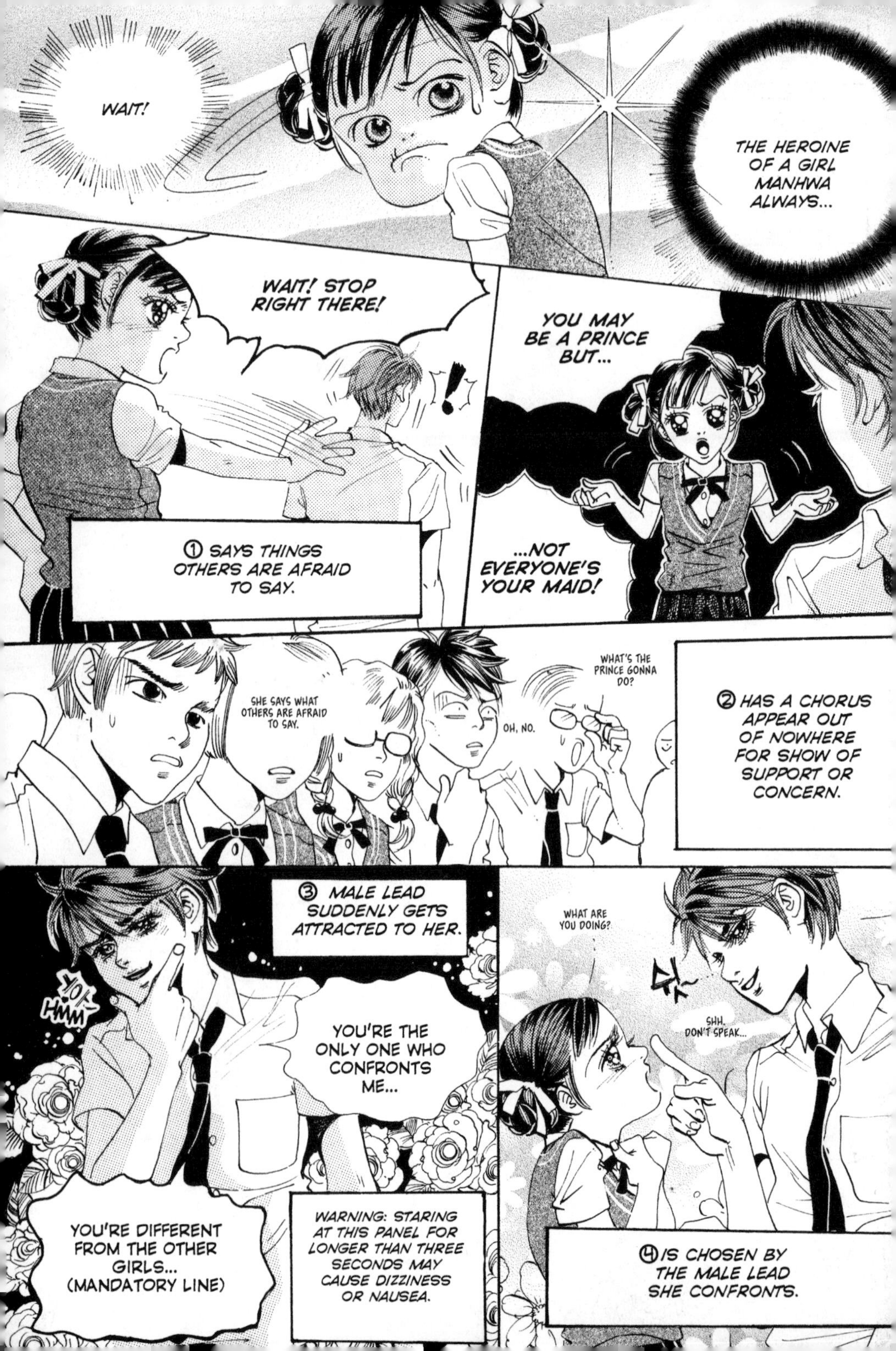
WAIT!
THE HEROINE OF A GIRL MANHWA ALWAYS...
WAIT! STOP RIGHT THERE!
① SAYS THINGS OTHERS ARE AFRAID TO SAY.
YOU MAY BE A PRINCE BUT...
...NOT EVERYONE'S YOUR MAID!
SHE SAYS WHAT OTHERS ARE AFRAID TO SAY.
OH, NO.
WHAT'S THE PRINCE GONNA DO?
② HAS A CHORUS APPEAR OUT OF NOWHERE FOR SHOW OF SUPPORT OR CONCERN.
③ MALE LEAD SUDDENLY GETS ATTRACTED TO HER.
HMM
YOU'RE THE ONLY ONE WHO CONFRONTS ME...
YOU'RE DIFFERENT FROM THE OTHER GIRLS... (MANDATORY LINE)
WARNING: STARING AT THIS PANEL FOR LONGER THAN THREE SECONDS MAY CAUSE DIZZINESS OR NAUSEA.
WHAT ARE YOU DOING?
SHH. DON'T SPEAK...
④ IS CHOSEN BY THE MALE LEAD SHE CONFRONTS.

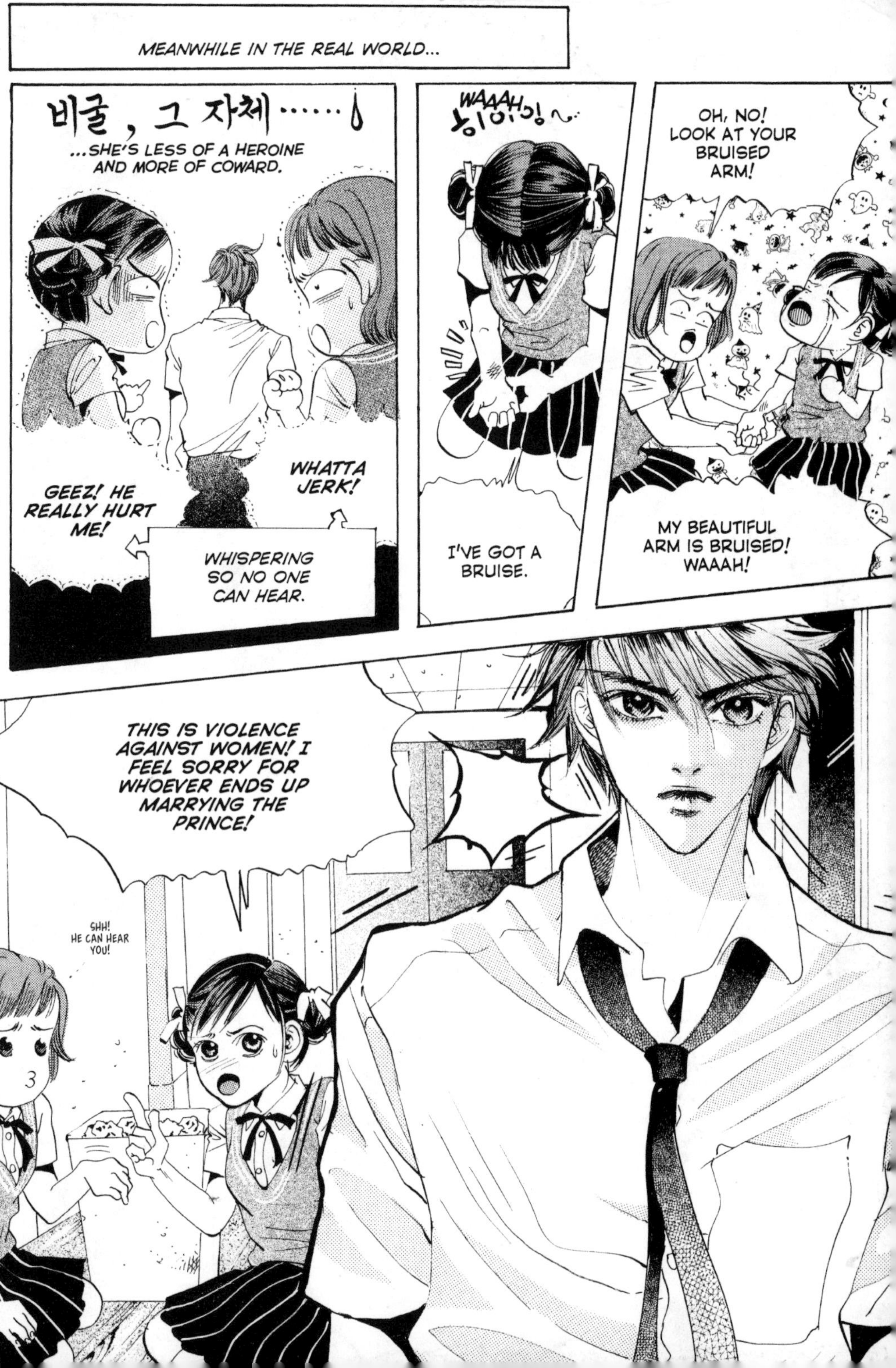
MEANWHILE IN THE REAL WORLD...
비굴, 그 자체……
...SHE'S LESS OF A HEROINE AND MORE OF COWARD.
GEEZ! HE REALLY HURT ME!
WHATTA JERK!
WHISPERING SO NO ONE CAN HEAR.
WAAAH
I'VE GOT A BRUISE.
OH, NO! LOOK AT YOUR BRUISED ARM!
MY BEAUTIFUL ARM IS BRUISED! WAAAH!
THIS IS VIOLENCE AGAINST WOMEN! I FEEL SORRY FOR WHOEVER ENDS UP MARRYING THE PRINCE!
SHH! HE CAN HEAR YOU!

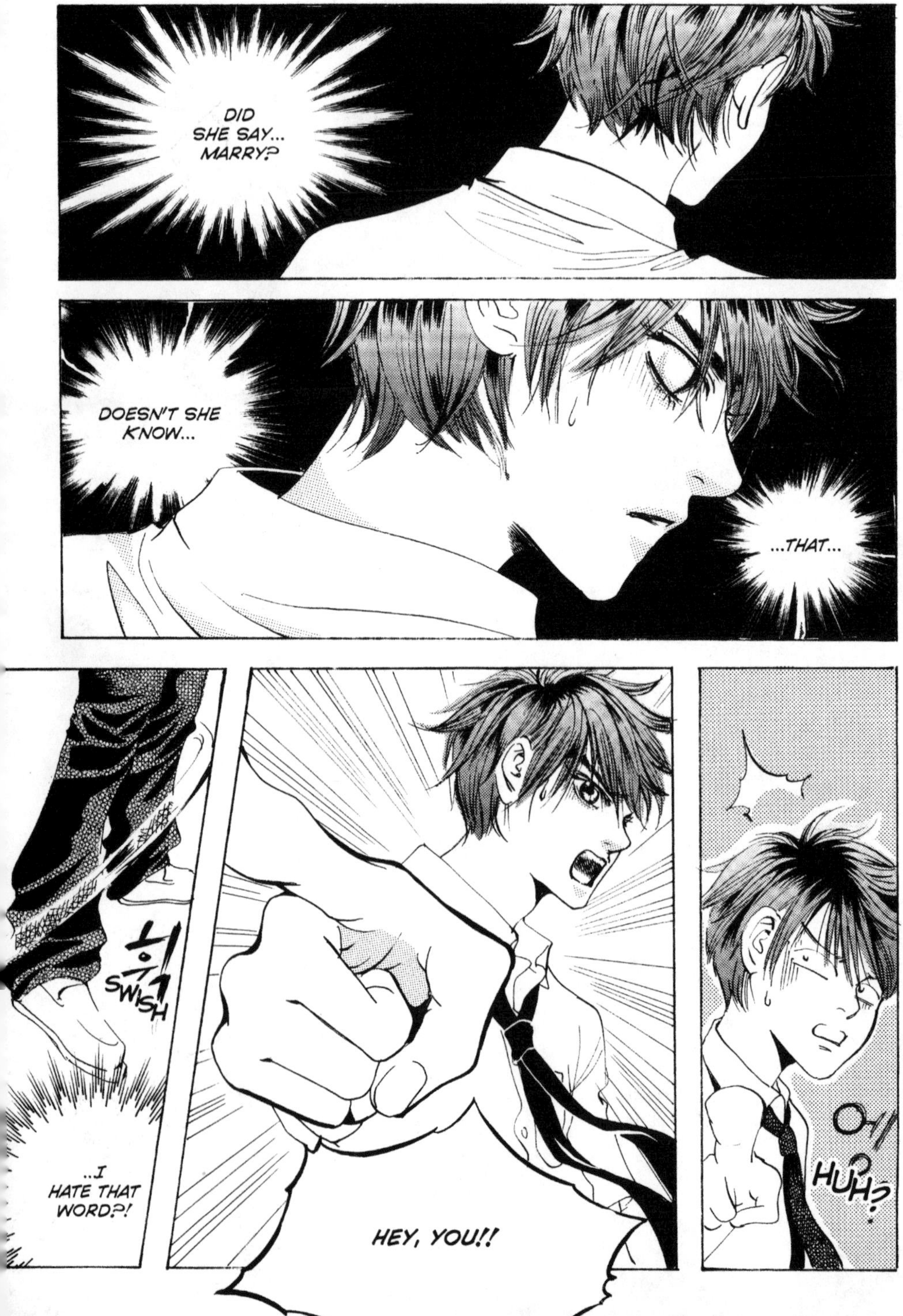
DID SHE SAY... MARRY?
DOESN'T SHE KNOW...
...THAT...
SWISH
..I HATE THAT WORD?!
HEY, YOU!!
HUH?

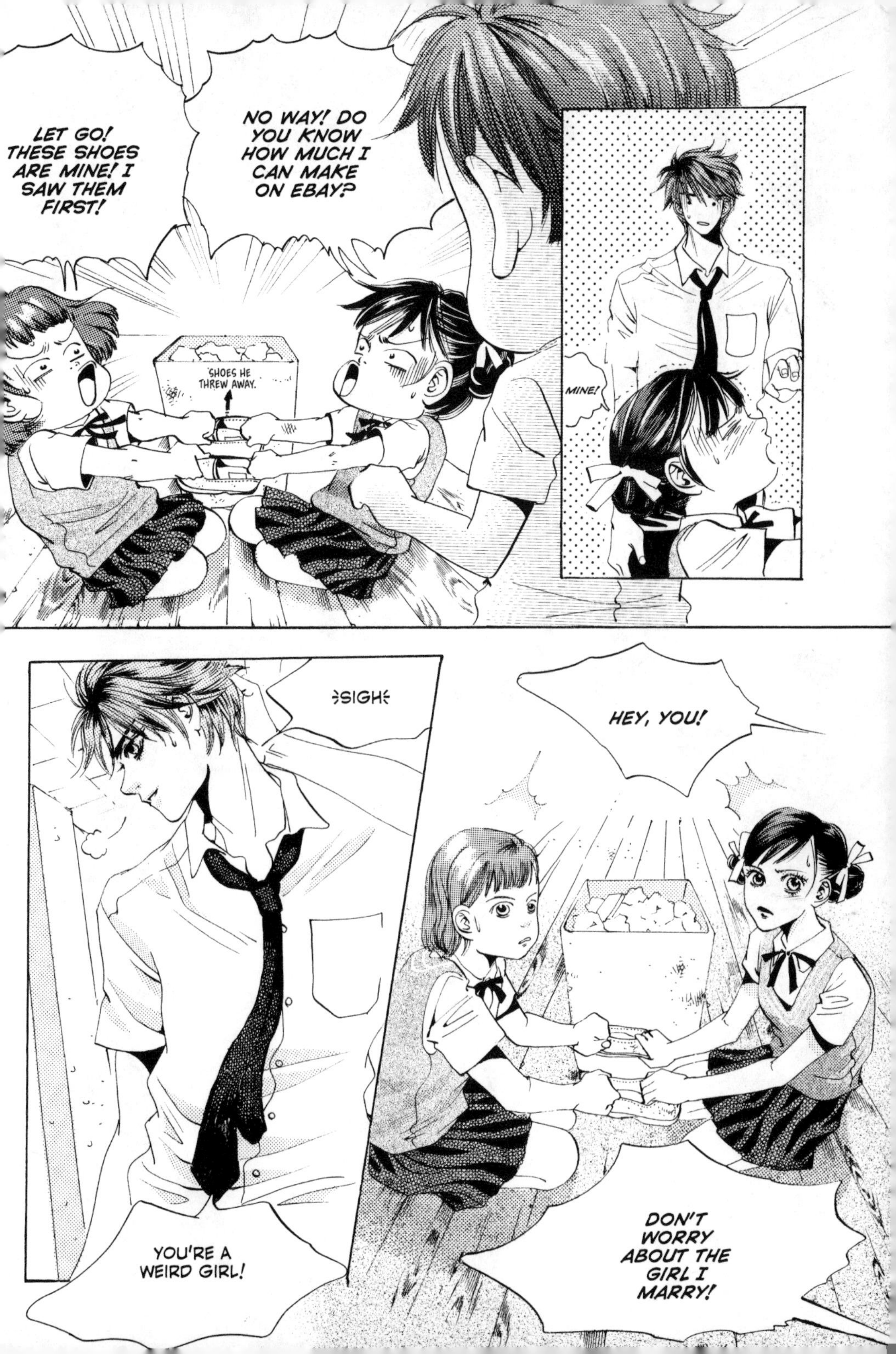
LET GO! THESE SHOES ARE MINE! I SAW THEM FIRST!
NO WAY! DO YOU KNOW HOW MUCH I CAN MAKE ON EBAY?
SHOES HE THREW AWAY.
MINE!
SIGH
YOU'RE A WEIRD GIRL!
HEY, YOU!
DON'T WORRY ABOUT THE GIRL I MARRY!

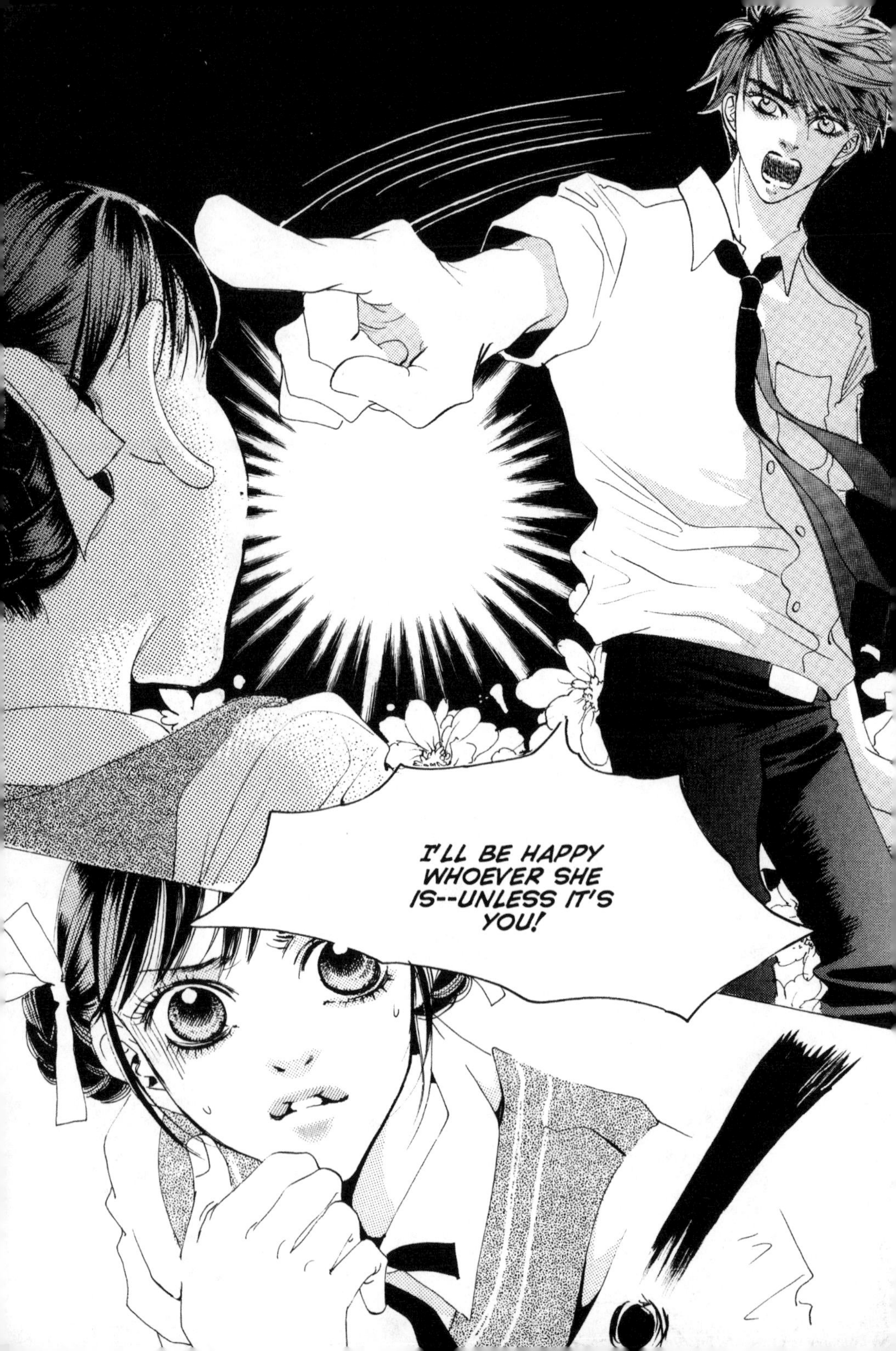
I'LL BE HAPPY WHOEVER SHE IS--UNLESS IT'S YOU!

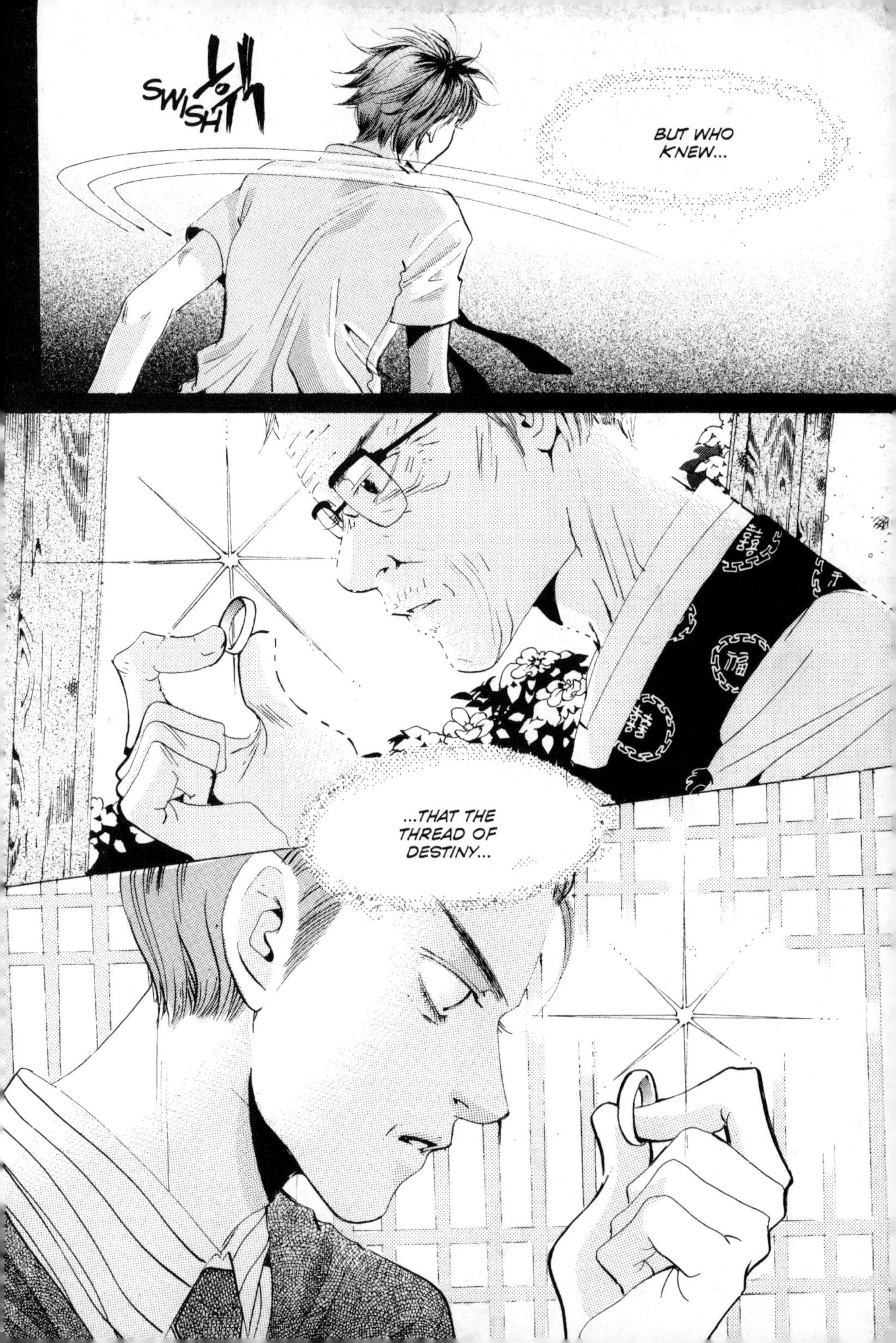
SWISH
BUT WHO KNEW...
...THAT THE THREAD OF DESTINY...

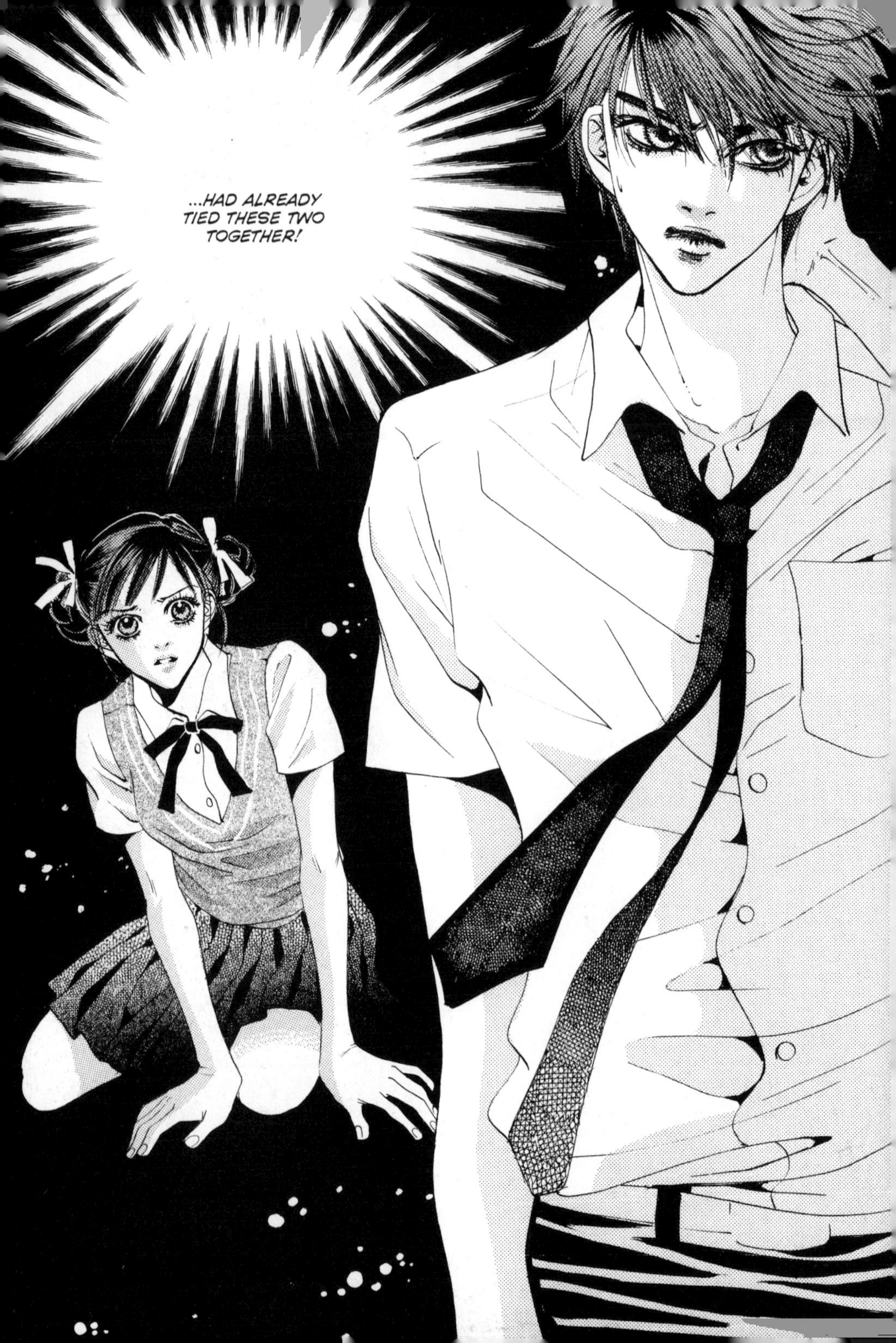
...HAD ALREADY
TIED THESE TWO
TOGETHER!

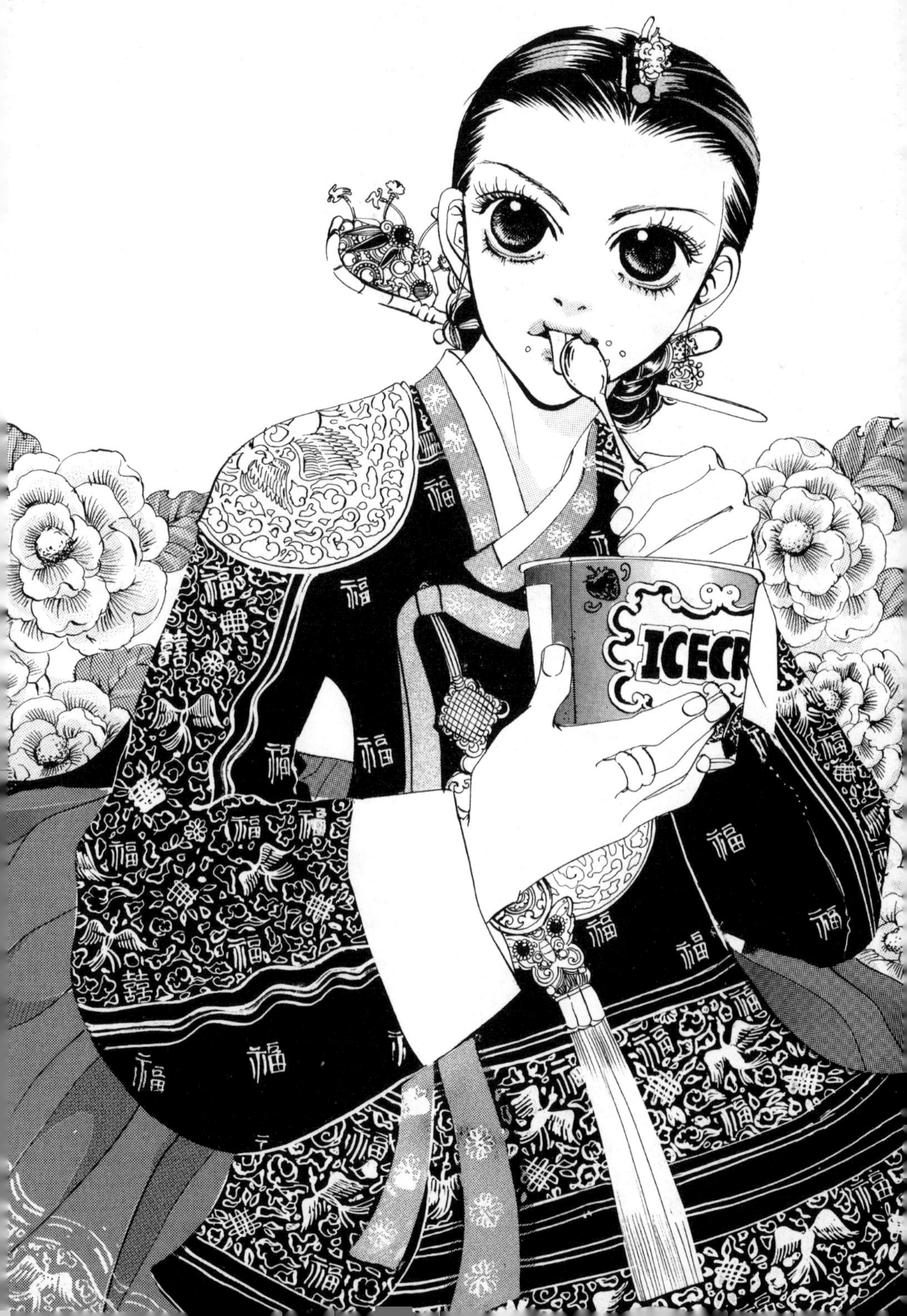
ICECR

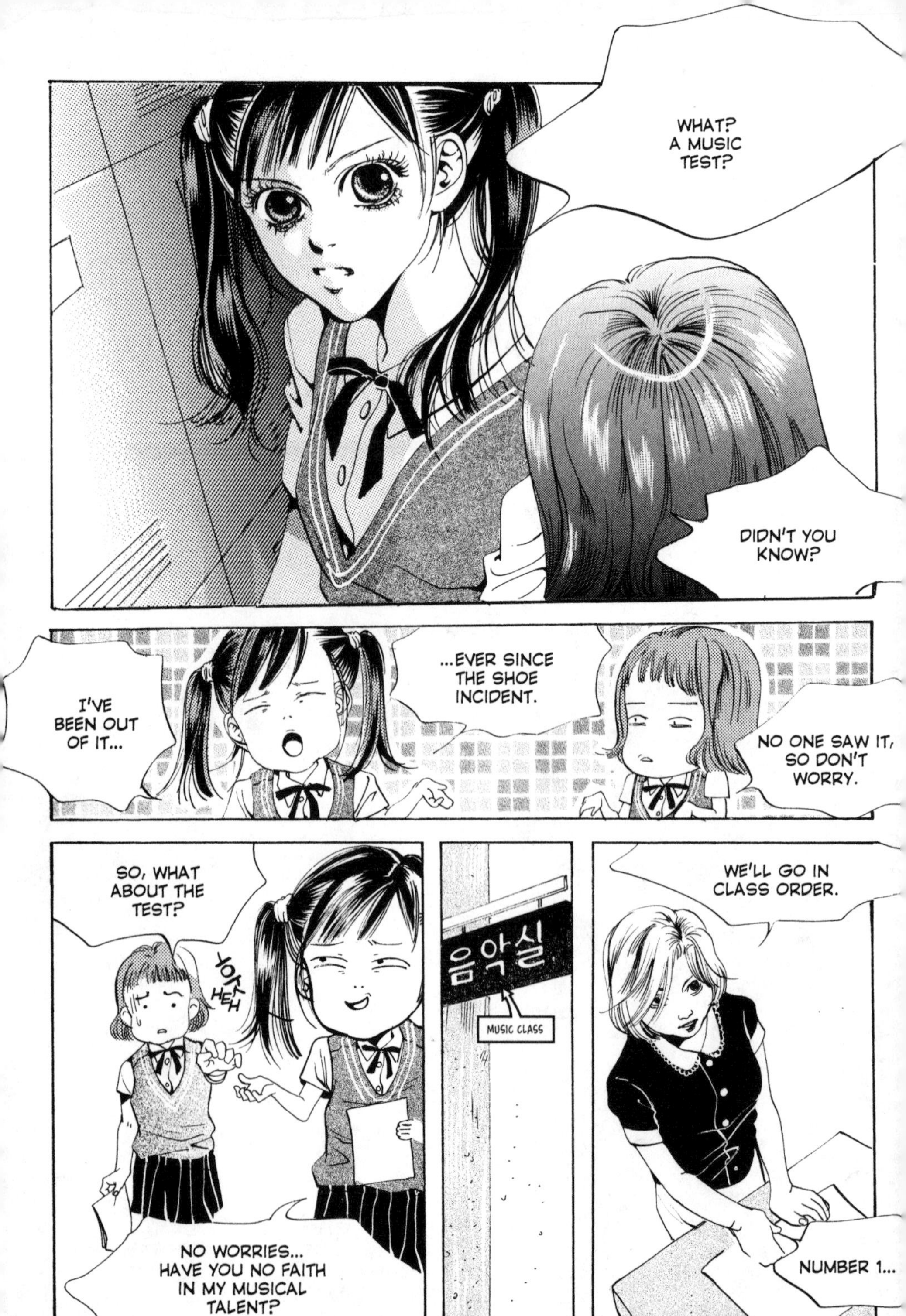
WHAT? A MUSIC TEST?
DIDN'T YOU KNOW?
I'VE BEEN OUT OF IT...
...EVER SINCE THE SHOE INCIDENT.
NO ONE SAW IT, SO DON'T WORRY.
SO, WHAT ABOUT THE TEST?
HEH
NO WORRIES... HAVE YOU NO FAITH IN MY MUSICAL TALENT?
음악실
MUSIC CLASS
WE'LL GO IN CLASS ORDER.
NUMBER 1...

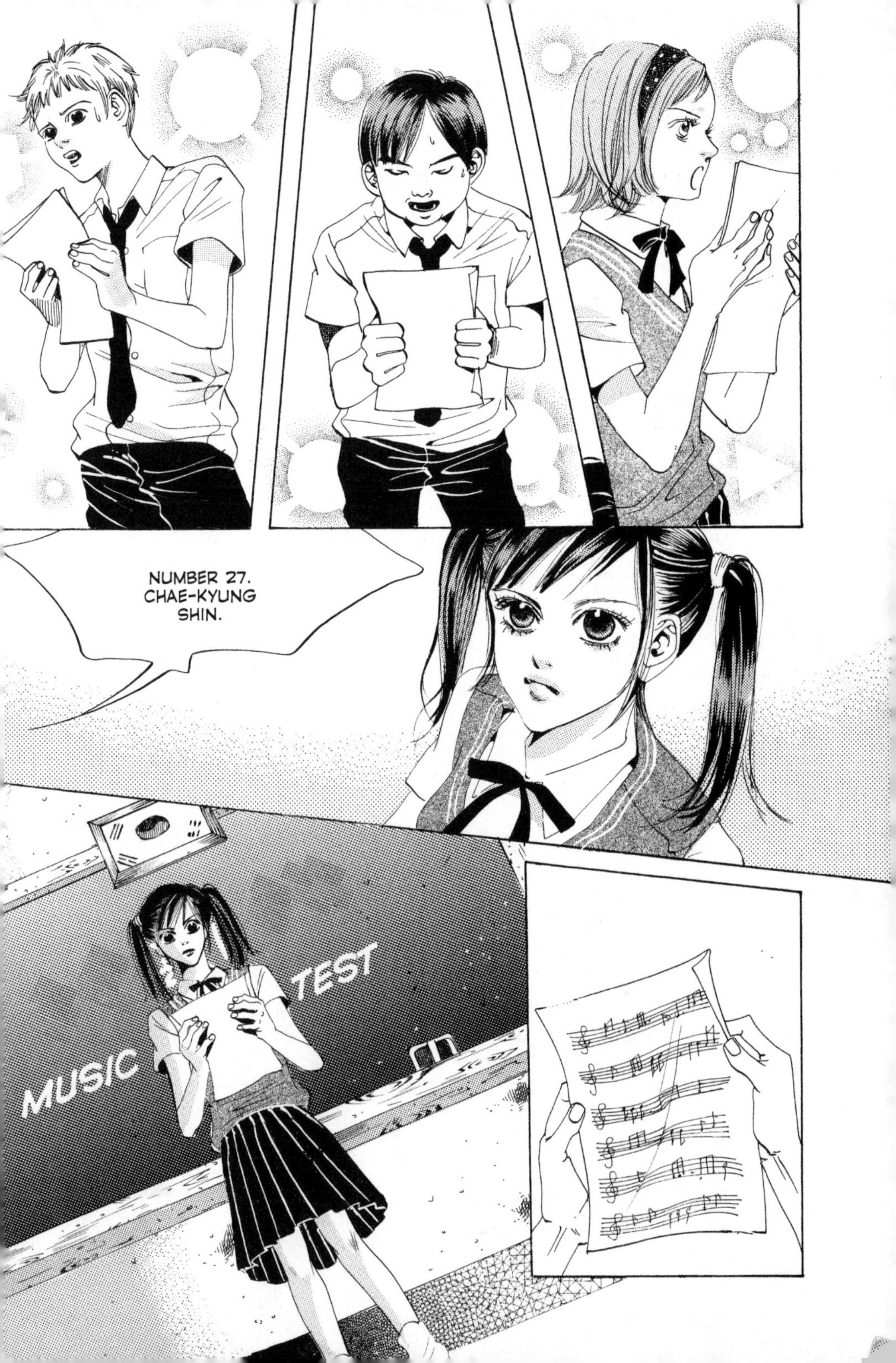
NUMBER 27. CHAE-KYUNG SHIN.
MUSIC
TEST

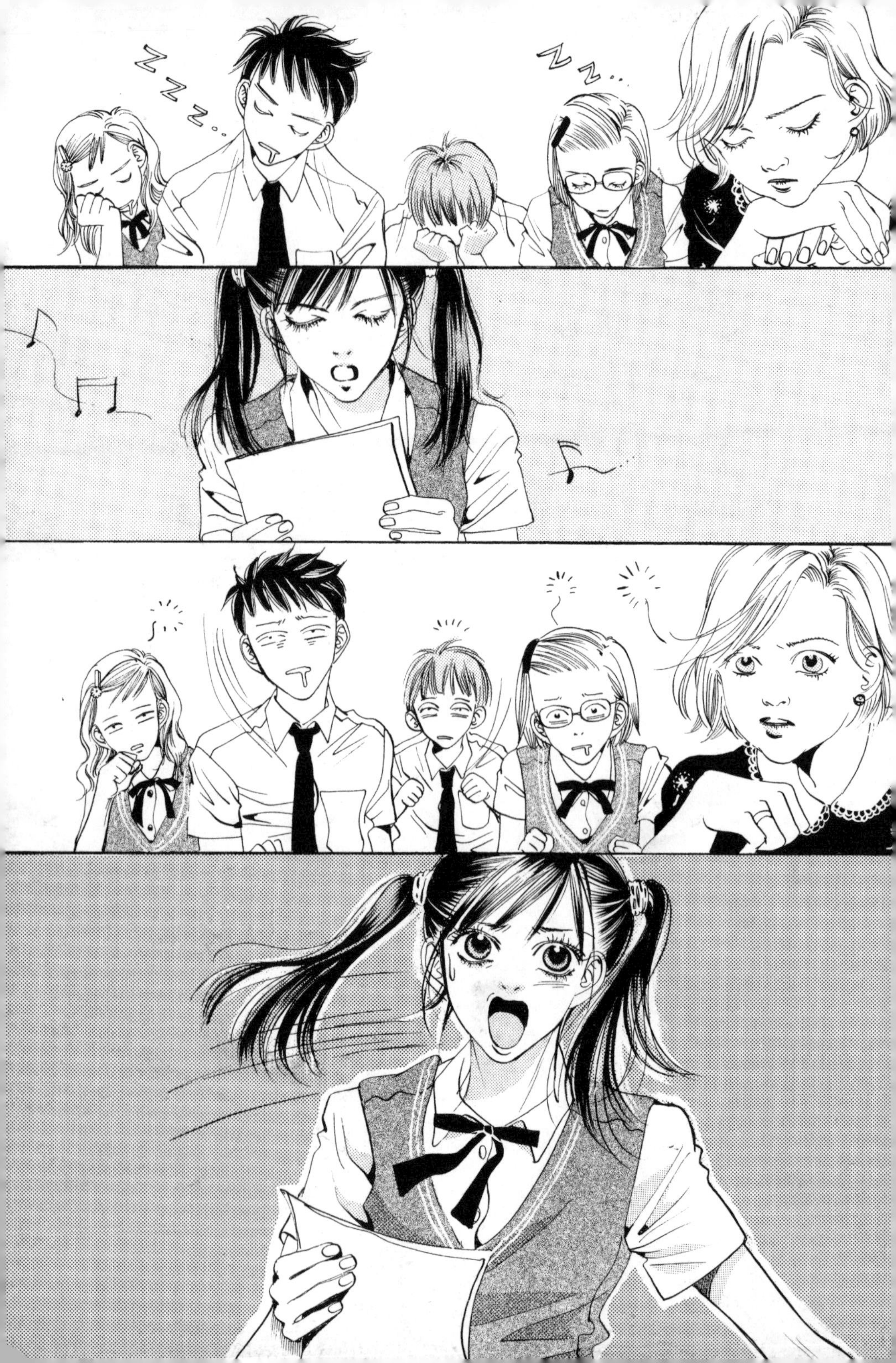
ZZZ...
ZZ...

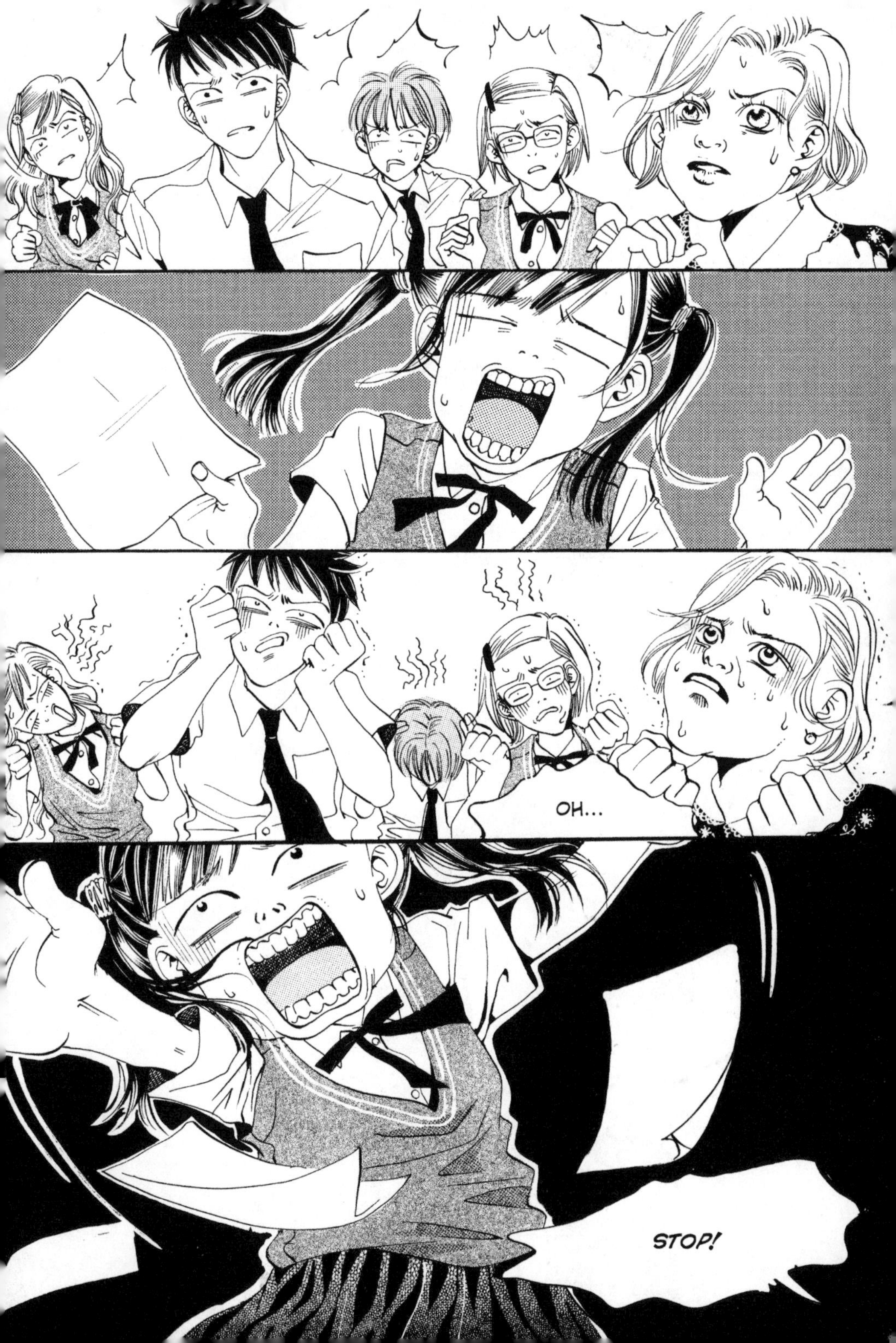
OH...
STOP!

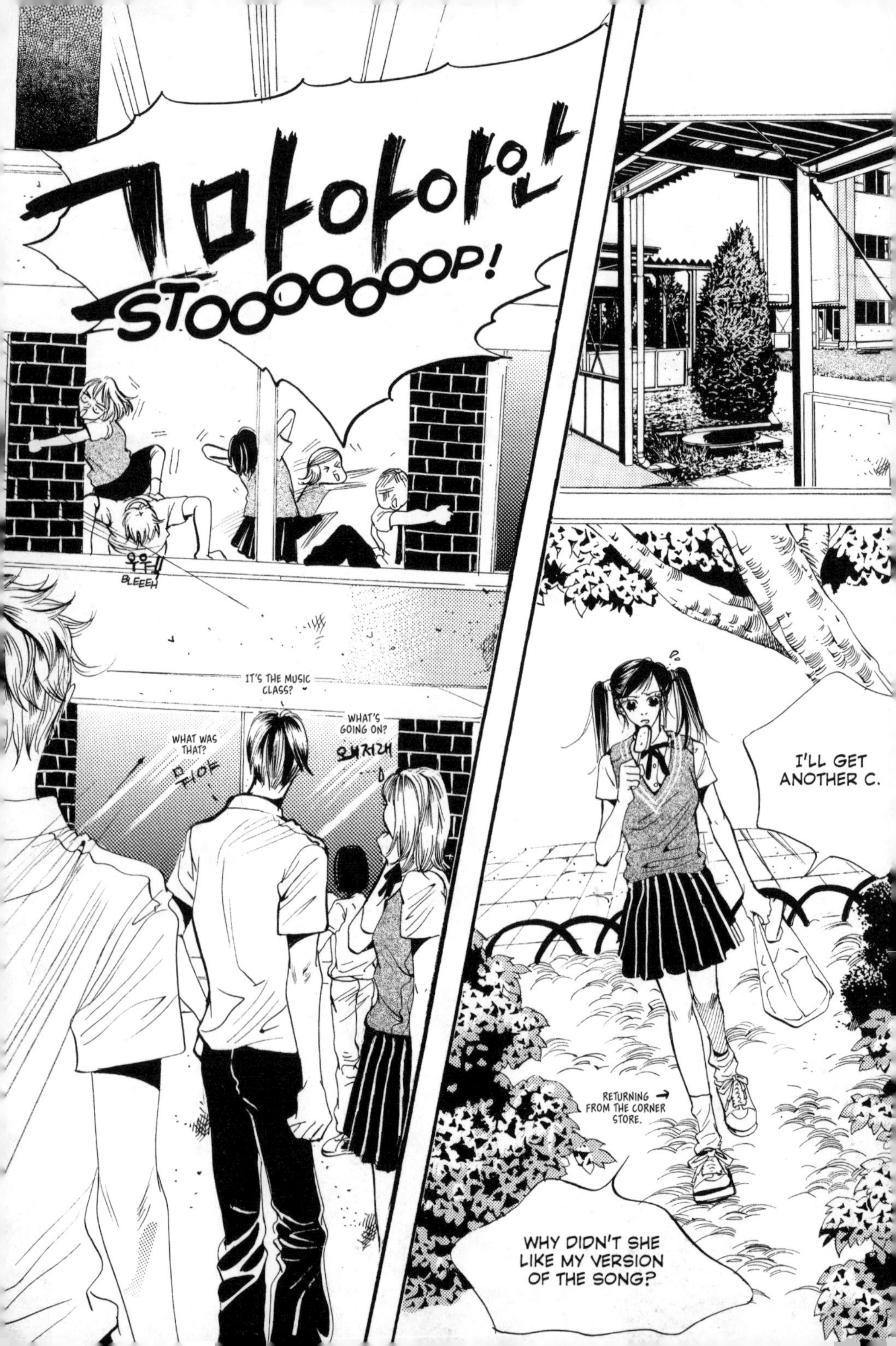
ㄱ마아아안
STOOOOOOOOP!
우우!!
BLEEEH
IT'S THE MUSIC CLASS?
WHAT WAS THAT?
뭐야
WHAT'S GOING ON?
왜저래
I'LL GET ANOTHER C.
RETURNING FROM THE CORNER STORE.
WHY DIDN'T SHE LIKE MY VERSION OF THE SONG?

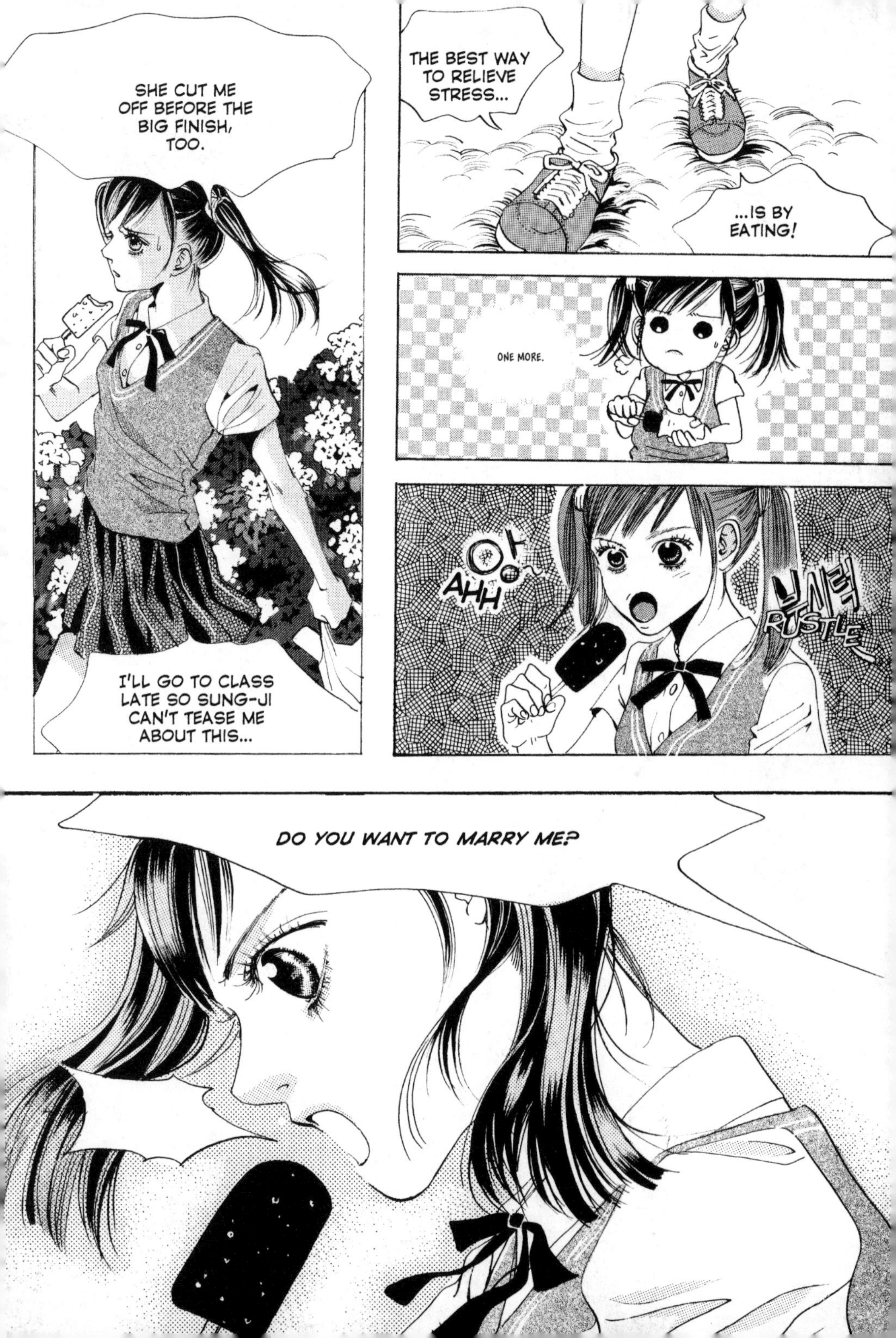
SHE CUT ME OFF BEFORE THE BIG FINISH, TOO.
I'LL GO TO CLASS LATE SO SUNG-JI CAN'T TEASE ME ABOUT THIS...
THE BEST WAY TO RELIEVE STRESS...
...IS BY EATING!
ONE MORE.
AHH
RUSTLE
DO YOU WANT TO MARRY ME?

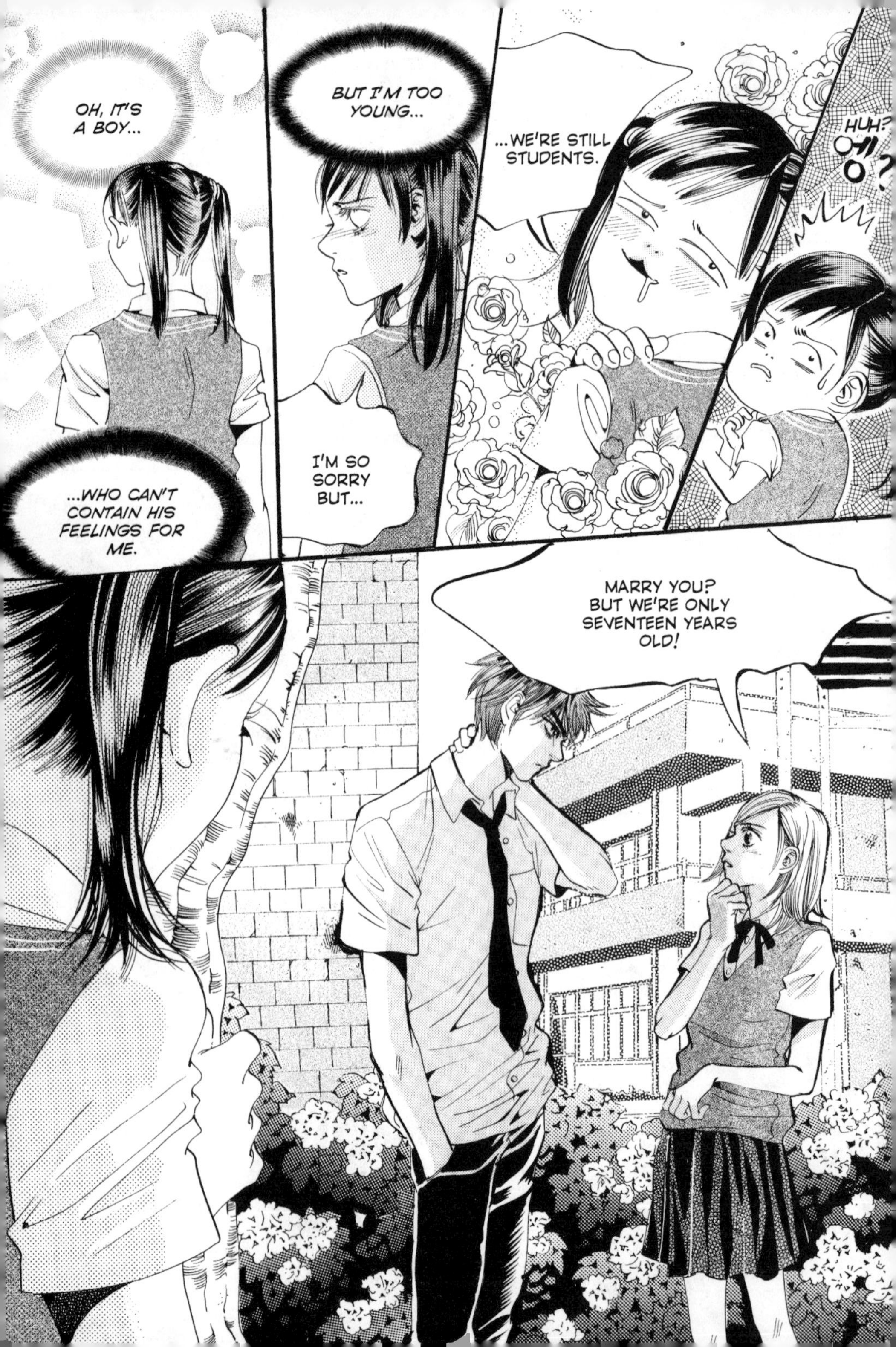
OH, IT'S A BOY...
...WHO CAN'T CONTAIN HIS FEELINGS FOR ME.
BUT I'M TOO YOUNG...
I'M SO SORRY BUT...
...WE'RE STILL STUDENTS.
HUH?
MARRY YOU? BUT WE'RE ONLY SEVENTEEN YEARS OLD!

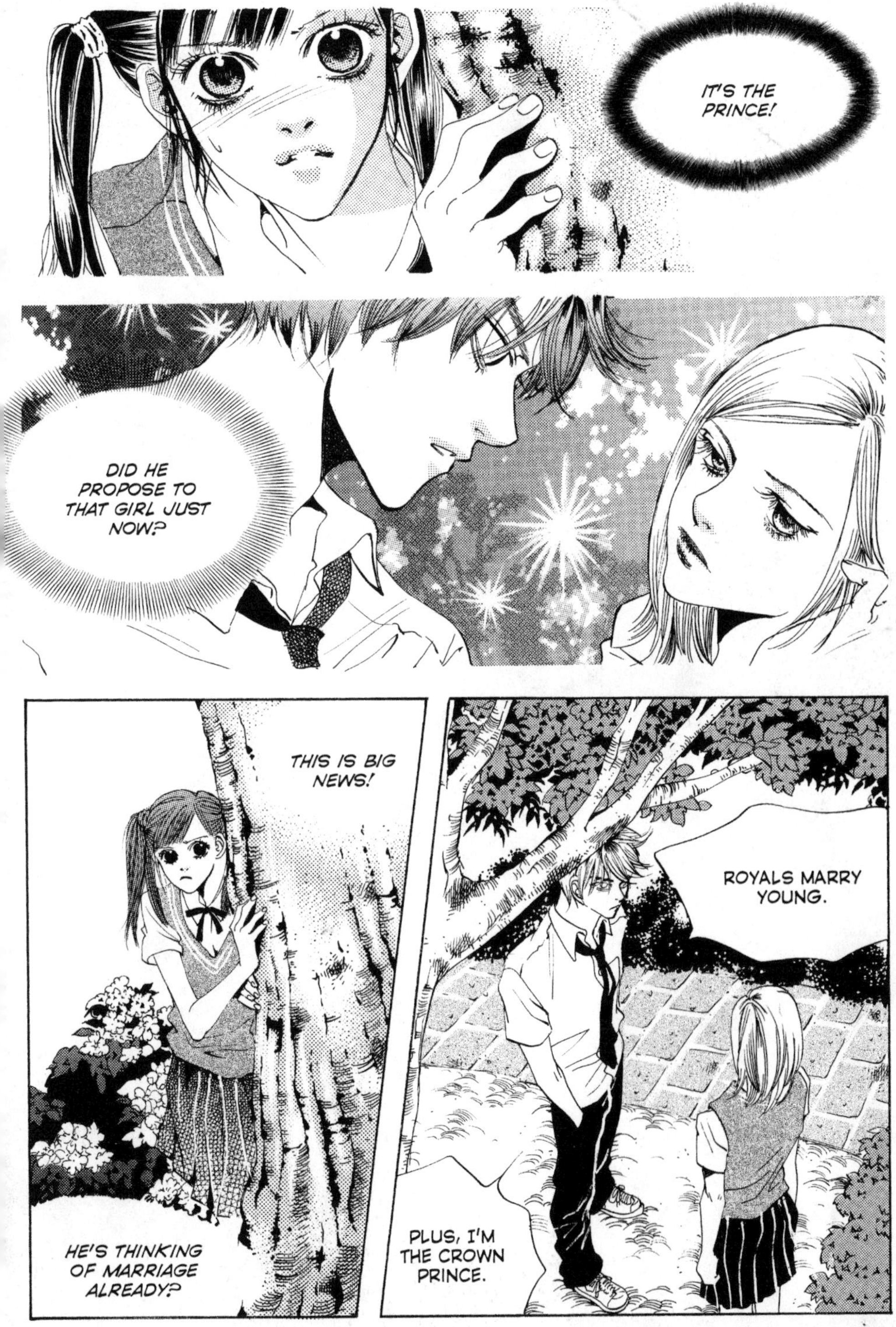
IT'S THE PRINCE!
DID HE PROPOSE TO THAT GIRL JUST NOW?
THIS IS BIG NEWS!
HE'S THINKING OF MARRIAGE ALREADY?
ROYALS MARRY YOUNG.
PLUS, I'M THE CROWN PRINCE.

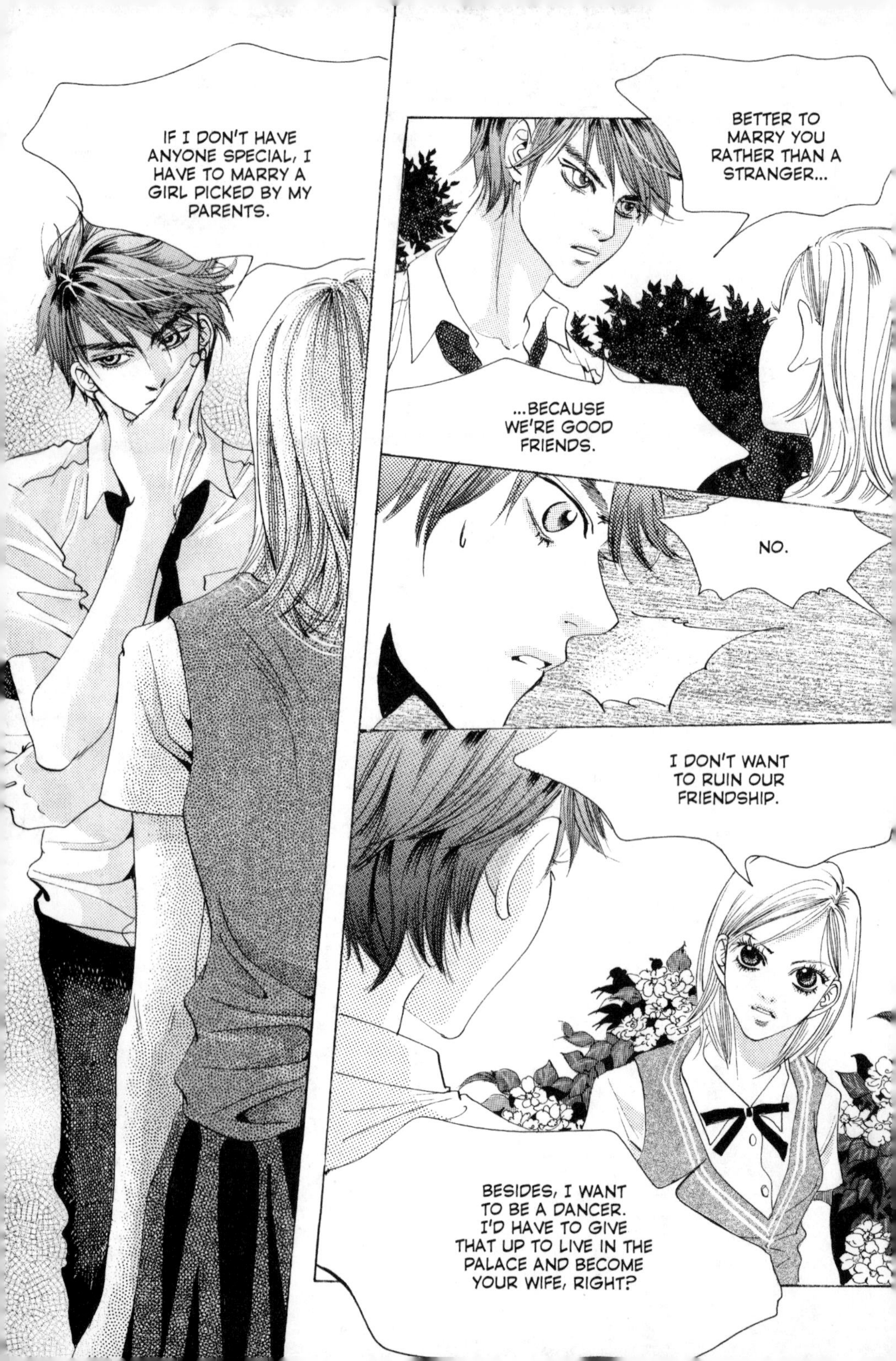
IF I DON'T HAVE ANYONE SPECIAL, I HAVE TO MARRY A GIRL PICKED BY MY PARENTS.
BETTER TO MARRY YOU RATHER THAN A STRANGER...
...BECAUSE WE'RE GOOD FRIENDS.
NO.
I DON'T WANT TO RUIN OUR FRIENDSHIP.
BESIDES, I WANT TO BE A DANCER. I'D HAVE TO GIVE THAT UP TO LIVE IN THE PALACE AND BECOME YOUR WIFE, RIGHT?

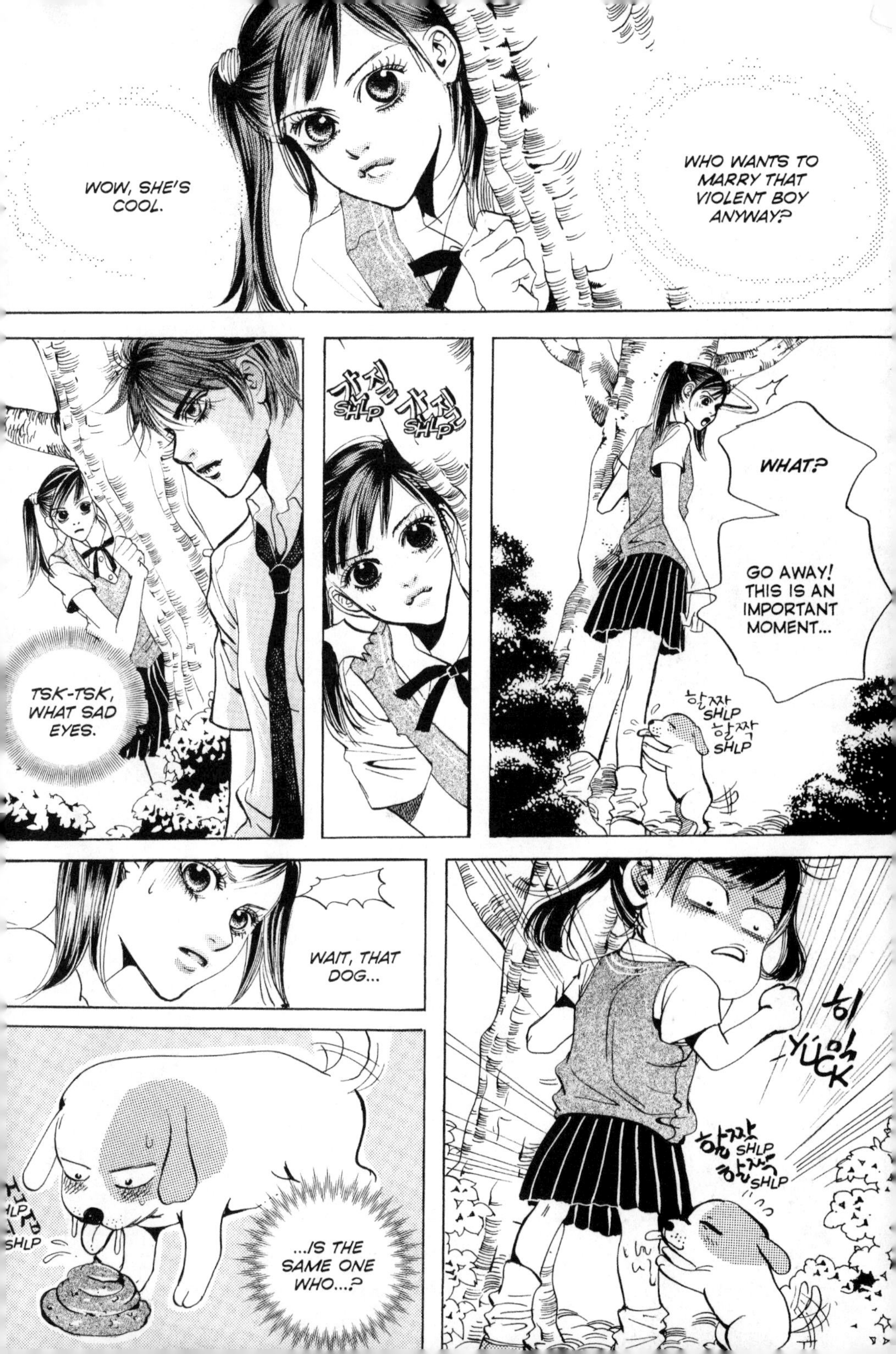
WOW, SHE'S COOL.
WHO WANTS TO MARRY THAT VIOLENT BOY ANYWAY?
TSK-TSK, WHAT SAD EYES.
가질 SHLP 가질 SHLP
WHAT?
GO AWAY! THIS IS AN IMPORTANT MOMENT...
할짜 SHLP 할짝 SHLP
WAIT, THAT DOG...
SHLP SHLP
...IS THE SAME ONE WHO...?
히악 YUCK
할짝 SHLP 할짝 SHLP

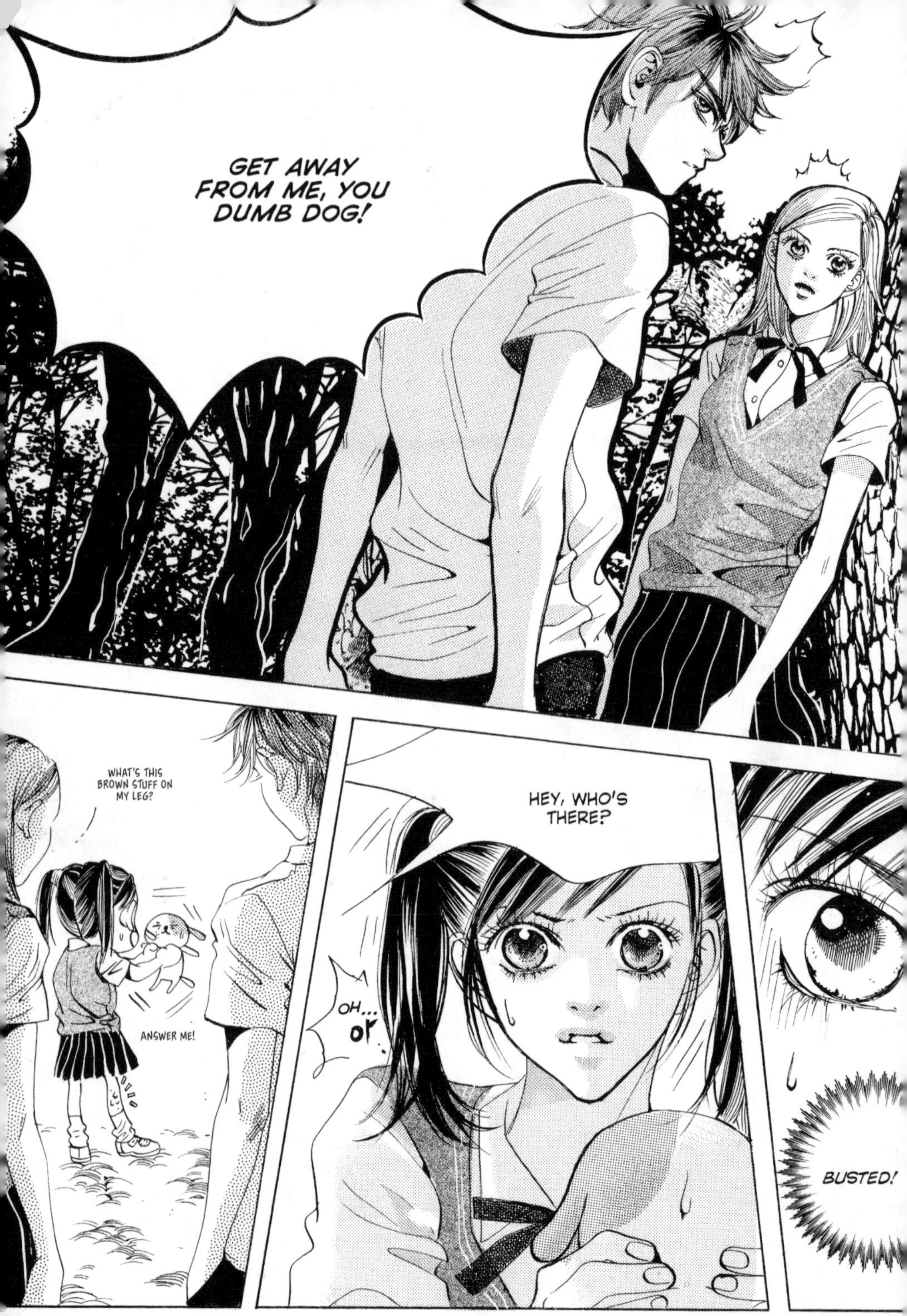
GET AWAY FROM ME, YOU DUMB DOG!
WHAT'S THIS BROWN STUFF ON MY LEG?
ANSWER ME!
HEY, WHO'S THERE?
OH... OH...
BUSTED!

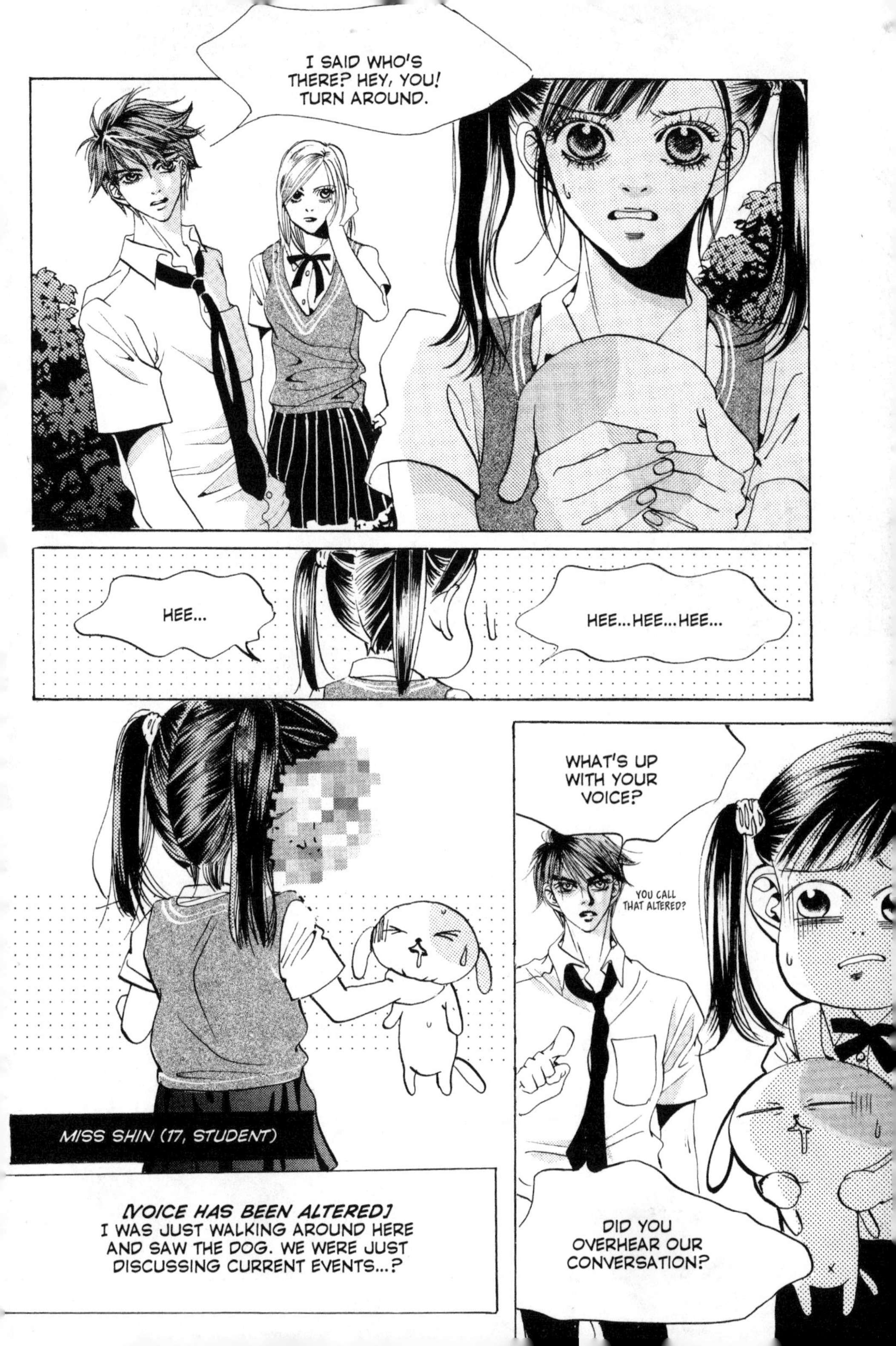
I SAID WHO'S THERE? HEY, YOU! TURN AROUND.
HEE...
HEE...HEE...HEE...
MISS SHIN (17, STUDENT)
[VOICE HAS BEEN ALTERED]
I WAS JUST WALKING AROUND HERE AND SAW THE DOG. WE WERE JUST DISCUSSING CURRENT EVENTS...?
WHAT'S UP WITH YOUR VOICE?
YOU CALL THAT ALTERED?
DID YOU OVERHEAR OUR CONVERSATION?

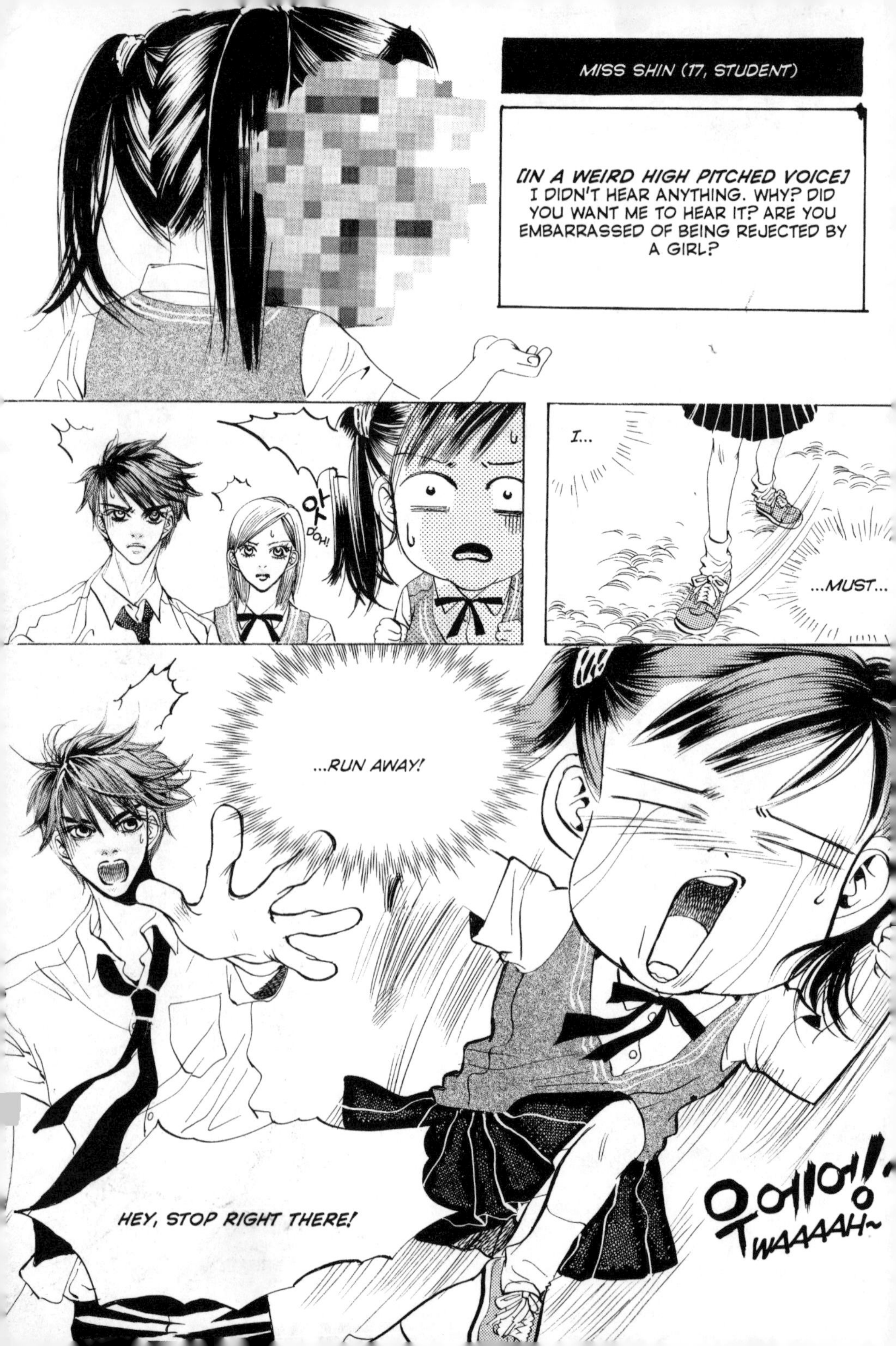
MISS SHIN (17, STUDENT)
[IN A WEIRD HIGH PITCHED VOICE] I DIDN'T HEAR ANYTHING. WHY? DID YOU WANT ME TO HEAR IT? ARE YOU EMBARRASSED OF BEING REJECTED BY A GIRL?
악
DOH!
I...
...MUST...
...RUN AWAY!
HEY, STOP RIGHT THERE!
우에엥!
WAAAAH~

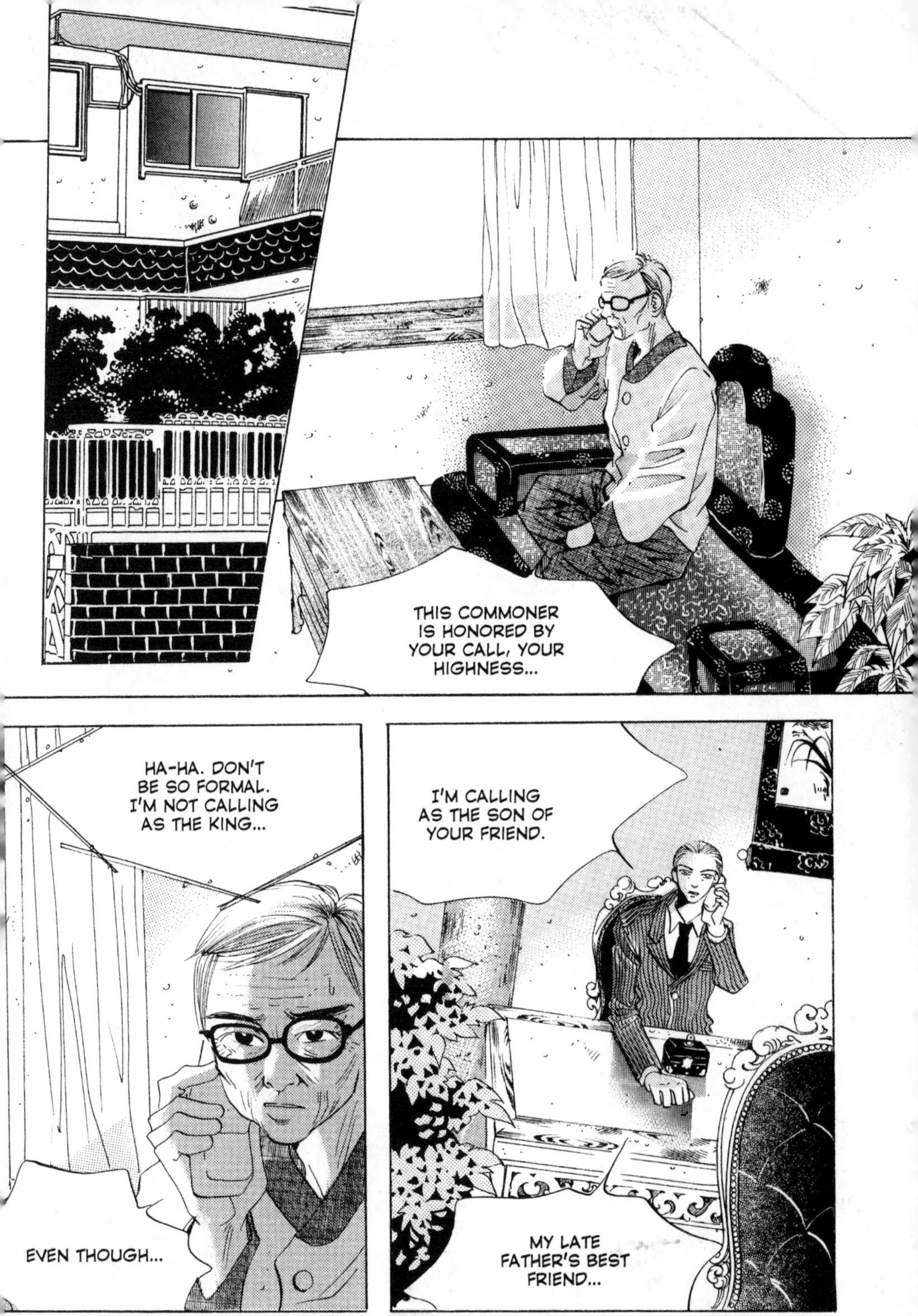
THIS COMMONER IS HONORED BY YOUR CALL, YOUR HIGHNESS...
HA-HA. DON'T BE SO FORMAL. I'M NOT CALLING AS THE KING...
EVEN THOUGH...
I'M CALLING AS THE SON OF YOUR FRIEND.
MY LATE FATHER'S BEST FRIEND...

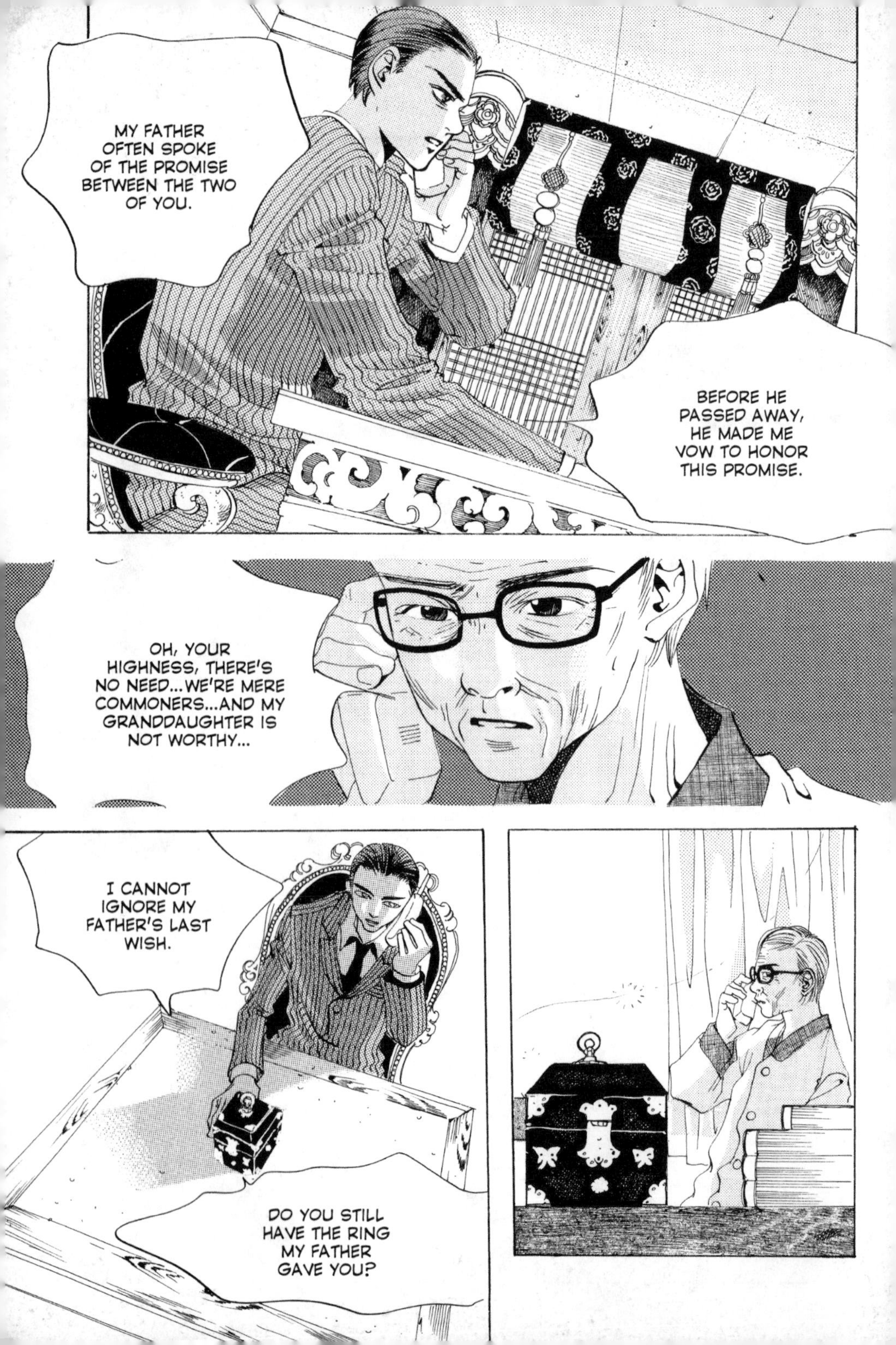

MY FATHER OFTEN SPOKE OF THE PROMISE BETWEEN THE TWO OF YOU.
BEFORE HE PASSED AWAY, HE MADE ME VOW TO HONOR THIS PROMISE.
OH, YOUR HIGHNESS, THERE'S NO NEED...WE'RE MERE COMMONERS...AND MY GRANDDAUGHTER IS NOT WORTHY...
I CANNOT IGNORE MY FATHER'S LAST WISH.
DO YOU STILL HAVE THE RING MY FATHER GAVE YOU?

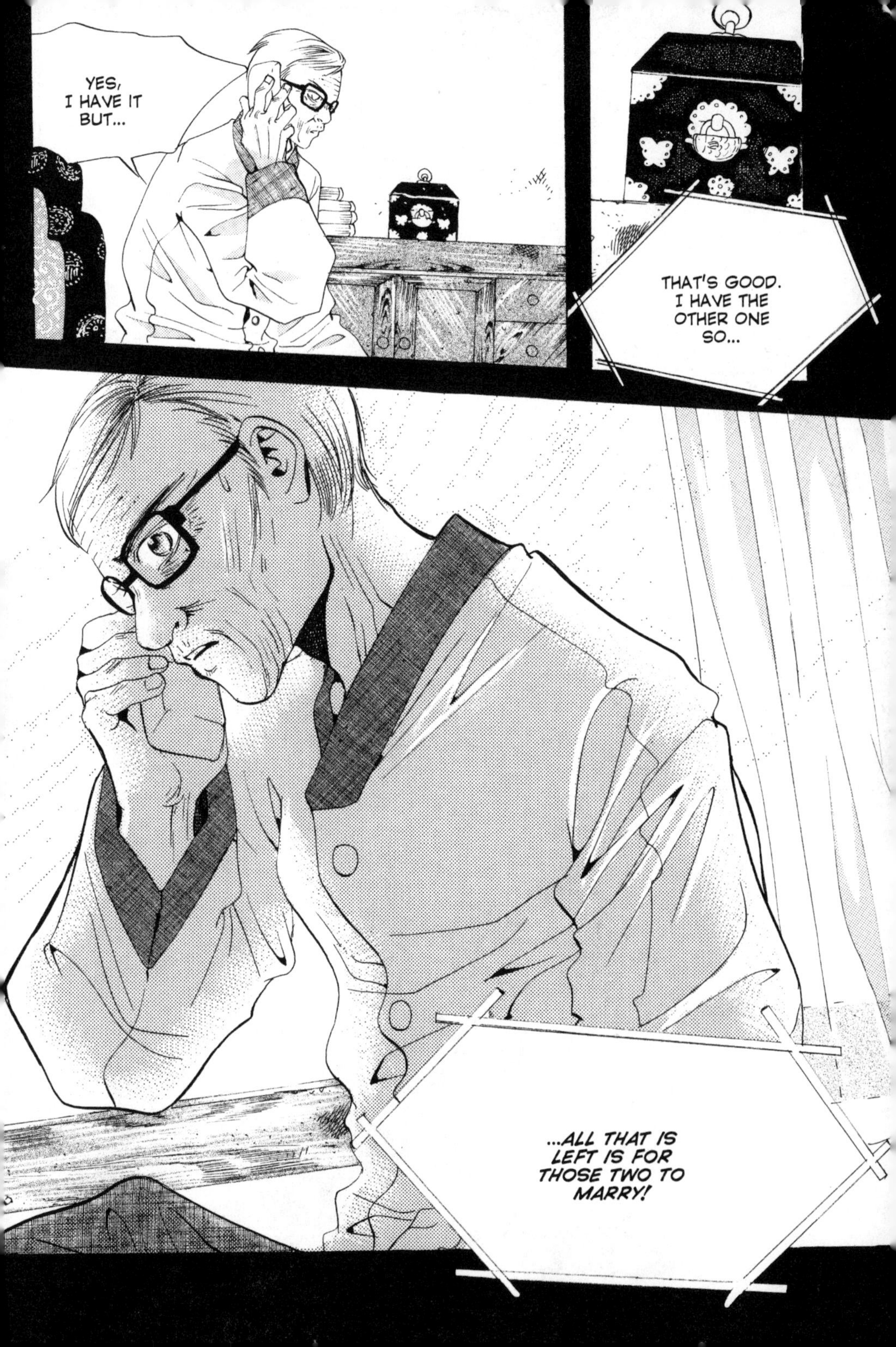
YES, I HAVE IT BUT...
THAT'S GOOD. I HAVE THE OTHER ONE SO...
...ALL THAT IS LEFT IS FOR THOSE TWO TO MARRY!

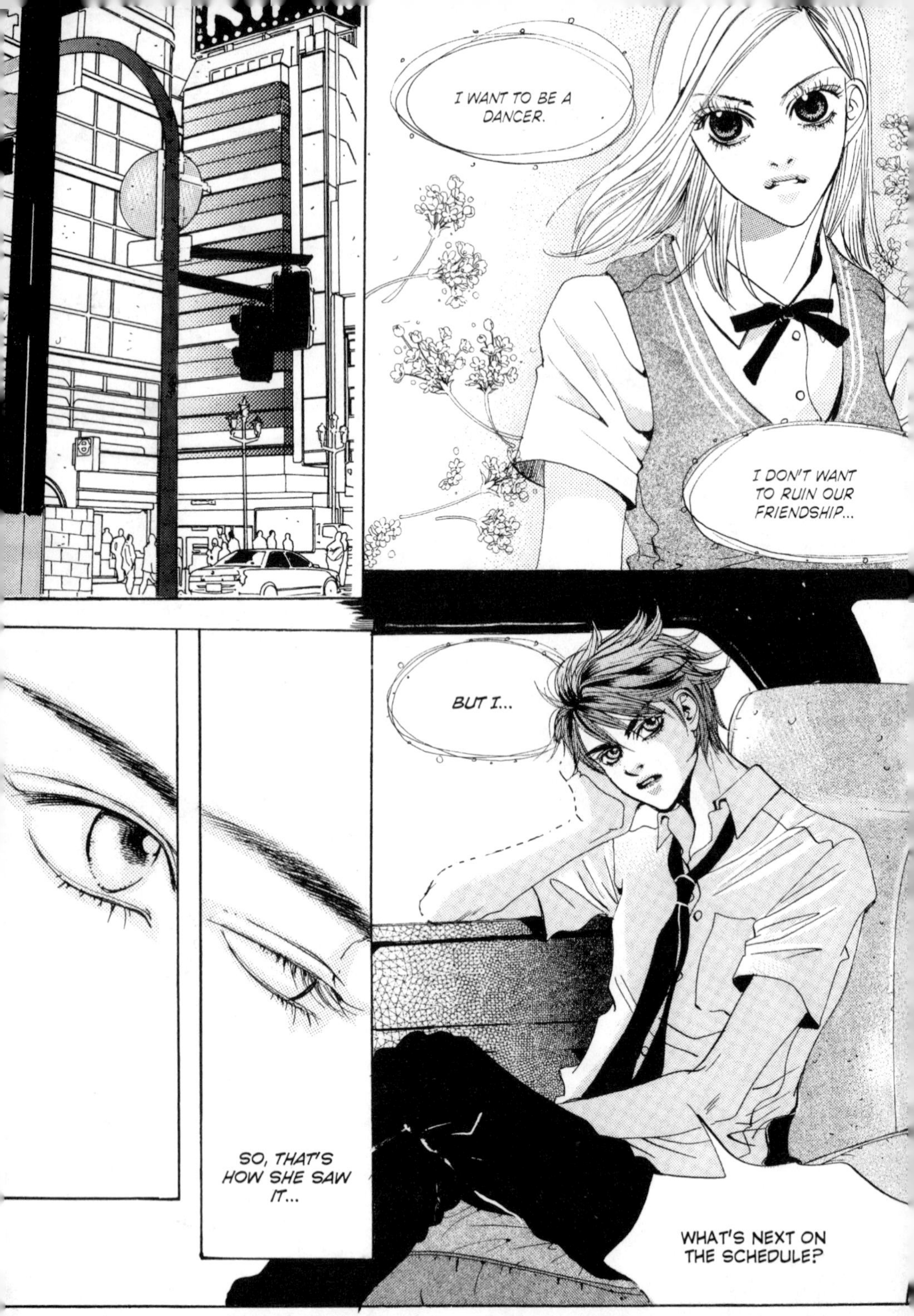
I WANT TO BE A DANCER.
I DON'T WANT TO RUIN OUR FRIENDSHIP...
BUT I...
SO, THAT'S HOW SHE SAW IT...
WHAT'S NEXT ON THE SCHEDULE?

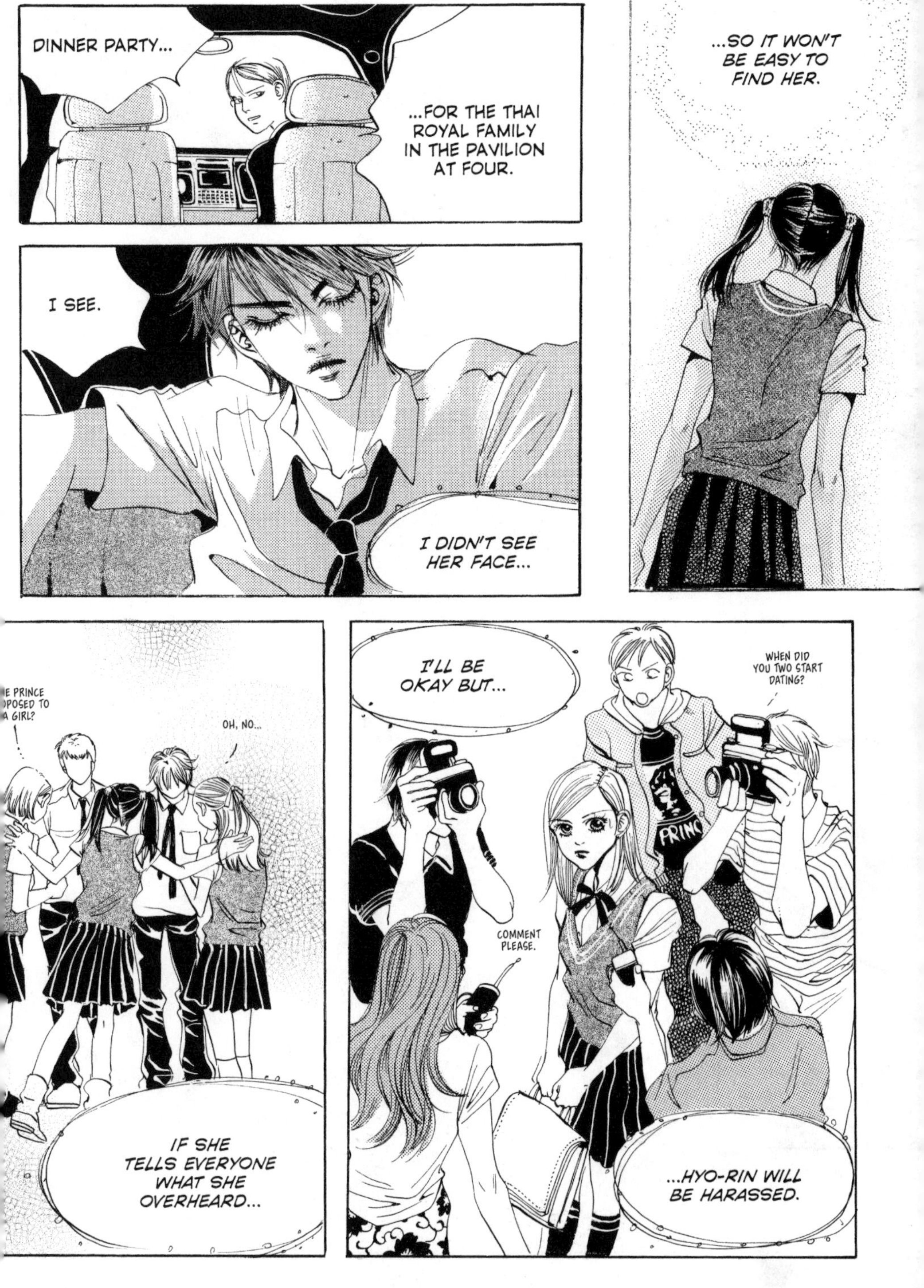
DINNER PARTY...
...FOR THE THAI ROYAL FAMILY IN THE PAVILION AT FOUR.
I SEE.
I DIDN'T SEE HER FACE...
...SO IT WON'T BE EASY TO FIND HER.
E PRINCE OPOSED TO A GIRL?
OH, NO...
IF SHE TELLS EVERYONE WHAT SHE OVERHEARD...
I'LL BE OKAY BUT...
WHEN DID YOU TWO START DATING?
COMMENT PLEASE.
...HYO-RIN WILL BE HARASSED.

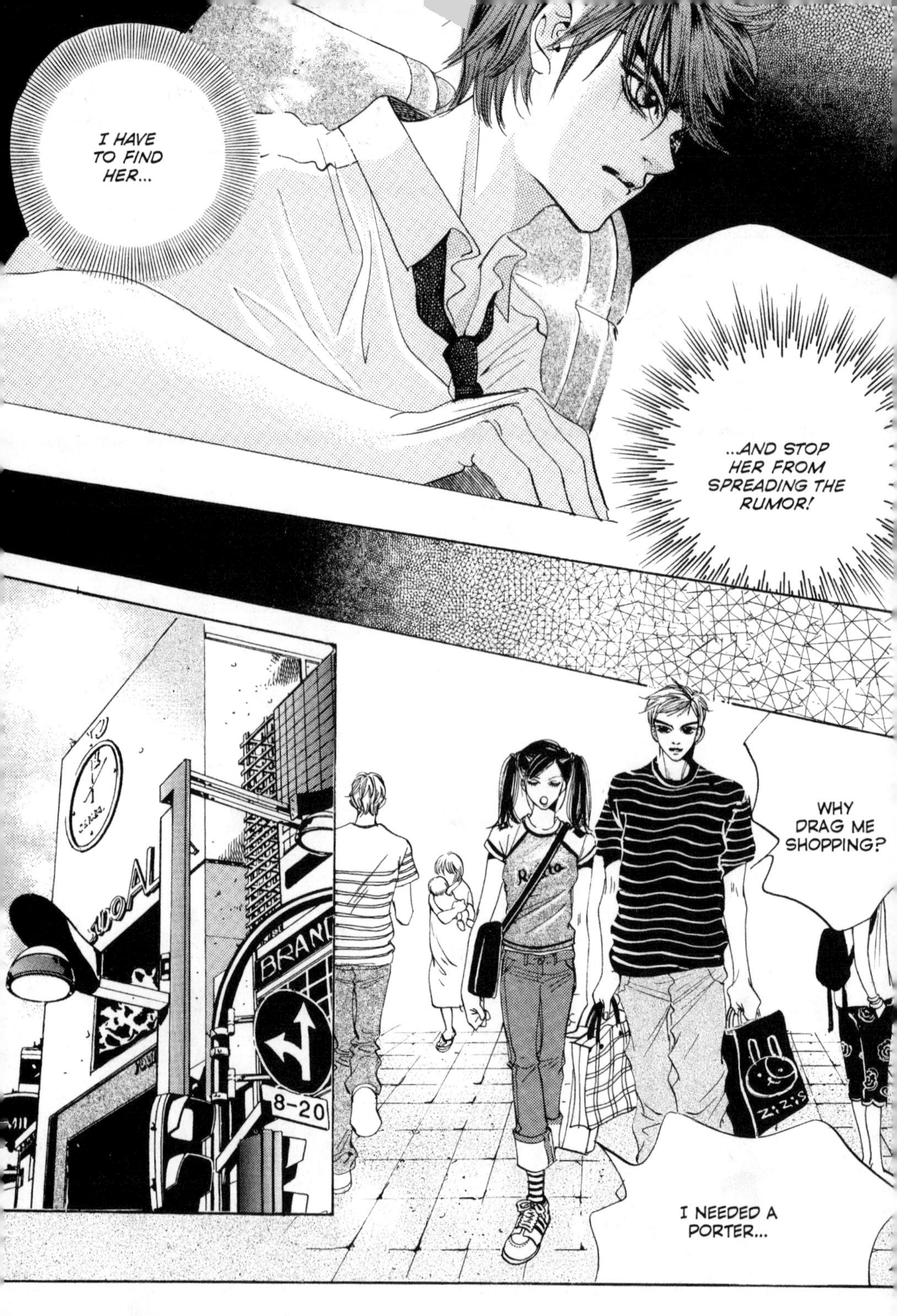
I HAVE TO FIND HER...
...AND STOP HER FROM SPREADING THE RUMOR!
WHY DRAG ME SHOPPING?
I NEEDED A PORTER...
BRAND
8-20
Z·Z·Z·S

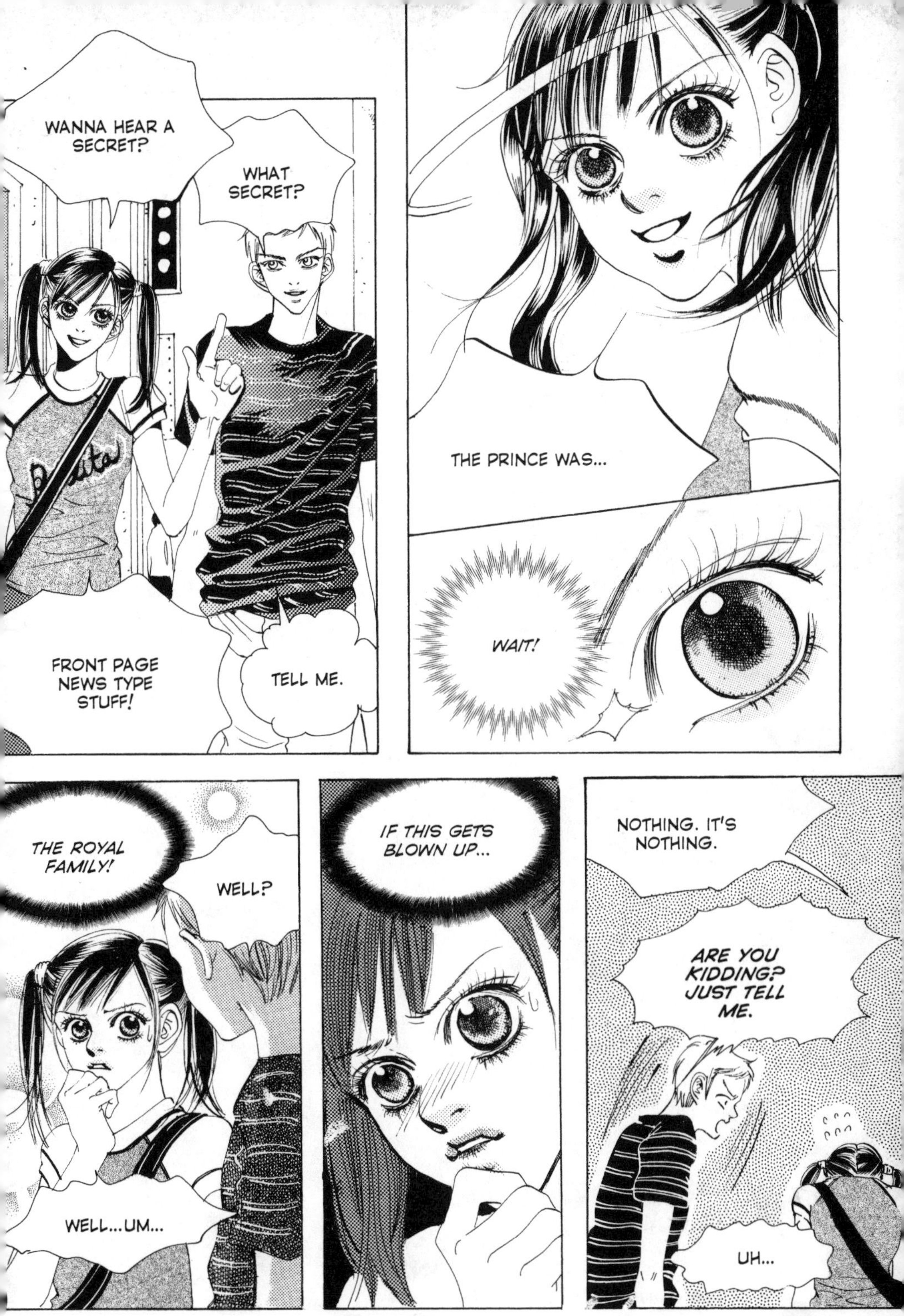
WANNA HEAR A SECRET?
WHAT SECRET?
FRONT PAGE NEWS TYPE STUFF!
TELL ME.
THE PRINCE WAS...
WAIT!
THE ROYAL FAMILY!
WELL?
WELL...UM...
IF THIS GETS BLOWN UP...
NOTHING. IT'S NOTHING.
ARE YOU KIDDING? JUST TELL ME.
UH...

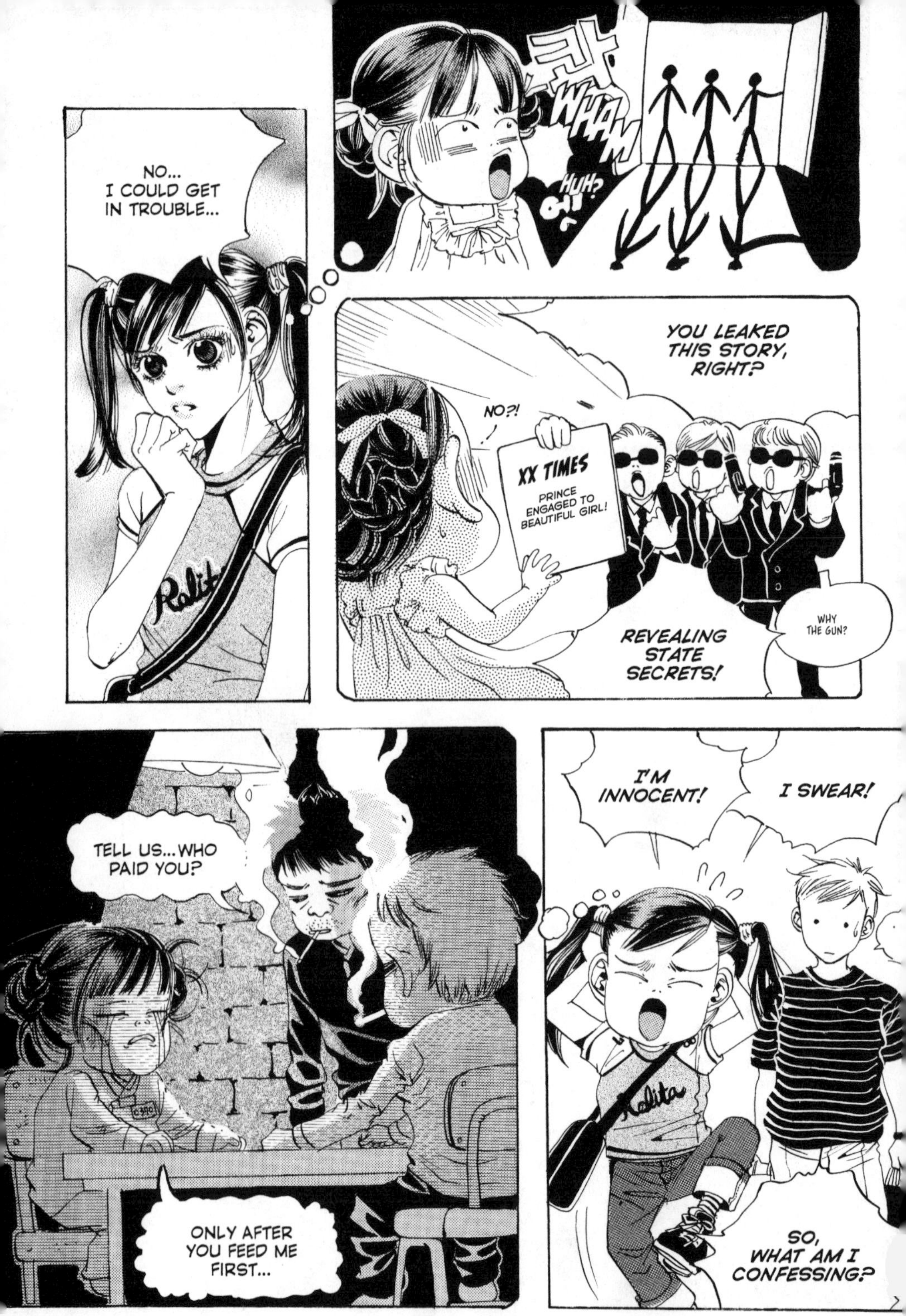
NO... I COULD GET IN TROUBLE...
WHAM
HUH?
YOU LEAKED THIS STORY, RIGHT?
NO?!
XX TIMES
PRINCE ENGAGED TO BEAUTIFUL GIRL!
REVEALING STATE SECRETS!
WHY THE GUN?
TELL US...WHO PAID YOU?
ONLY AFTER YOU FEED ME FIRST...
I'M INNOCENT!
I SWEAR!
SO, WHAT AM I CONFESSING?

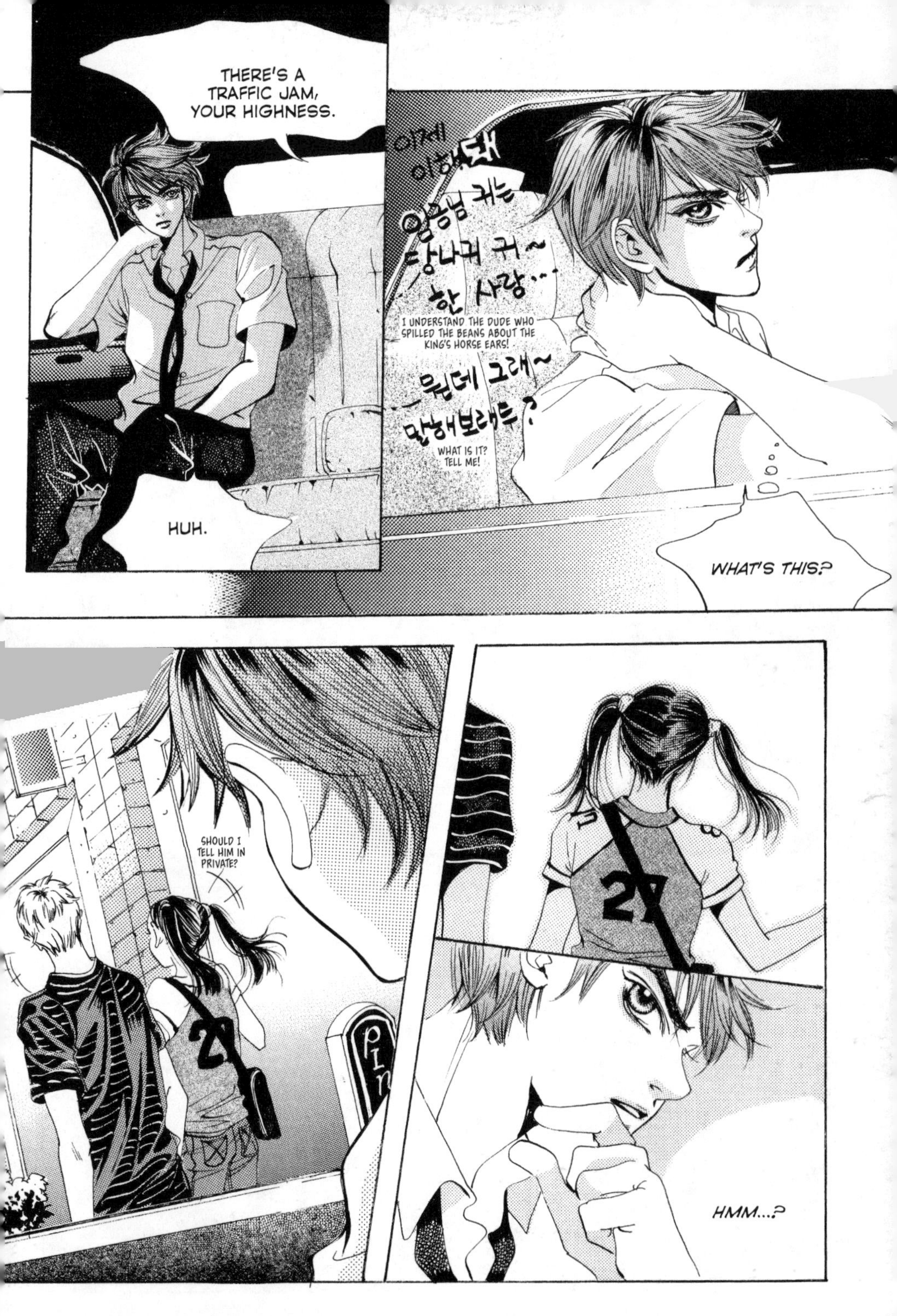
THERE'S A TRAFFIC JAM, YOUR HIGHNESS.
HUH.
이제 이해돼 임금님 귀는 당나귀 귀~ 한 사람...
I UNDERSTAND THE DUDE WHO SPILLED THE BEANS ABOUT THE KING'S HORSE EARS!
뭔데 그래~ 말해보래두?
WHAT IS IT? TELL ME!
WHAT'S THIS?
SHOULD I TELL HIM IN PRIVATE?
HMM...?

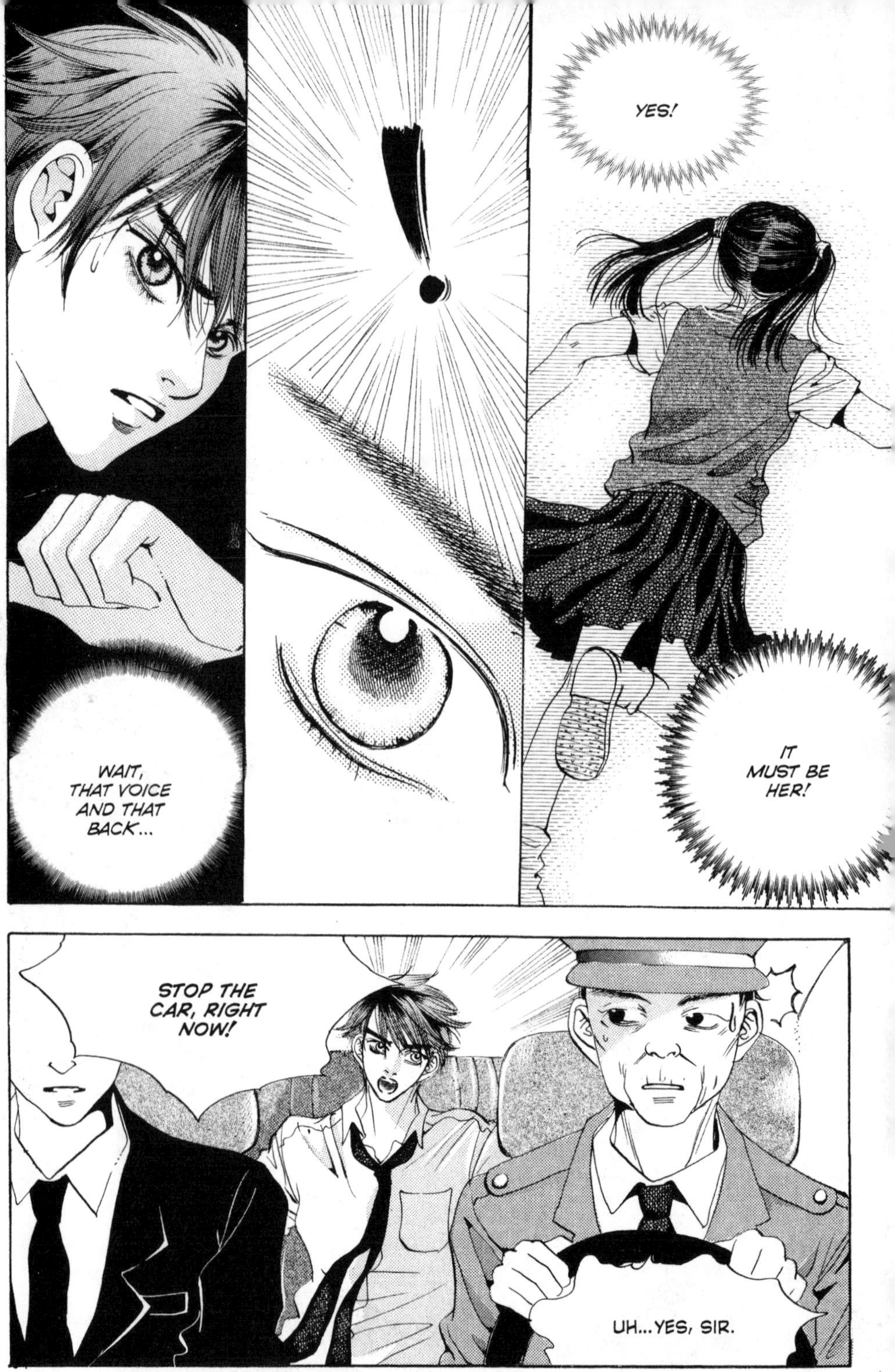
WAIT, THAT VOICE AND THAT BACK...
!
YES!
IT MUST BE HER!
STOP THE CAR, RIGHT NOW!
UH...YES, SIR.

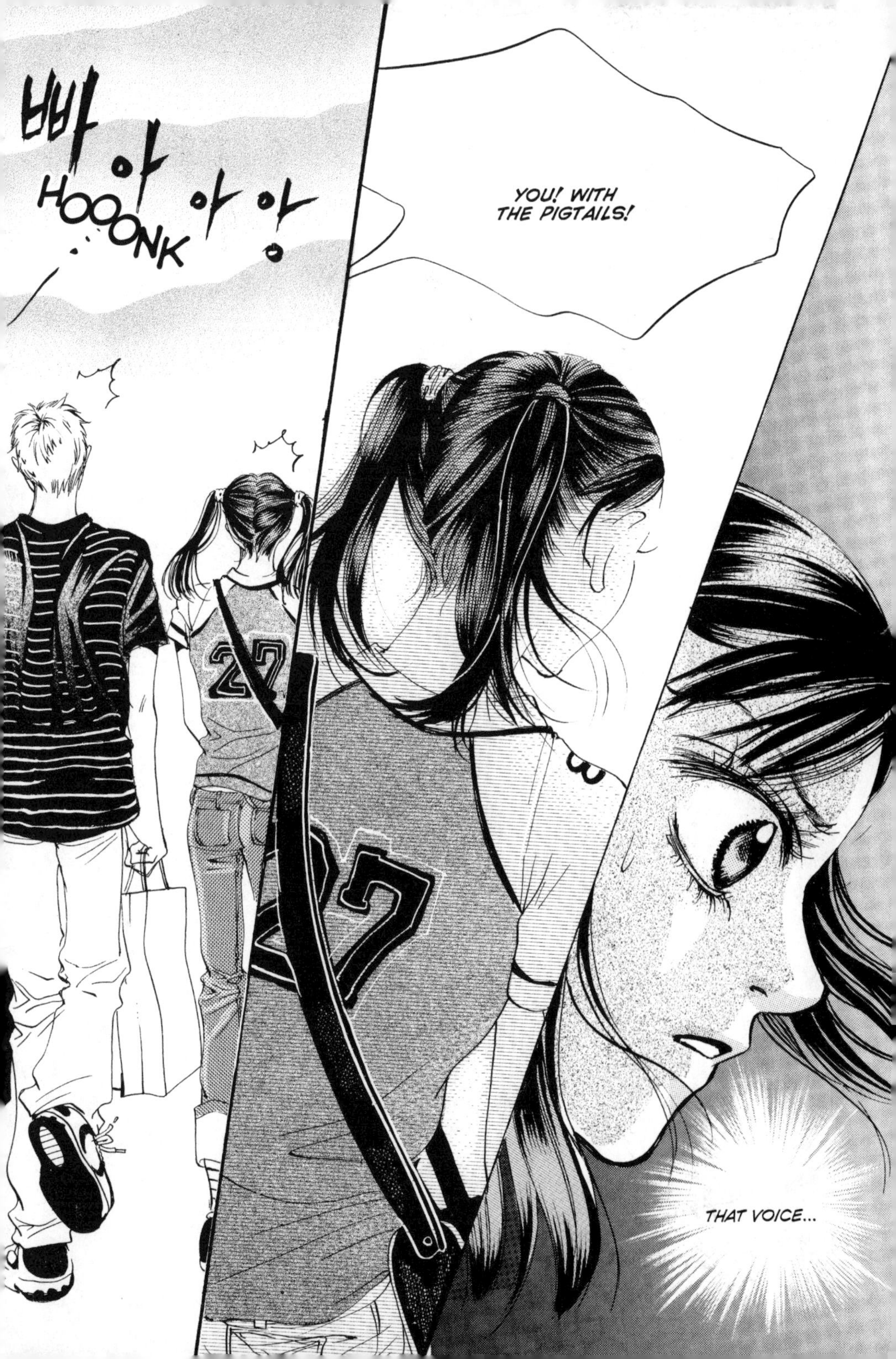
빠아아앙
HOOONK
YOU! WITH
THE PIGTAILS!
THAT VOICE...

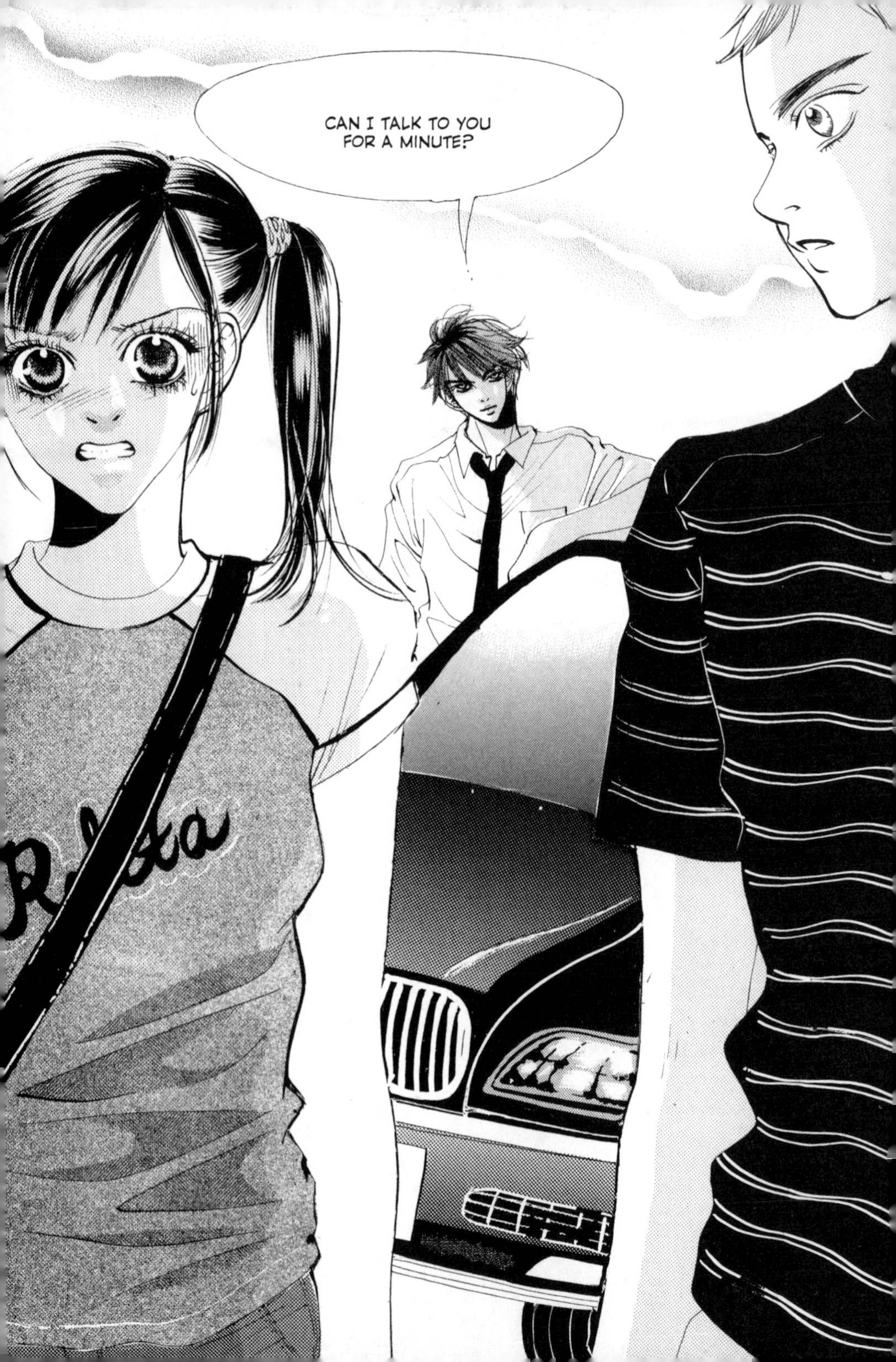
CAN I TALK TO YOU FOR A MINUTE?

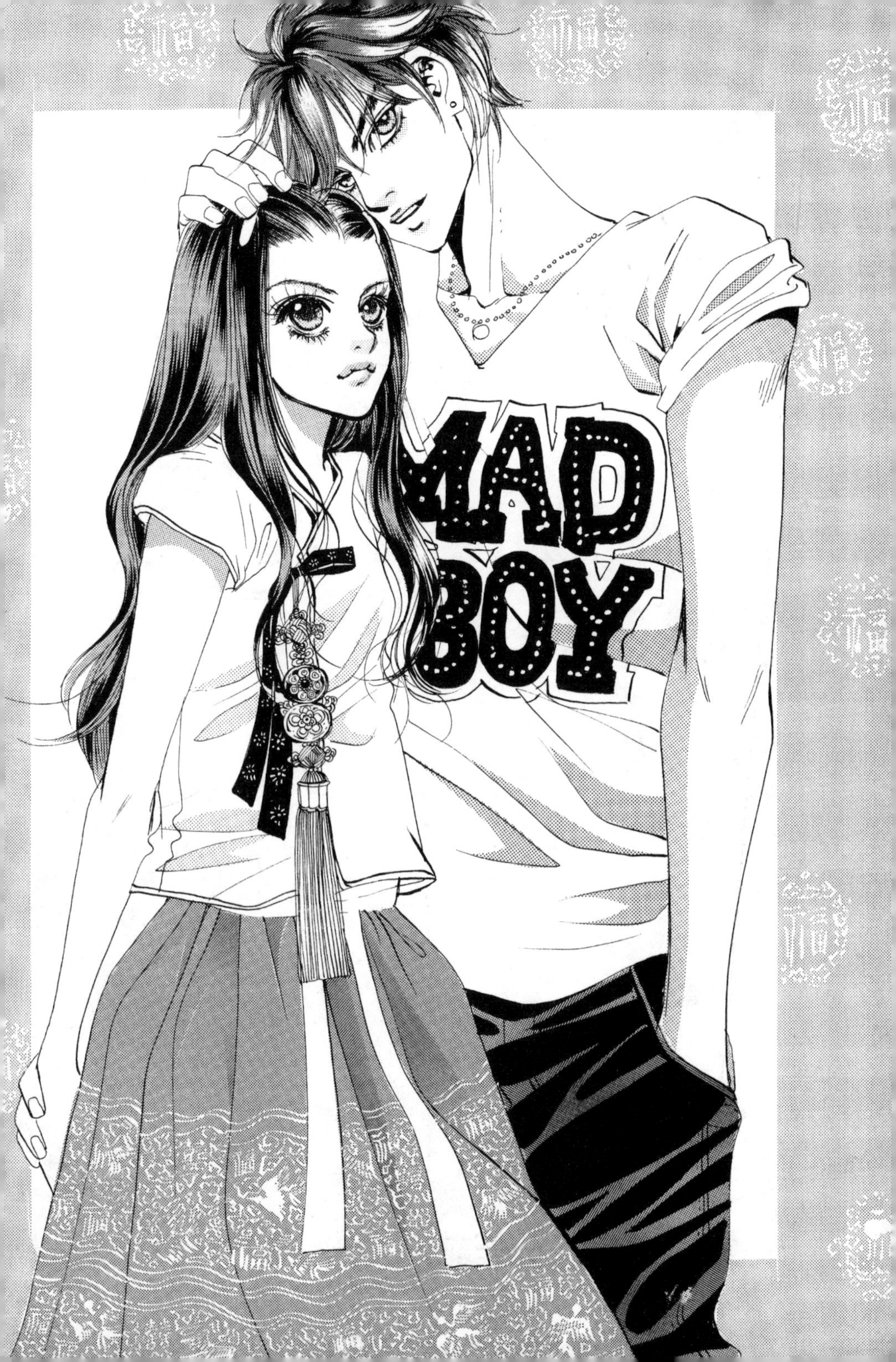
MAD
BOY

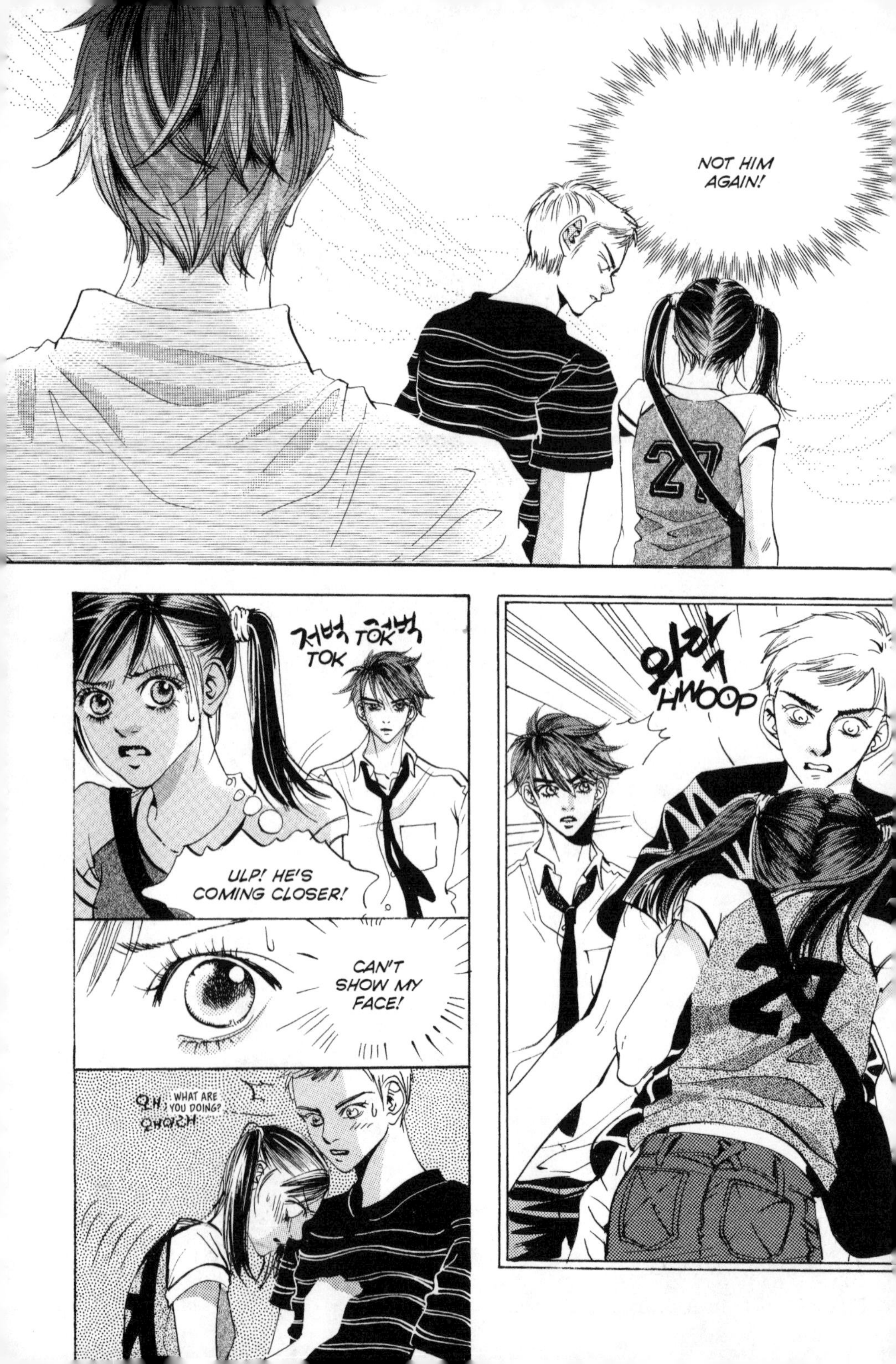
NOT HIM AGAIN!
저벅 저벅
TOK TOK
ULP! HE'S COMING CLOSER!
CAN'T SHOW MY FACE!
왜 왜이래
WHAT ARE YOU DOING?
와락
HWOOP

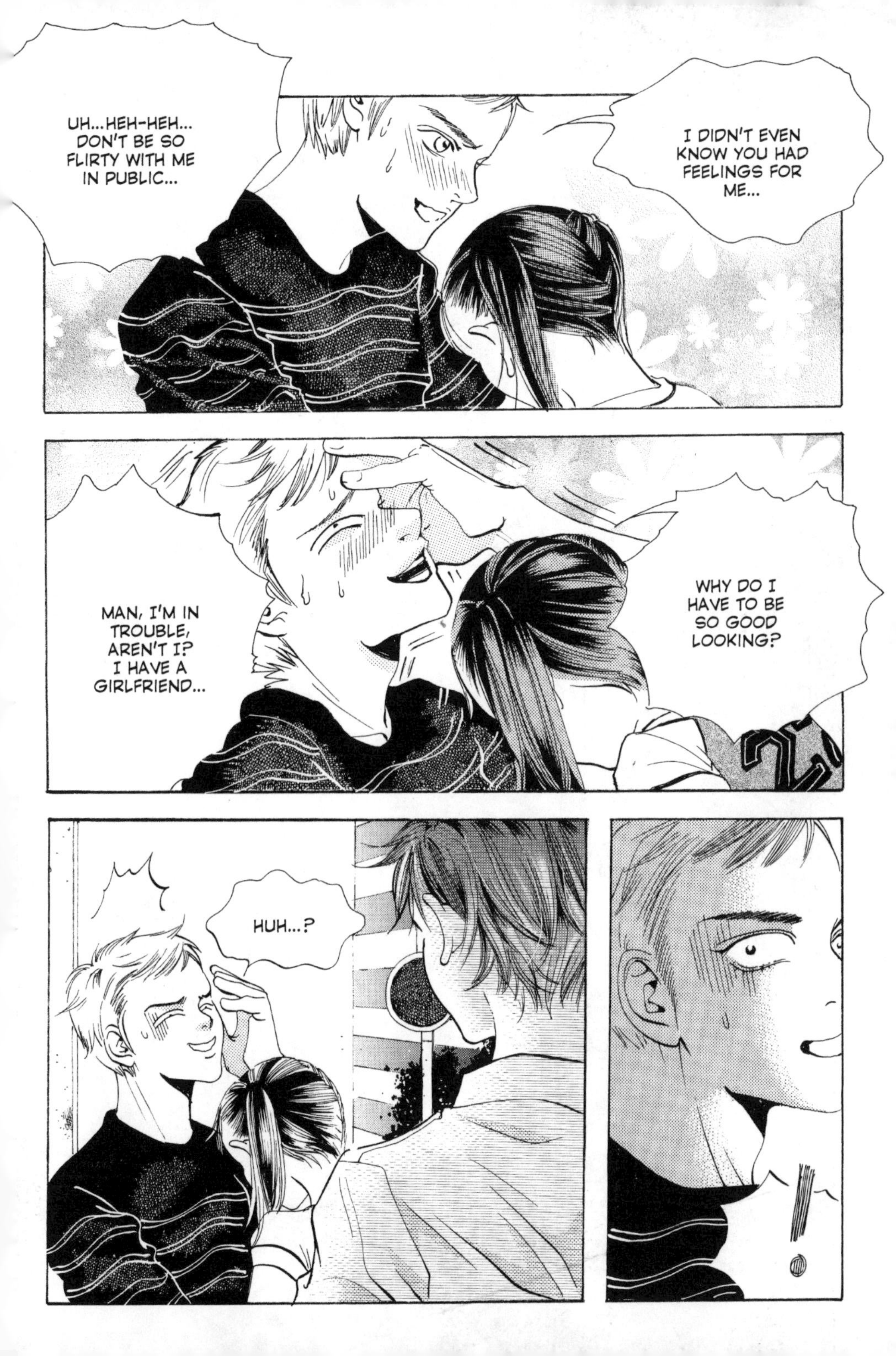
UH...HEH-HEH... DON'T BE SO FLIRTY WITH ME IN PUBLIC...
I DIDN'T EVEN KNOW YOU HAD FEELINGS FOR ME...
MAN, I'M IN TROUBLE, AREN'T I? I HAVE A GIRLFRIEND...
WHY DO I HAVE TO BE SO GOOD LOOKING?
HUH...?

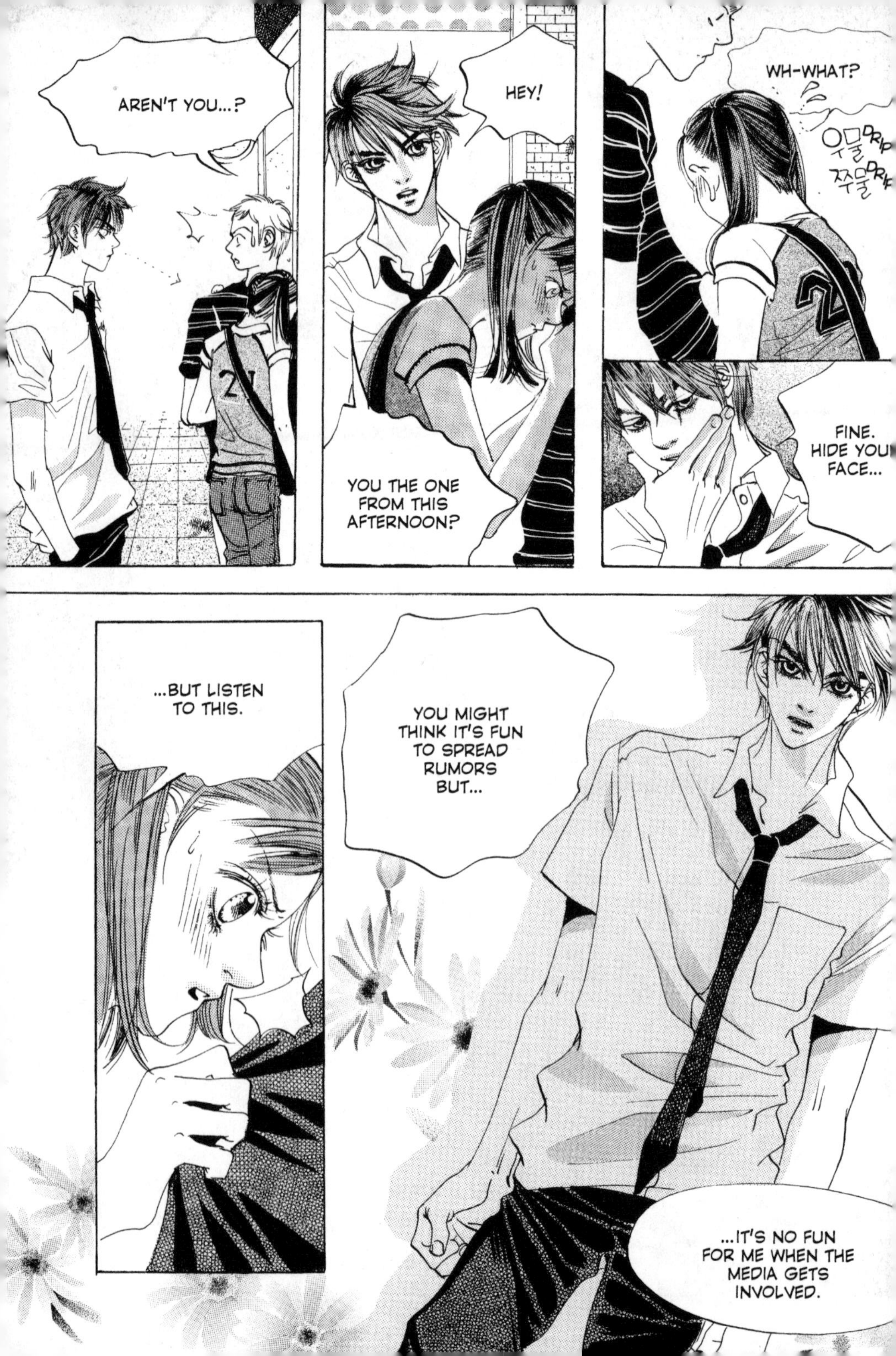
AREN'T YOU...?
HEY!
YOU THE ONE FROM THIS AFTERNOON?
WH-WHAT?
우물 DRIP
쭈물 DRIP
FINE. HIDE YOU FACE...
...BUT LISTEN TO THIS.
YOU MIGHT THINK IT'S FUN TO SPREAD RUMORS BUT...
...IT'S NO FUN FOR ME WHEN THE MEDIA GETS INVOLVED.

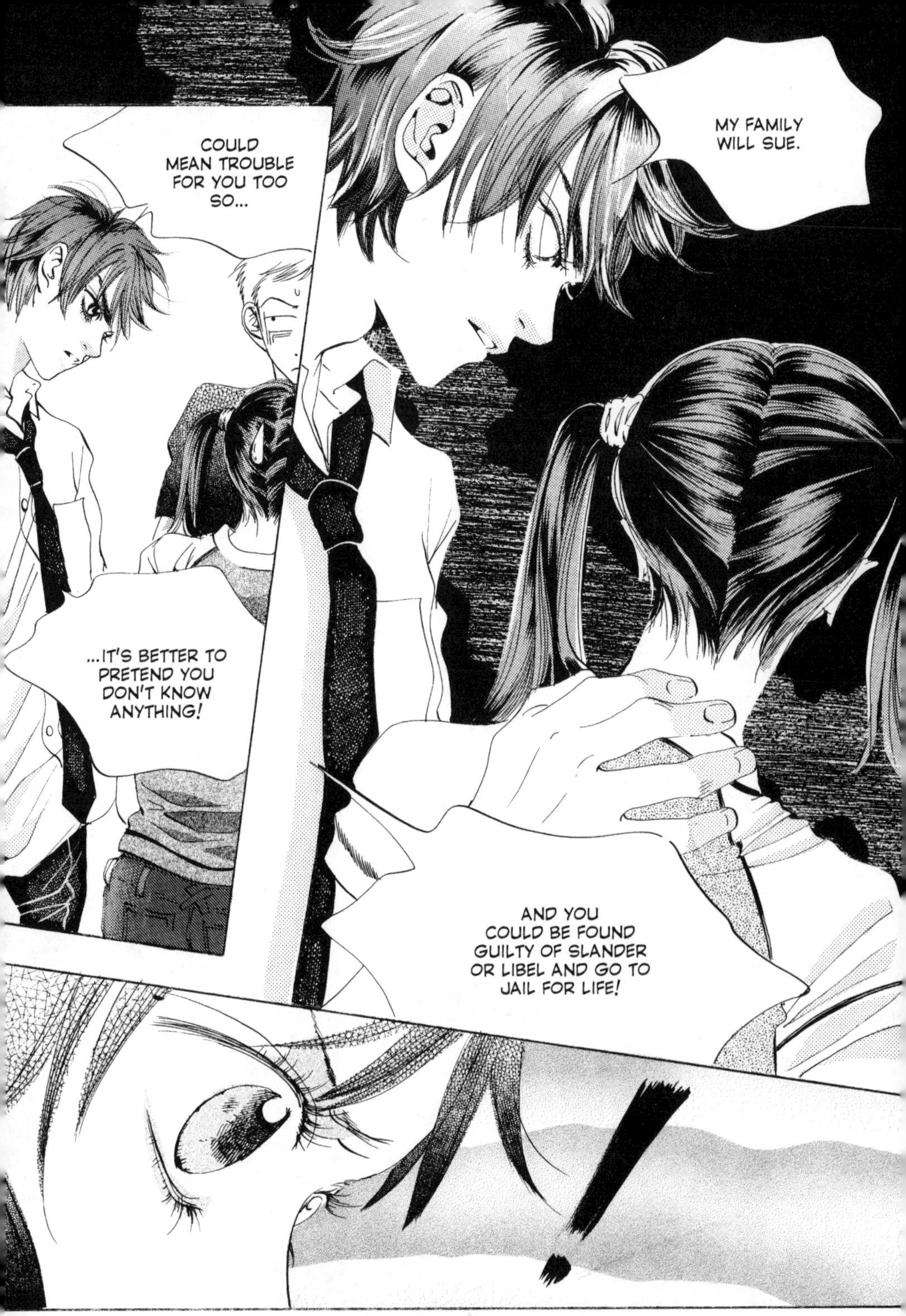
COULD MEAN TROUBLE FOR YOU TOO SO...
...IT'S BETTER TO PRETEND YOU DON'T KNOW ANYTHING!
MY FAMILY WILL SUE.
AND YOU COULD BE FOUND GUILTY OF SLANDER OR LIBEL AND GO TO JAIL FOR LIFE!

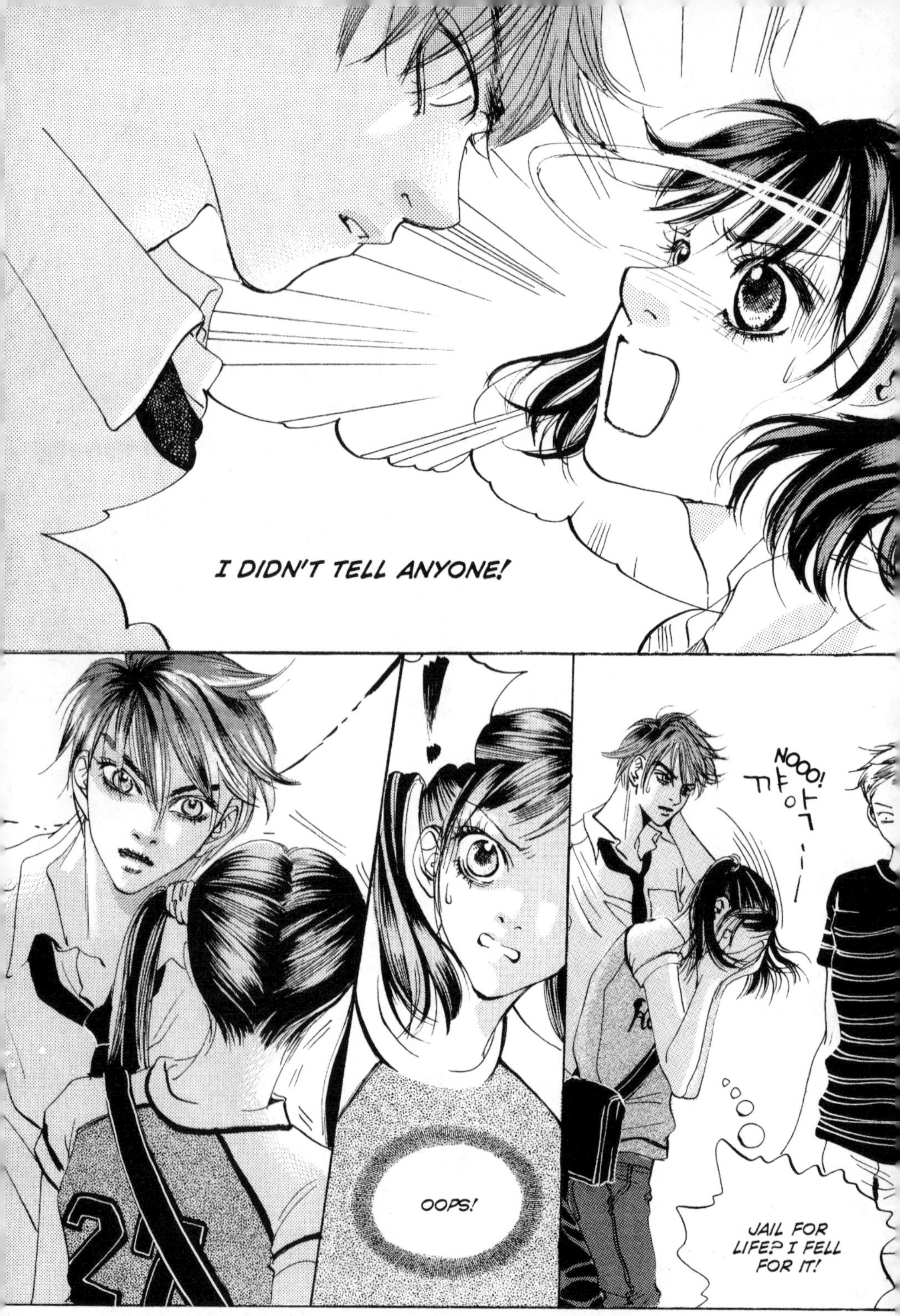
I DIDN'T TELL ANYONE!
!
OOPS!
NOOO!
JAIL FOR LIFE? I FELL FOR IT!

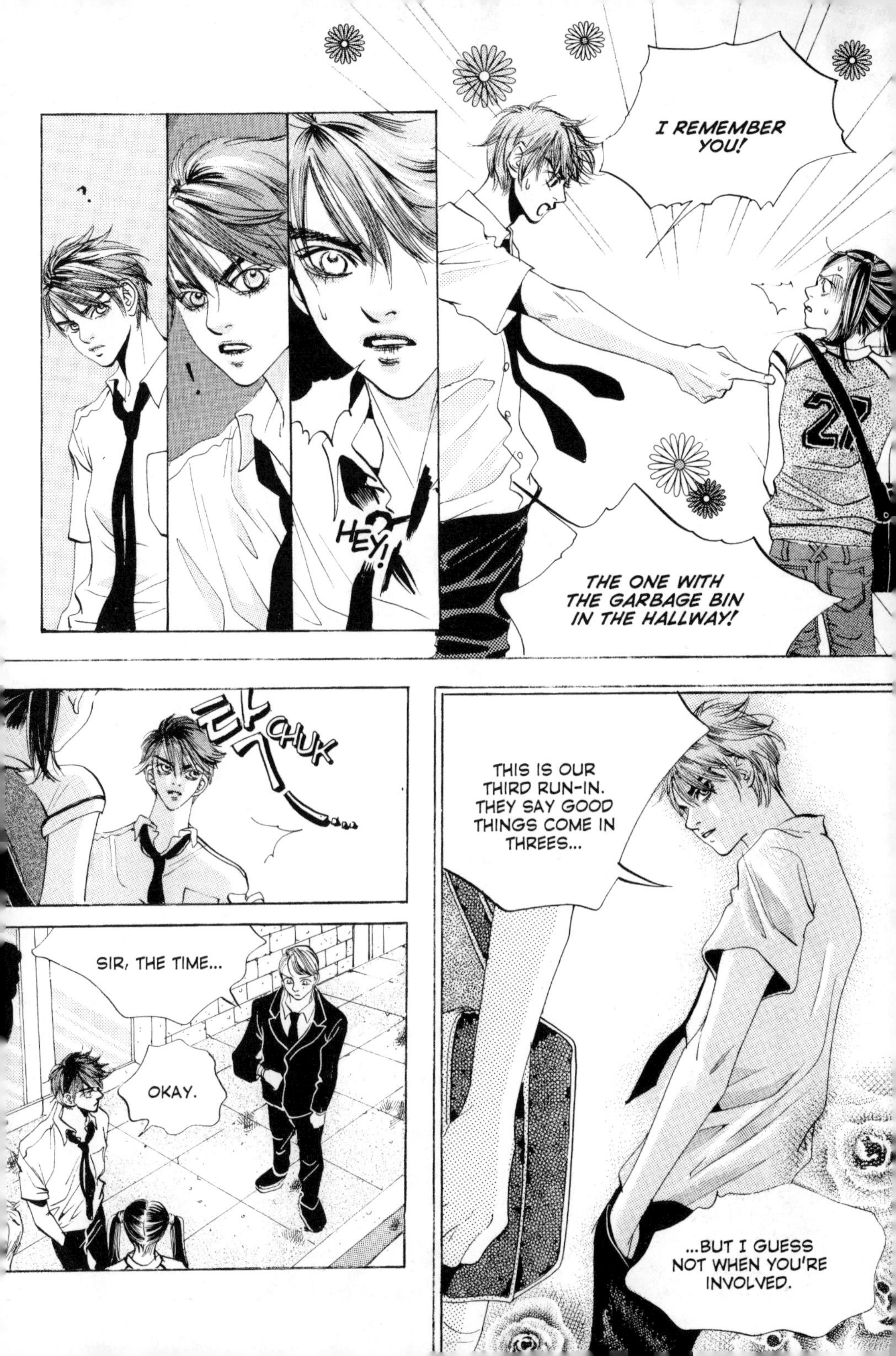
?
!
HEY!
I REMEMBER YOU!
THE ONE WITH THE GARBAGE BIN IN THE HALLWAY!
CHUK
SIR, THE TIME...
OKAY.
THIS IS OUR THIRD RUN-IN. THEY SAY GOOD THINGS COME IN THREES...
...BUT I GUESS NOT WHEN YOU'RE INVOLVED.

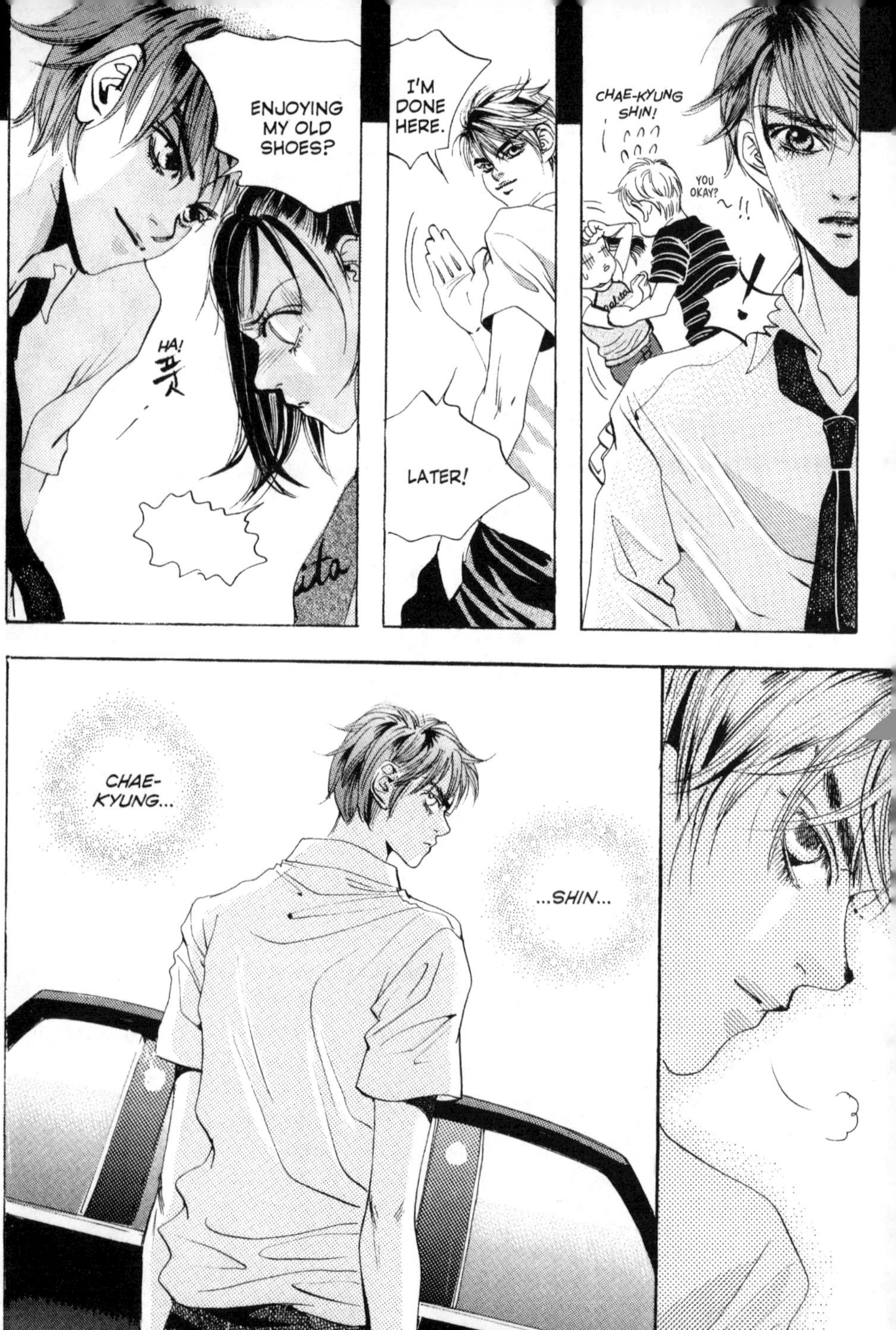
ENJOYING MY OLD SHOES?
HA!
픗
I'M DONE HERE.
LATER!
CHAE-KYUNG SHIN!
YOU OKAY?
!!
!
CHAE-KYUNG...
...SHIN...

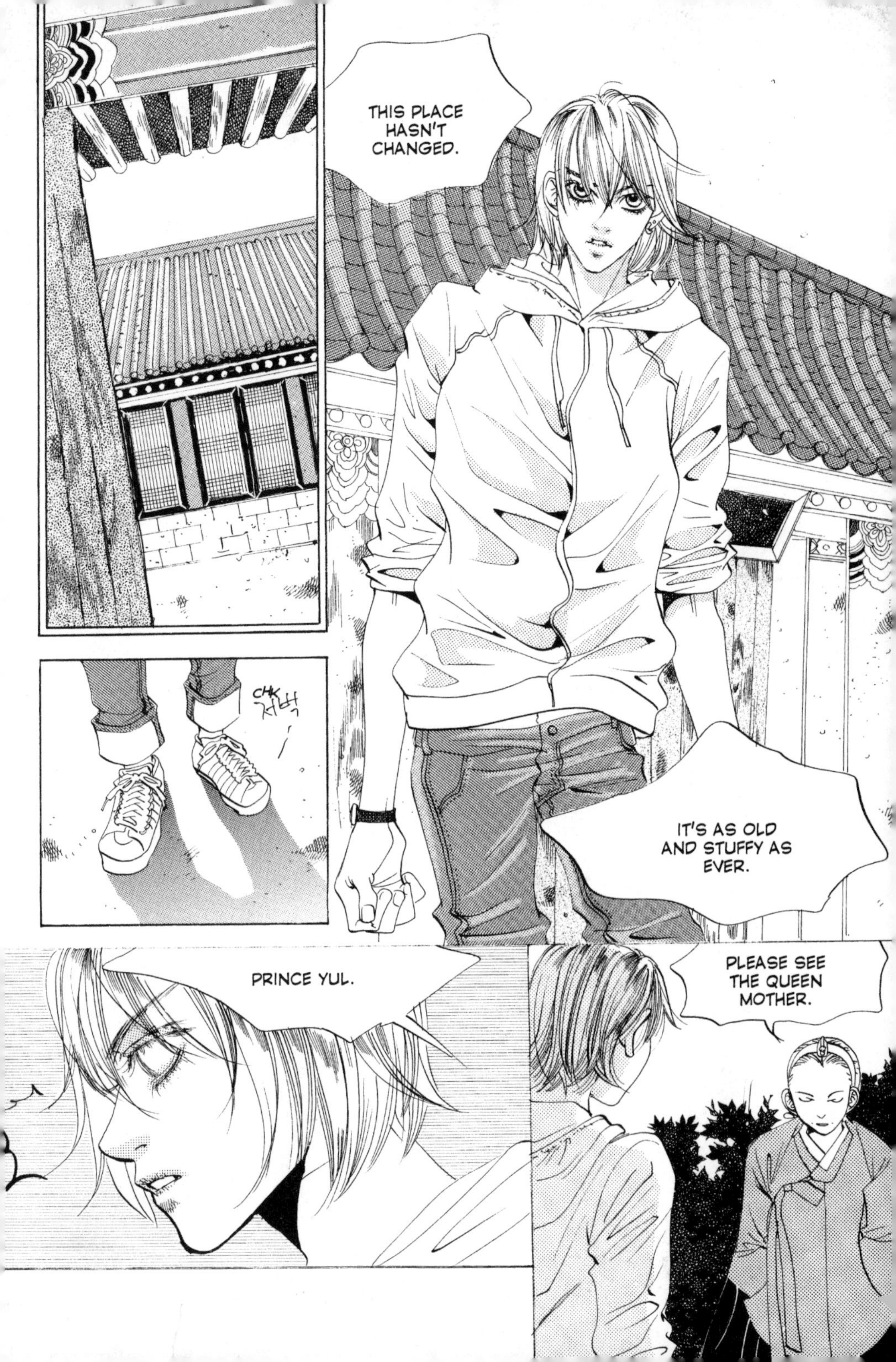
CHK
저벅
THIS PLACE HASN'T CHANGED.
IT'S AS OLD AND STUFFY AS EVER.
PRINCE YUL.
PLEASE SEE THE QUEEN MOTHER.

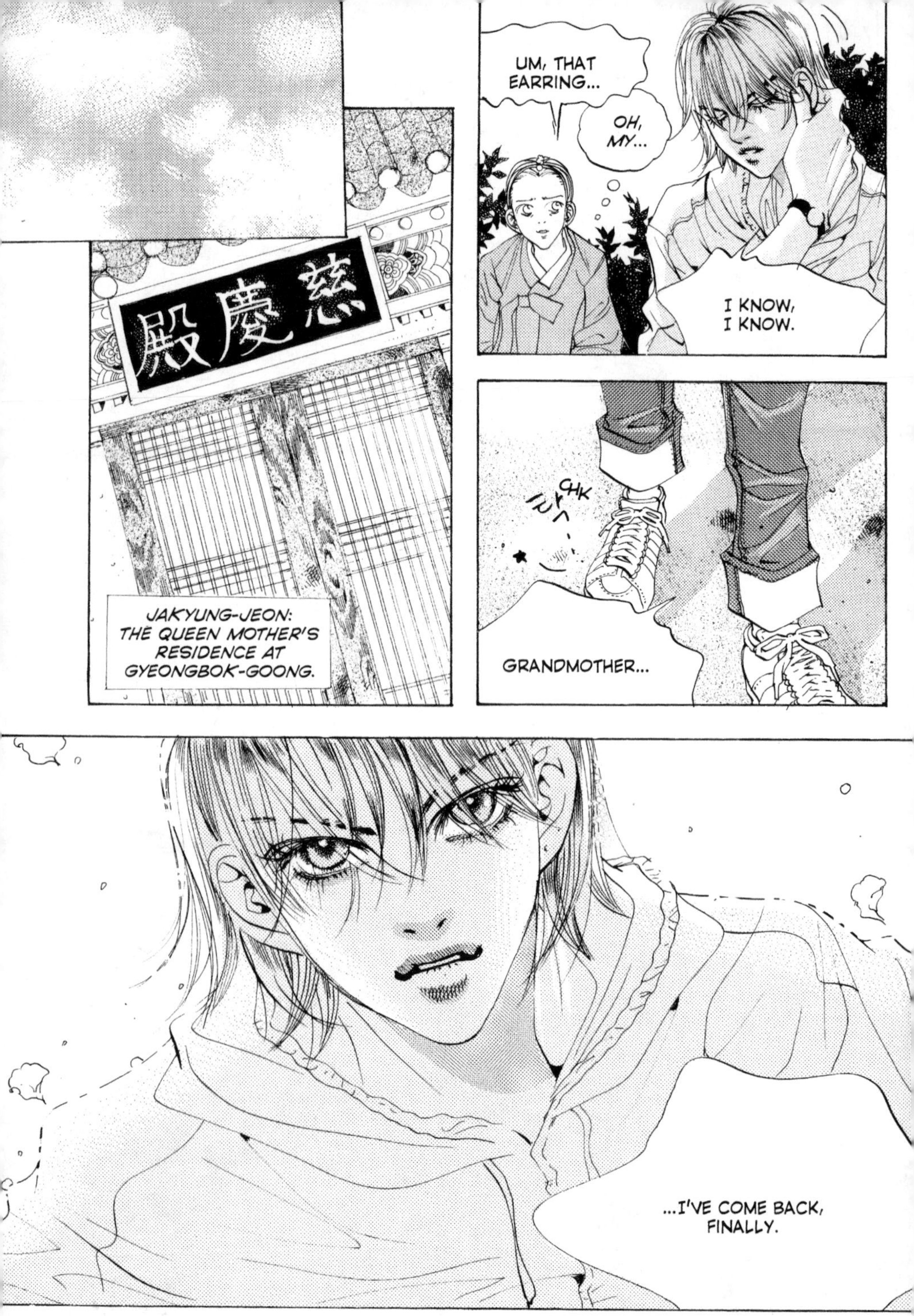

慈慶殿
JAKYUNG-JEON: THE QUEEN MOTHER'S RESIDENCE AT GYEONGBOK-GOONG.
UM, THAT EARRING...
OH, MY...
I KNOW, I KNOW.
CHK
GRANDMOTHER...
...I'VE COME BACK, FINALLY.

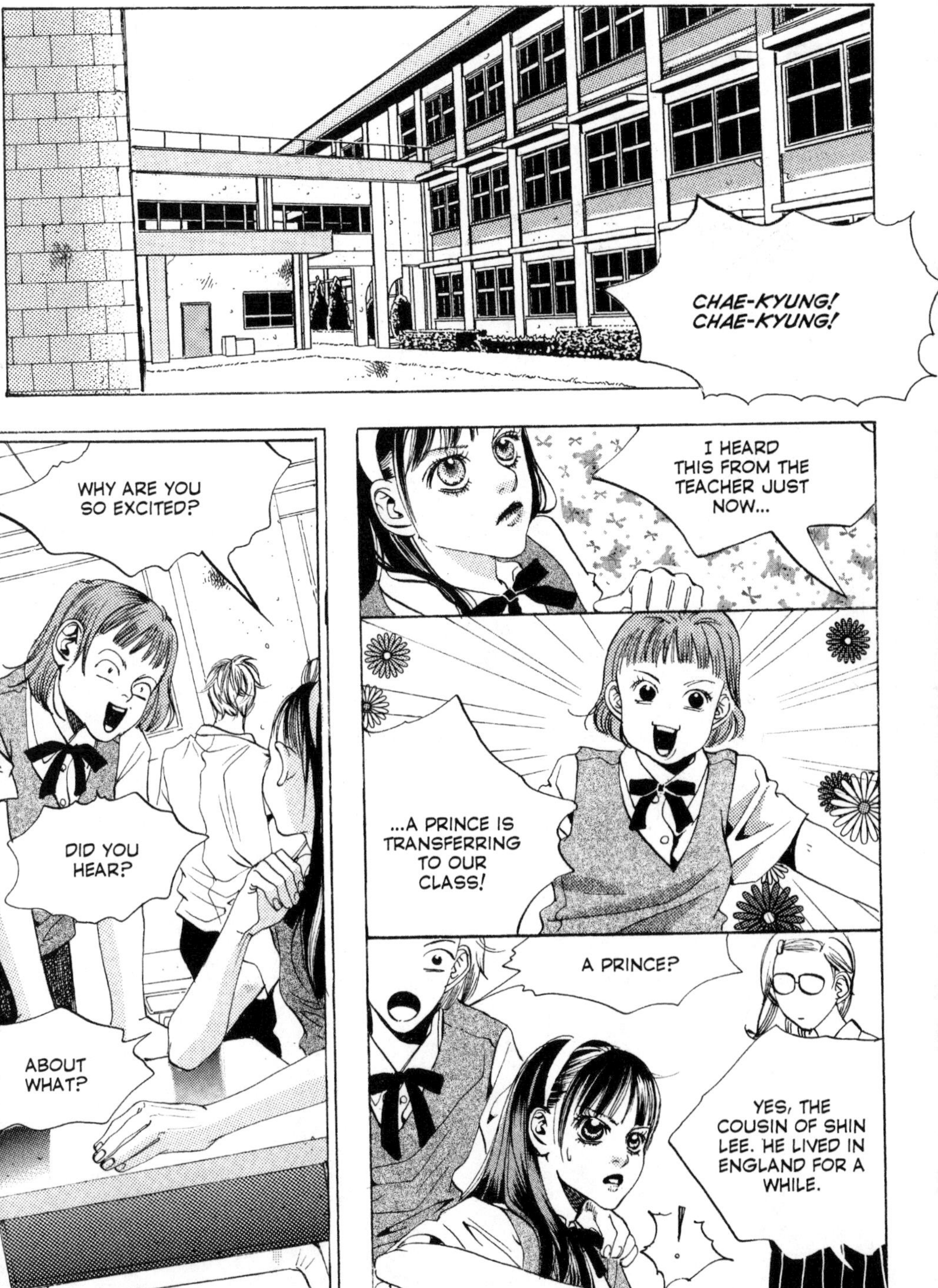
CHAE-KYUNG! CHAE-KYUNG!
WHY ARE YOU SO EXCITED?
DID YOU HEAR?
ABOUT WHAT?
I HEARD THIS FROM THE TEACHER JUST NOW...
...A PRINCE IS TRANSFERRING TO OUR CLASS!
A PRINCE?
YES, THE COUSIN OF SHIN LEE. HE LIVED IN ENGLAND FOR A WHILE.
!

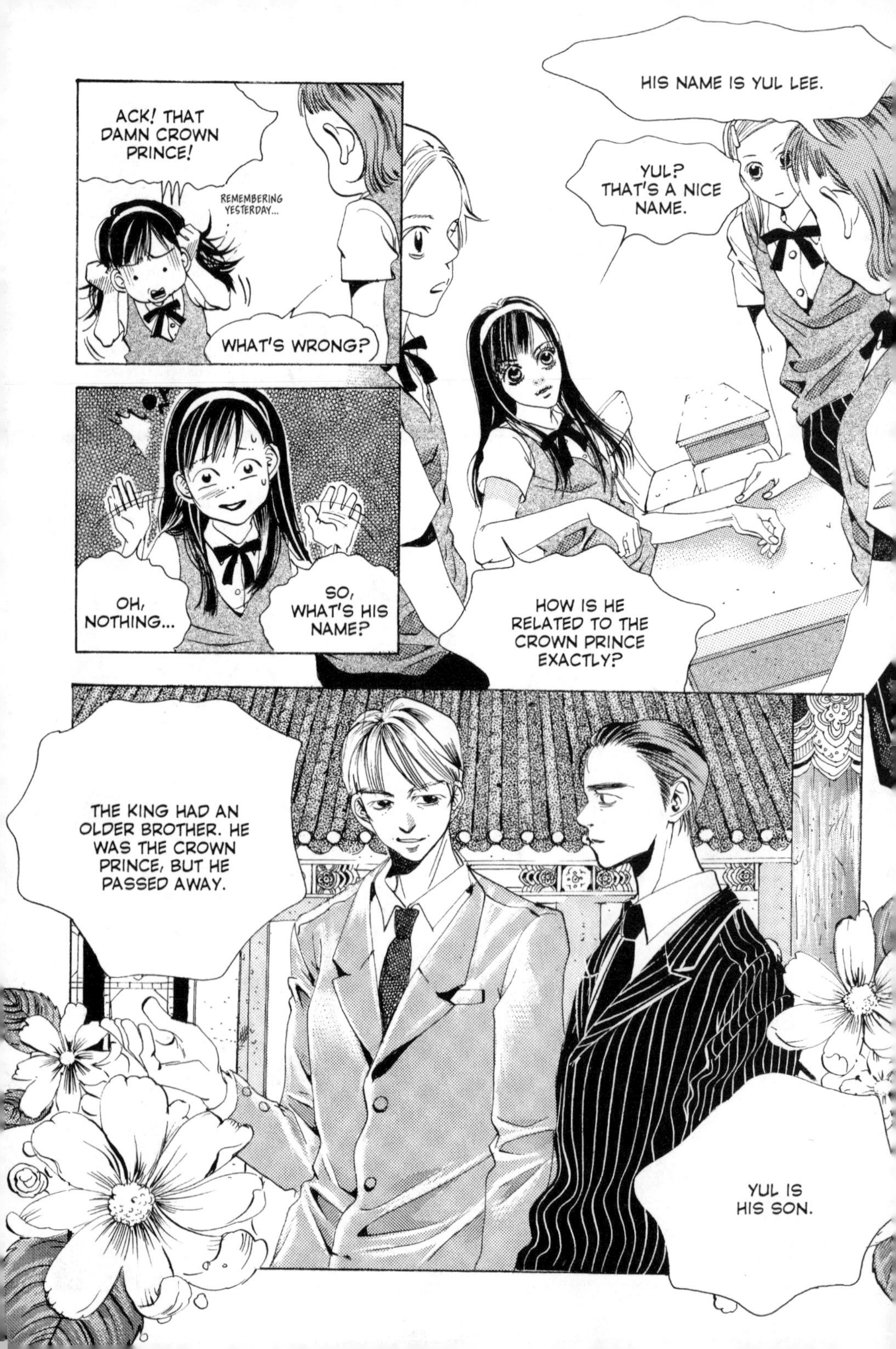
ACK! THAT DAMN CROWN PRINCE!
REMEMBERING YESTERDAY...
WHAT'S WRONG?
OH, NOTHING...
SO, WHAT'S HIS NAME?
HIS NAME IS YUL LEE.
YUL? THAT'S A NICE NAME.
HOW IS HE RELATED TO THE CROWN PRINCE EXACTLY?
THE KING HAD AN OLDER BROTHER. HE WAS THE CROWN PRINCE, BUT HE PASSED AWAY.
YUL IS HIS SON.

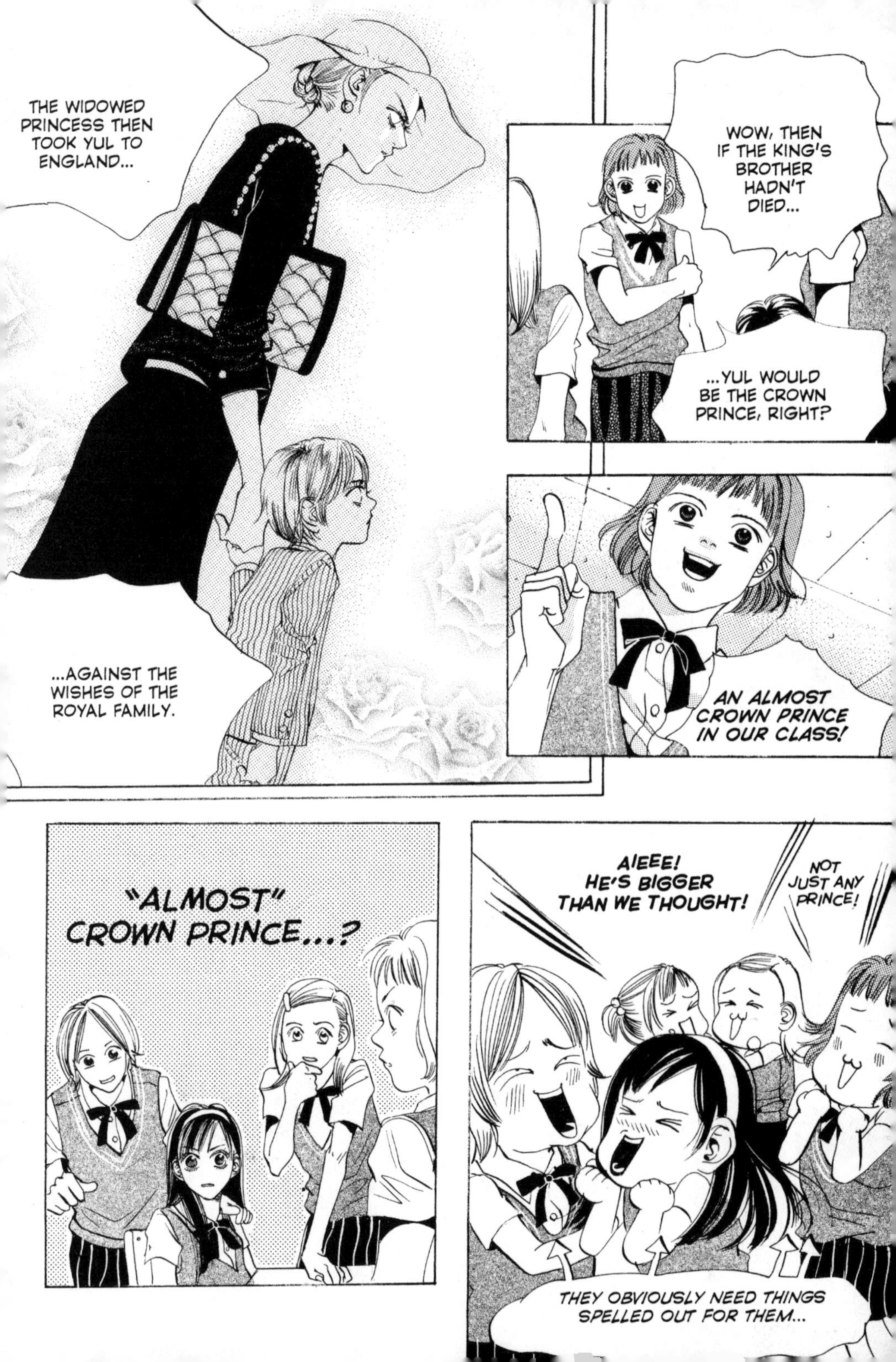
THE WIDOWED PRINCESS THEN TOOK YUL TO ENGLAND...
...AGAINST THE WISHES OF THE ROYAL FAMILY.
WOW, THEN IF THE KING'S BROTHER HADN'T DIED...
...YUL WOULD BE THE CROWN PRINCE, RIGHT?
AN ALMOST CROWN PRINCE IN OUR CLASS!
"ALMOST" CROWN PRINCE...?
AIEEE! HE'S BIGGER THAN WE THOUGHT!
NOT JUST ANY PRINCE!
THEY OBVIOUSLY NEED THINGS SPELLED OUT FOR THEM...

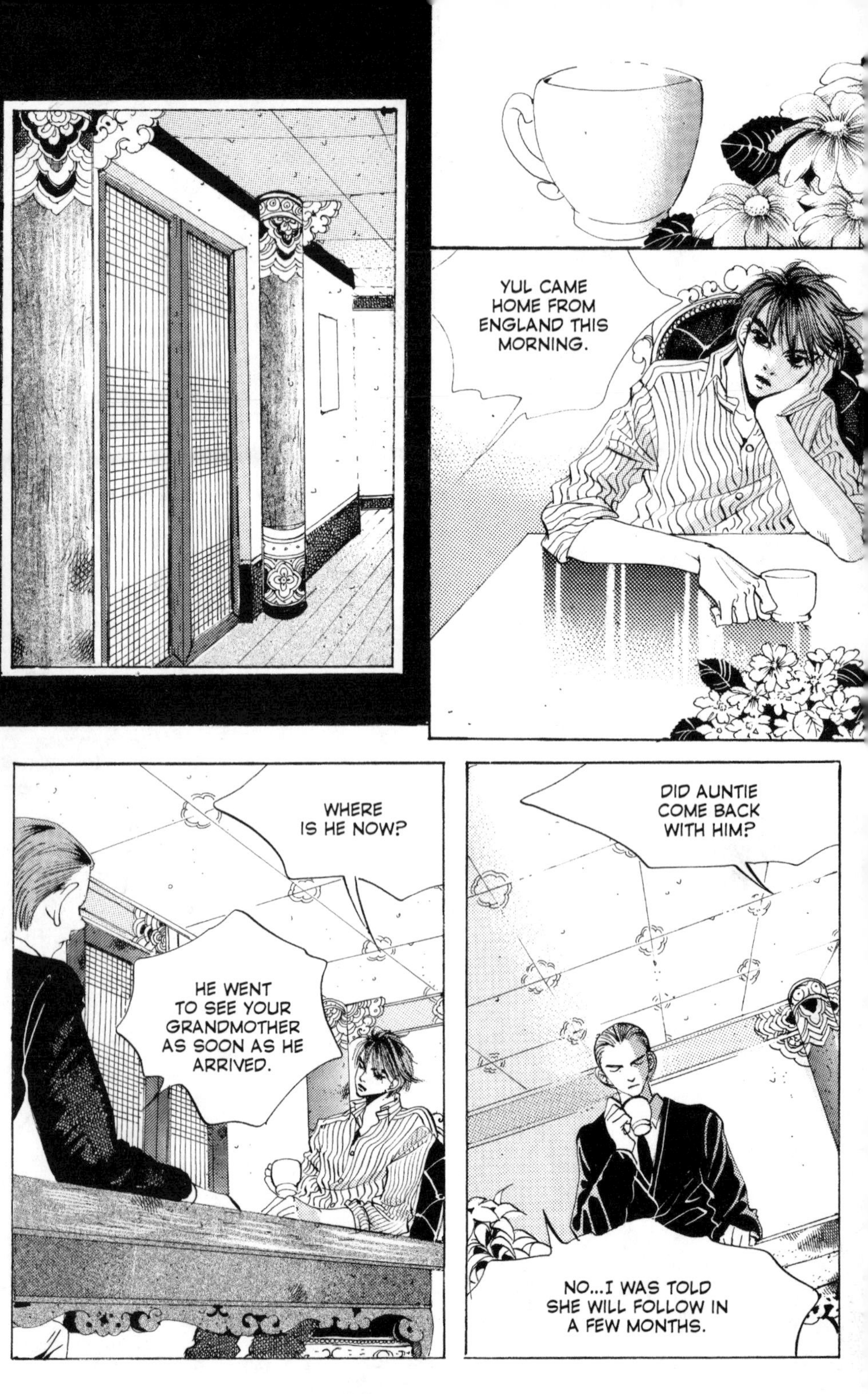
YUL CAME HOME FROM ENGLAND THIS MORNING.
WHERE IS HE NOW?
HE WENT TO SEE YOUR GRANDMOTHER AS SOON AS HE ARRIVED.
DID AUNTIE COME BACK WITH HIM?
NO...I WAS TOLD SHE WILL FOLLOW IN A FEW MONTHS.

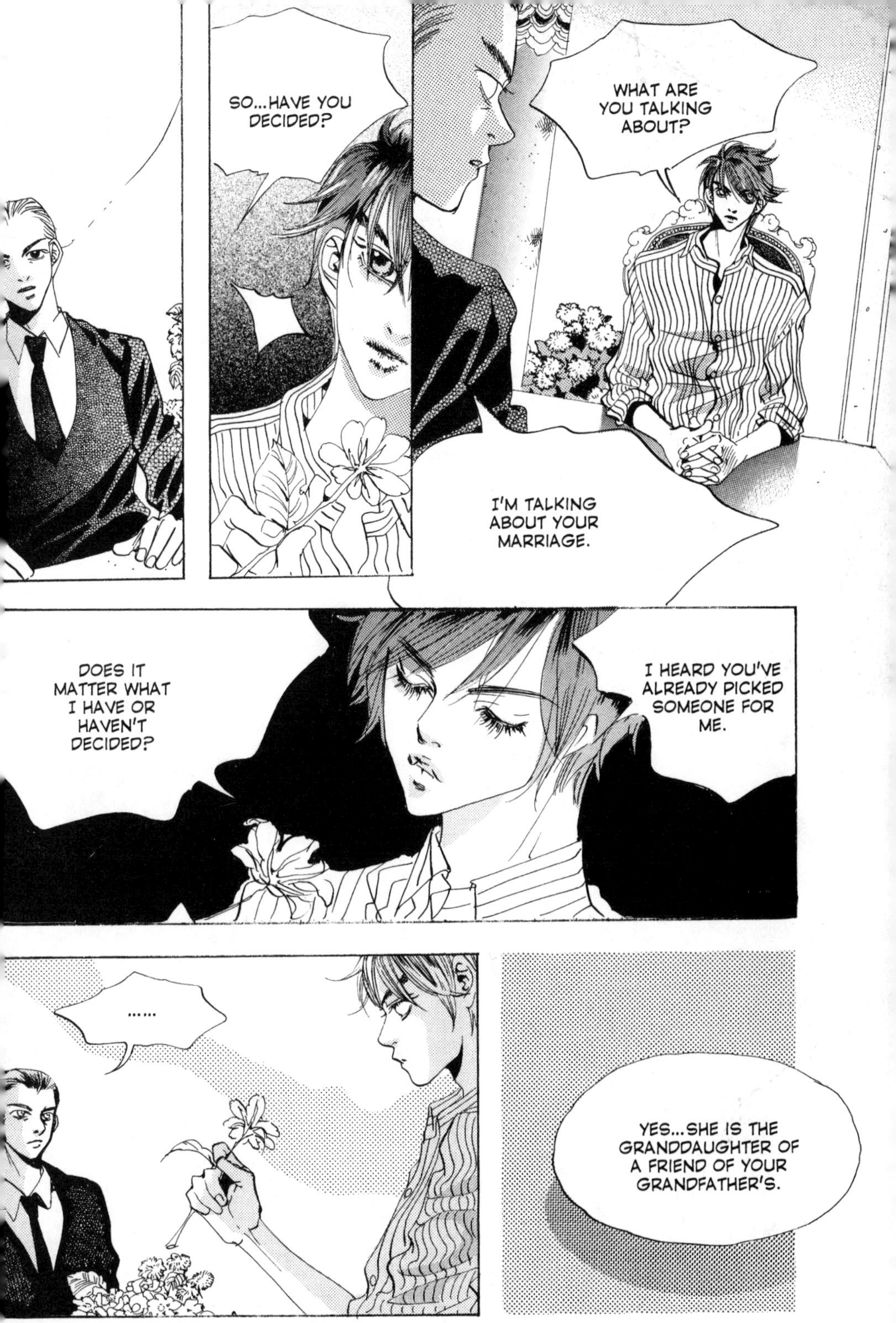
SO...HAVE YOU DECIDED?
WHAT ARE YOU TALKING ABOUT?
I'M TALKING ABOUT YOUR MARRIAGE.
DOES IT MATTER WHAT I HAVE OR HAVEN'T DECIDED?
I HEARD YOU'VE ALREADY PICKED SOMEONE FOR ME.
......
YES...SHE IS THE GRANDDAUGHTER OF A FRIEND OF YOUR GRANDFATHER'S.

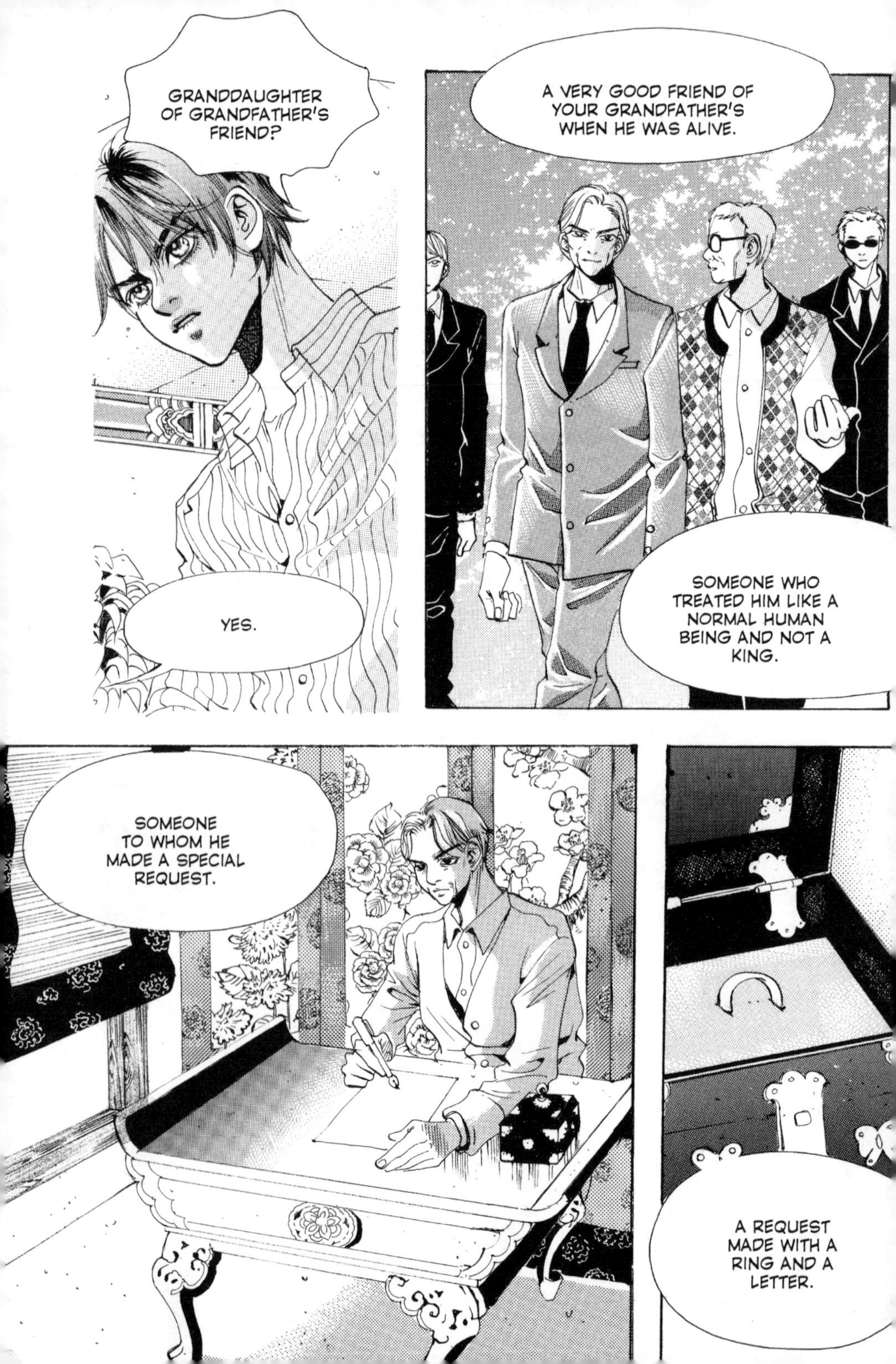
GRANDDAUGHTER OF GRANDFATHER'S FRIEND?
YES.
A VERY GOOD FRIEND OF YOUR GRANDFATHER'S WHEN HE WAS ALIVE.
SOMEONE WHO TREATED HIM LIKE A NORMAL HUMAN BEING AND NOT A KING.
SOMEONE TO WHOM HE MADE A SPECIAL REQUEST.
A REQUEST MADE WITH A RING AND A LETTER.

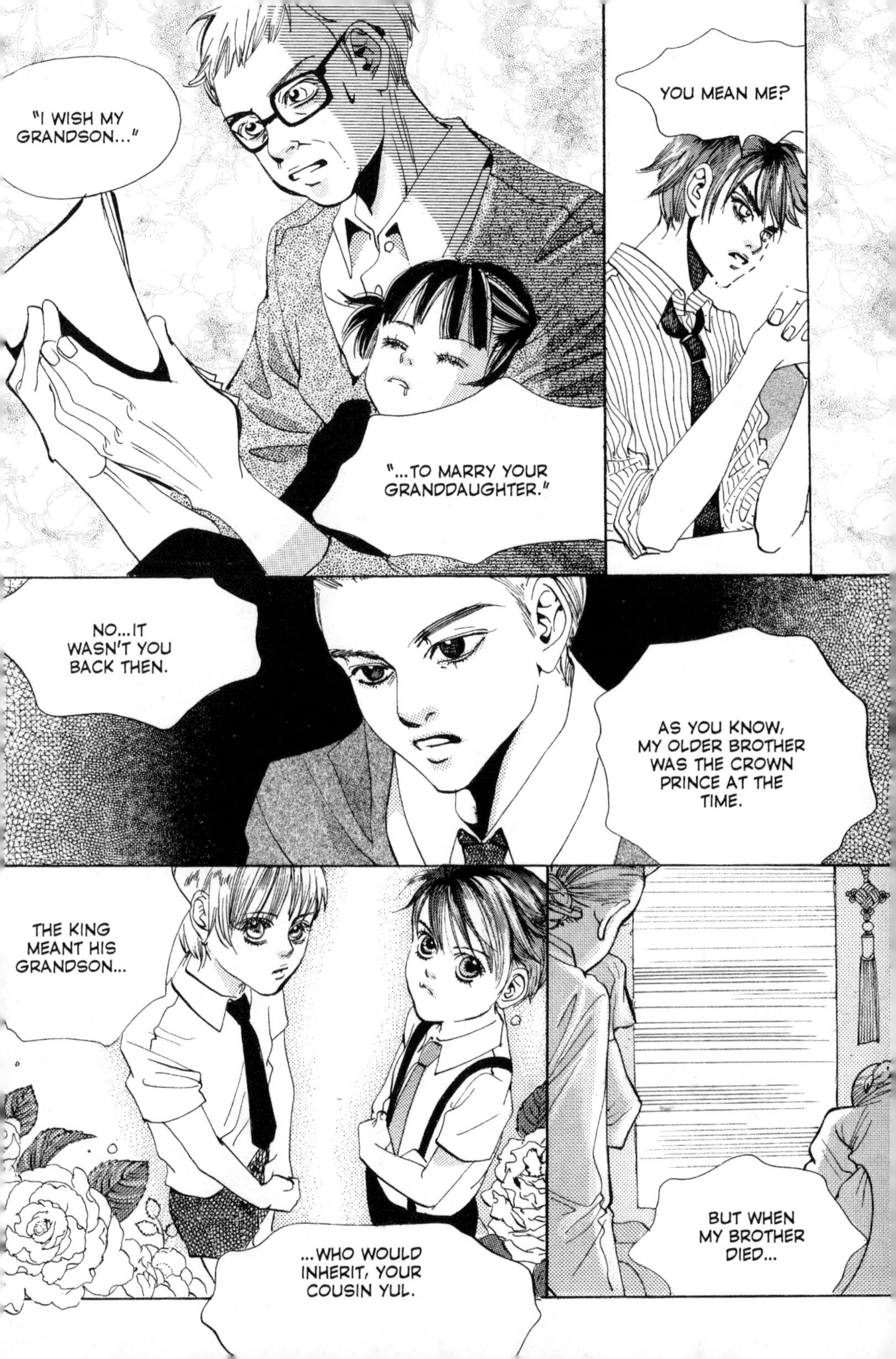
"I WISH MY GRANDSON..."
"...TO MARRY YOUR GRANDDAUGHTER."
YOU MEAN ME?
NO...IT WASN'T YOU BACK THEN.
AS YOU KNOW, MY OLDER BROTHER WAS THE CROWN PRINCE AT THE TIME.
THE KING MEANT HIS GRANDSON...
...WHO WOULD INHERIT, YOUR COUSIN YUL.
BUT WHEN MY BROTHER DIED...

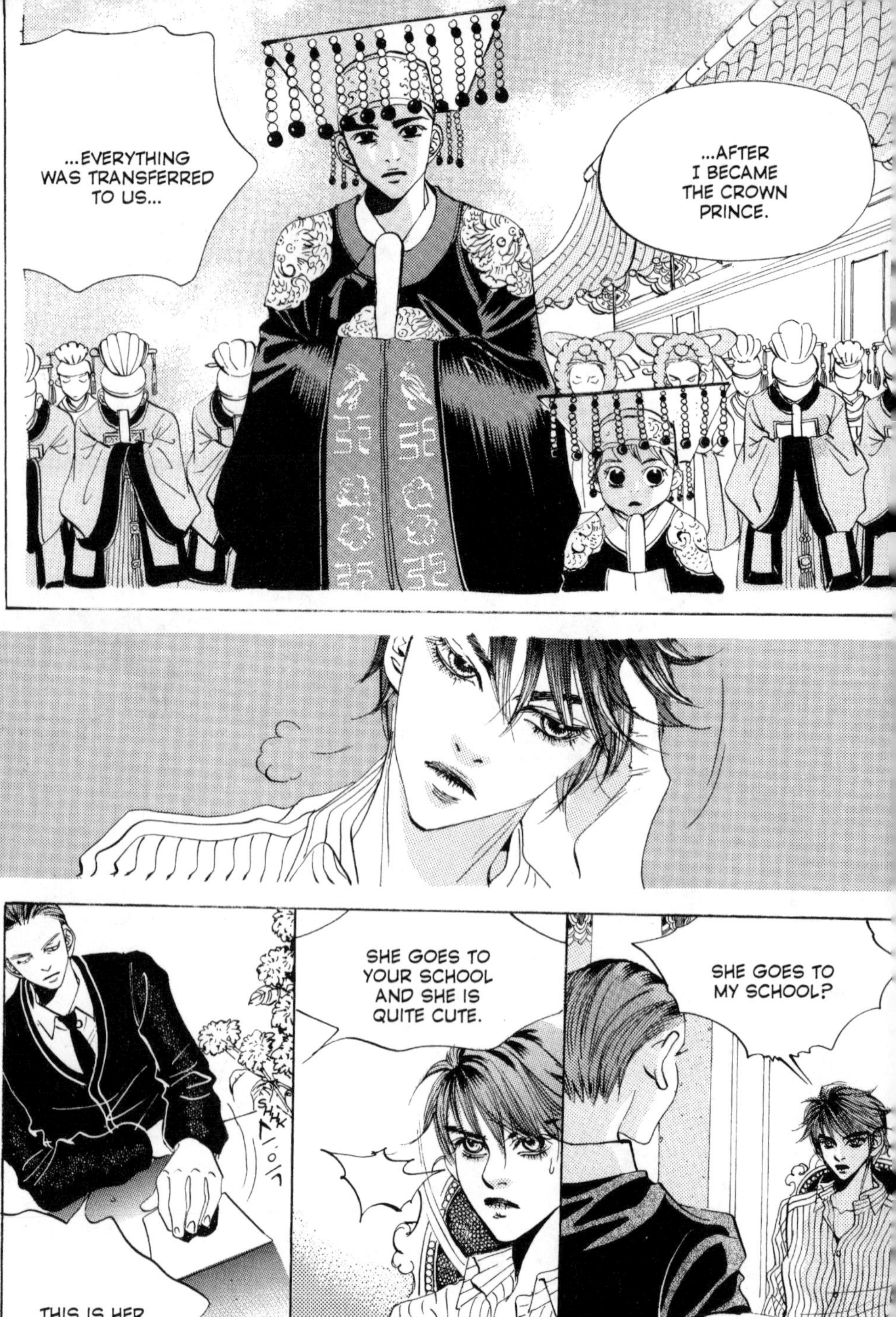
...EVERYTHING WAS TRANSFERRED TO US...
...AFTER I BECAME THE CROWN PRINCE.
SHIK
THIS IS HER PICTURE.
SHE GOES TO YOUR SCHOOL AND SHE IS QUITE CUTE.
SHE GOES TO MY SCHOOL?
THAT'S RIGHT.

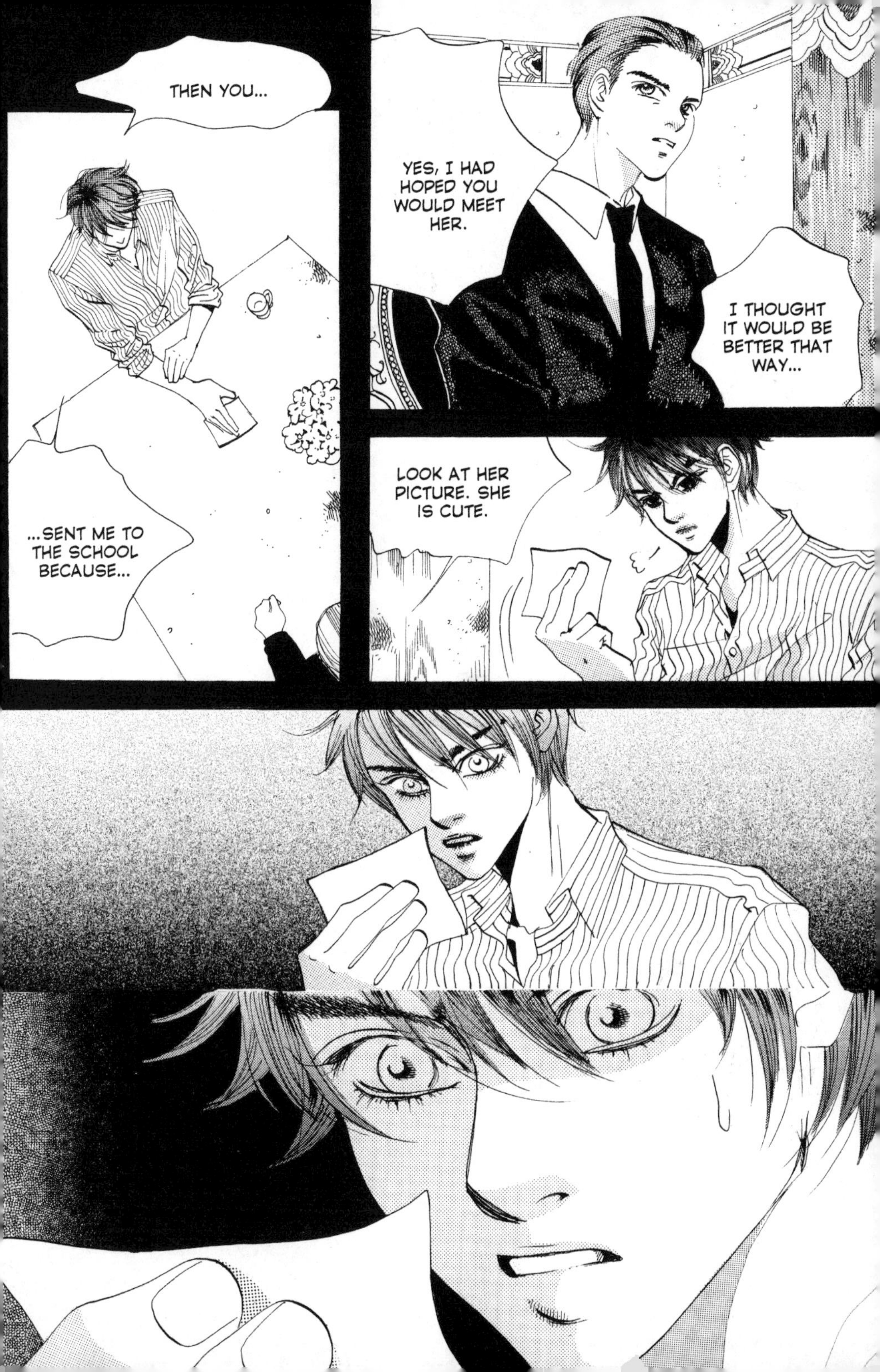
THEN YOU...
...SENT ME TO THE SCHOOL BECAUSE...
YES, I HAD HOPED YOU WOULD MEET HER.
I THOUGHT IT WOULD BE BETTER THAT WAY...
LOOK AT HER PICTURE. SHE IS CUTE.

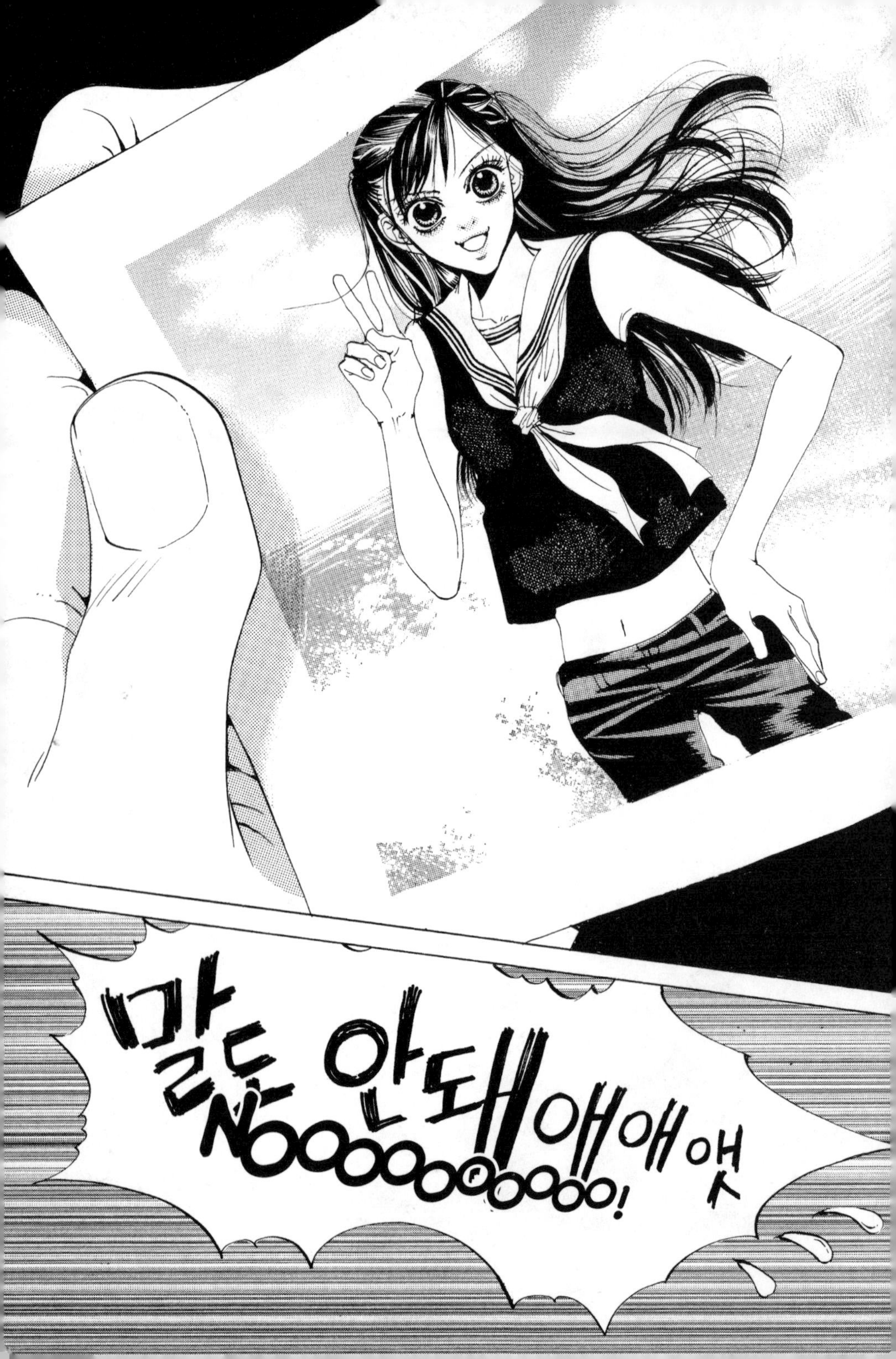
말도 안돼애애애앳
NOOOOOOOOOOOOO!

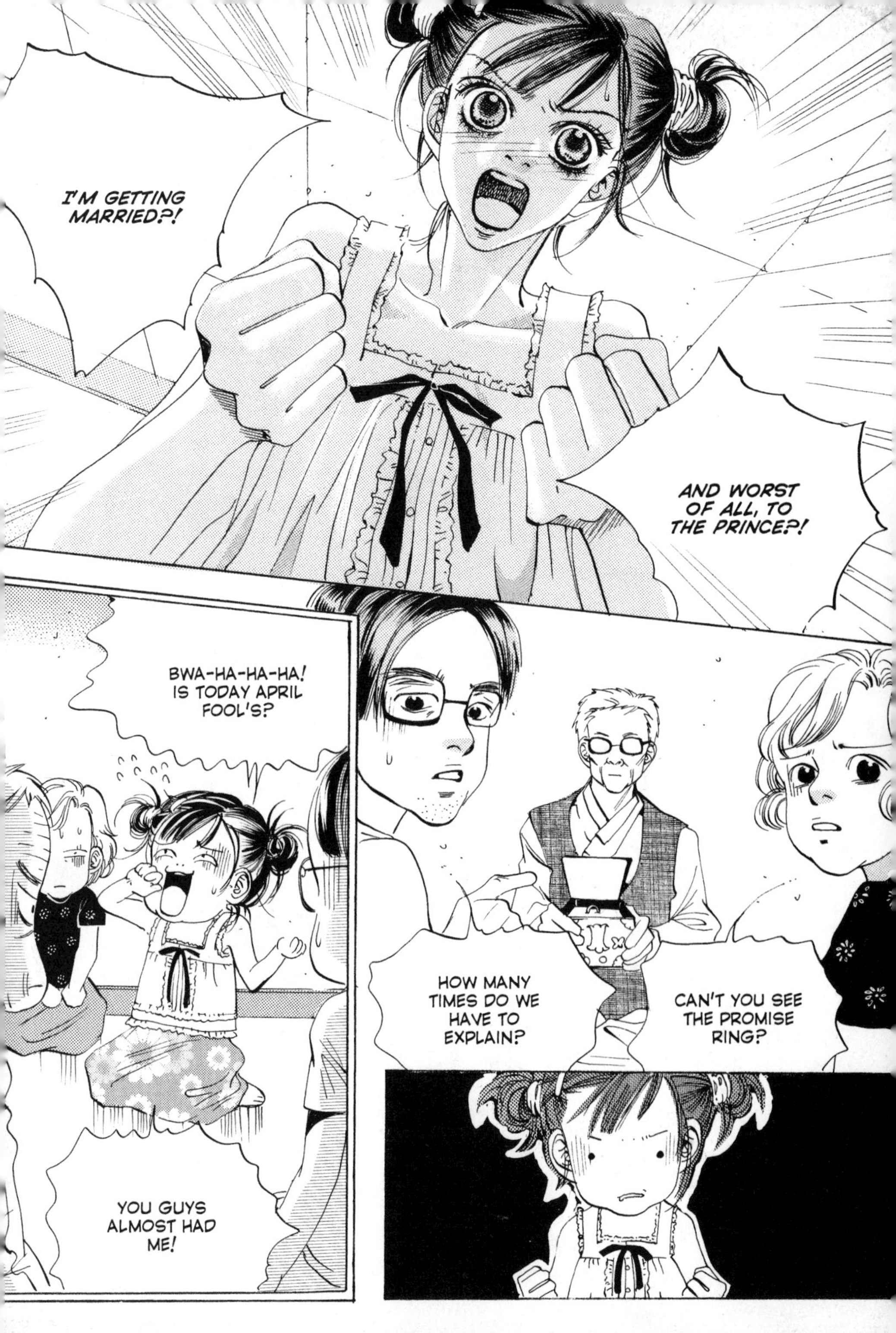
I'M GETTING MARRIED?!
AND WORST OF ALL, TO THE PRINCE?!
BWA-HA-HA-HA! IS TODAY APRIL FOOL'S?
YOU GUYS ALMOST HAD ME!
HOW MANY TIMES DO WE HAVE TO EXPLAIN?
CAN'T YOU SEE THE PROMISE RING?

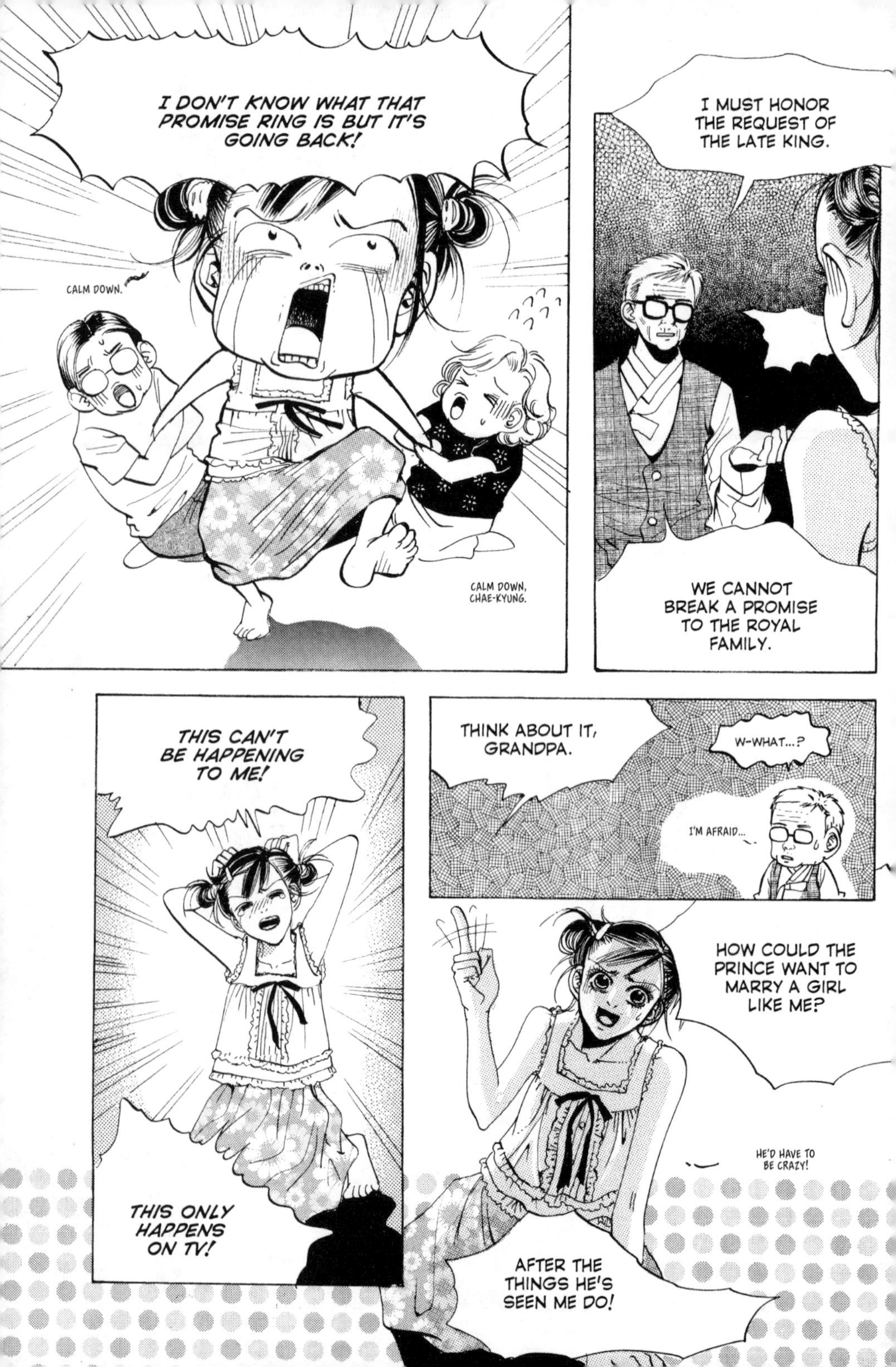
I DON'T KNOW WHAT THAT PROMISE RING IS BUT IT'S GOING BACK!
CALM DOWN.
CALM DOWN, CHAE-KYUNG.
I MUST HONOR THE REQUEST OF THE LATE KING.
WE CANNOT BREAK A PROMISE TO THE ROYAL FAMILY.
THIS CAN'T BE HAPPENING TO ME!
THIS ONLY HAPPENS ON TV!
THINK ABOUT IT, GRANDPA.
W-WHAT...?
I'M AFRAID...
HOW COULD THE PRINCE WANT TO MARRY A GIRL LIKE ME?
HE'D HAVE TO BE CRAZY!
AFTER THE THINGS HE'S SEEN ME DO!

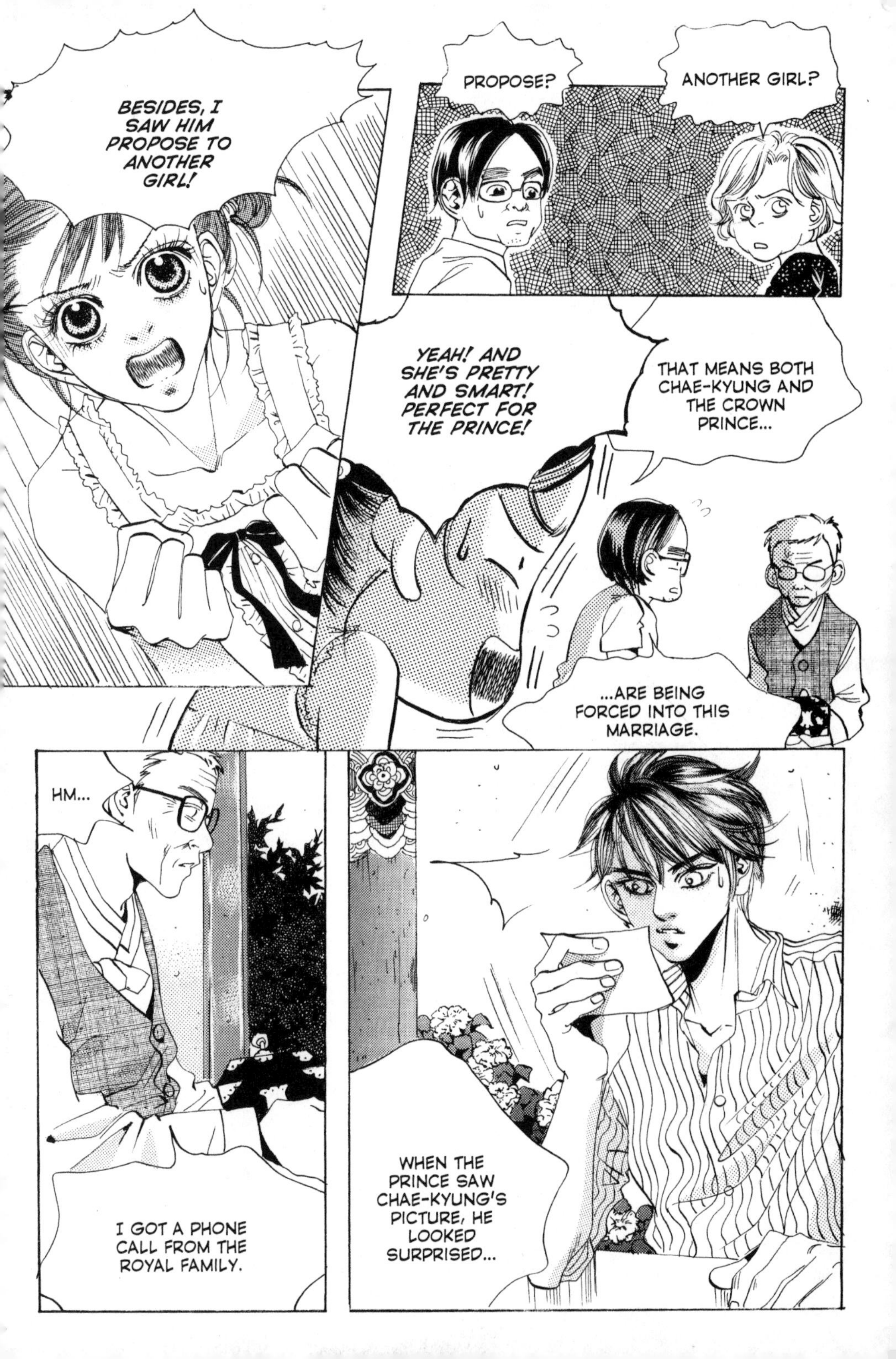
BESIDES, I SAW HIM PROPOSE TO ANOTHER GIRL!
PROPOSE?
ANOTHER GIRL?
YEAH! AND SHE'S PRETTY AND SMART! PERFECT FOR THE PRINCE!
THAT MEANS BOTH CHAE-KYUNG AND THE CROWN PRINCE...
...ARE BEING FORCED INTO THIS MARRIAGE.
HM...
I GOT A PHONE CALL FROM THE ROYAL FAMILY.
WHEN THE PRINCE SAW CHAE-KYUNG'S PICTURE, HE LOOKED SURPRISED...

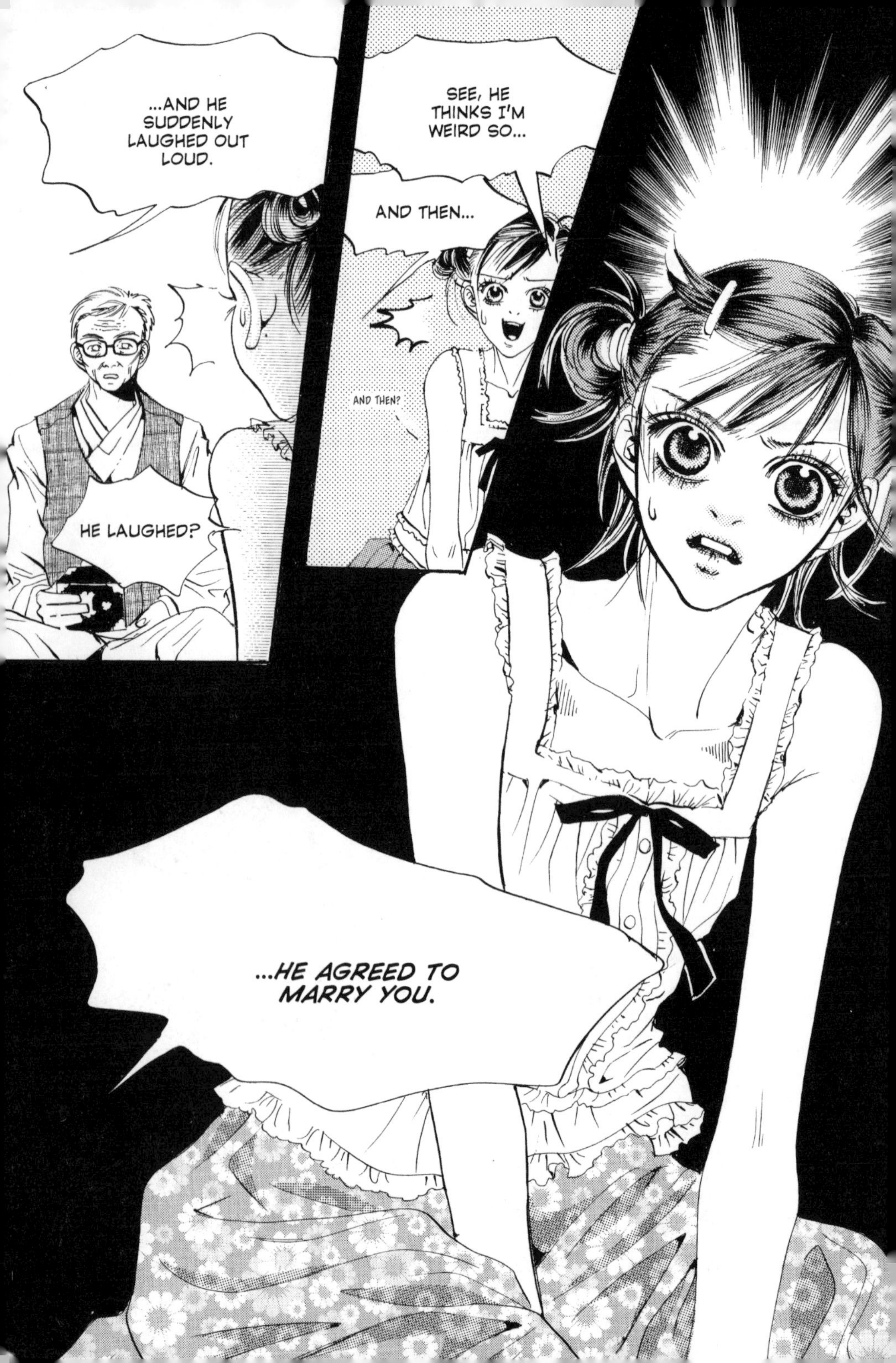
...AND HE SUDDENLY LAUGHED OUT LOUD.
HE LAUGHED?
SEE, HE THINKS I'M WEIRD SO...
AND THEN...
AND THEN?
...HE AGREED TO MARRY YOU.

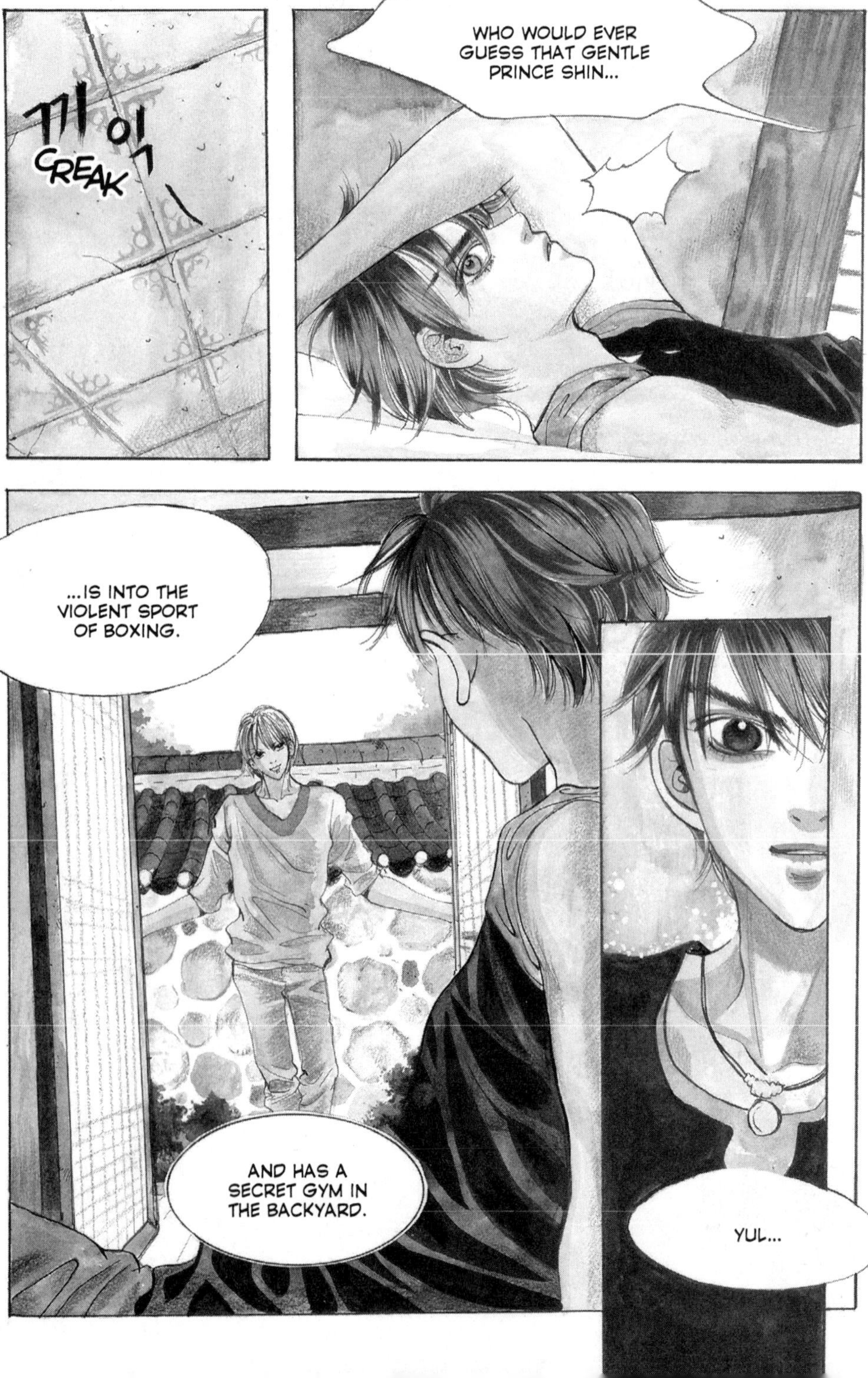
끼이익
CREAK
WHO WOULD EVER GUESS THAT GENTLE PRINCE SHIN...
...IS INTO THE VIOLENT SPORT OF BOXING.
AND HAS A SECRET GYM IN THE BACKYARD.
YUL...

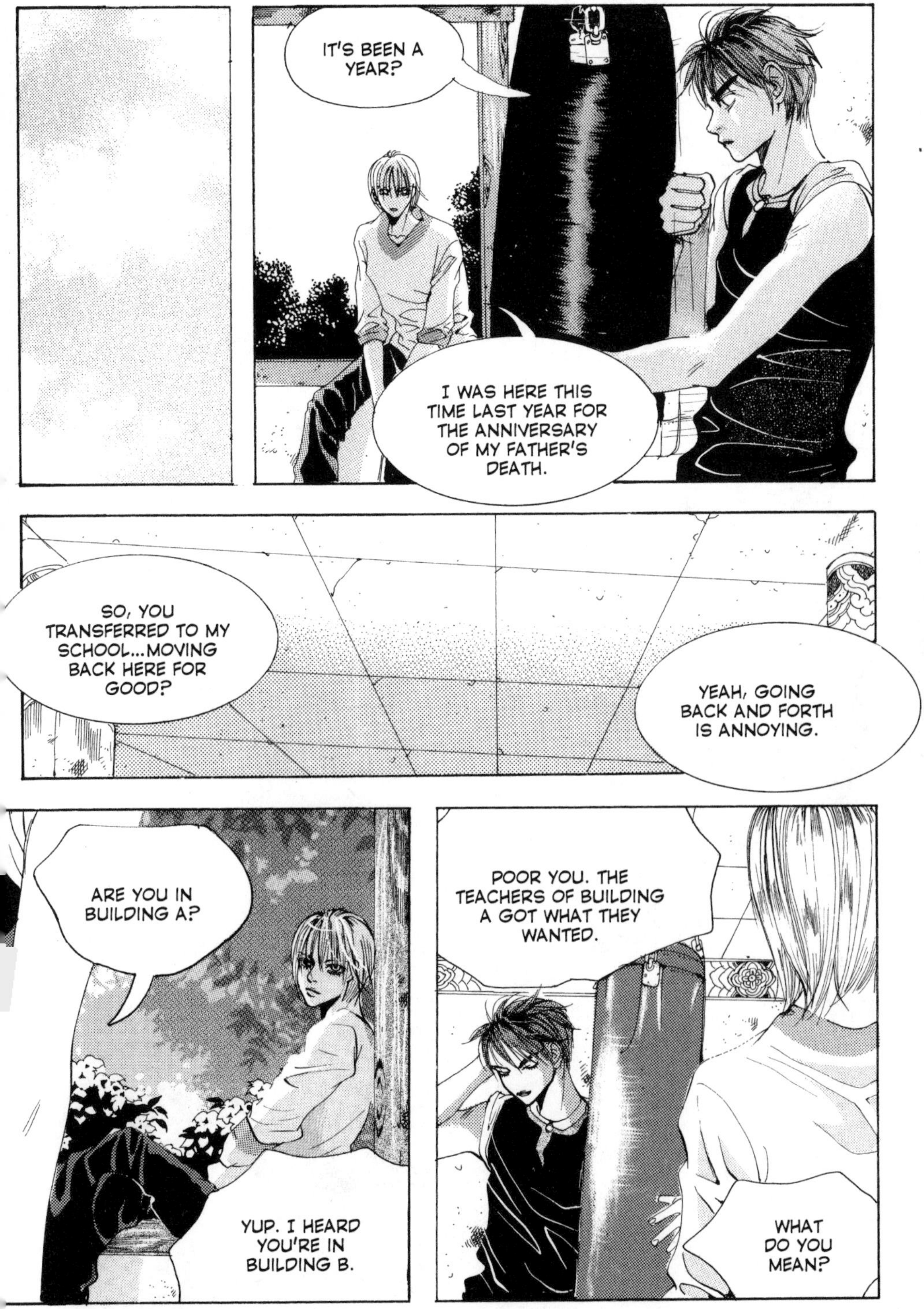
IT'S BEEN A YEAR?
I WAS HERE THIS TIME LAST YEAR FOR THE ANNIVERSARY OF MY FATHER'S DEATH.
SO, YOU TRANSFERRED TO MY SCHOOL...MOVING BACK HERE FOR GOOD?
YEAH, GOING BACK AND FORTH IS ANNOYING.
ARE YOU IN BUILDING A?
YUP. I HEARD YOU'RE IN BUILDING B.
POOR YOU. THE TEACHERS OF BUILDING A GOT WHAT THEY WANTED.
WHAT DO YOU MEAN?

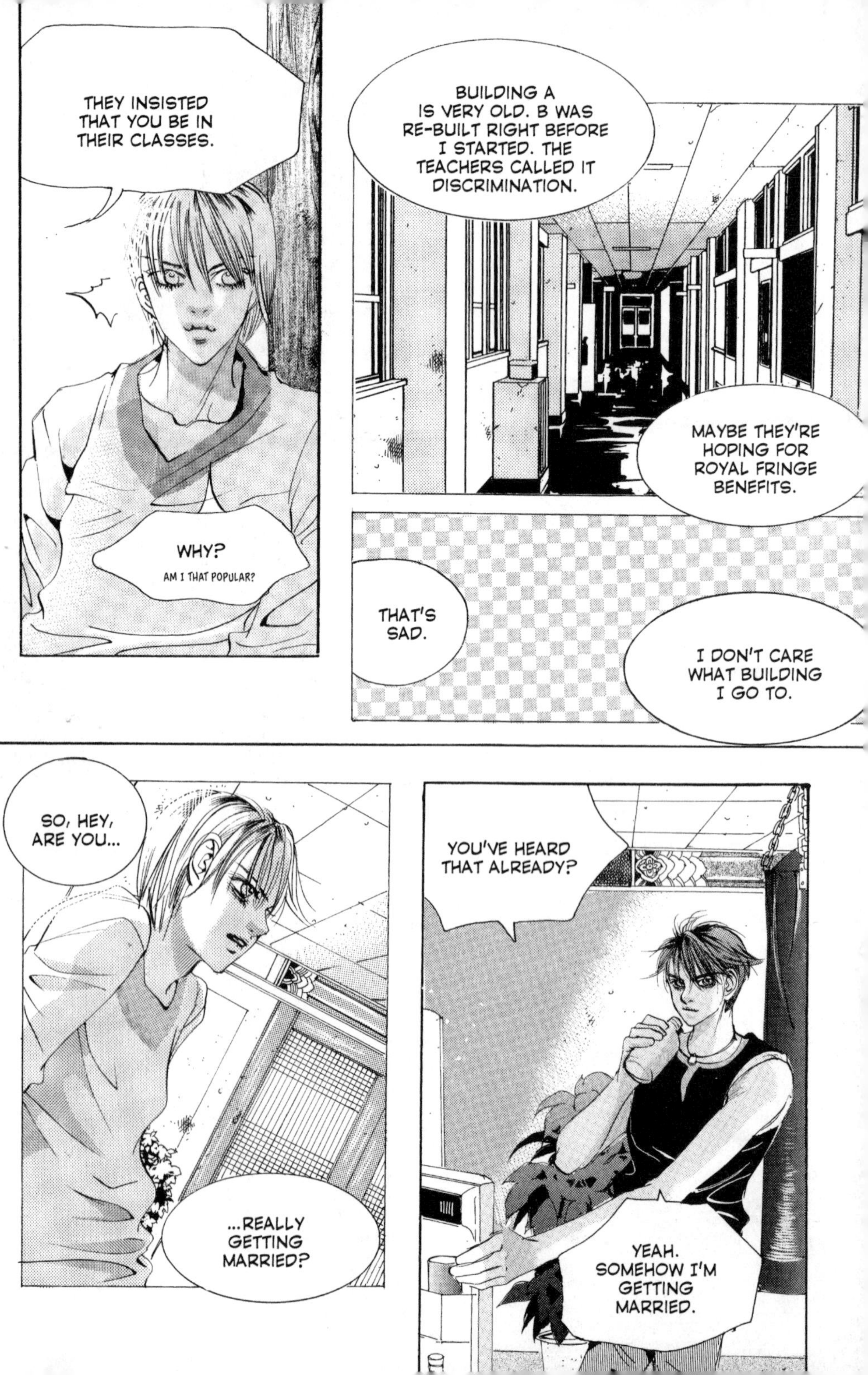
THEY INSISTED THAT YOU BE IN THEIR CLASSES.
WHY?
AM I THAT POPULAR?
BUILDING A IS VERY OLD. B WAS RE-BUILT RIGHT BEFORE I STARTED. THE TEACHERS CALLED IT DISCRIMINATION.
MAYBE THEY'RE HOPING FOR ROYAL FRINGE BENEFITS.
THAT'S SAD.
I DON'T CARE WHAT BUILDING I GO TO.
SO, HEY, ARE YOU...
...REALLY GETTING MARRIED?
YOU'VE HEARD THAT ALREADY?
YEAH. SOMEHOW I'M GETTING MARRIED.

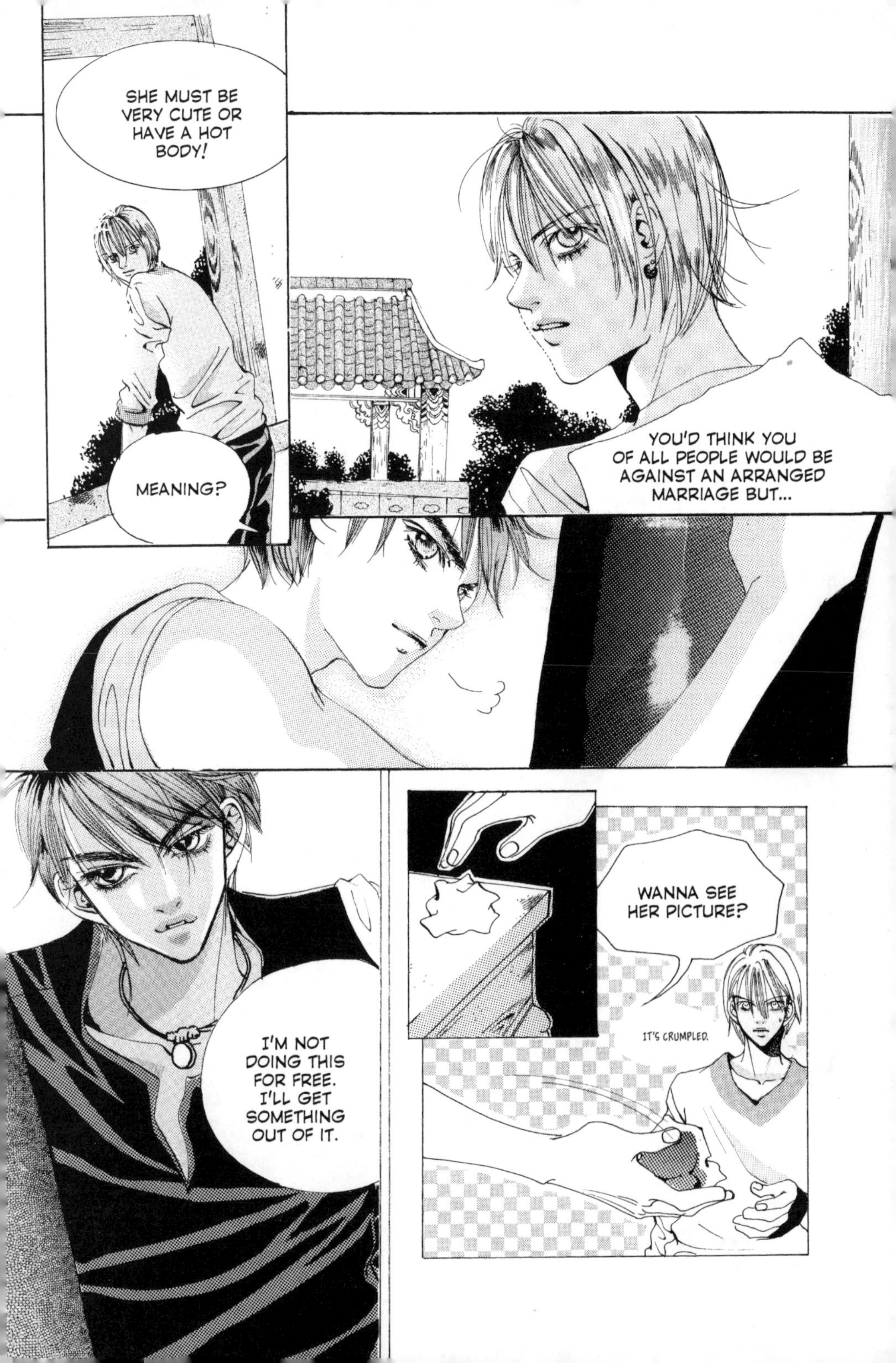
SHE MUST BE VERY CUTE OR HAVE A HOT BODY!
MEANING?
YOU'D THINK YOU OF ALL PEOPLE WOULD BE AGAINST AN ARRANGED MARRIAGE BUT...
I'M NOT DOING THIS FOR FREE. I'LL GET SOMETHING OUT OF IT.
WANNA SEE HER PICTURE?
IT'S CRUMPLED.

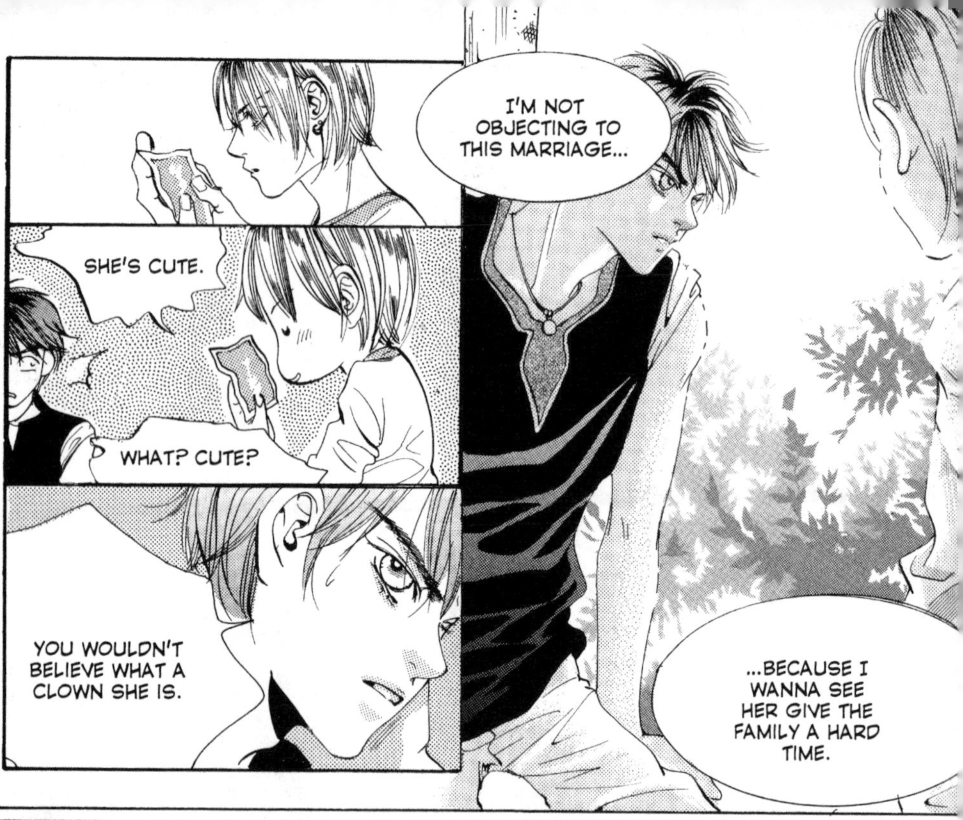
SHE'S CUTE.
WHAT? CUTE?
YOU WOULDN'T BELIEVE WHAT A CLOWN SHE IS.
I'M NOT OBJECTING TO THIS MARRIAGE...
...BECAUSE I WANNA SEE HER GIVE THE FAMILY A HARD TIME.

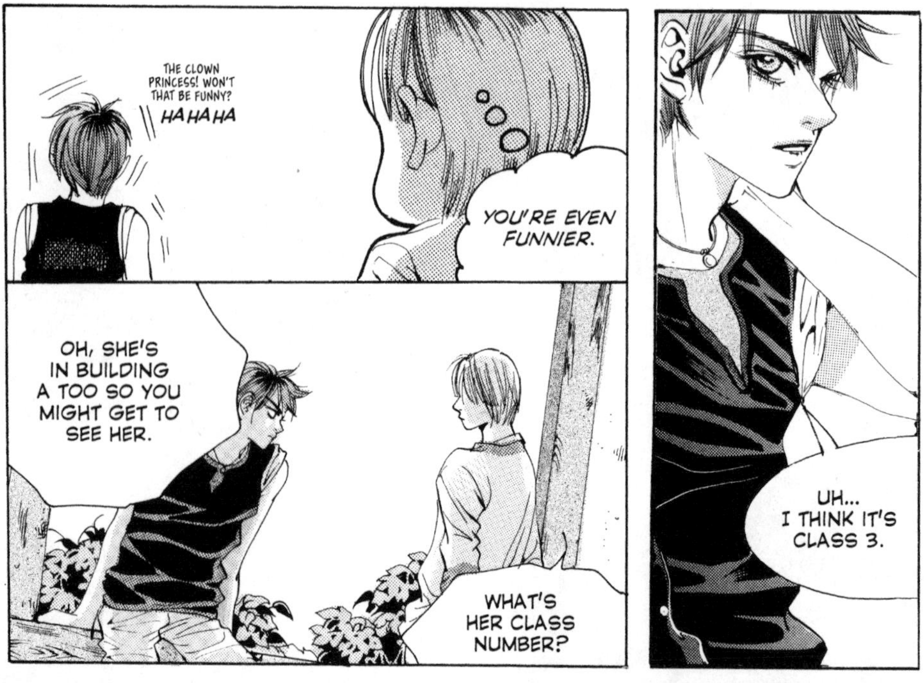
THE CLOWN PRINCESS! WON'T THAT BE FUNNY?
HA HA HA
YOU'RE EVEN FUNNIER.
OH, SHE'S IN BUILDING A TOO SO YOU MIGHT GET TO SEE HER.
WHAT'S HER CLASS NUMBER?
UH... I THINK IT'S CLASS 3.

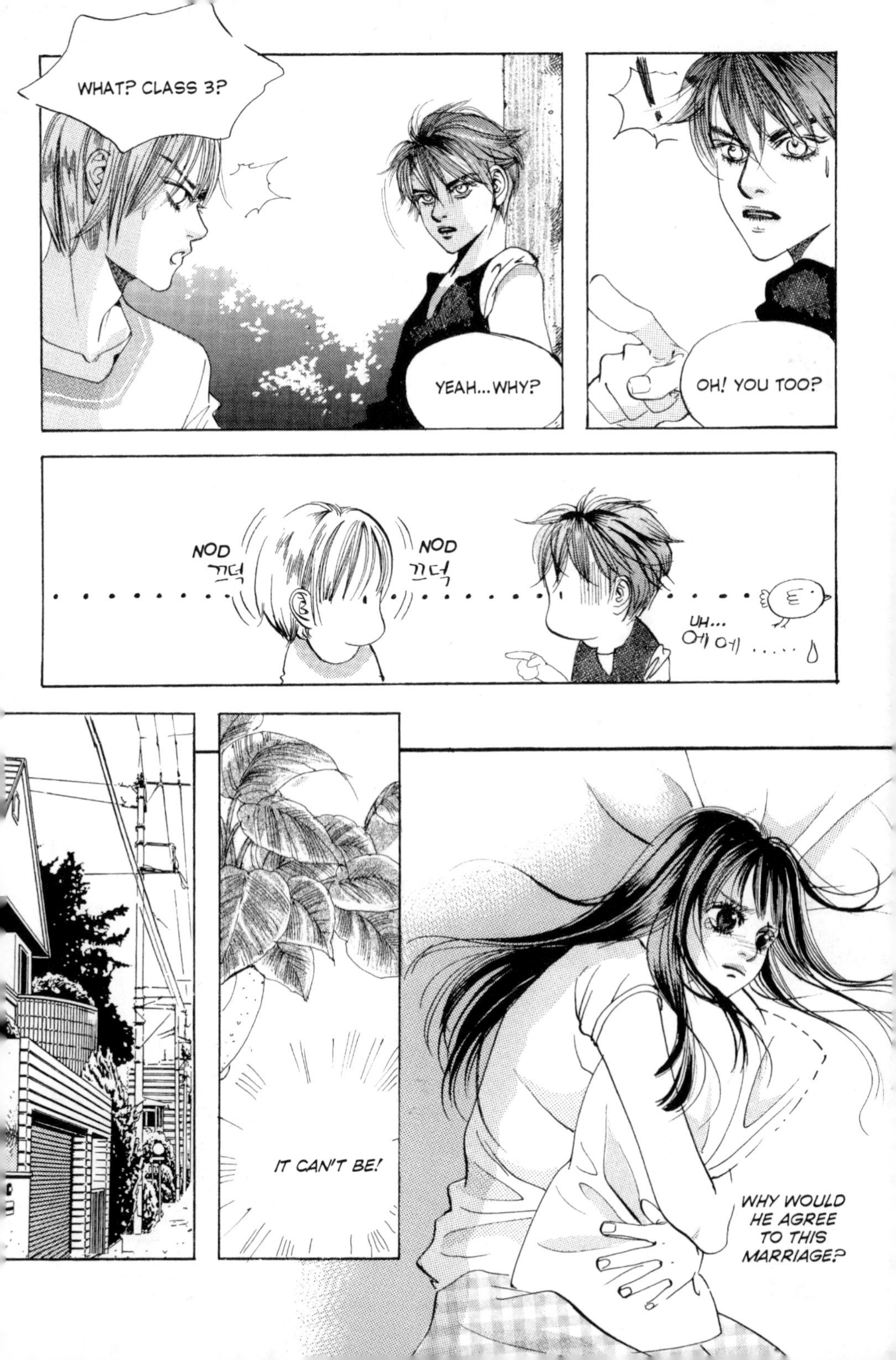
WHAT? CLASS 3?
YEAH...WHY?
OH! YOU TOO?
NOD
끄덕
NOD
끄덕
UH...
에에 .....
IT CAN'T BE!
WHY WOULD HE AGREE TO THIS MARRIAGE?

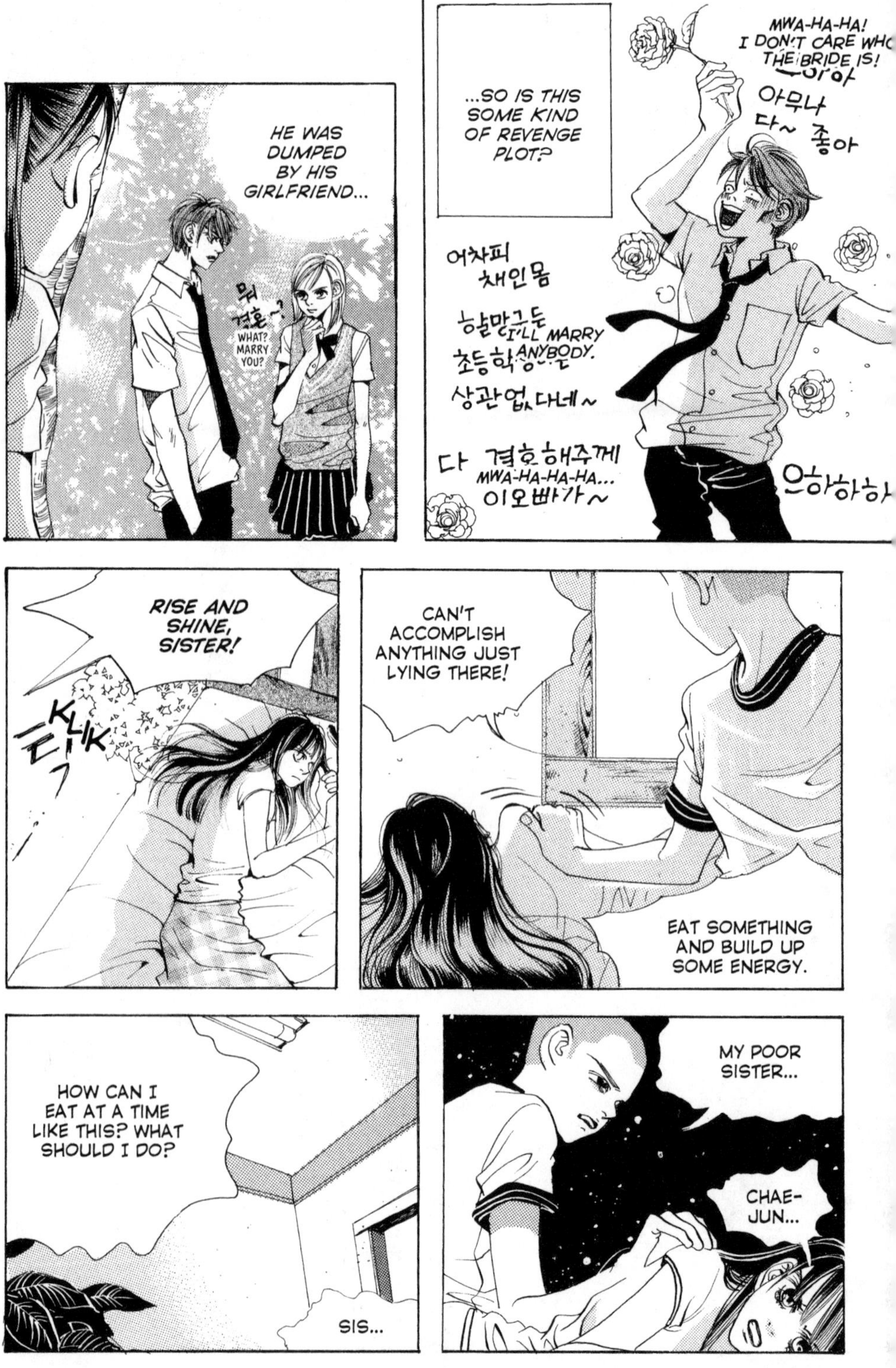
HE WAS DUMPED BY HIS GIRLFRIEND...
뭐 결혼~?
WHAT? MARRY YOU?
...SO IS THIS SOME KIND OF REVENGE PLOT?
MWA-HA-HA! I DON'T CARE WHO THE BRIDE IS!
아무나 다~ 좋아
어차피 채인몸
I'LL MARRY ANYBODY.
상관없다네~
MWA-HA-HA-HA...
이오빠가~
RISE AND SHINE, SISTER!
KLIK
CAN'T ACCOMPLISH ANYTHING JUST LYING THERE!
EAT SOMETHING AND BUILD UP SOME ENERGY.
HOW CAN I EAT AT A TIME LIKE THIS? WHAT SHOULD I DO?
SIS...
MY POOR SISTER...
CHAE-JUN...

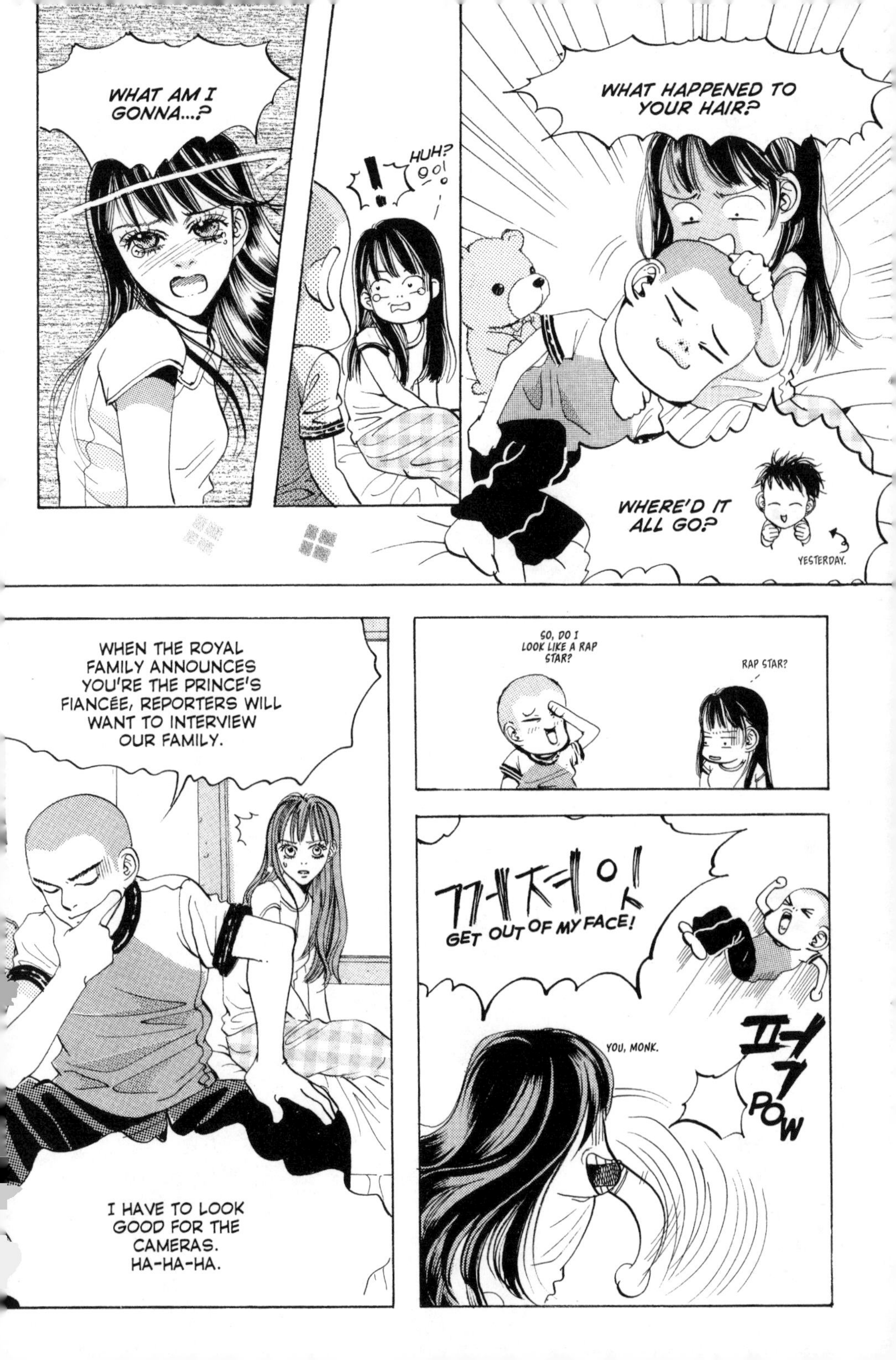
WHAT AM I GONNA...?
HUH?
WHAT HAPPENED TO YOUR HAIR?
WHERE'D IT ALL GO?
YESTERDAY.
WHEN THE ROYAL FAMILY ANNOUNCES YOU'RE THE PRINCE'S FIANCÉE, REPORTERS WILL WANT TO INTERVIEW OUR FAMILY.
I HAVE TO LOOK GOOD FOR THE CAMERAS. HA-HA-HA.
SO, DO I LOOK LIKE A RAP STAR?
RAP STAR?
GET OUT OF MY FACE!
YOU, MONK.
퍽
POW

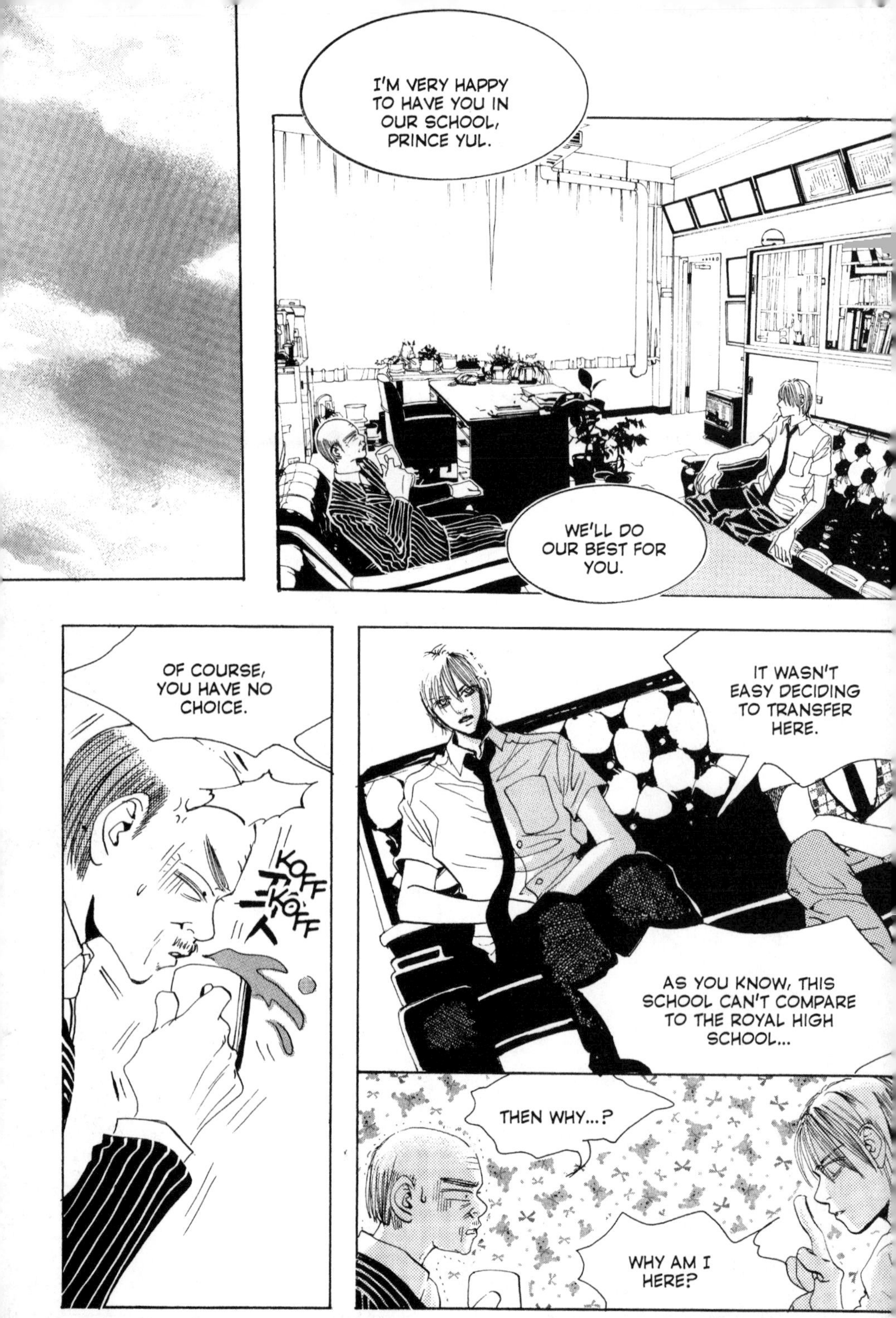
I'M VERY HAPPY TO HAVE YOU IN OUR SCHOOL, PRINCE YUL.
WE'LL DO OUR BEST FOR YOU.
OF COURSE, YOU HAVE NO CHOICE.
KOFF KOFF
IT WASN'T EASY DECIDING TO TRANSFER HERE.
AS YOU KNOW, THIS SCHOOL CAN'T COMPARE TO THE ROYAL HIGH SCHOOL...
THEN WHY...?
WHY AM I HERE?

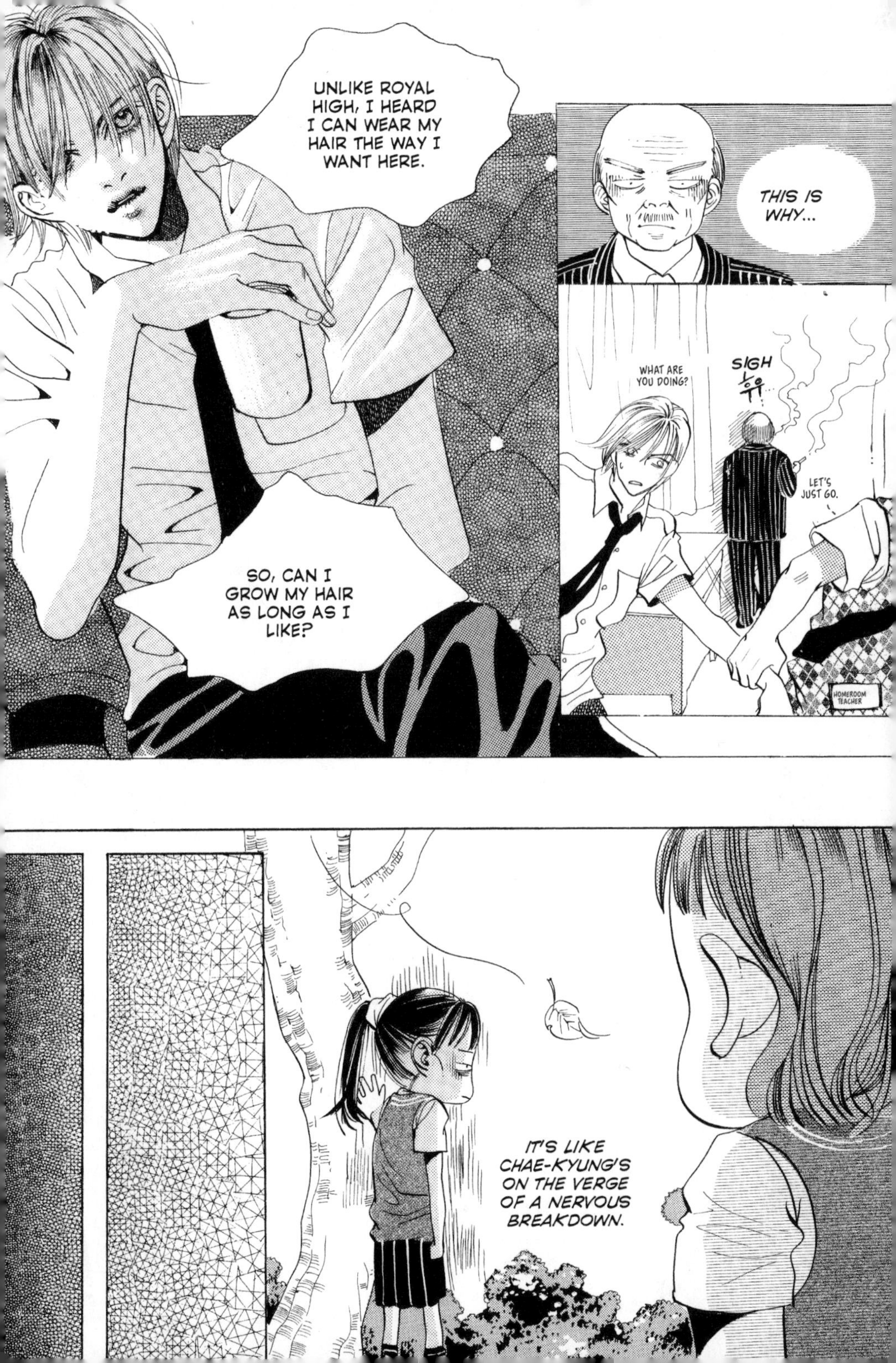
UNLIKE ROYAL HIGH, I HEARD I CAN WEAR MY HAIR THE WAY I WANT HERE.
SO, CAN I GROW MY HAIR AS LONG AS I LIKE?
THIS IS WHY...
WHAT ARE YOU DOING?
SIGH
휴유...
LET'S JUST GO.
HOMEROOM TEACHER
IT'S LIKE CHAE-KYUNG'S ON THE VERGE OF A NERVOUS BREAKDOWN.

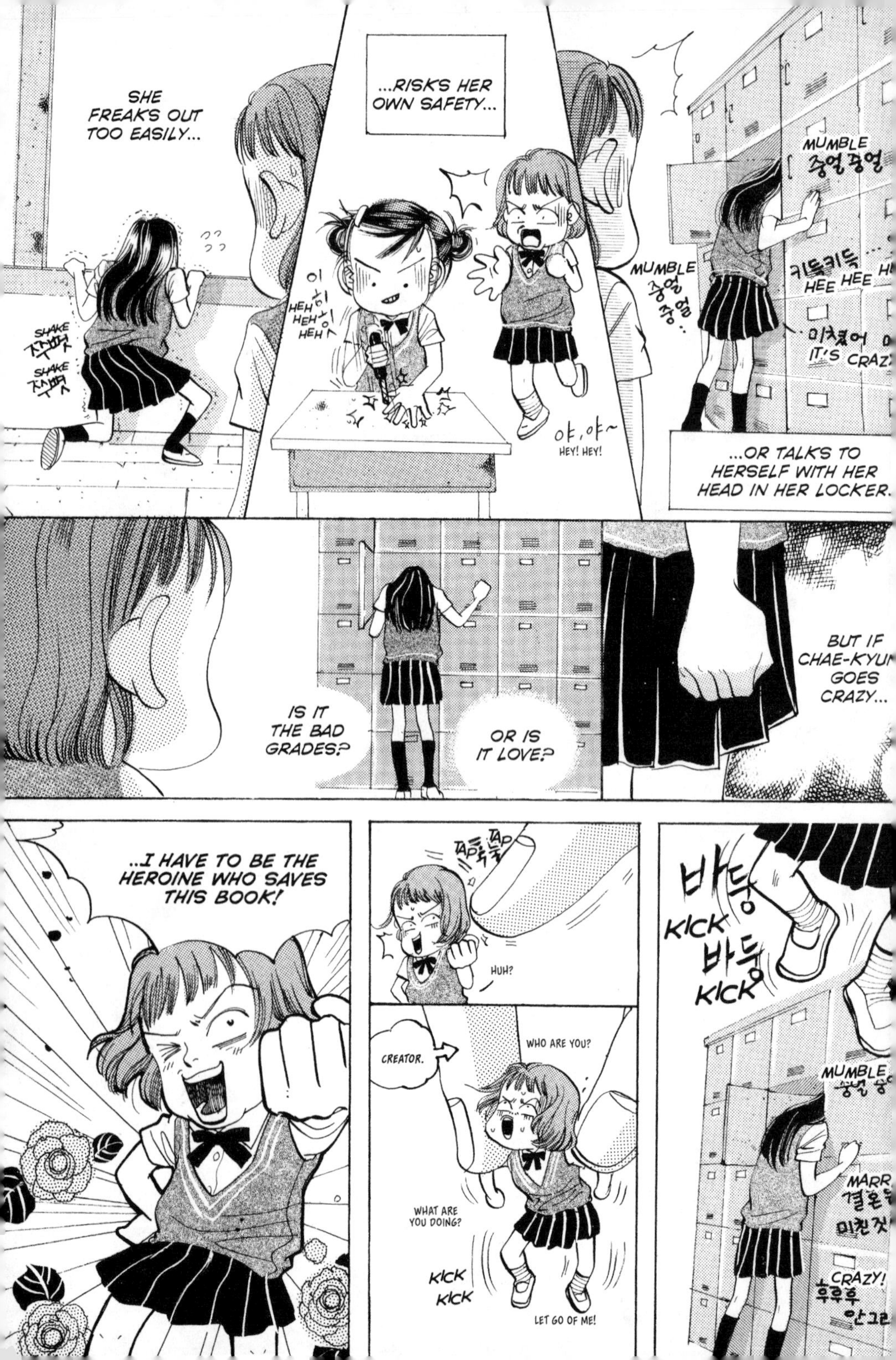
SHE FREAKS OUT TOO EASILY...
SHAKE
SHAKE
...RISKS HER OWN SAFETY...
HEH HEH HEH HEH
야, 야~
HEY! HEY!
MUMBLE
중얼 중얼
MUMBLE
중얼중얼
키득키득
HEE HEE HE
미쳤어
IT'S CRAZ
...OR TALKS TO HERSELF WITH HER HEAD IN HER LOCKER.
IS IT THE BAD GRADES?
OR IS IT LOVE?
BUT IF CHAE-KYU GOES CRAZY...
...I HAVE TO BE THE HEROINE WHO SAVES THIS BOOK!
TAP TAP
HUH?
CREATOR.
WHO ARE YOU?
WHAT ARE YOU DOING?
KICK KICK
LET GO OF ME!
바동
KICK
바동
KICK
MUMBLE
MARR
CRAZY!

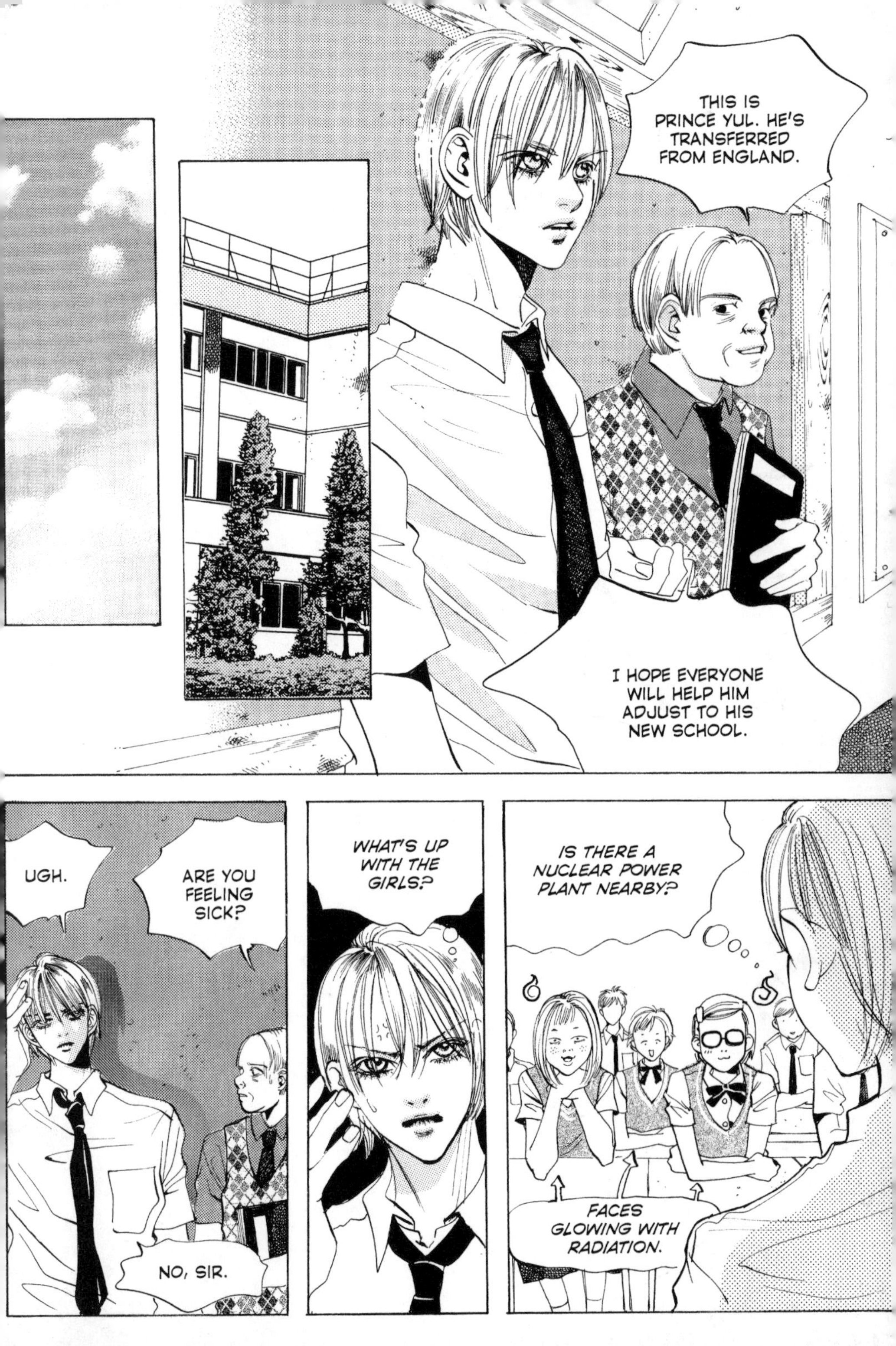
THIS IS PRINCE YUL. HE'S TRANSFERRED FROM ENGLAND.
I HOPE EVERYONE WILL HELP HIM ADJUST TO HIS NEW SCHOOL.
UGH.
ARE YOU FEELING SICK?
NO, SIR.
WHAT'S UP WITH THE GIRLS?
IS THERE A NUCLEAR POWER PLANT NEARBY?
FACES GLOWING WITH RADIATION.

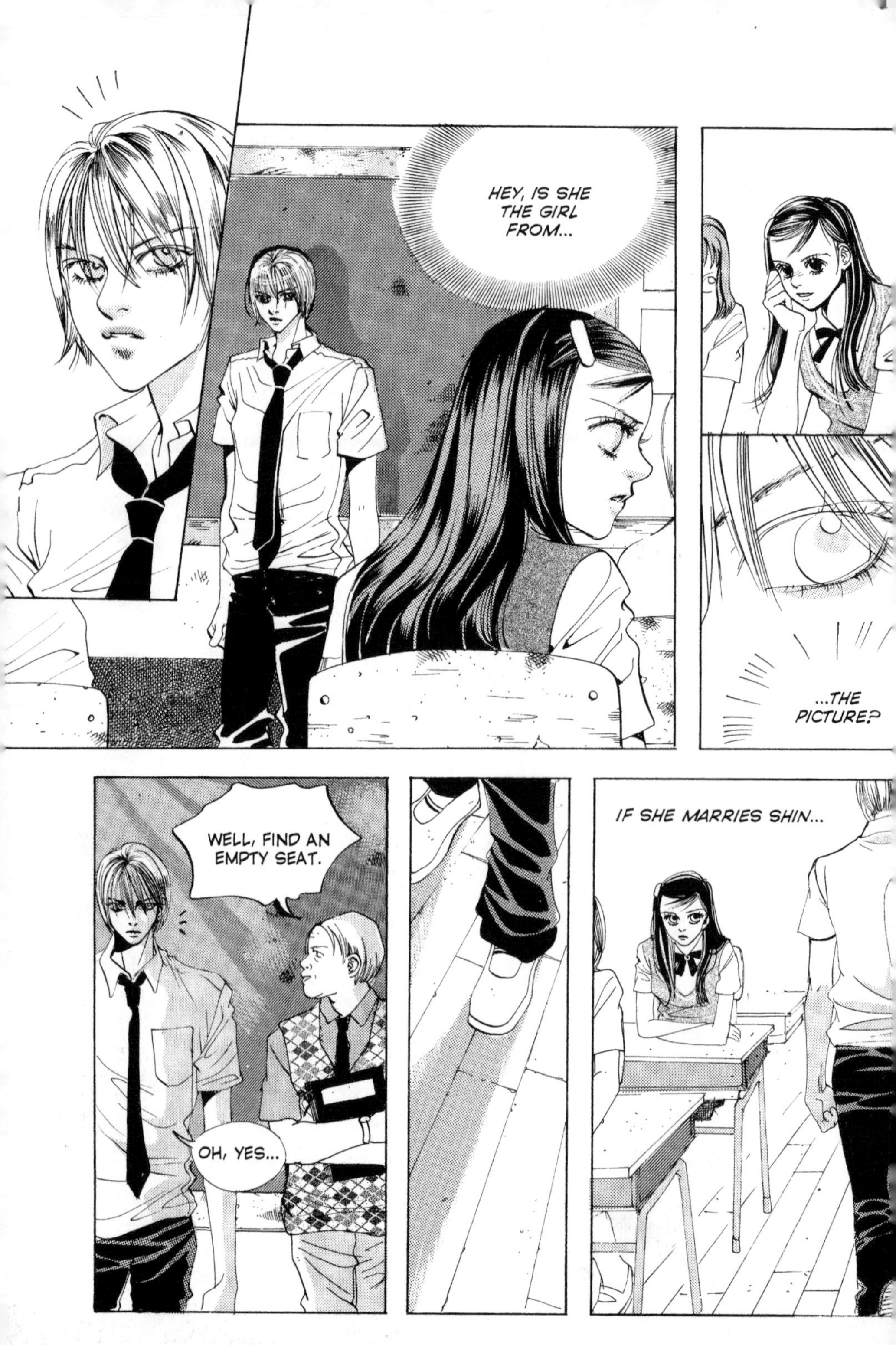
HEY, IS SHE THE GIRL FROM...
...THE PICTURE?
WELL, FIND AN EMPTY SEAT.
OH, YES...
IF SHE MARRIES SHIN...

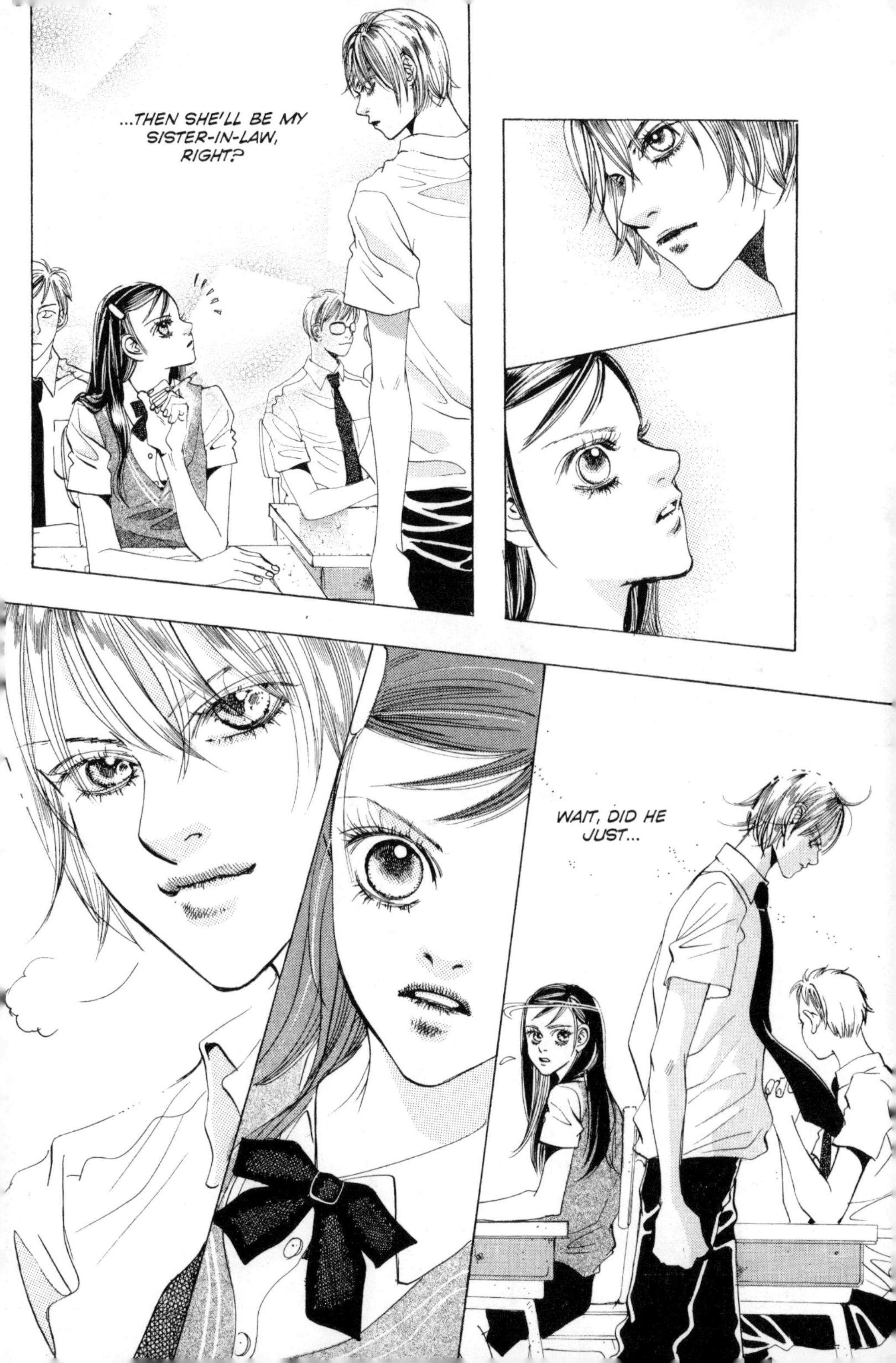
...THEN SHE'LL BE MY SISTER-IN-LAW, RIGHT?
WAIT, DID HE JUST...

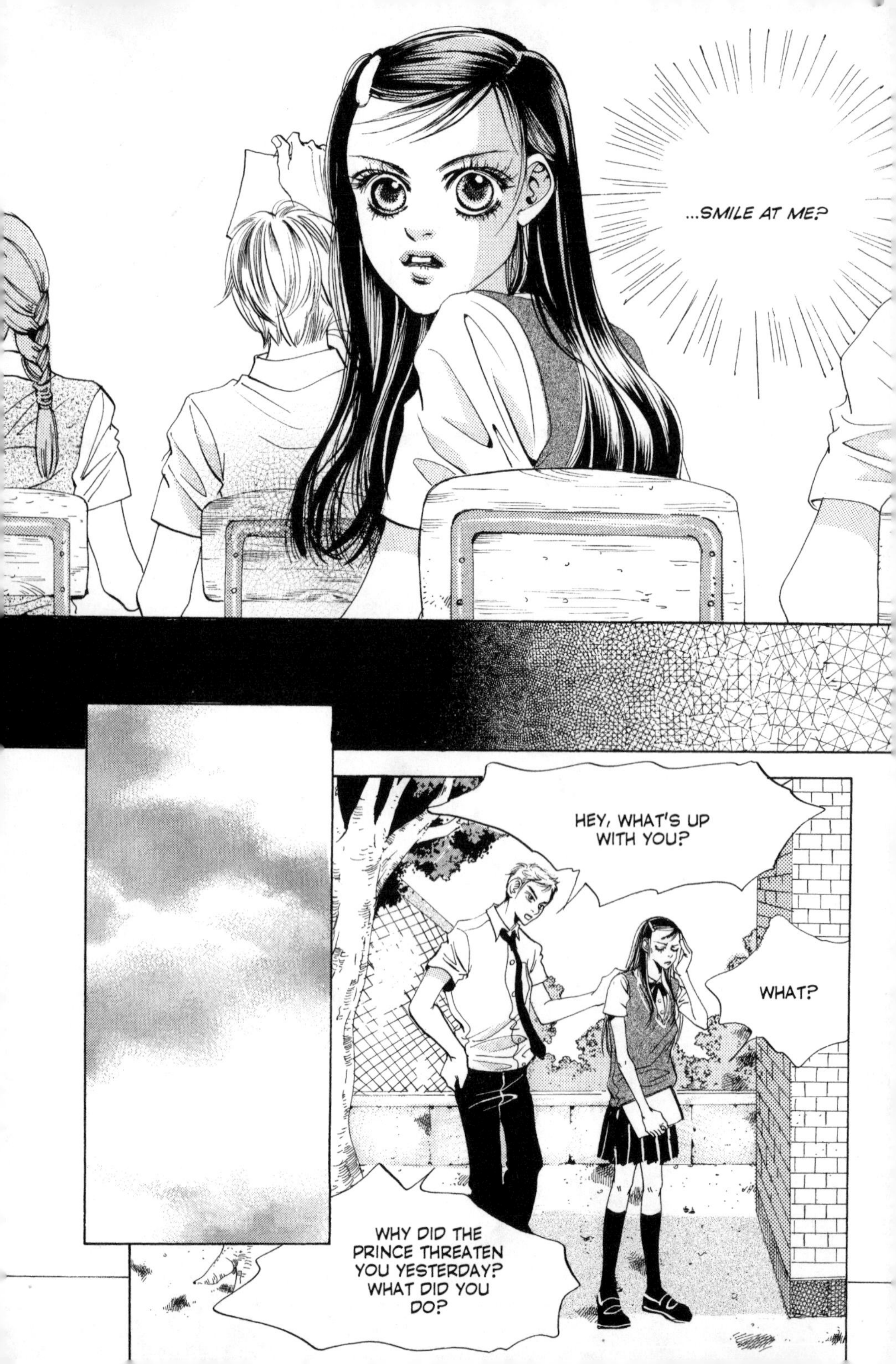
...SMILE AT ME?
HEY, WHAT'S UP WITH YOU?
WHAT?
WHY DID THE PRINCE THREATEN YOU YESTERDAY? WHAT DID YOU DO?

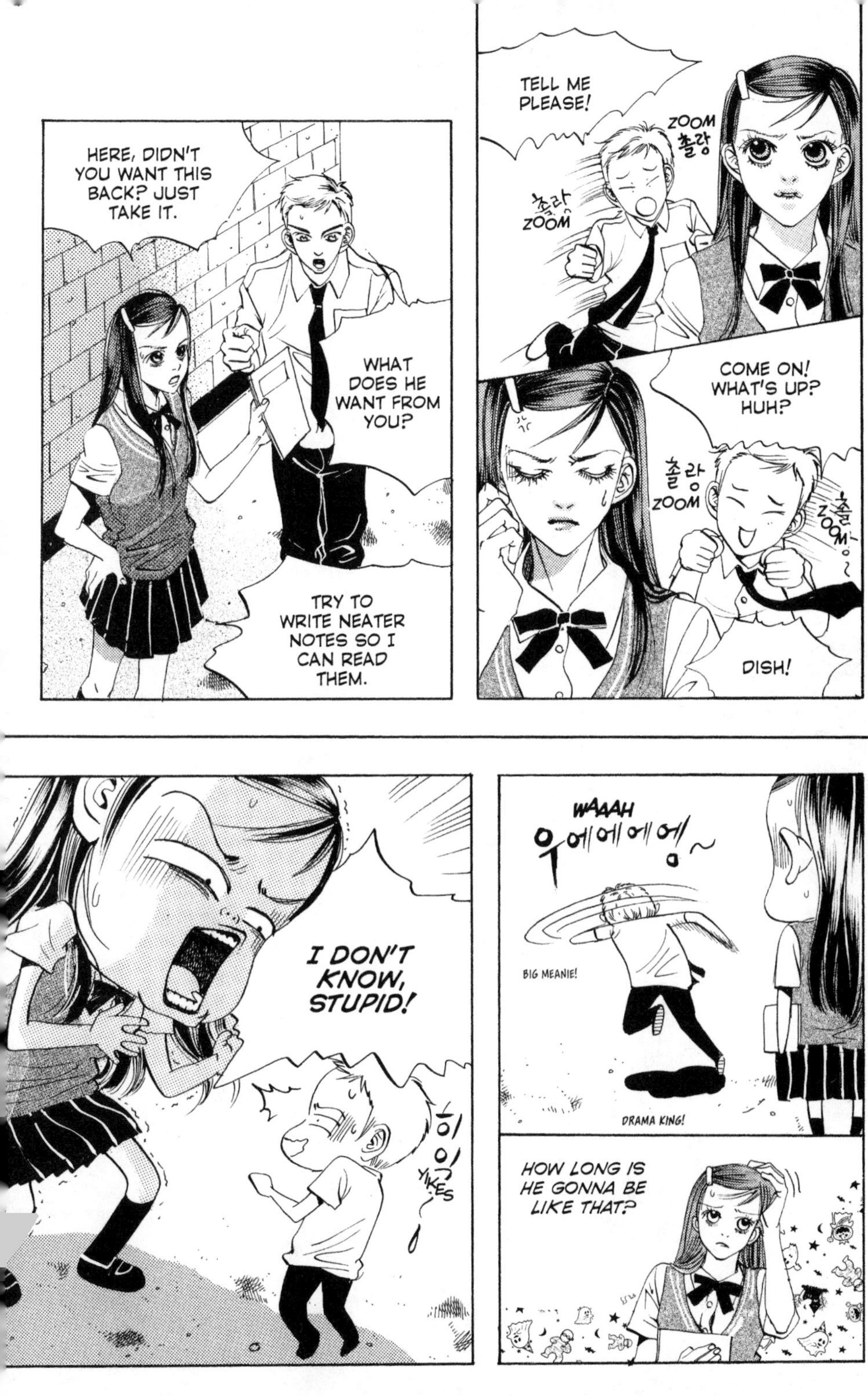
HERE, DIDN'T YOU WANT THIS BACK? JUST TAKE IT.
WHAT DOES HE WANT FROM YOU?
TRY TO WRITE NEATER NOTES SO I CAN READ THEM.
TELL ME PLEASE!
촐랑
ZOOM
ZOOM
촐랑
COME ON! WHAT'S UP? HUH?
촐랑
ZOOM
촐랑
ZOOM
DISH!
I DON'T KNOW, STUPID!
히익
YIKES
WAAAH
우에에에엥~
BIG MEANIE!
DRAMA KING!
HOW LONG IS HE GONNA BE LIKE THAT?

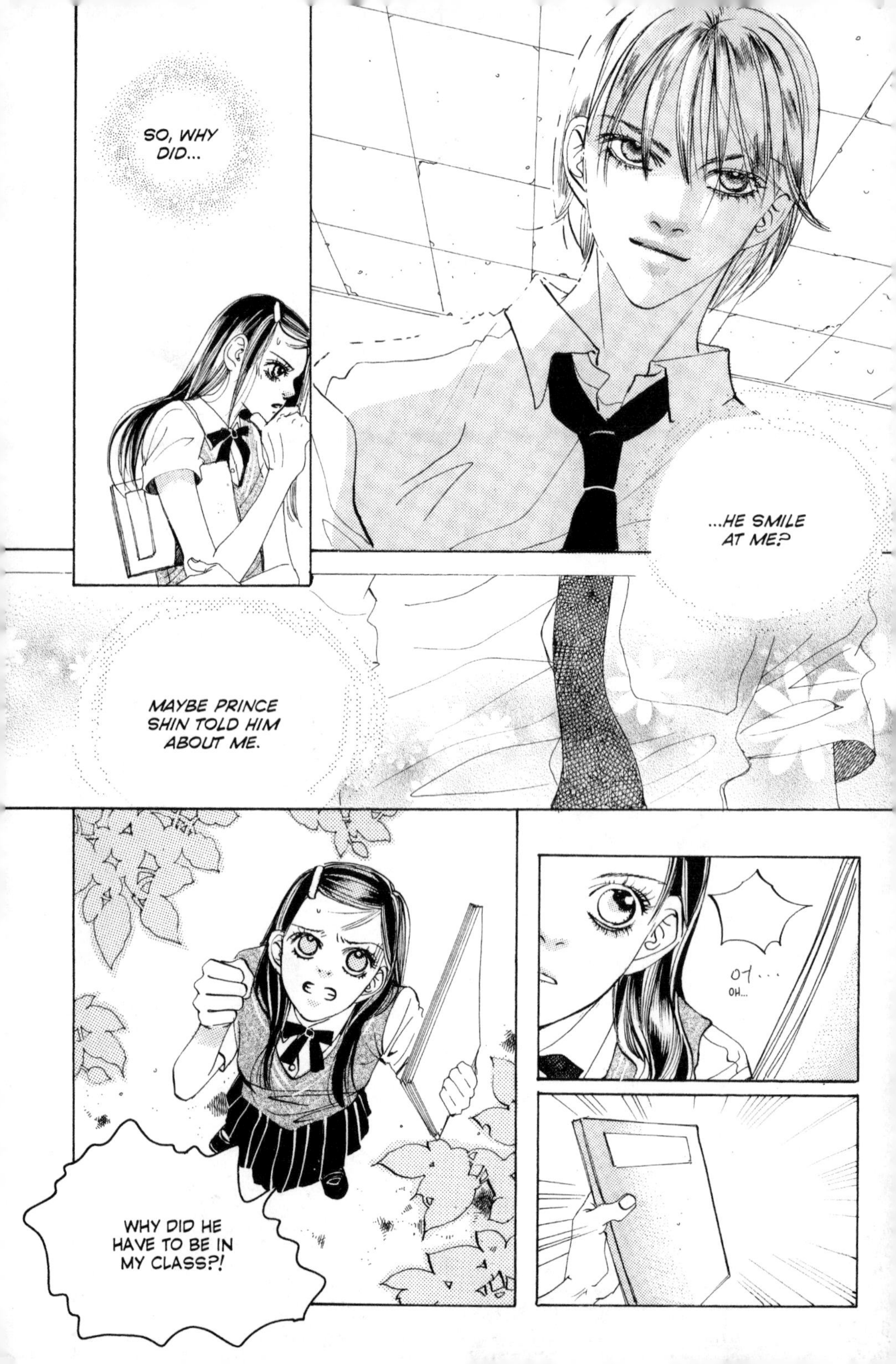
SO, WHY DID...
...HE SMILE AT ME?
MAYBE PRINCE SHIN TOLD HIM ABOUT ME.
WHY DID HE HAVE TO BE IN MY CLASS?!
어...
OH...

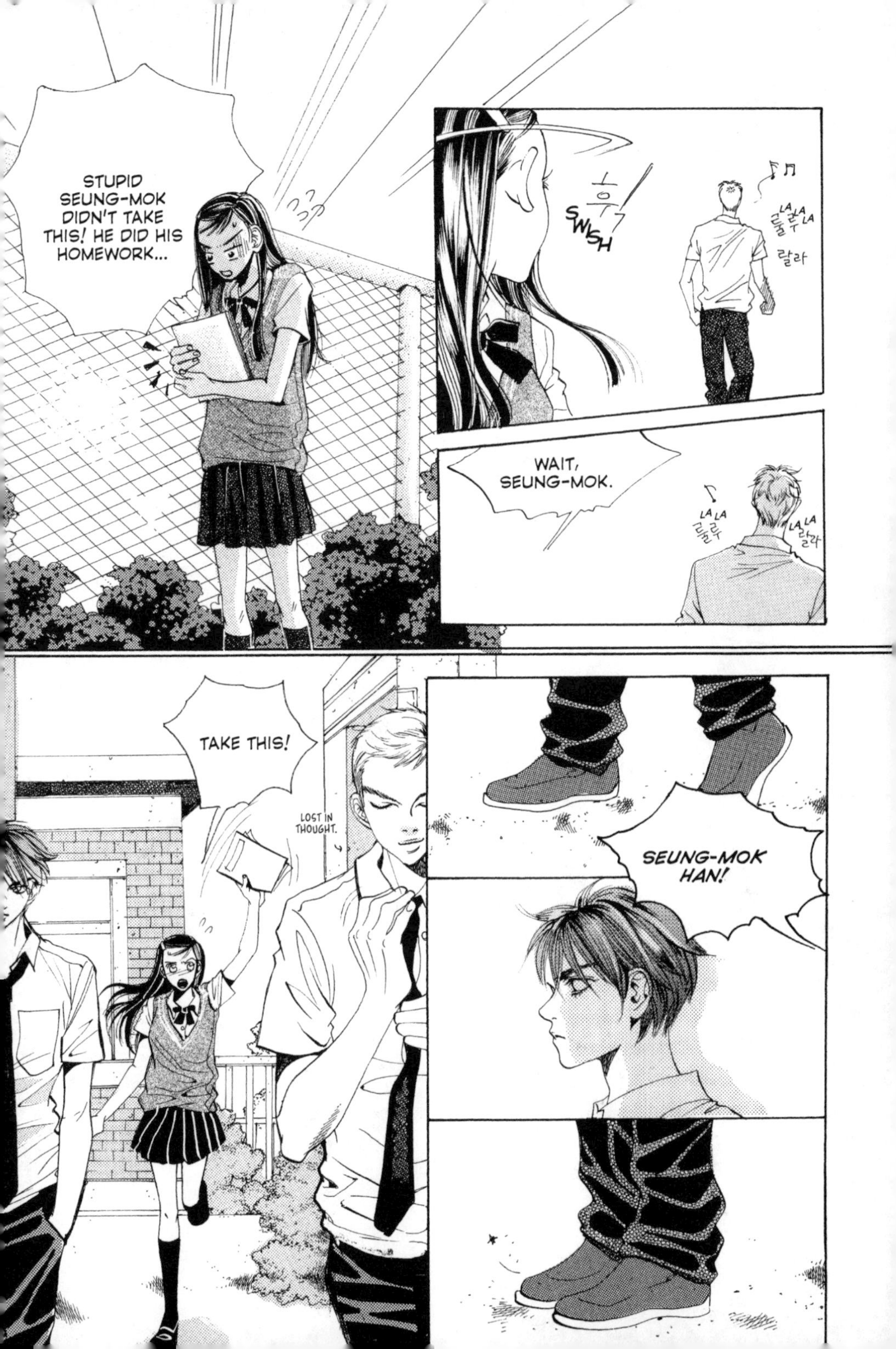
STUPID SEUNG-MOK DIDN'T TAKE THIS! HE DID HIS HOMEWORK...
SWISH
LA LA LA
랄라
WAIT, SEUNG-MOK.
LA LA
LA LA 랄라
TAKE THIS!
LOST IN THOUGHT.
SEUNG-MOK HAN!

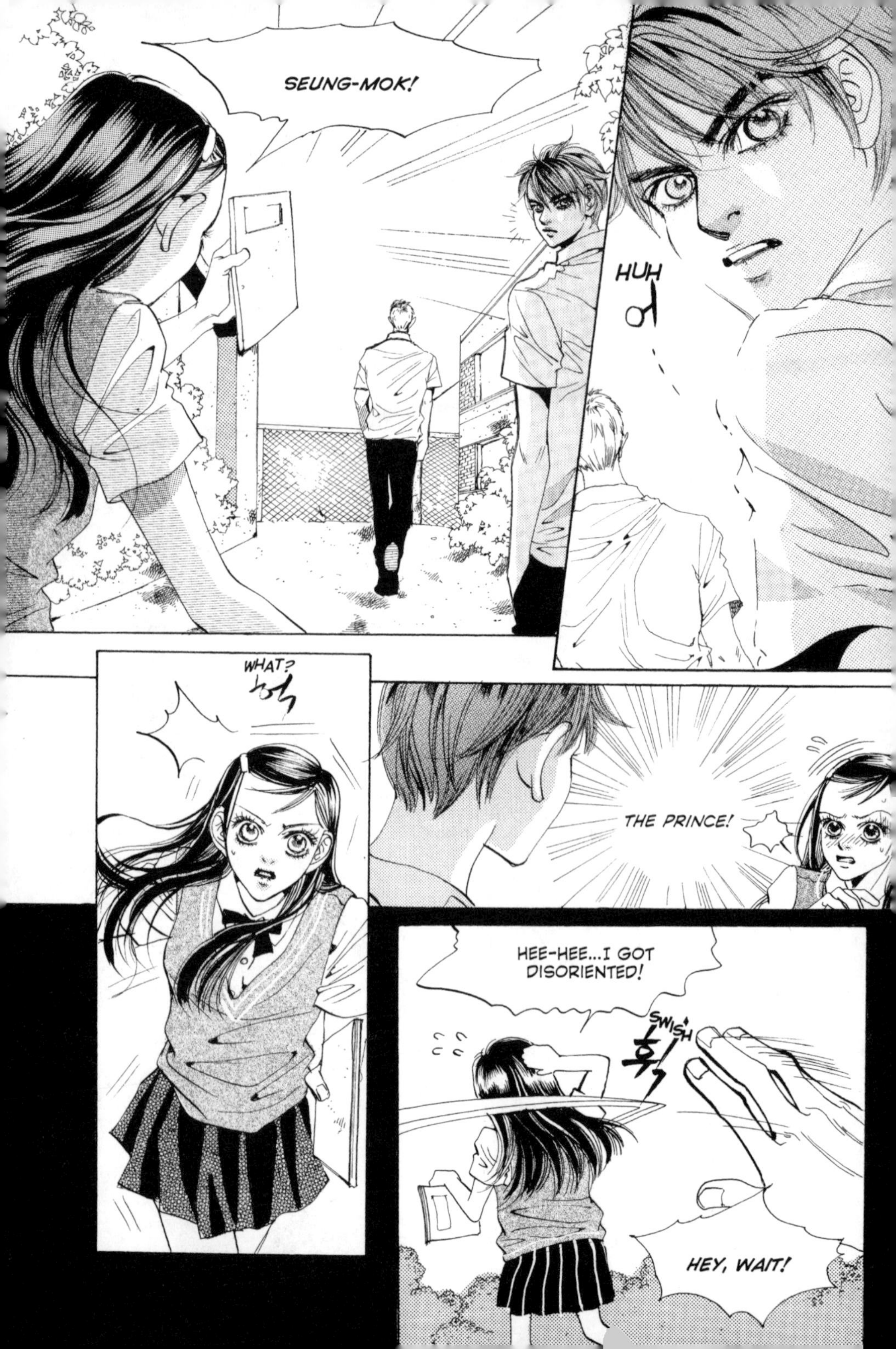
SEUNG-MOK!
HUH
허
WHAT?
헉
THE PRINCE!
HEE-HEE...I GOT DISORIENTED!
SWISH
휙
HEY, WAIT!

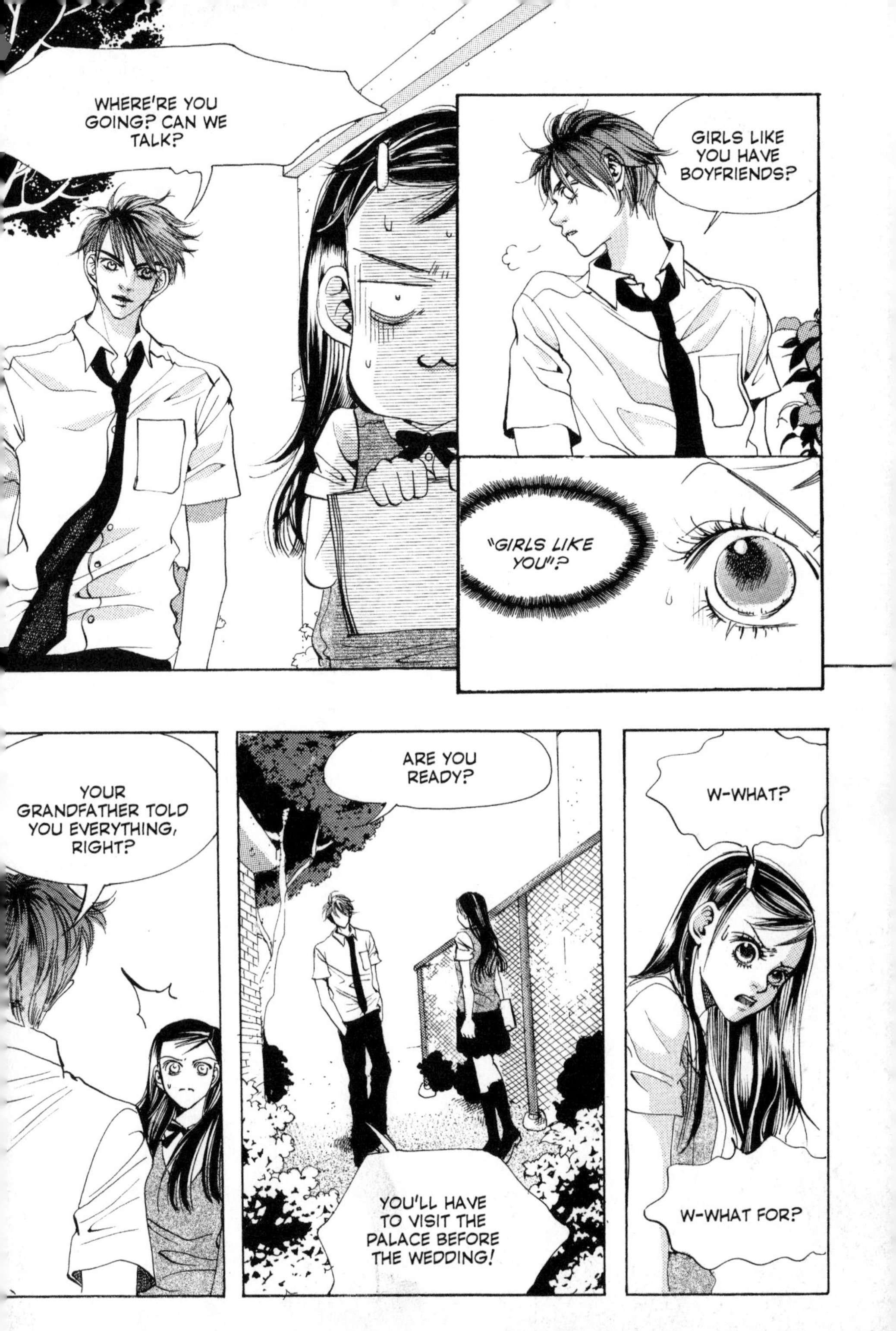
WHERE'RE YOU GOING? CAN WE TALK?
GIRLS LIKE YOU HAVE BOYFRIENDS?
"GIRLS LIKE YOU"?
YOUR GRANDFATHER TOLD YOU EVERYTHING, RIGHT?
ARE YOU READY?
YOU'LL HAVE TO VISIT THE PALACE BEFORE THE WEDDING!
W-WHAT?
W-WHAT FOR?

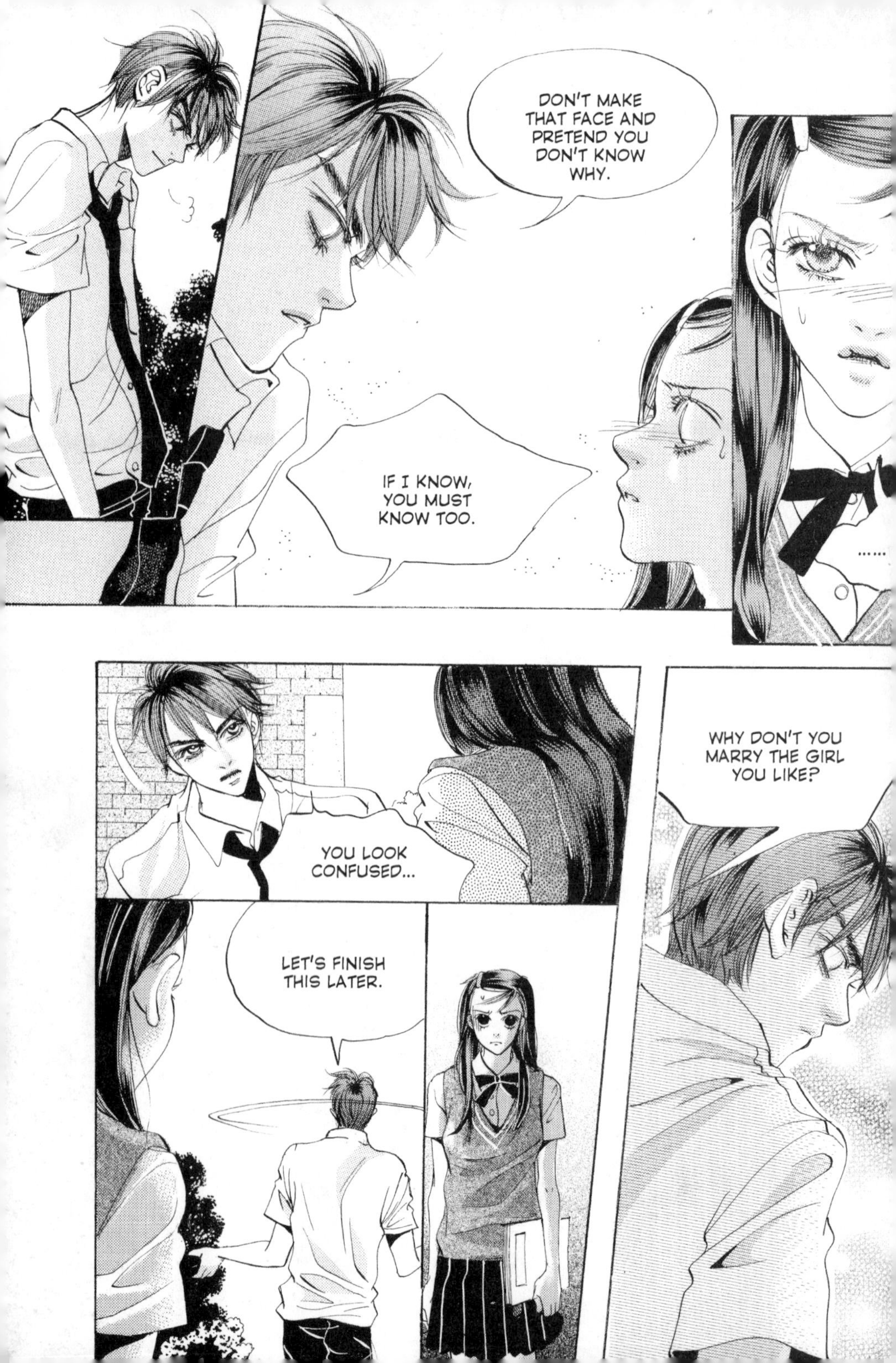
DON'T MAKE THAT FACE AND PRETEND YOU DON'T KNOW WHY.
IF I KNOW, YOU MUST KNOW TOO.
......
YOU LOOK CONFUSED...
LET'S FINISH THIS LATER.
WHY DON'T YOU MARRY THE GIRL YOU LIKE?

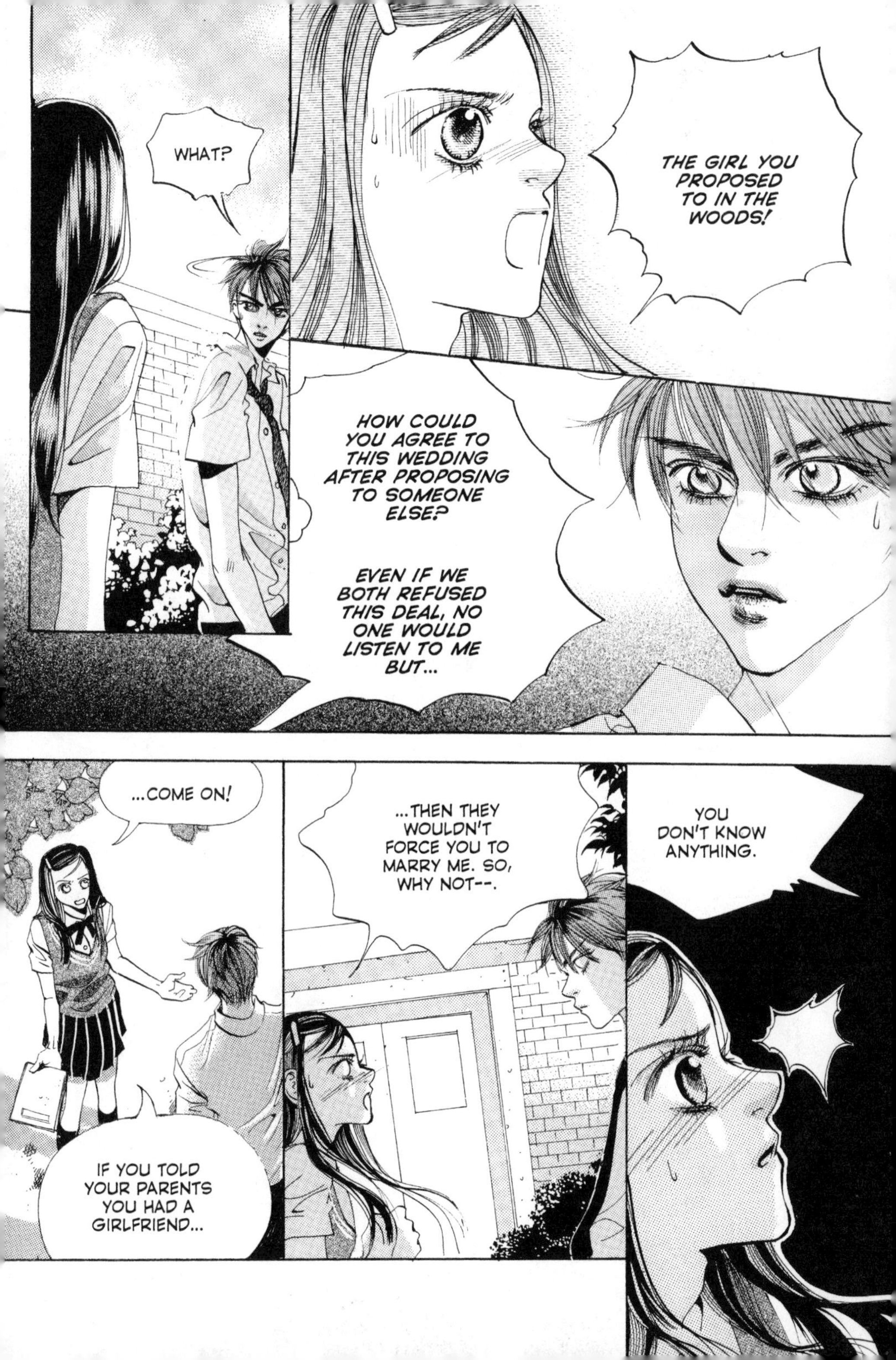
WHAT?
THE GIRL YOU PROPOSED TO IN THE WOODS!
HOW COULD YOU AGREE TO THIS WEDDING AFTER PROPOSING TO SOMEONE ELSE?
EVEN IF WE BOTH REFUSED THIS DEAL, NO ONE WOULD LISTEN TO ME BUT...
...COME ON!
IF YOU TOLD YOUR PARENTS YOU HAD A GIRLFRIEND...
...THEN THEY WOULDN'T FORCE YOU TO MARRY ME. SO, WHY NOT--.
YOU DON'T KNOW ANYTHING.

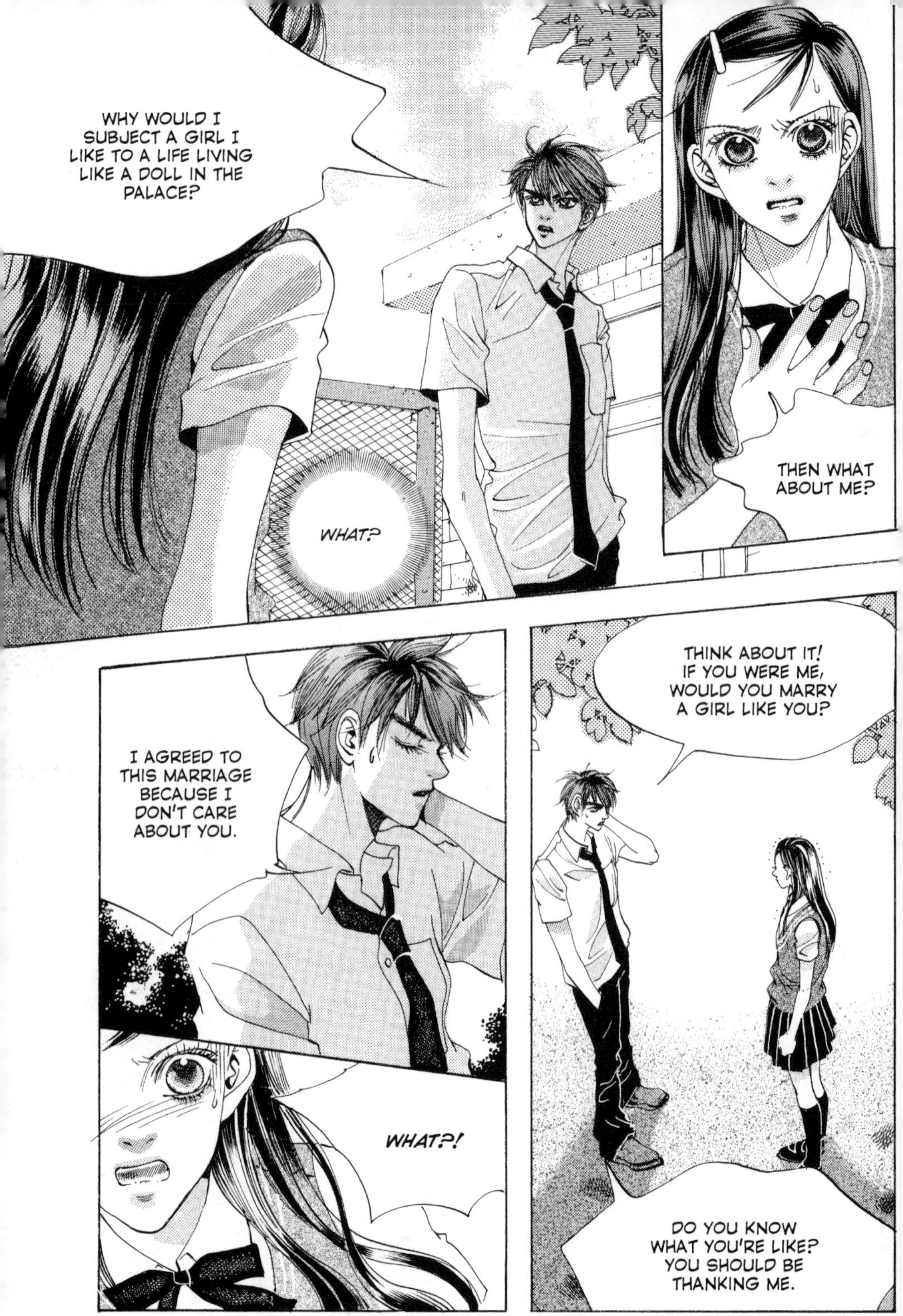
WHY WOULD I SUBJECT A GIRL I LIKE TO A LIFE LIVING LIKE A DOLL IN THE PALACE?
WHAT?
THEN WHAT ABOUT ME?
I AGREED TO THIS MARRIAGE BECAUSE I DON'T CARE ABOUT YOU.
WHAT?!
THINK ABOUT IT! IF YOU WERE ME, WOULD YOU MARRY A GIRL LIKE YOU?
DO YOU KNOW WHAT YOU'RE LIKE? YOU SHOULD BE THANKING ME.

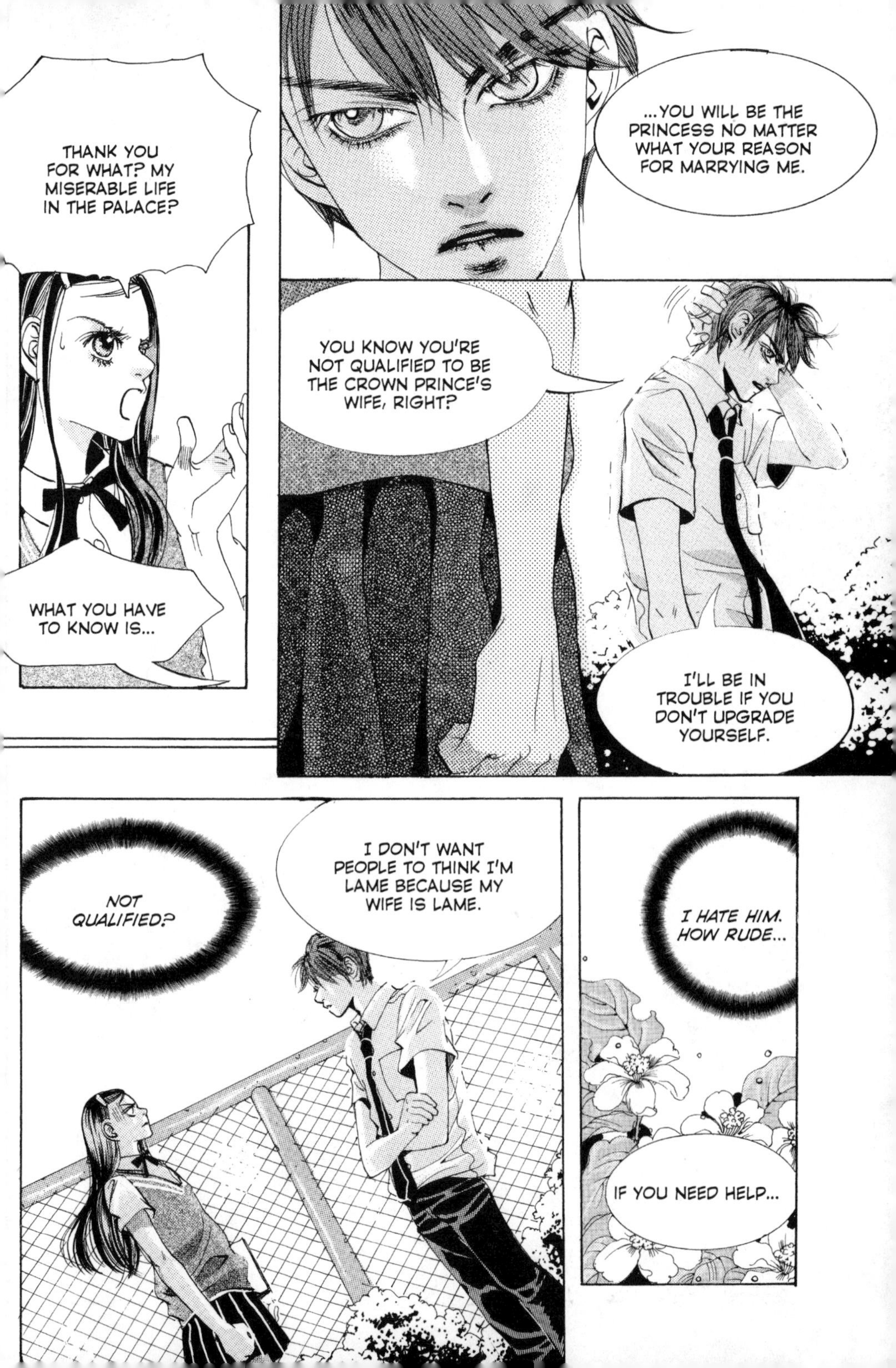
THANK YOU FOR WHAT? MY MISERABLE LIFE IN THE PALACE?
WHAT YOU HAVE TO KNOW IS...
...YOU WILL BE THE PRINCESS NO MATTER WHAT YOUR REASON FOR MARRYING ME.
YOU KNOW YOU'RE NOT QUALIFIED TO BE THE CROWN PRINCE'S WIFE, RIGHT?
I'LL BE IN TROUBLE IF YOU DON'T UPGRADE YOURSELF.
NOT QUALIFIED?
I DON'T WANT PEOPLE TO THINK I'M LAME BECAUSE MY WIFE IS LAME.
I HATE HIM. HOW RUDE...
IF YOU NEED HELP...

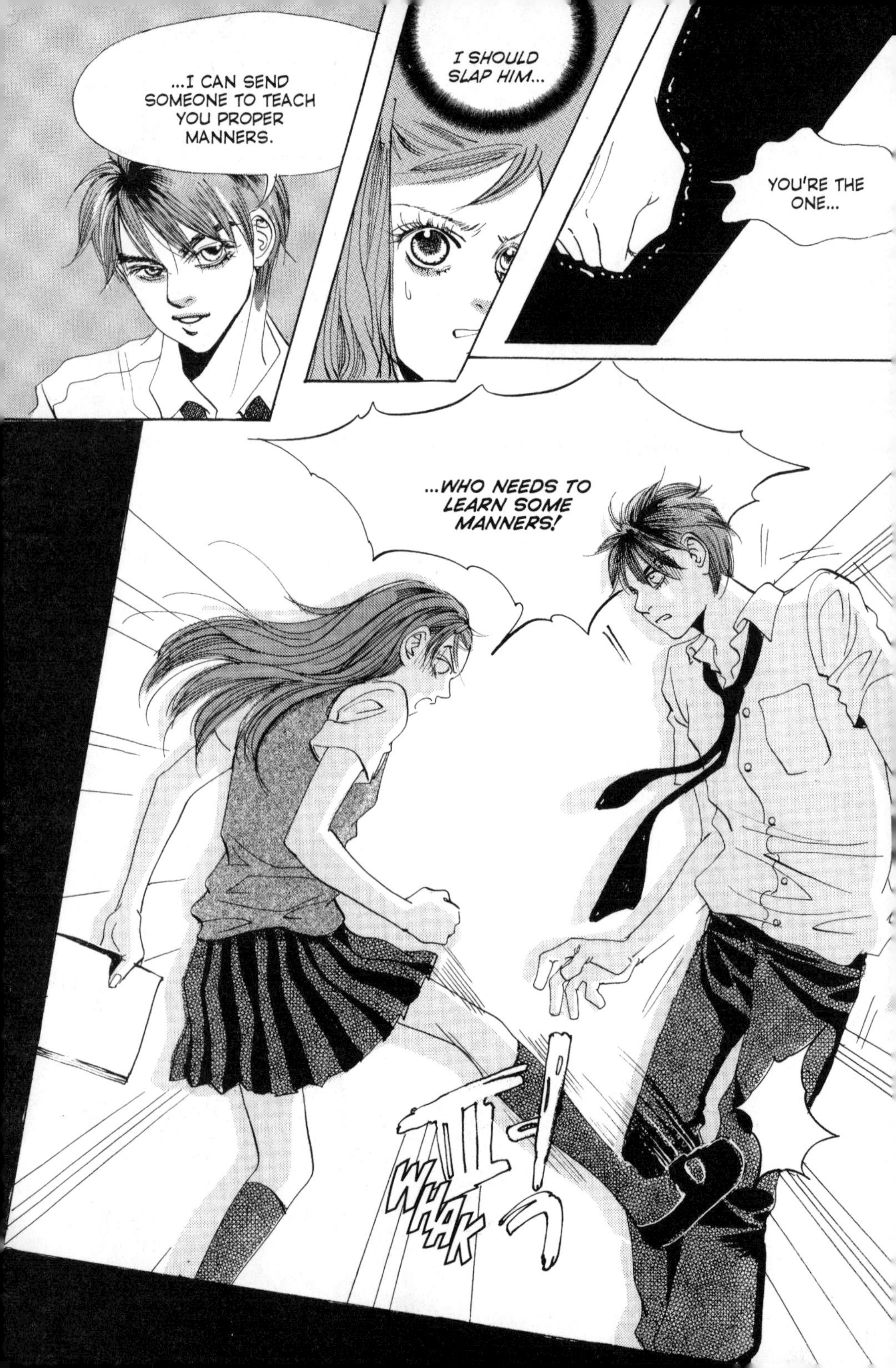

...I CAN SEND SOMEONE TO TEACH YOU PROPER MANNERS.
I SHOULD SLAP HIM...
YOU'RE THE ONE...
...WHO NEEDS TO LEARN SOME MANNERS!
WHAK

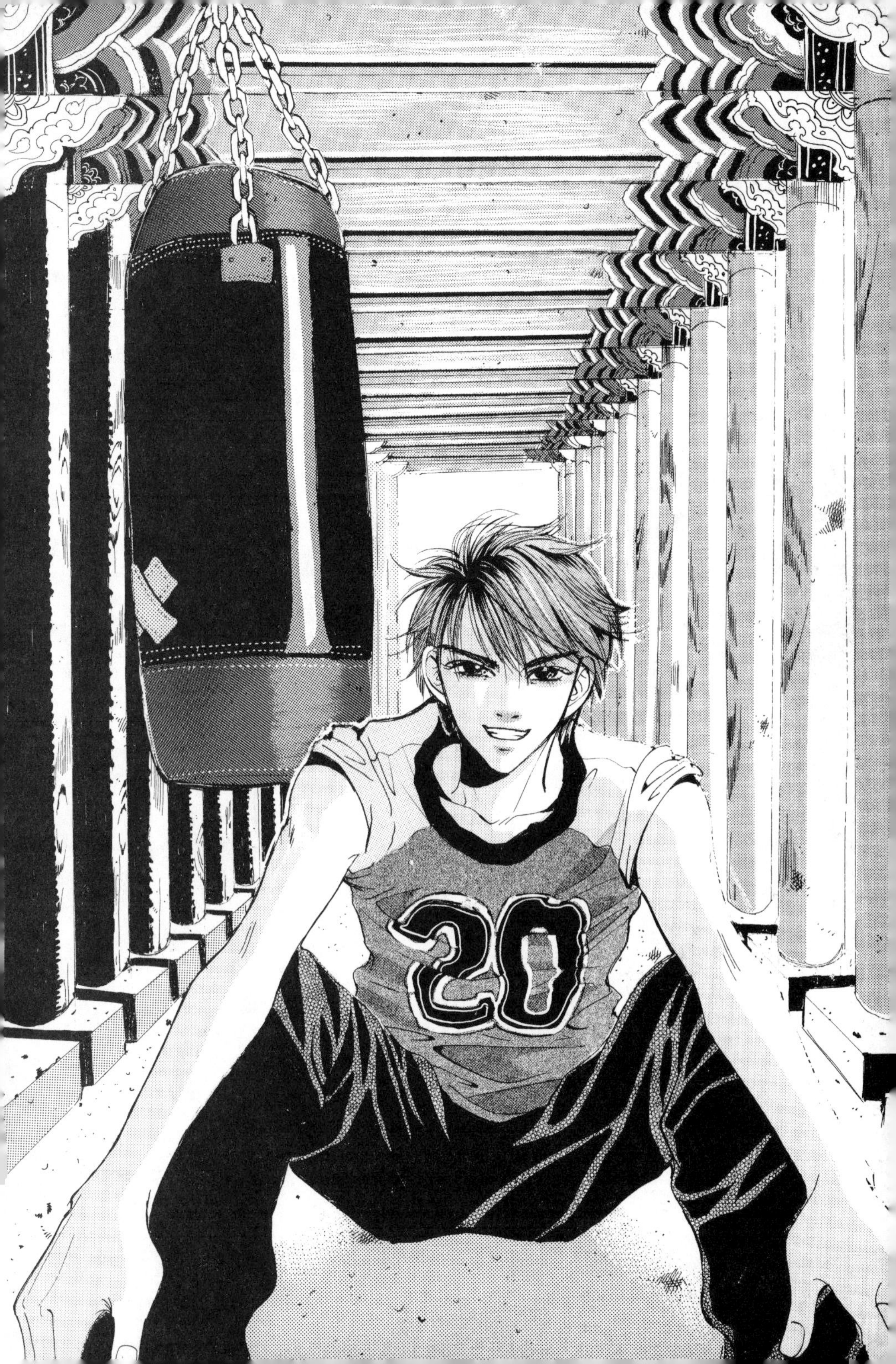

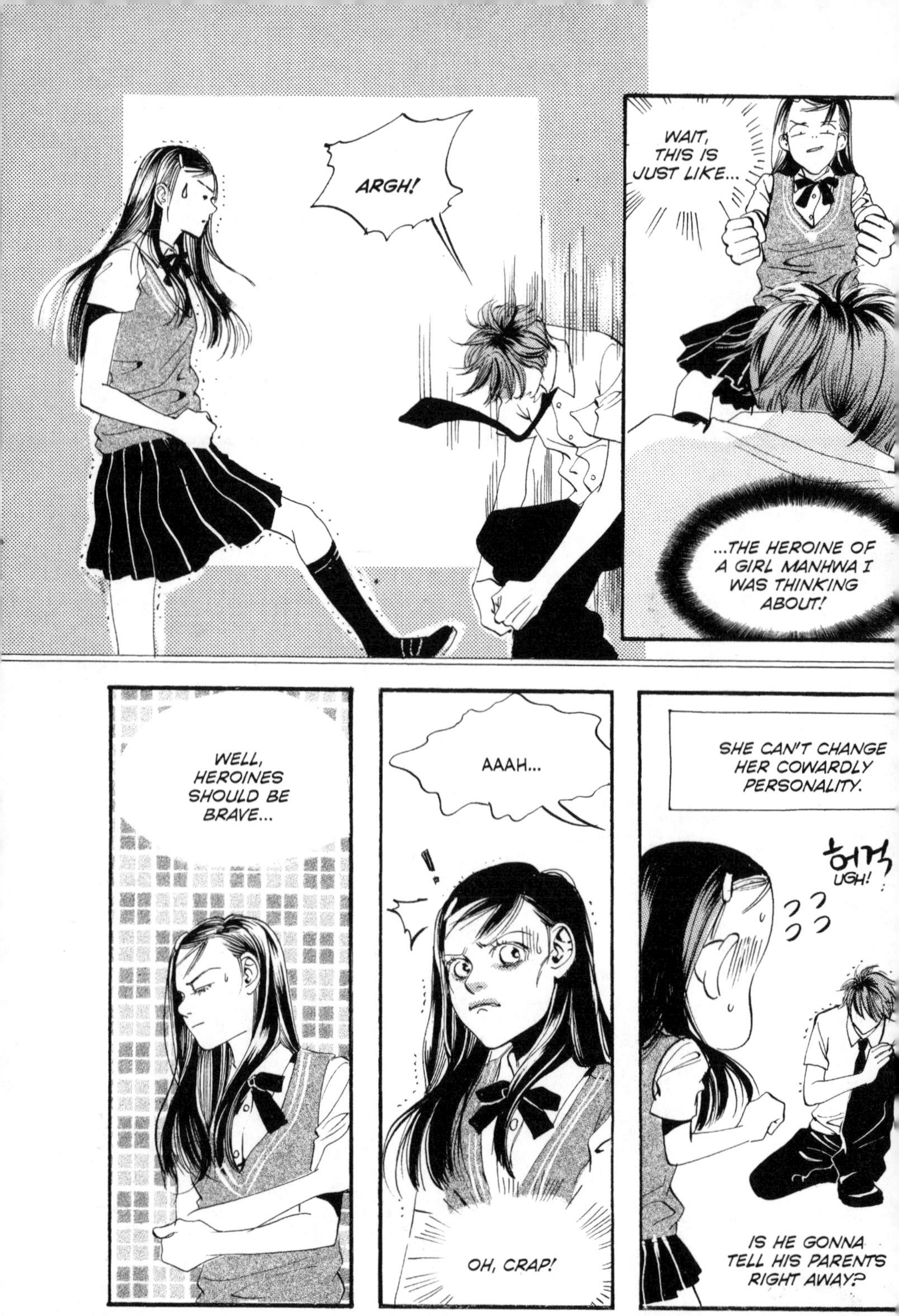
ARGH!
WAIT, THIS IS JUST LIKE...
...THE HEROINE OF A GIRL MANHWA I WAS THINKING ABOUT!
WELL, HEROINES SHOULD BE BRAVE...
AAAH...
!
OH, CRAP!
SHE CAN'T CHANGE HER COWARDLY PERSONALITY.
허걱
UGH!
IS HE GONNA TELL HIS PARENTS RIGHT AWAY?

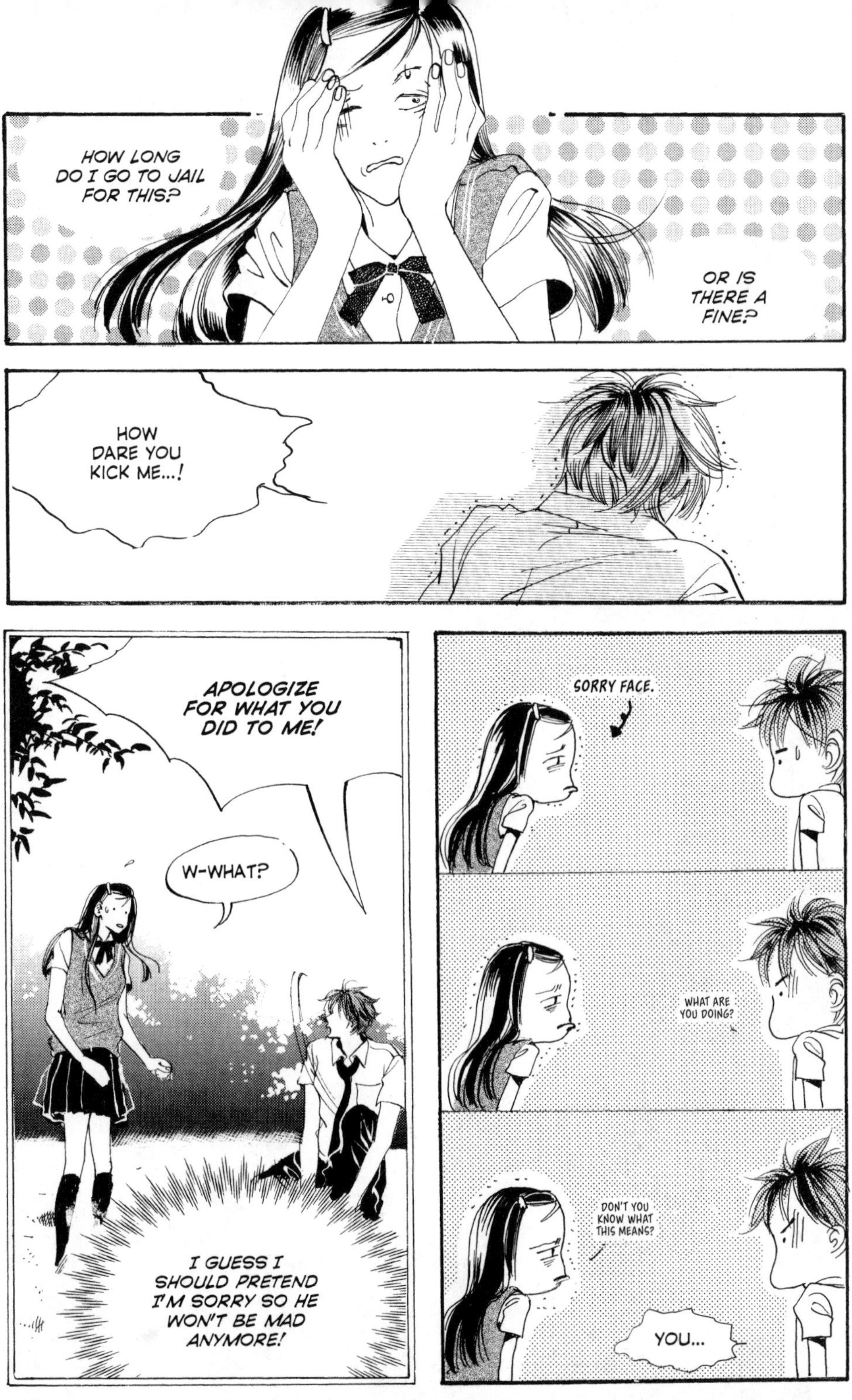
HOW LONG DO I GO TO JAIL FOR THIS?
OR IS THERE A FINE?
HOW DARE YOU KICK ME...!
APOLOGIZE FOR WHAT YOU DID TO ME!
W-WHAT?
I GUESS I SHOULD PRETEND I'M SORRY SO HE WON'T BE MAD ANYMORE!
SORRY FACE.
WHAT ARE YOU DOING?
DON'T YOU KNOW WHAT THIS MEANS?
YOU...

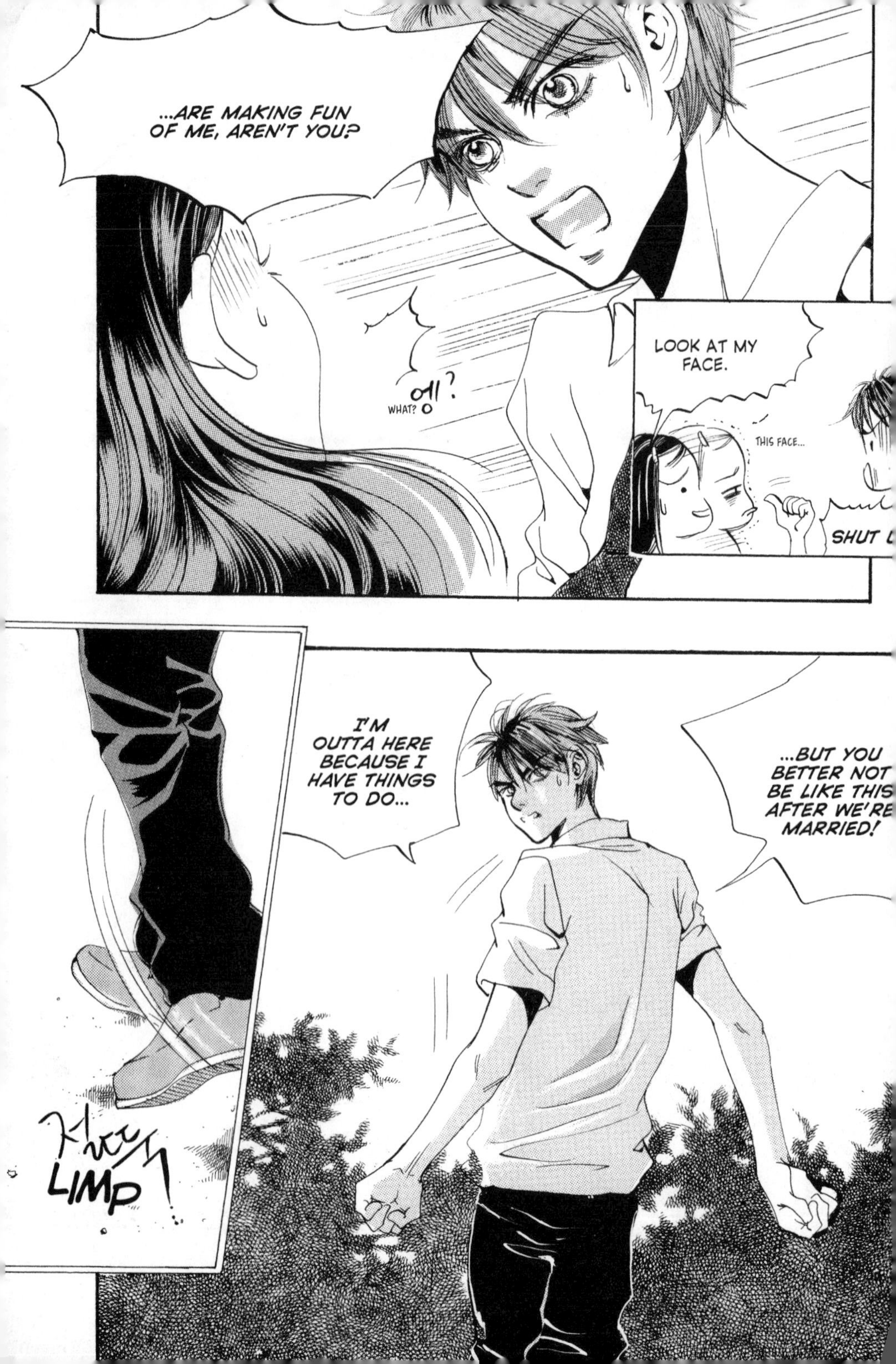
...ARE MAKING FUN OF ME, AREN'T YOU?
에?
WHAT?
LOOK AT MY FACE.
THIS FACE...
SHUT
I'M OUTTA HERE BECAUSE I HAVE THINGS TO DO...
...BUT YOU BETTER NOT BE LIKE THIS AFTER WE'RE MARRIED!
LIMP

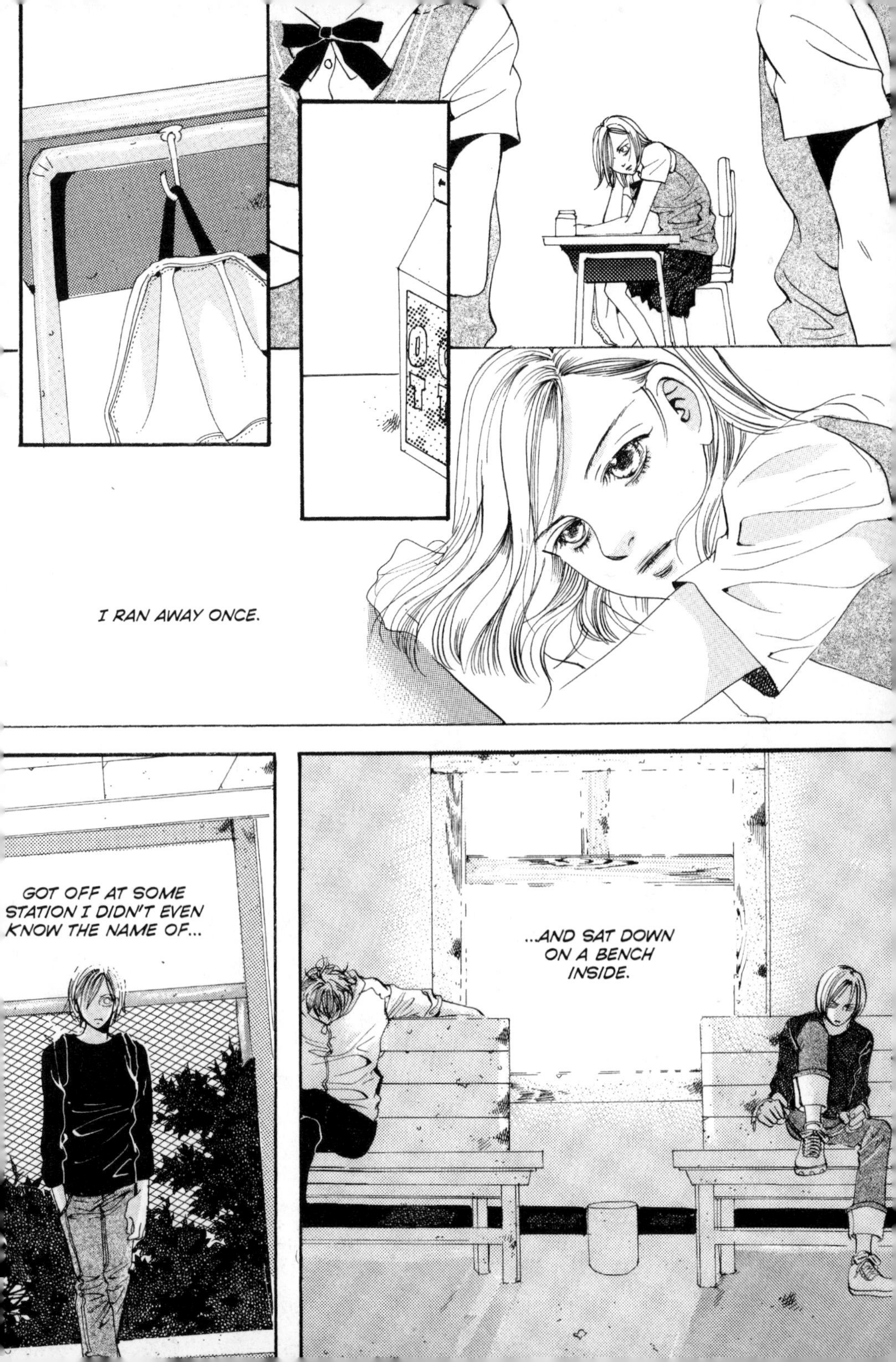
I RAN AWAY ONCE.
GOT OFF AT SOME STATION I DIDN'T EVEN KNOW THE NAME OF...
...AND SAT DOWN ON A BENCH INSIDE.

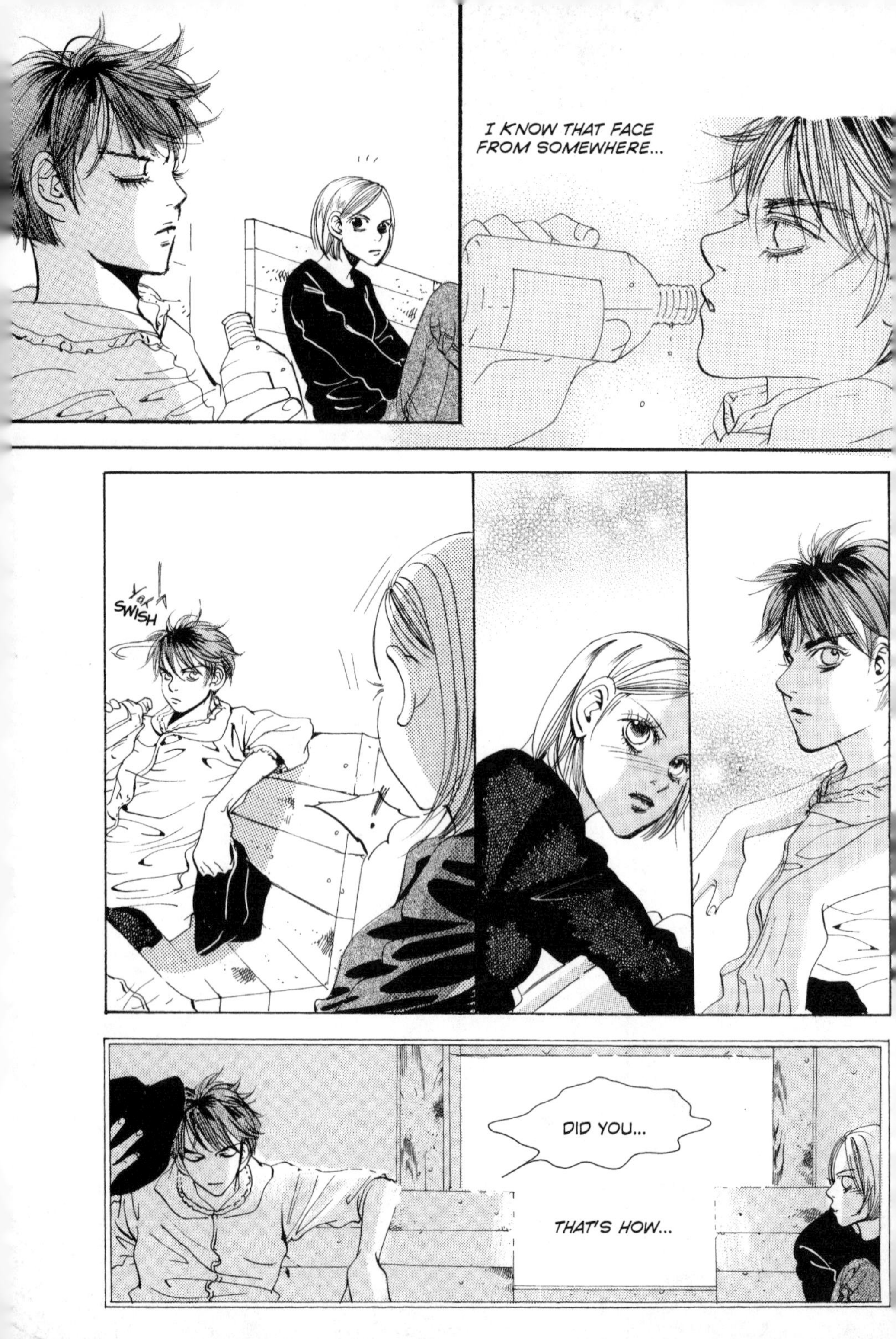
I KNOW THAT FACE FROM SOMEWHERE...
SWISH
DID YOU...
THAT'S HOW...

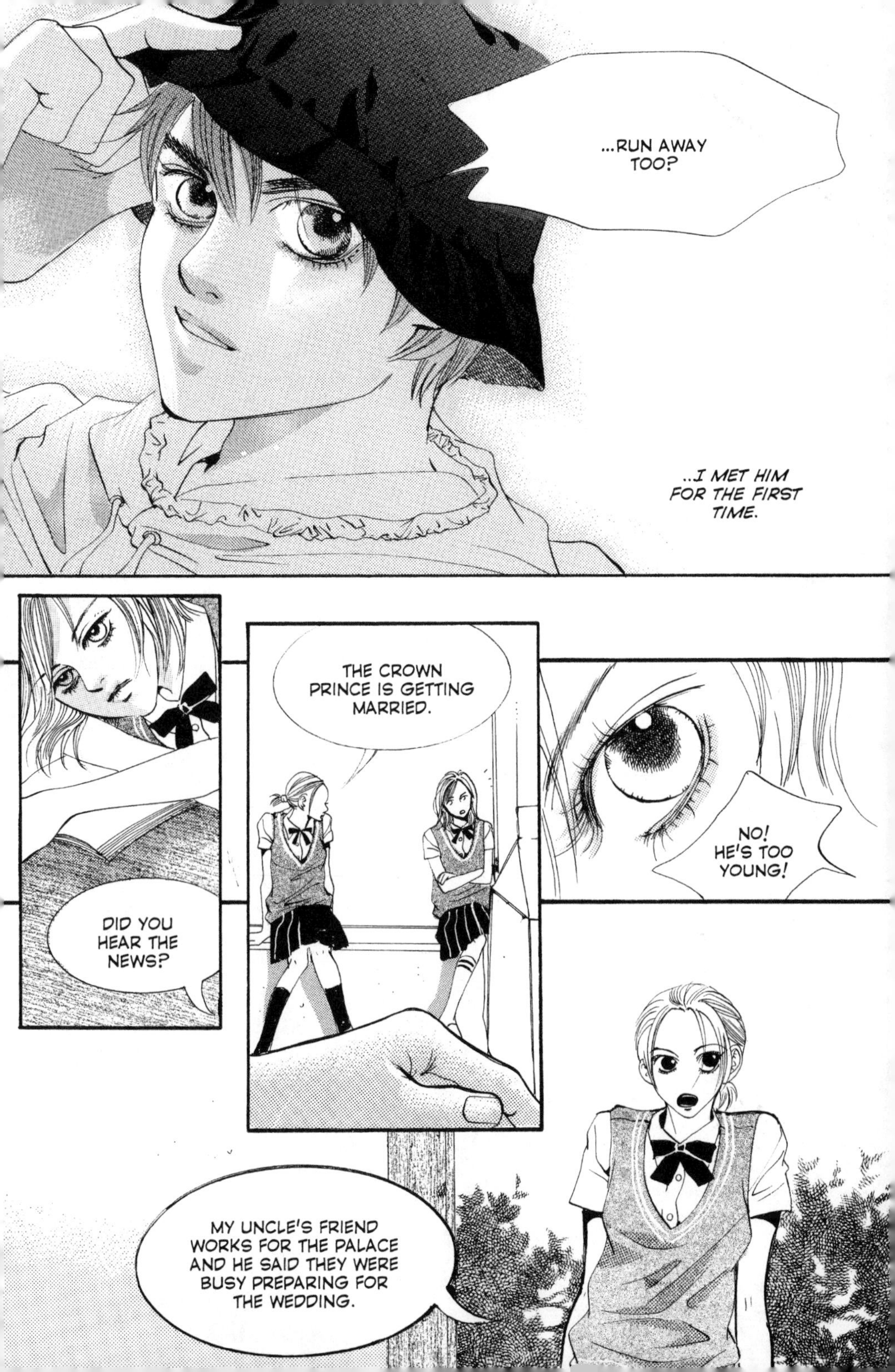
...RUN AWAY TOO?
...I MET HIM FOR THE FIRST TIME.
DID YOU HEAR THE NEWS?
THE CROWN PRINCE IS GETTING MARRIED.
NO! HE'S TOO YOUNG!
MY UNCLE'S FRIEND WORKS FOR THE PALACE AND HE SAID THEY WERE BUSY PREPARING FOR THE WEDDING.

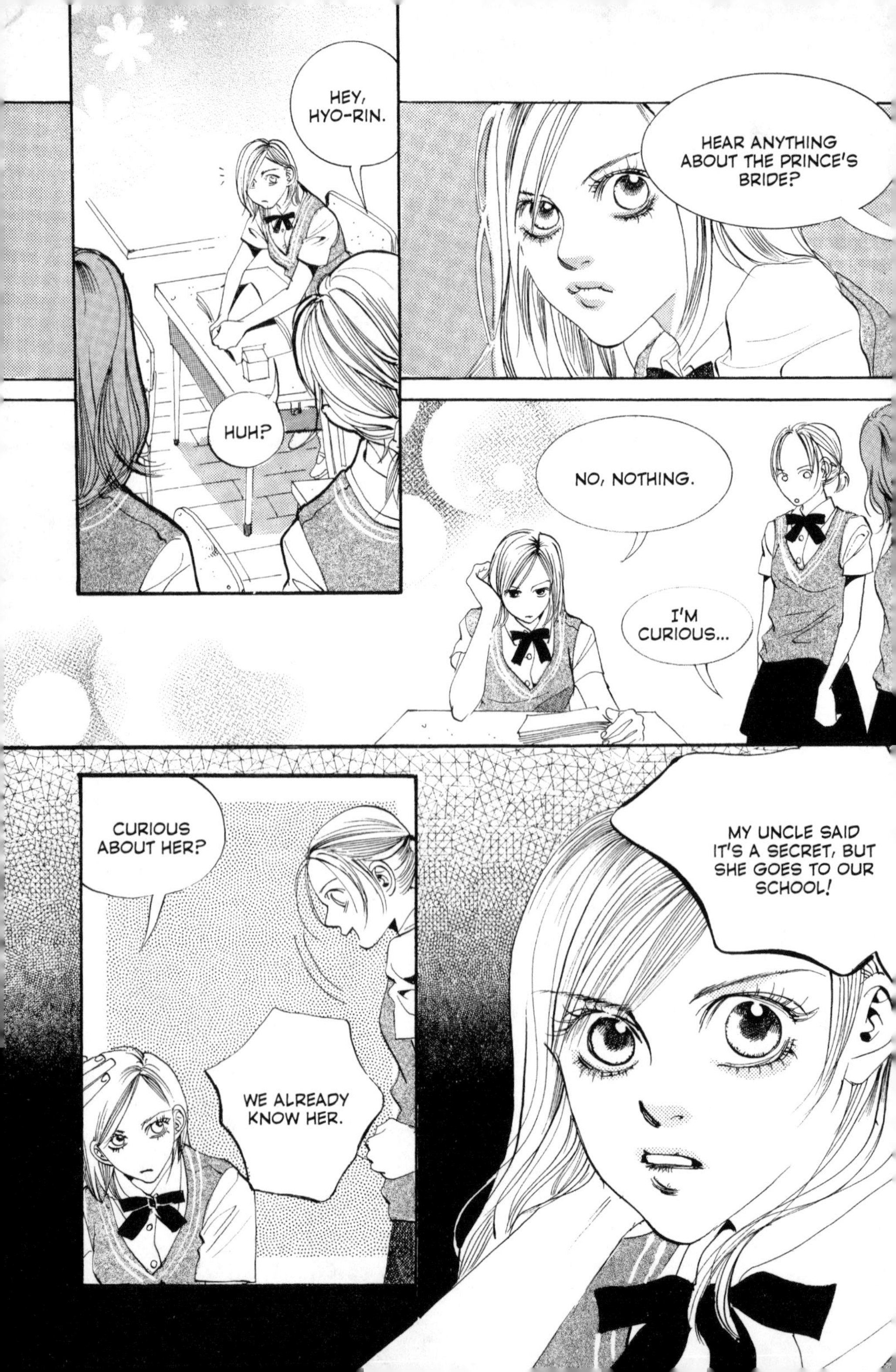
HEY, HYO-RIN.
HUH?
HEAR ANYTHING ABOUT THE PRINCE'S BRIDE?
NO, NOTHING.
I'M CURIOUS...
CURIOUS ABOUT HER?
WE ALREADY KNOW HER.
MY UNCLE SAID IT'S A SECRET, BUT SHE GOES TO OUR SCHOOL!

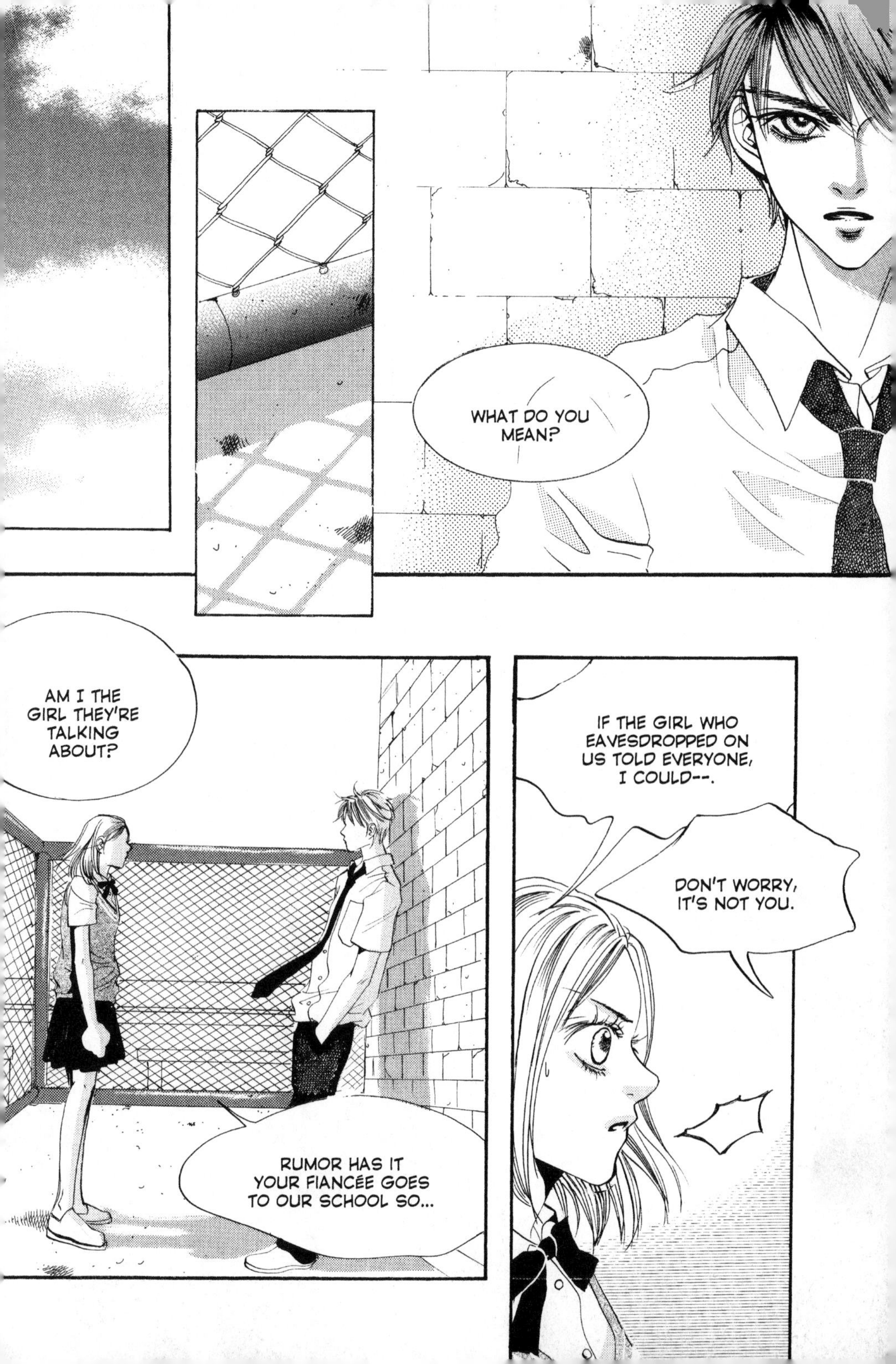
WHAT DO YOU MEAN?
AM I THE GIRL THEY'RE TALKING ABOUT?
RUMOR HAS IT YOUR FIANCÉE GOES TO OUR SCHOOL SO...
IF THE GIRL WHO EAVESDROPPED ON US TOLD EVERYONE, I COULD--.
DON'T WORRY, IT'S NOT YOU.

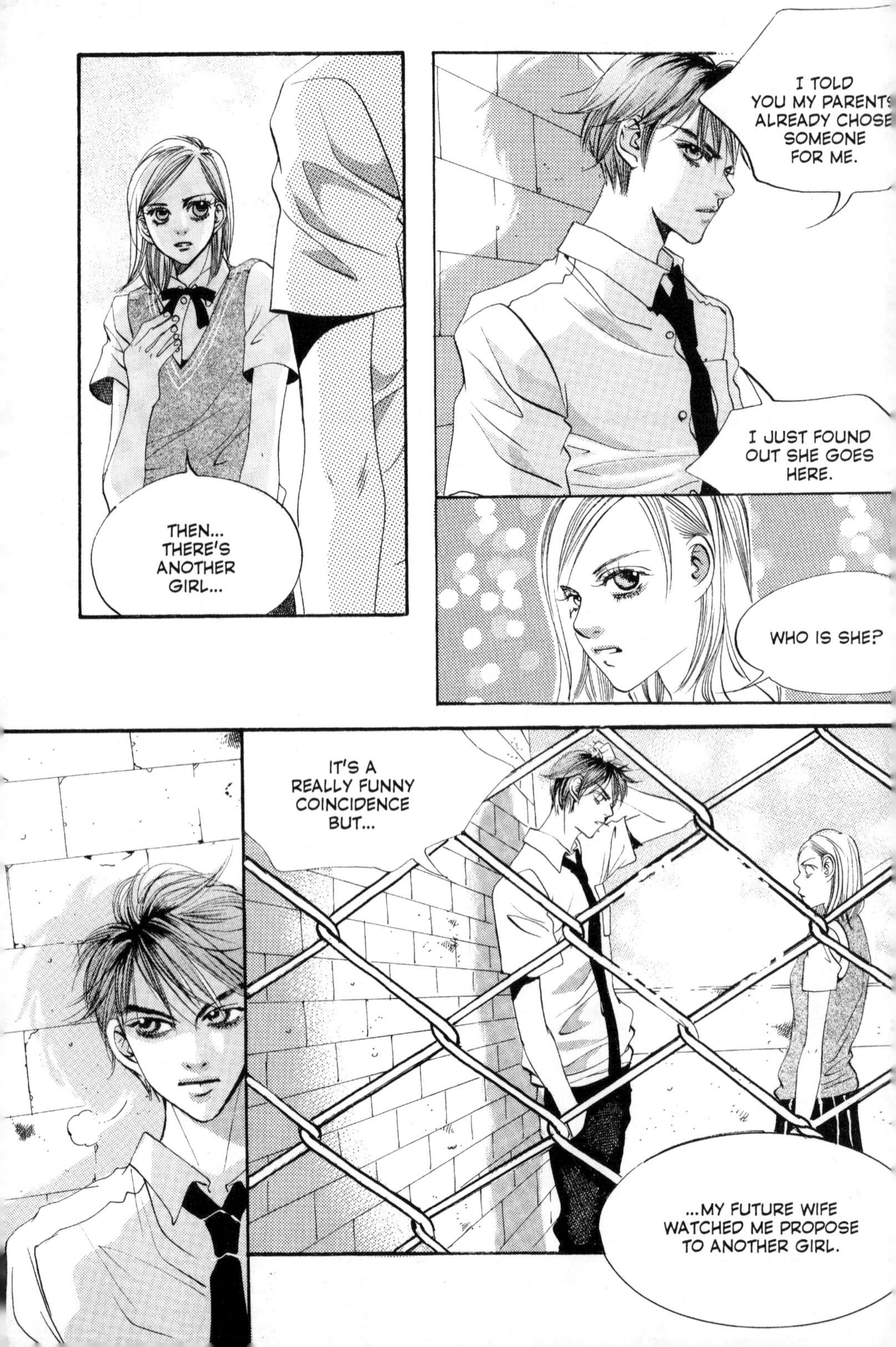
THEN... THERE'S ANOTHER GIRL...
I TOLD YOU MY PARENTS ALREADY CHOSE SOMEONE FOR ME.
I JUST FOUND OUT SHE GOES HERE.
WHO IS SHE?
IT'S A REALLY FUNNY COINCIDENCE BUT...
...MY FUTURE WIFE WATCHED ME PROPOSE TO ANOTHER GIRL.

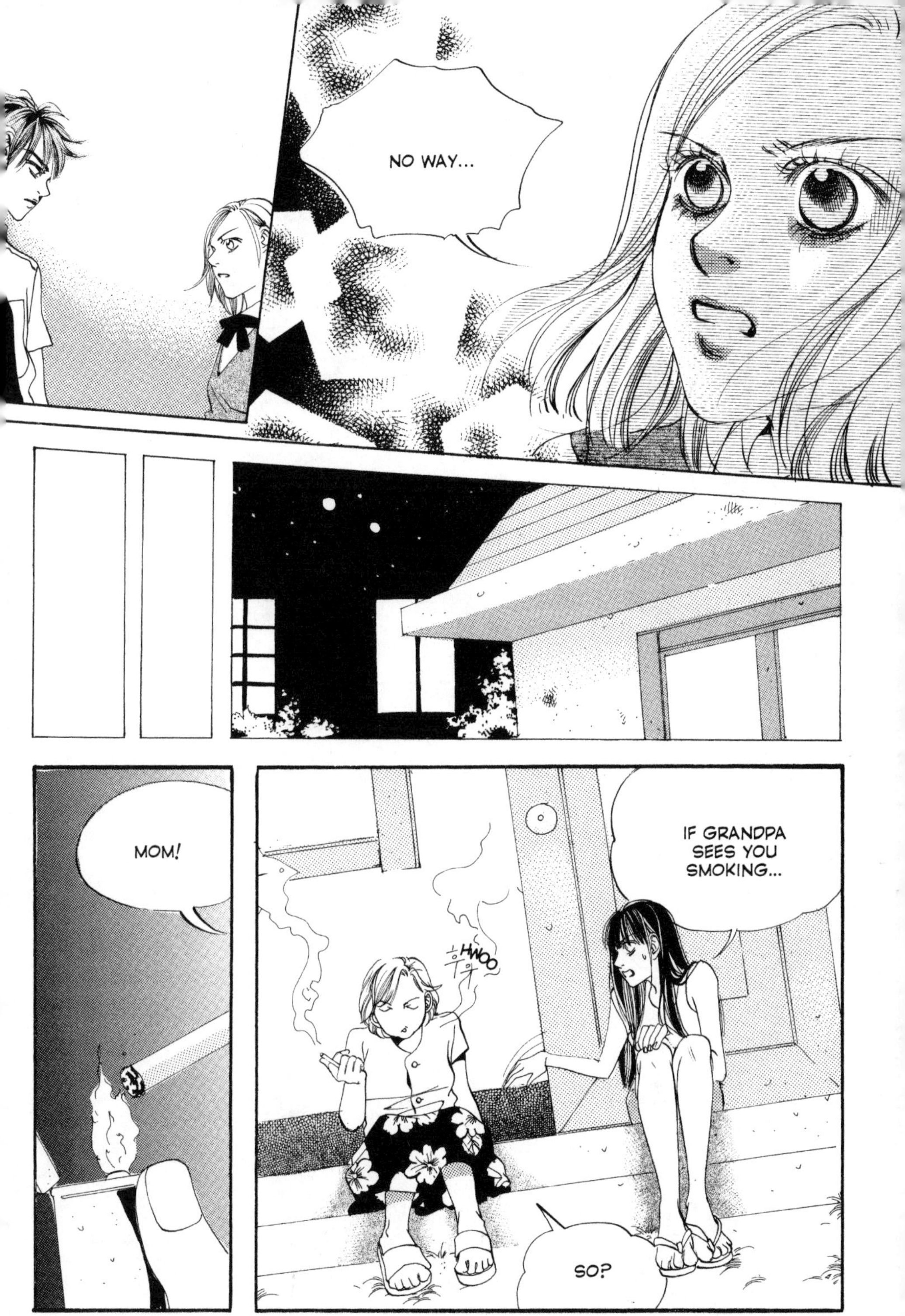
NO WAY...
MOM!
IF GRANDPA SEES YOU SMOKING...
HWOO
SO?

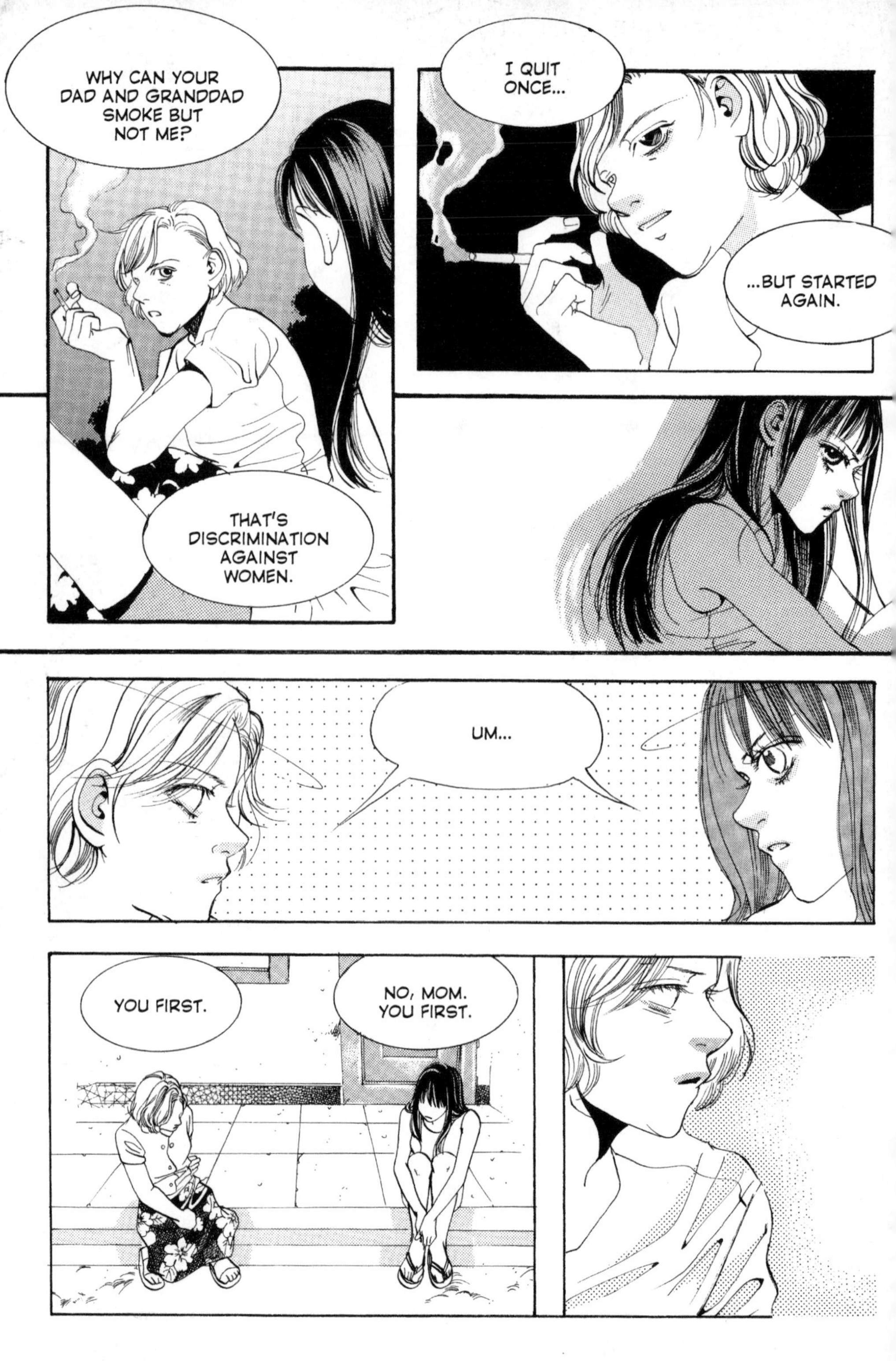
WHY CAN YOUR DAD AND GRANDDAD SMOKE BUT NOT ME?
THAT'S DISCRIMINATION AGAINST WOMEN.
I QUIT ONCE...
...BUT STARTED AGAIN.
UM...
YOU FIRST.
NO, MOM. YOU FIRST.

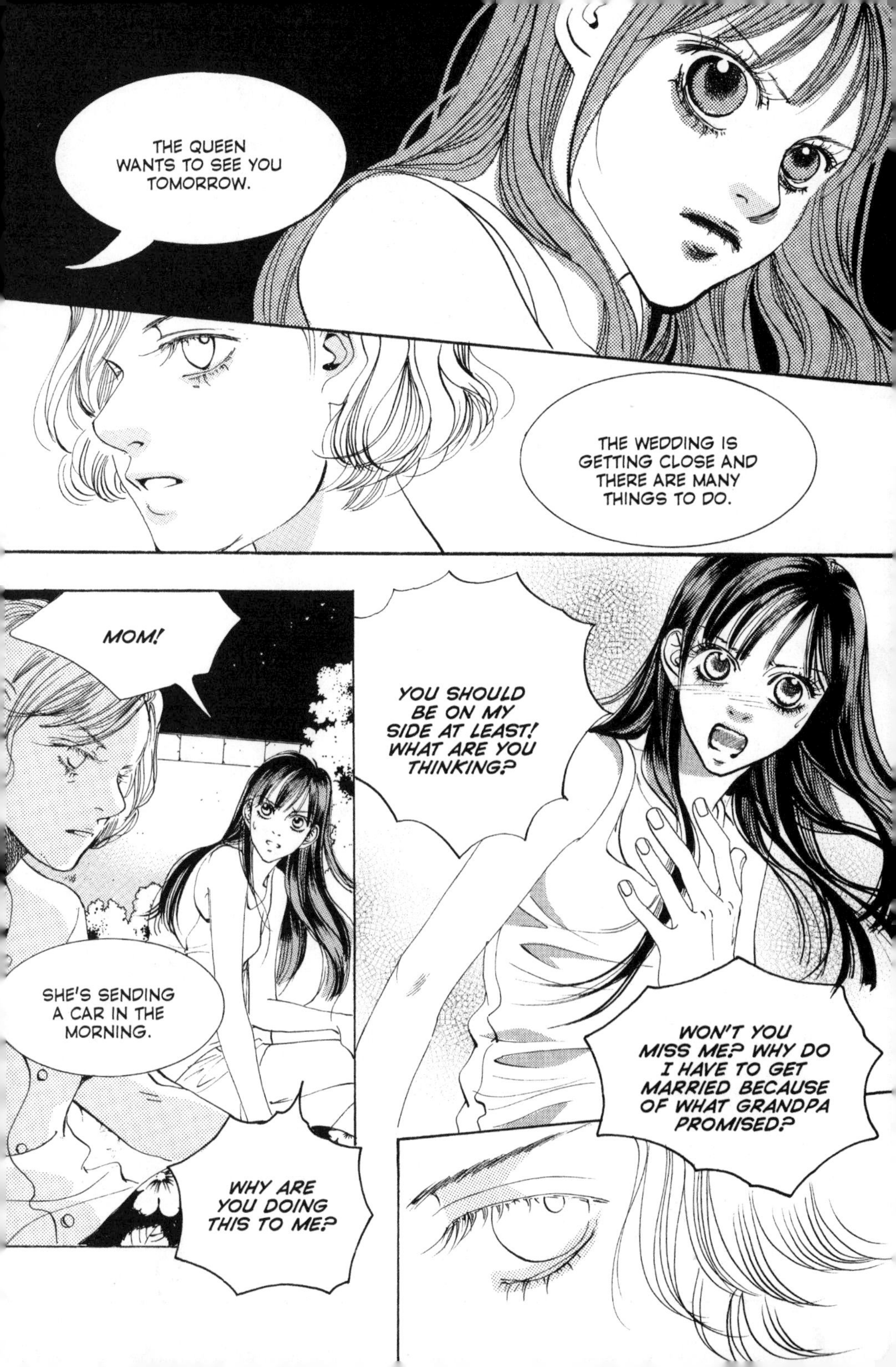
THE QUEEN WANTS TO SEE YOU TOMORROW.
THE WEDDING IS GETTING CLOSE AND THERE ARE MANY THINGS TO DO.
MOM!
SHE'S SENDING A CAR IN THE MORNING.
WHY ARE YOU DOING THIS TO ME?
YOU SHOULD BE ON MY SIDE AT LEAST! WHAT ARE YOU THINKING?
WON'T YOU MISS ME? WHY DO I HAVE TO GET MARRIED BECAUSE OF WHAT GRANDPA PROMISED?

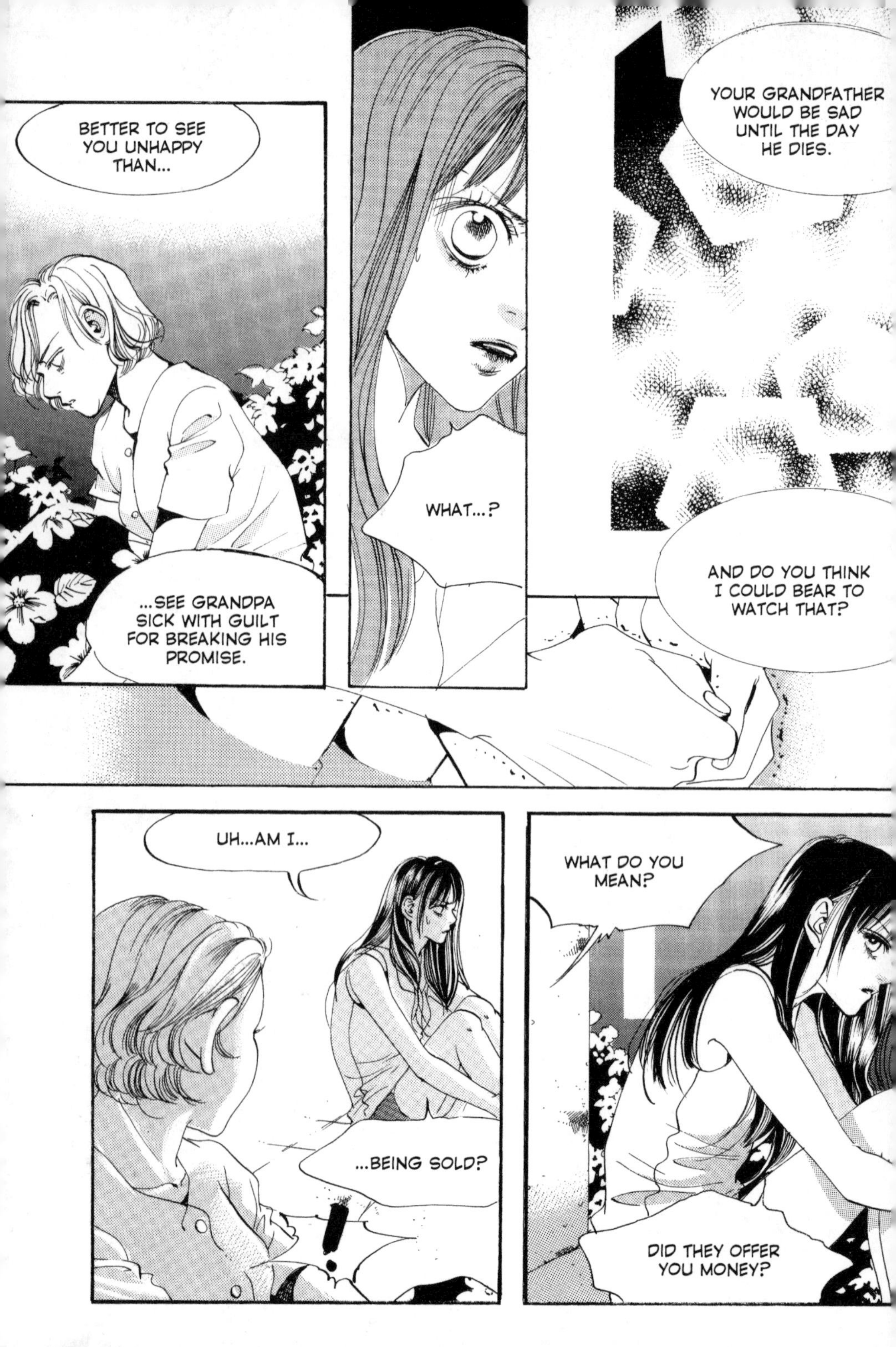
BETTER TO SEE YOU UNHAPPY THAN...
...SEE GRANDPA SICK WITH GUILT FOR BREAKING HIS PROMISE.
WHAT...?
YOUR GRANDFATHER WOULD BE SAD UNTIL THE DAY HE DIES.
AND DO YOU THINK I COULD BEAR TO WATCH THAT?
UH...AM I...
...BEING SOLD?
WHAT DO YOU MEAN?
DID THEY OFFER YOU MONEY?

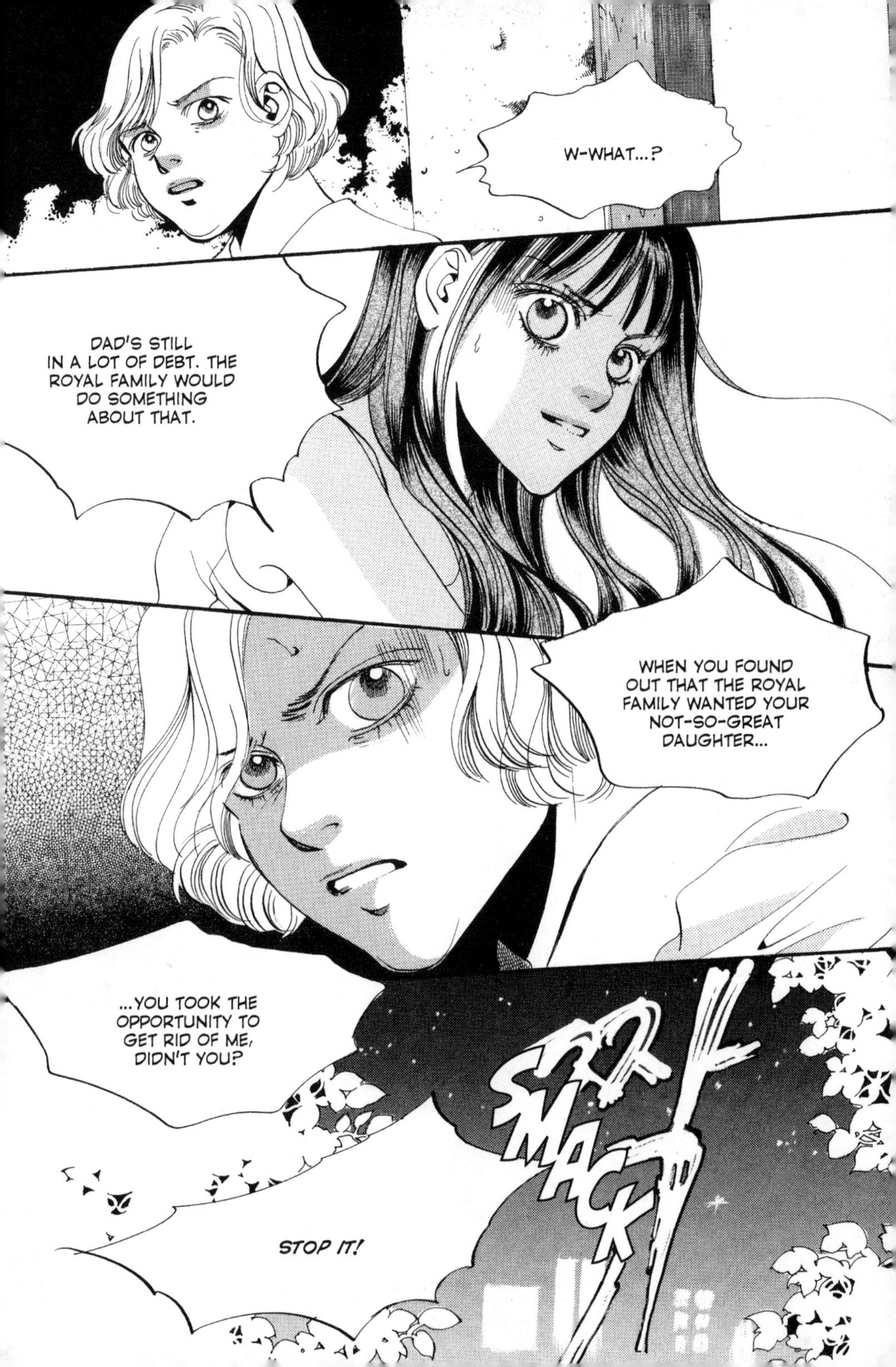
W-WHAT...?
DAD'S STILL IN A LOT OF DEBT. THE ROYAL FAMILY WOULD DO SOMETHING ABOUT THAT.
WHEN YOU FOUND OUT THAT THE ROYAL FAMILY WANTED YOUR NOT-SO-GREAT DAUGHTER...
...YOU TOOK THE OPPORTUNITY TO GET RID OF ME, DIDN'T YOU?
STOP IT!
SMACK

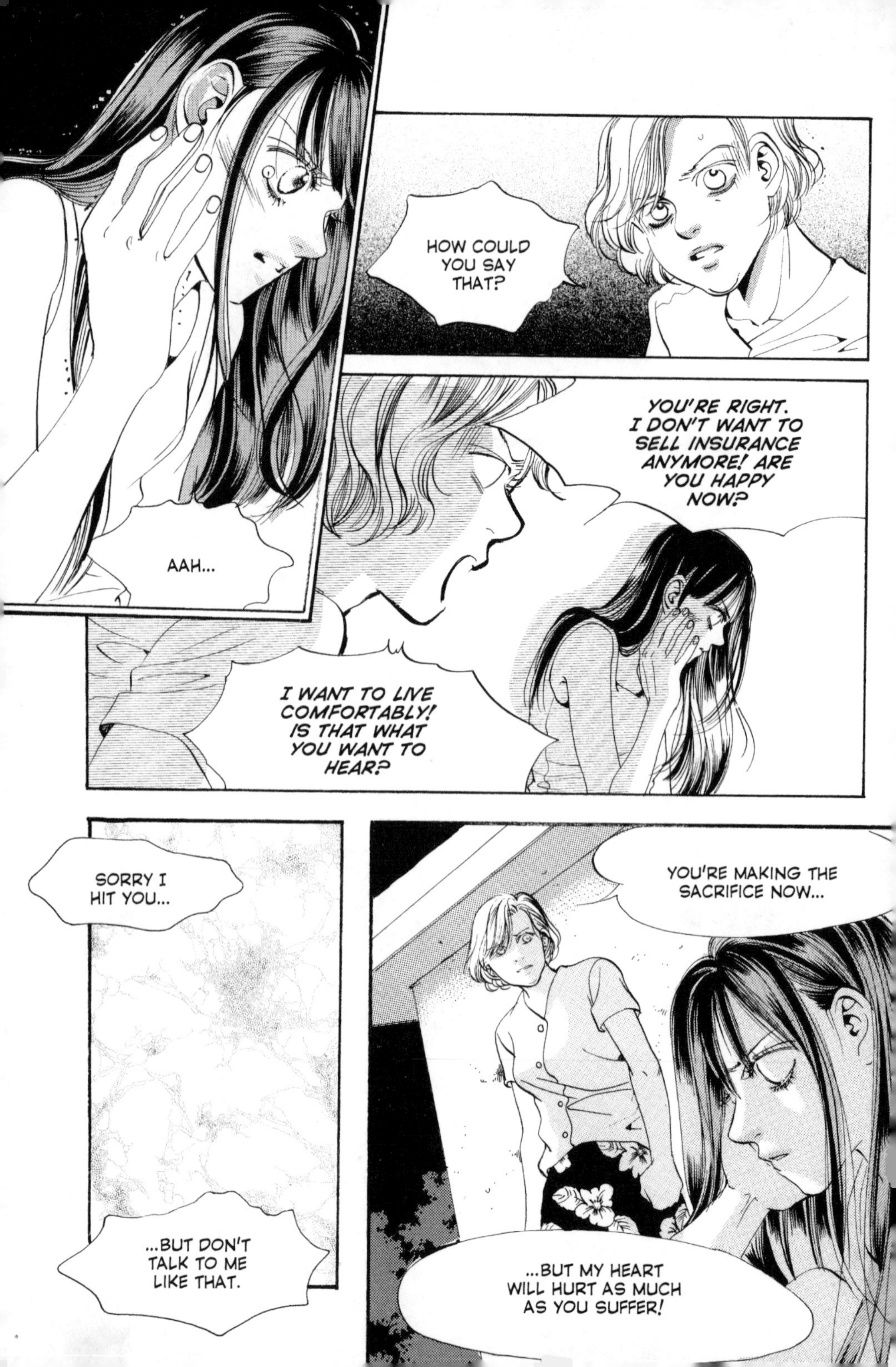
AAH...
HOW COULD YOU SAY THAT?
YOU'RE RIGHT. I DON'T WANT TO SELL INSURANCE ANYMORE! ARE YOU HAPPY NOW?
I WANT TO LIVE COMFORTABLY! IS THAT WHAT YOU WANT TO HEAR?
SORRY I HIT YOU...
...BUT DON'T TALK TO ME LIKE THAT.
YOU'RE MAKING THE SACRIFICE NOW...
...BUT MY HEART WILL HURT AS MUCH AS YOU SUFFER!

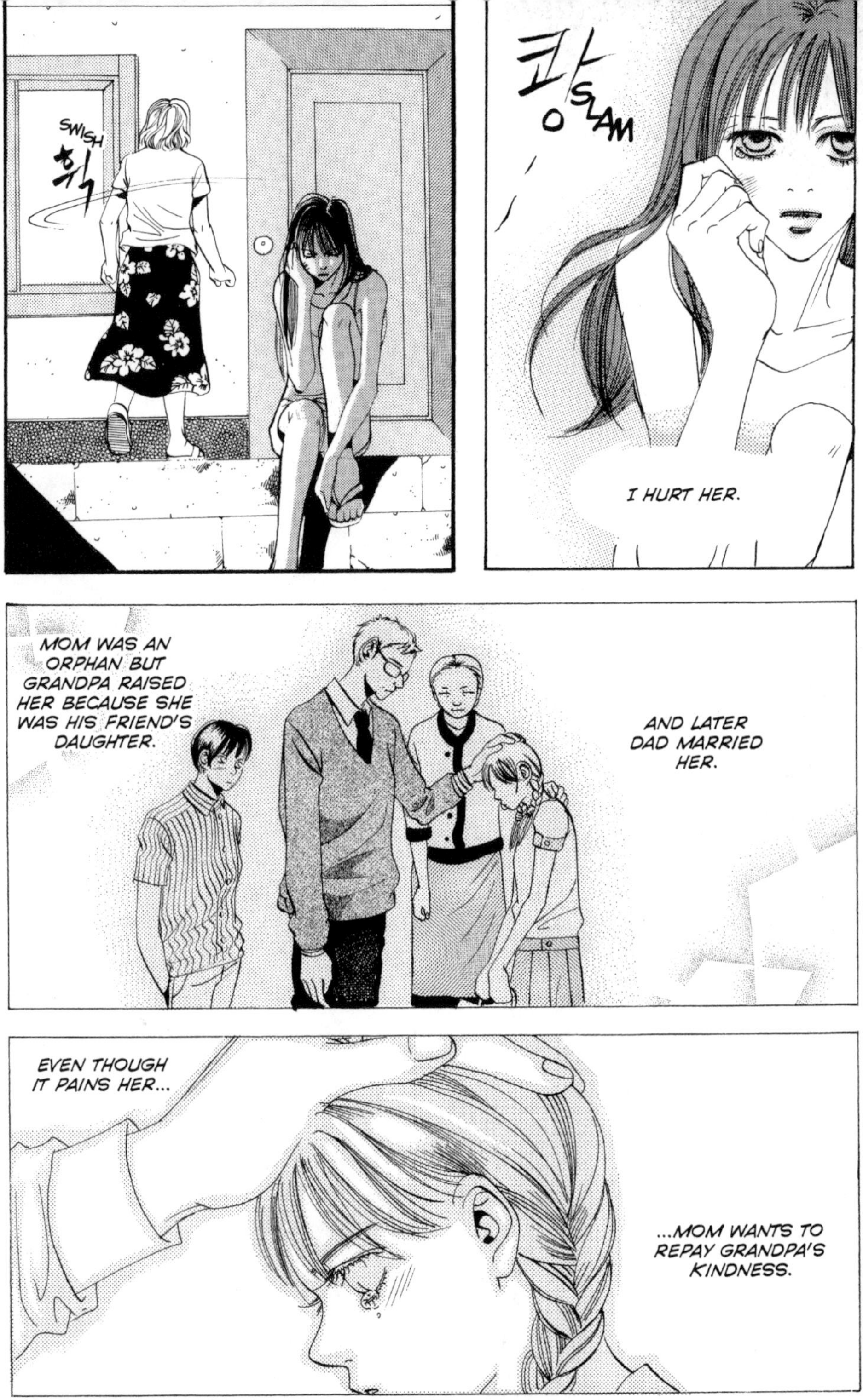
SWISH
휙
SLAM
I HURT HER.
MOM WAS AN ORPHAN BUT GRANDPA RAISED HER BECAUSE SHE WAS HIS FRIEND'S DAUGHTER.
AND LATER DAD MARRIED HER.
EVEN THOUGH IT PAINS HER...
...MOM WANTS TO REPAY GRANDPA'S KINDNESS.

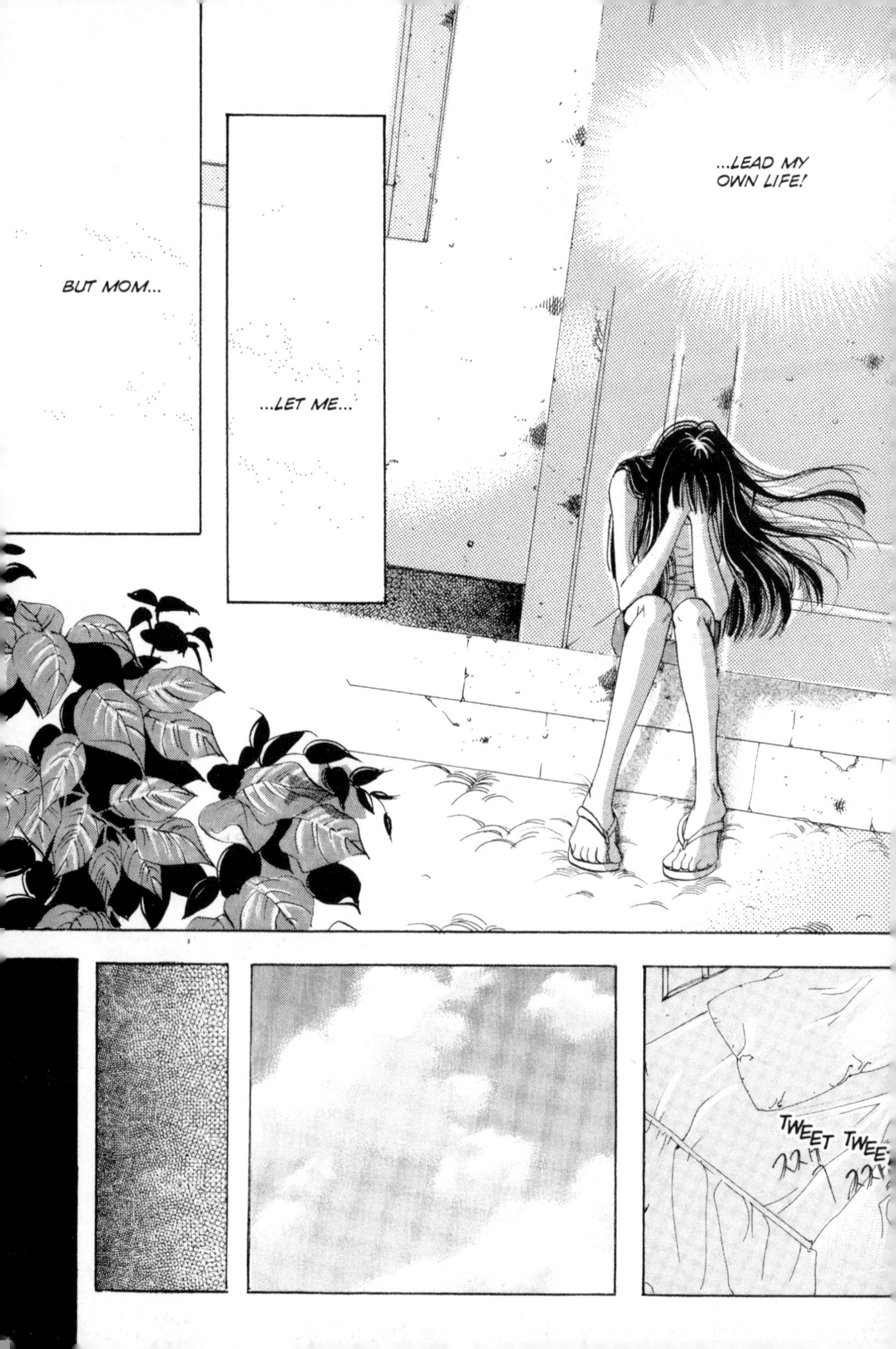
BUT MOM...
...LET ME...
...LEAD MY OWN LIFE!
TWEET TWEE

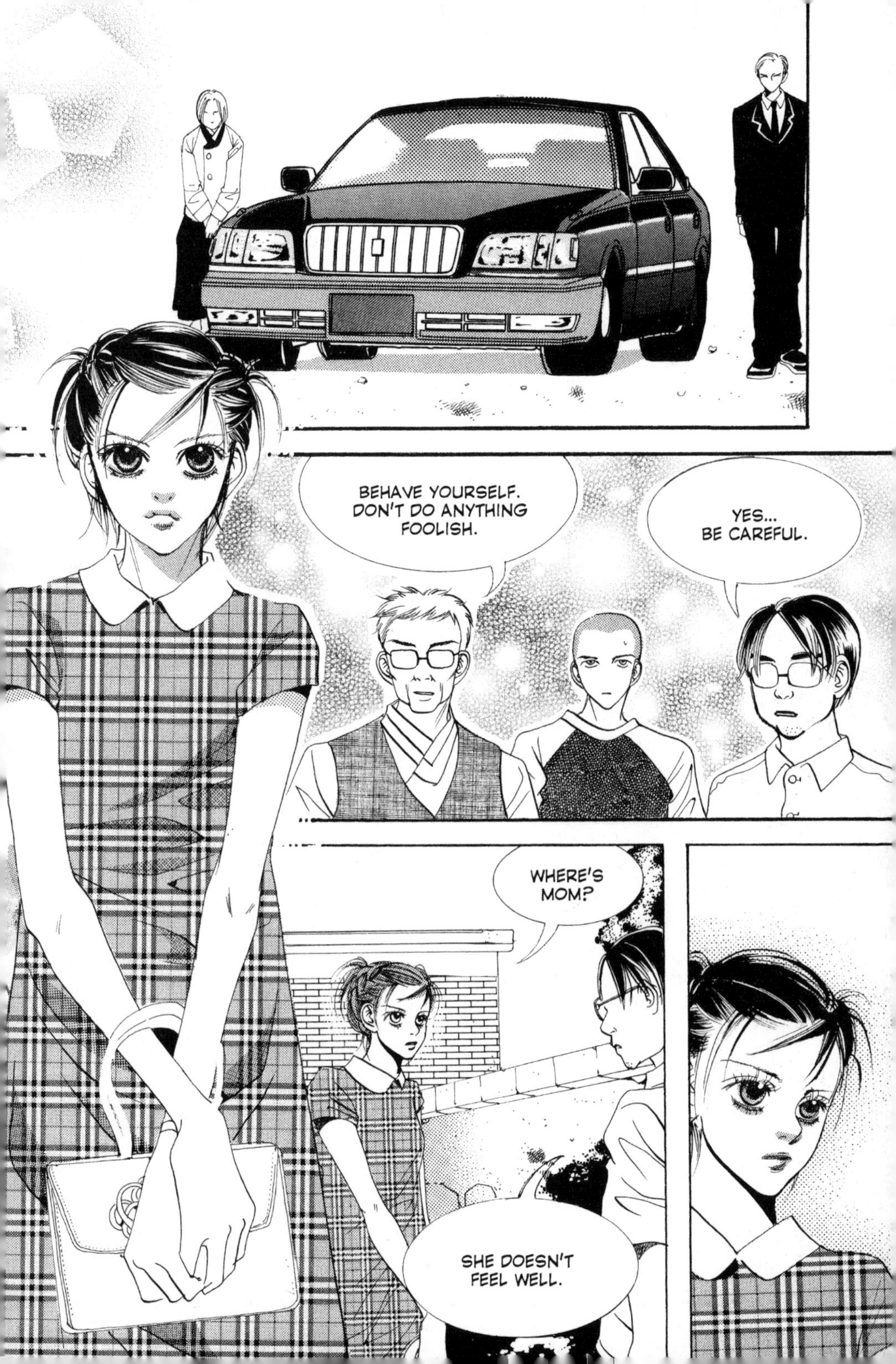
BEHAVE YOURSELF. DON'T DO ANYTHING FOOLISH.
YES... BE CAREFUL.
WHERE'S MOM?
SHE DOESN'T FEEL WELL.

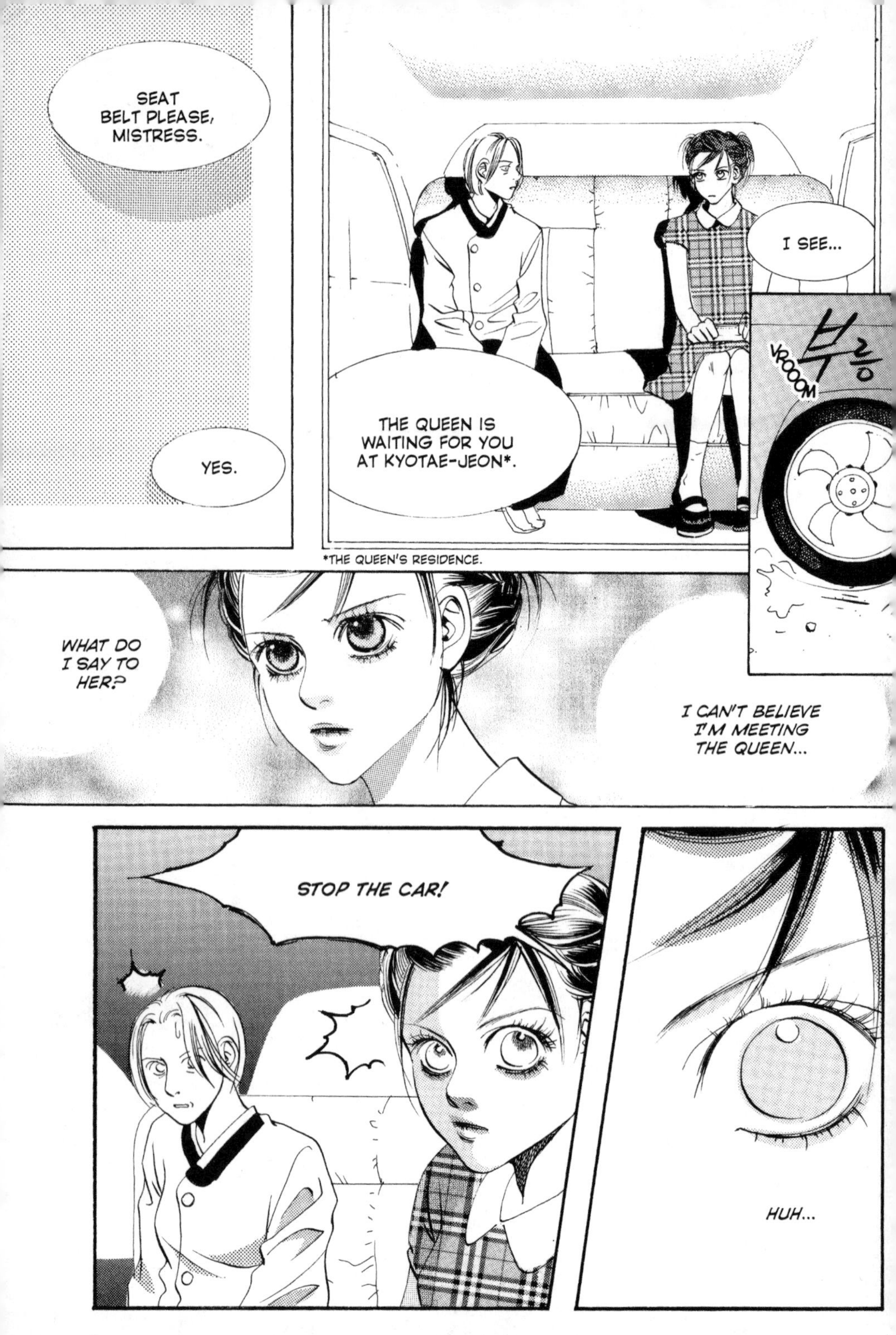
SEAT BELT PLEASE, MISTRESS.
YES.
THE QUEEN IS WAITING FOR YOU AT KYOTAE-JEON*.
I SEE...
부릉
VROOOM
WHAT DO I SAY TO HER?
I CAN'T BELIEVE I'M MEETING THE QUEEN...
STOP THE CAR!
HUH...

*THE QUEEN'S RESIDENCE.

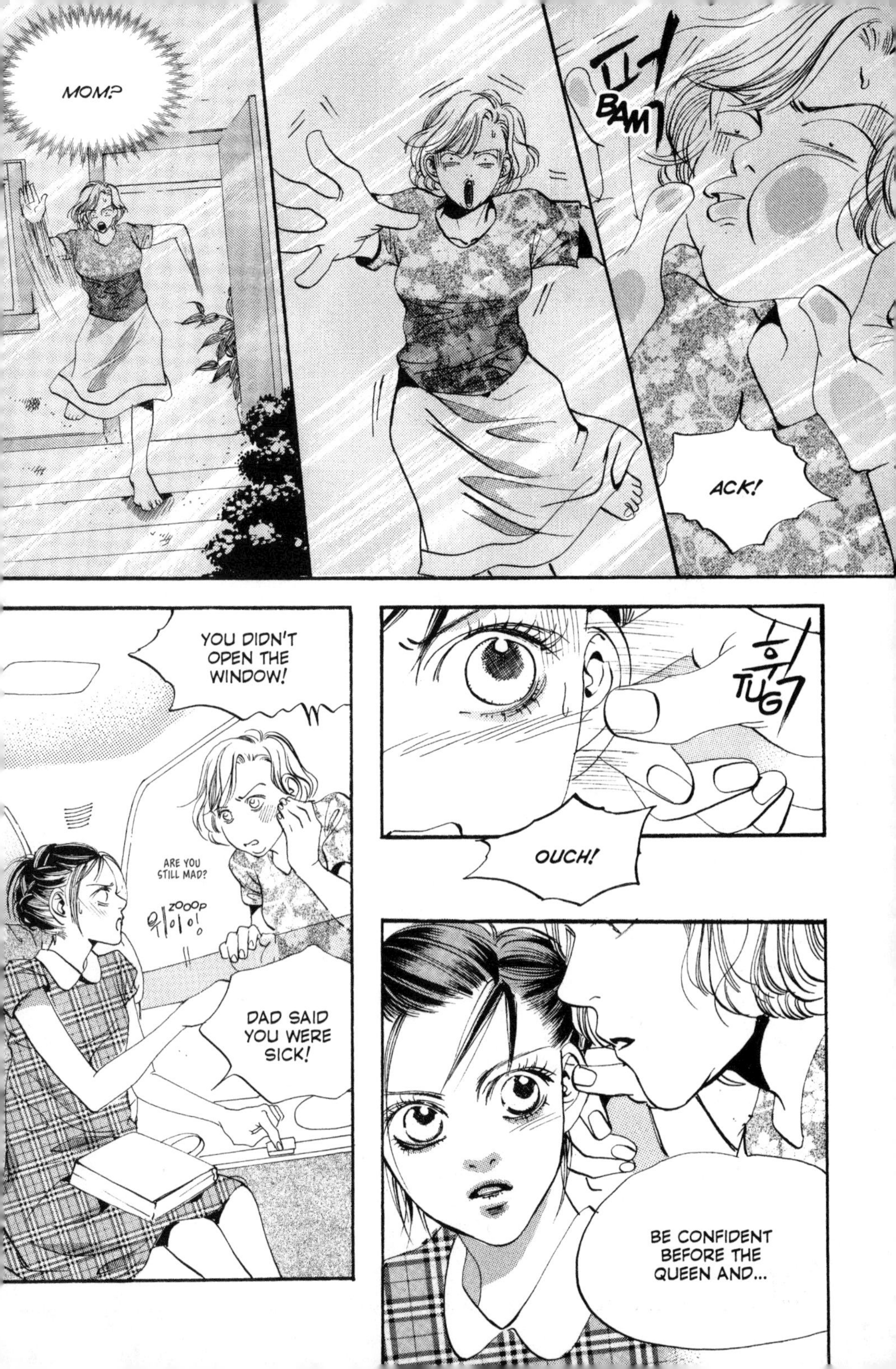
MOM?
BAM
ACK!
YOU DIDN'T OPEN THE WINDOW!
ARE YOU STILL MAD?
ZOOOP
DAD SAID YOU WERE SICK!
TUG
OUCH!
BE CONFIDENT BEFORE THE QUEEN AND...

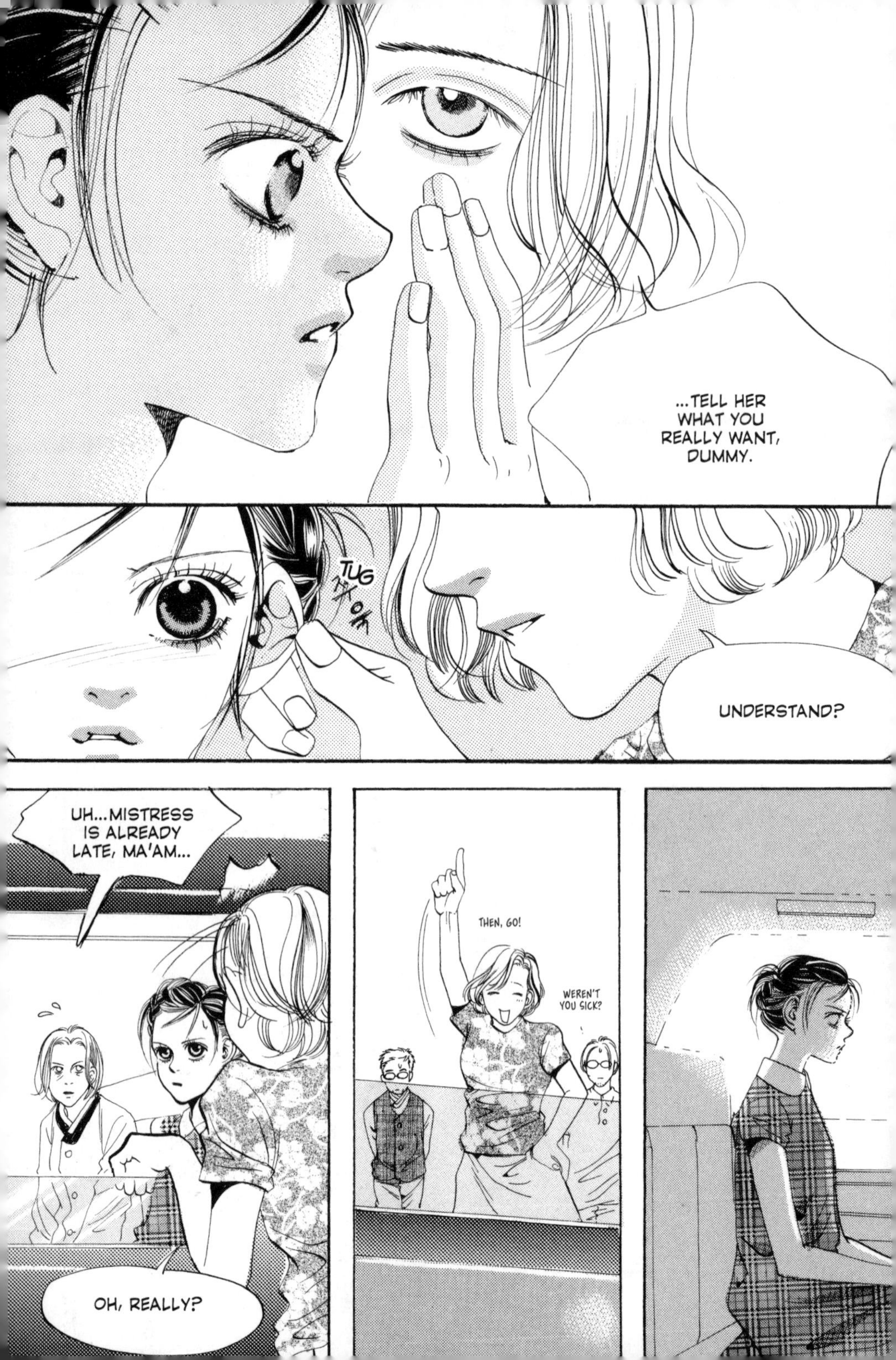
...TELL HER WHAT YOU REALLY WANT, DUMMY.
TUG
UNDERSTAND?
UH...MISTRESS IS ALREADY LATE, MA'AM...
OH, REALLY?
THEN, GO!
WEREN'T YOU SICK?

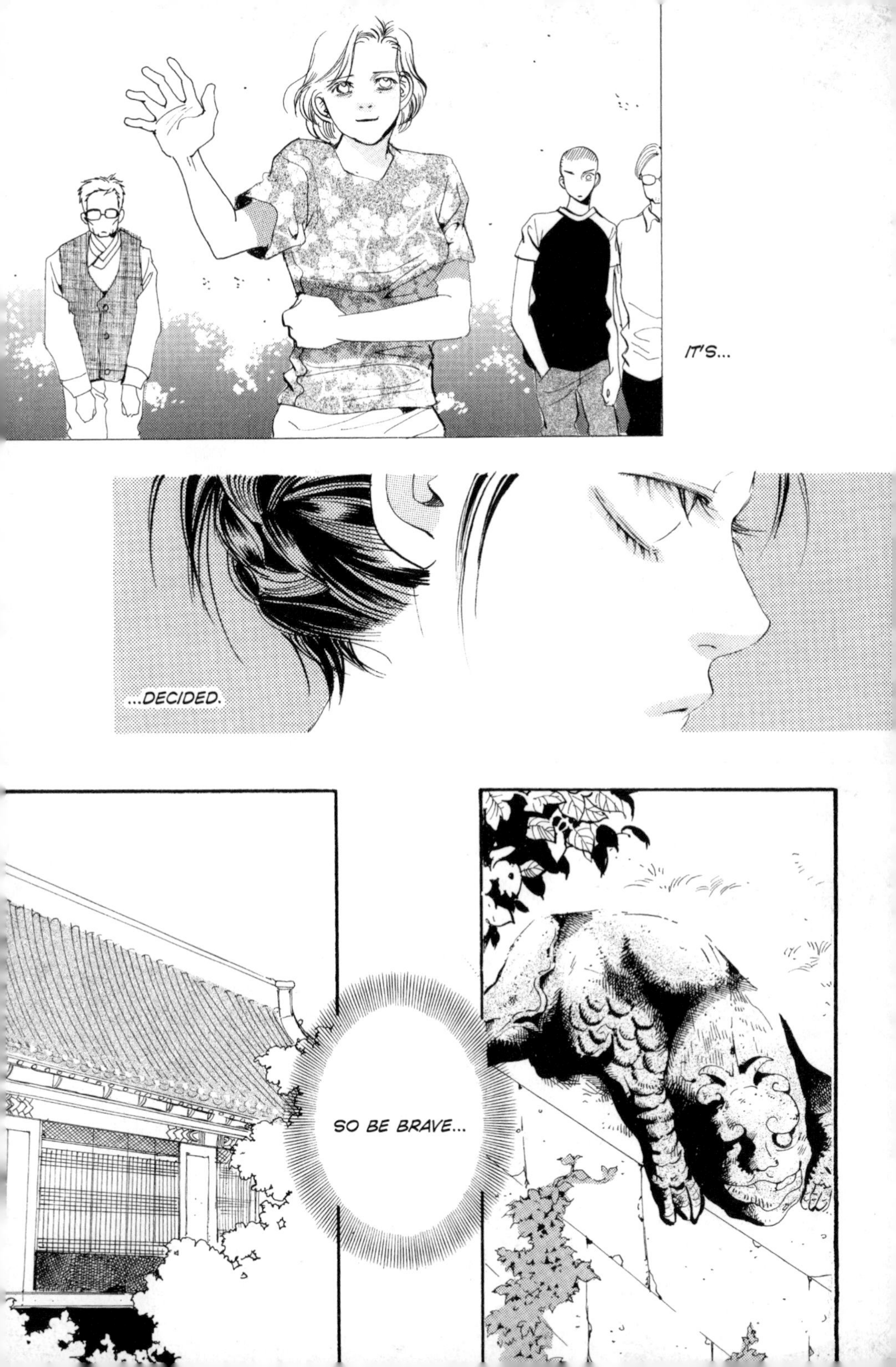
IT'S...
...DECIDED.
SO BE BRAVE...

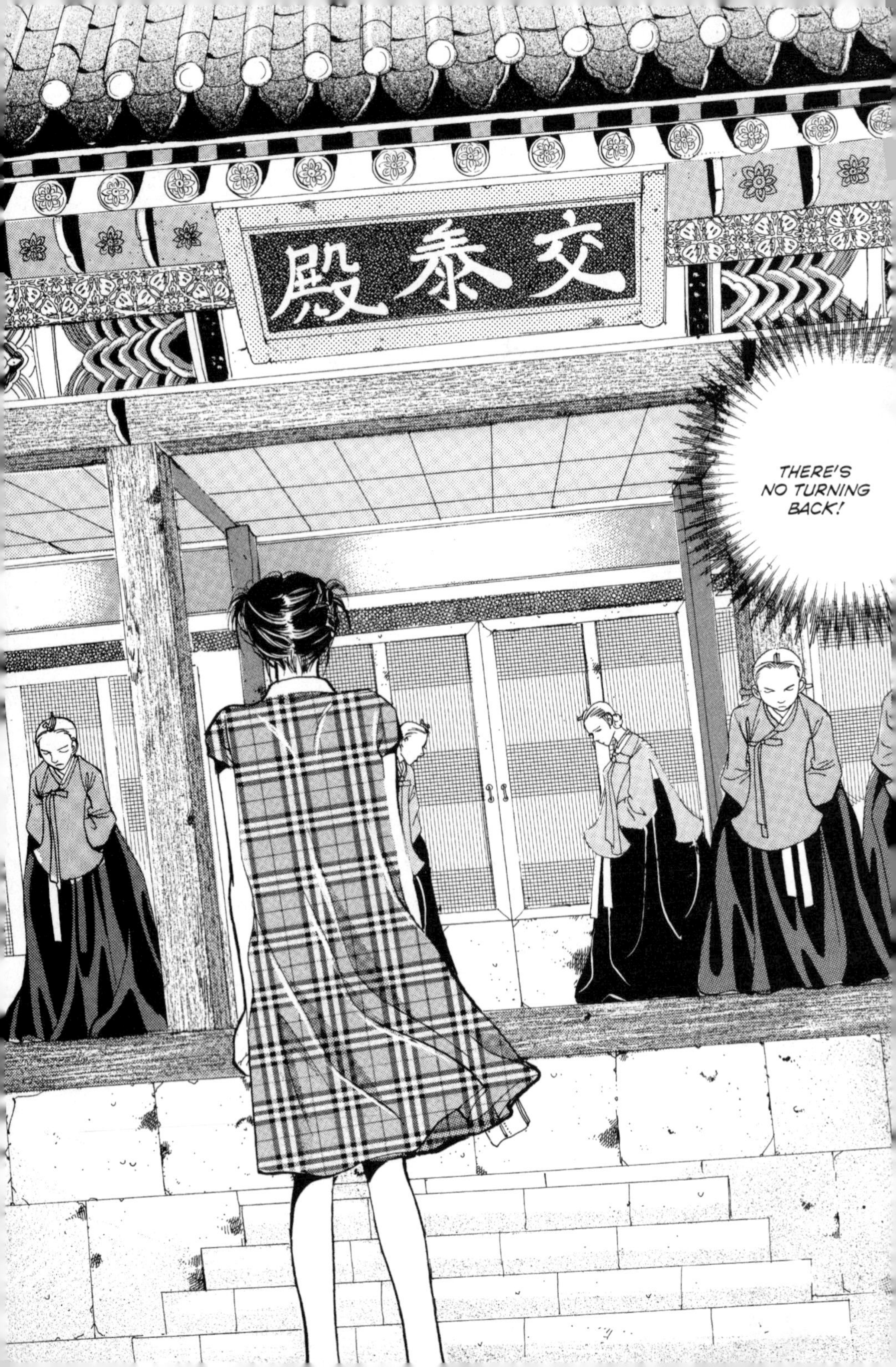
交泰殿
THERE'S NO TURNING BACK!

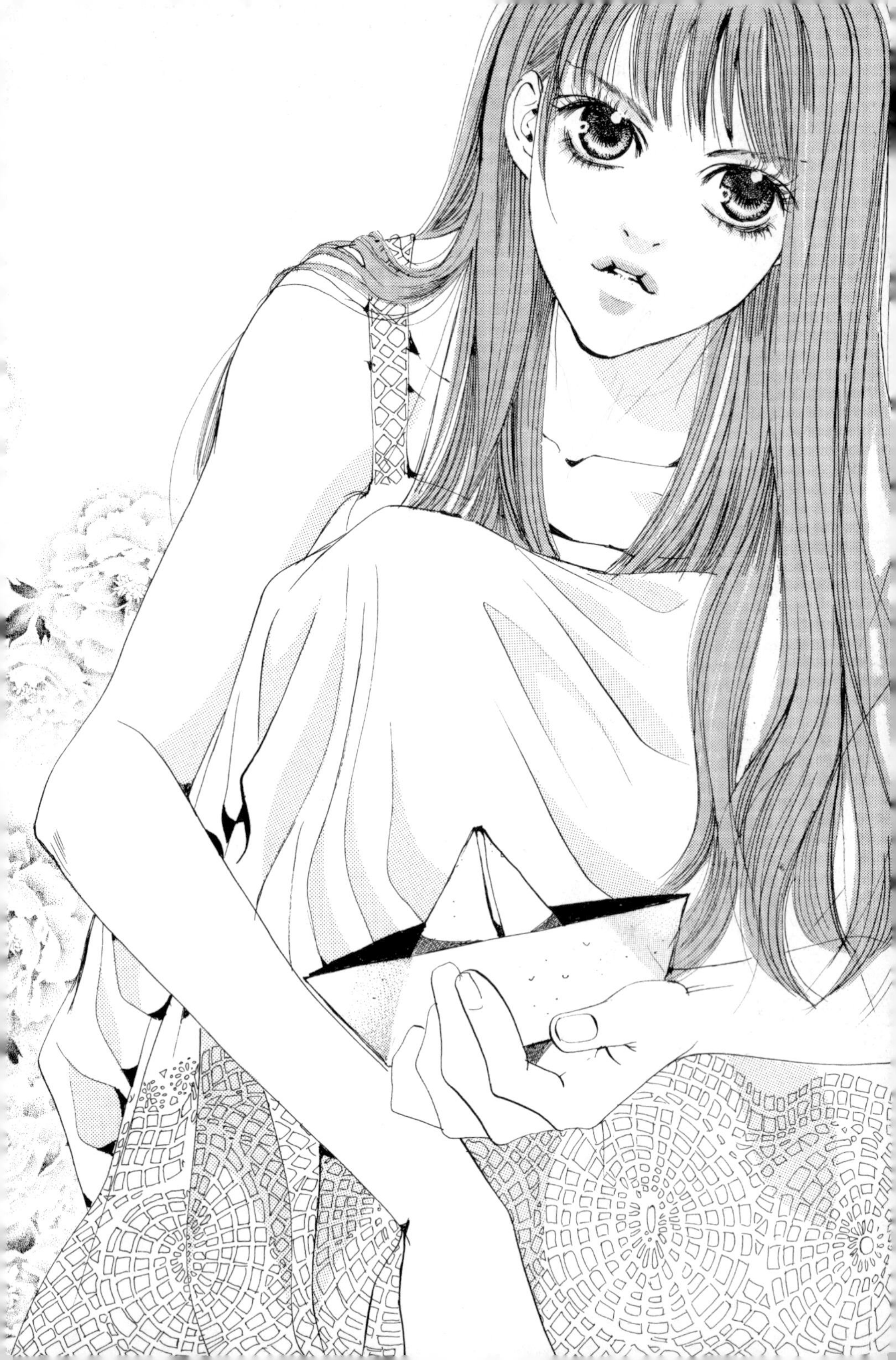

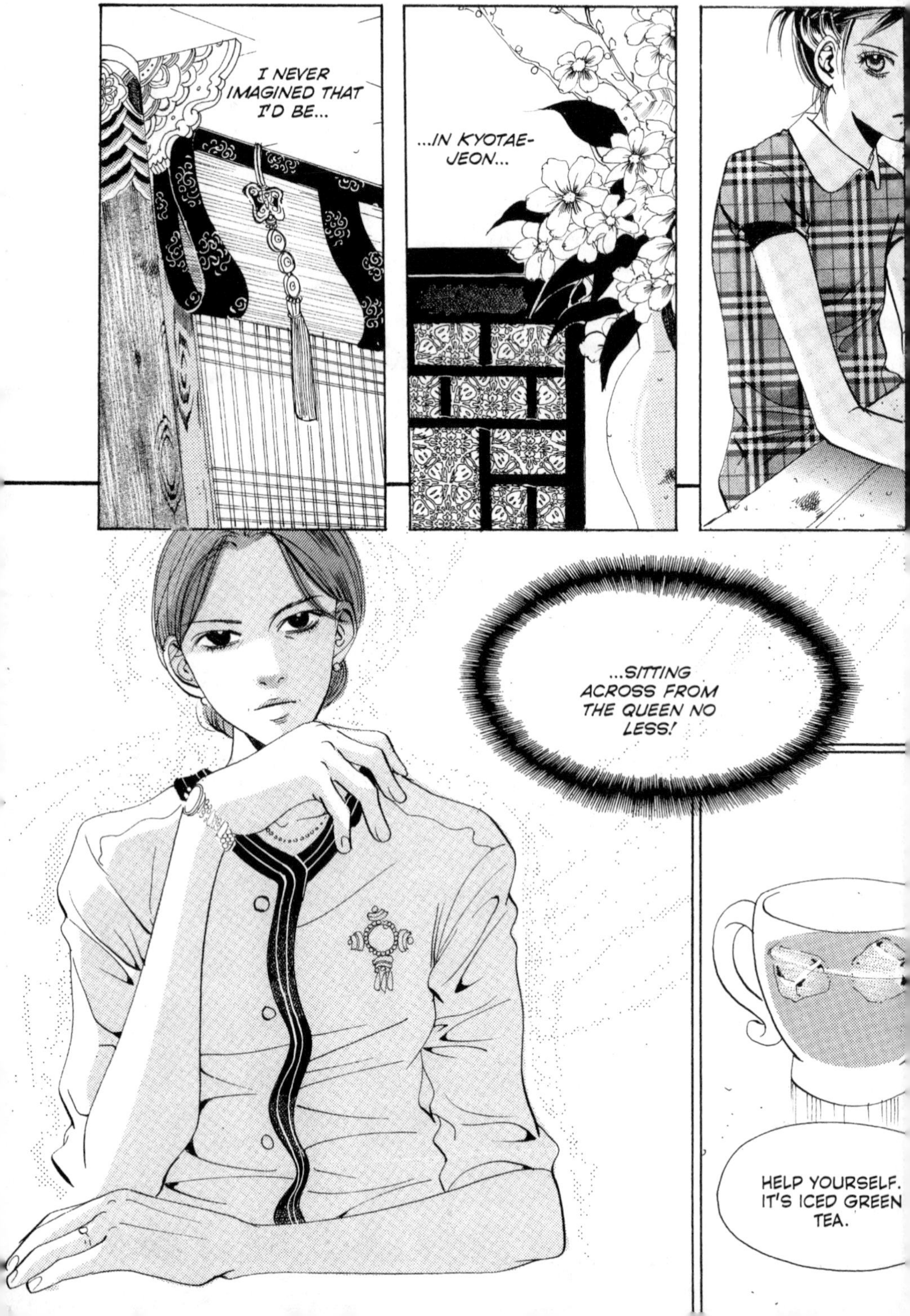
I NEVER IMAGINED THAT I'D BE...
...IN KYOTAE-JEON...
...SITTING ACROSS FROM THE QUEEN NO LESS!
HELP YOURSELF. IT'S ICED GREEN TEA.

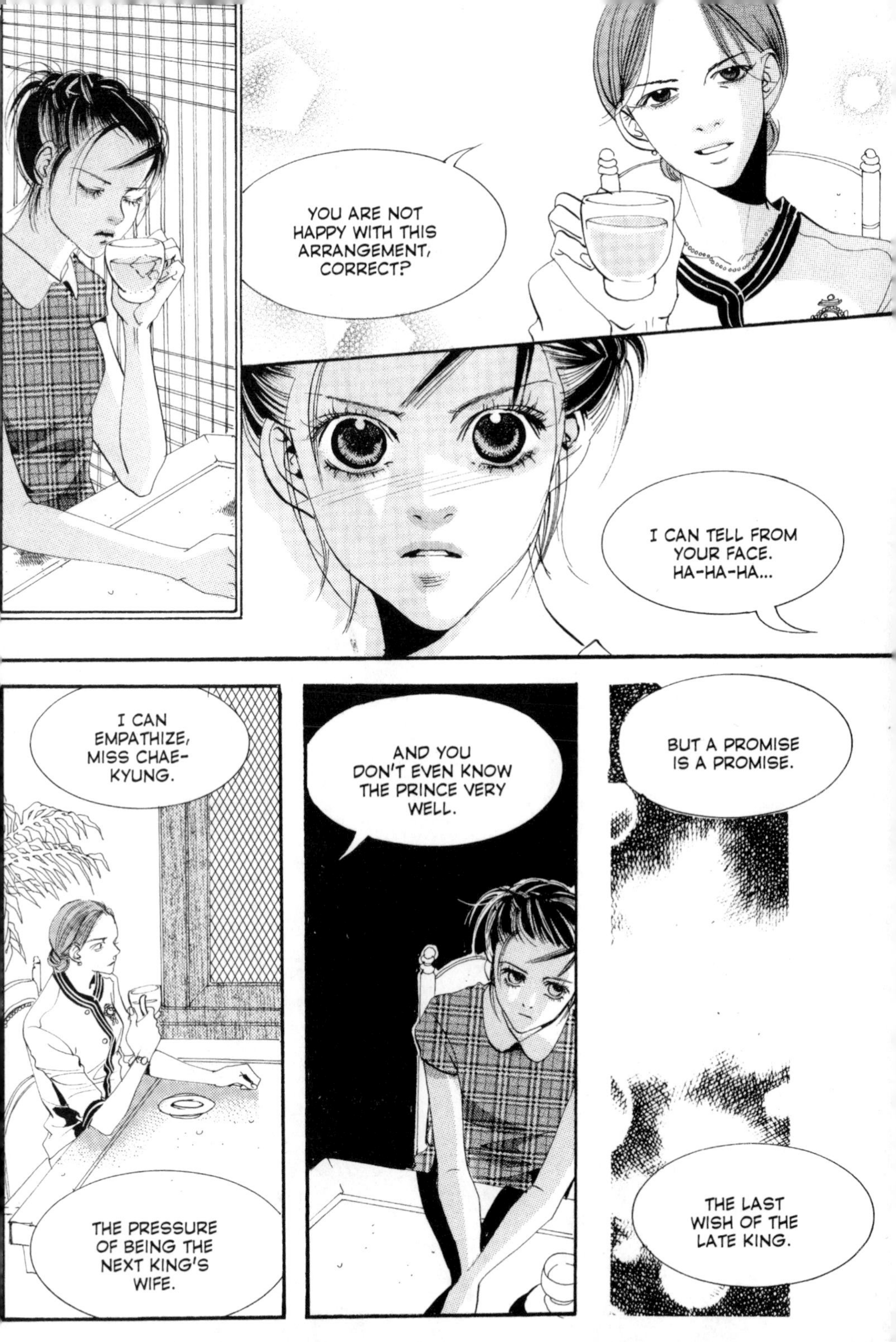
YOU ARE NOT HAPPY WITH THIS ARRANGEMENT, CORRECT?
I CAN TELL FROM YOUR FACE. HA-HA-HA...
I CAN EMPATHIZE, MISS CHAE-KYUNG.
THE PRESSURE OF BEING THE NEXT KING'S WIFE.
AND YOU DON'T EVEN KNOW THE PRINCE VERY WELL.
BUT A PROMISE IS A PROMISE.
THE LAST WISH OF THE LATE KING.

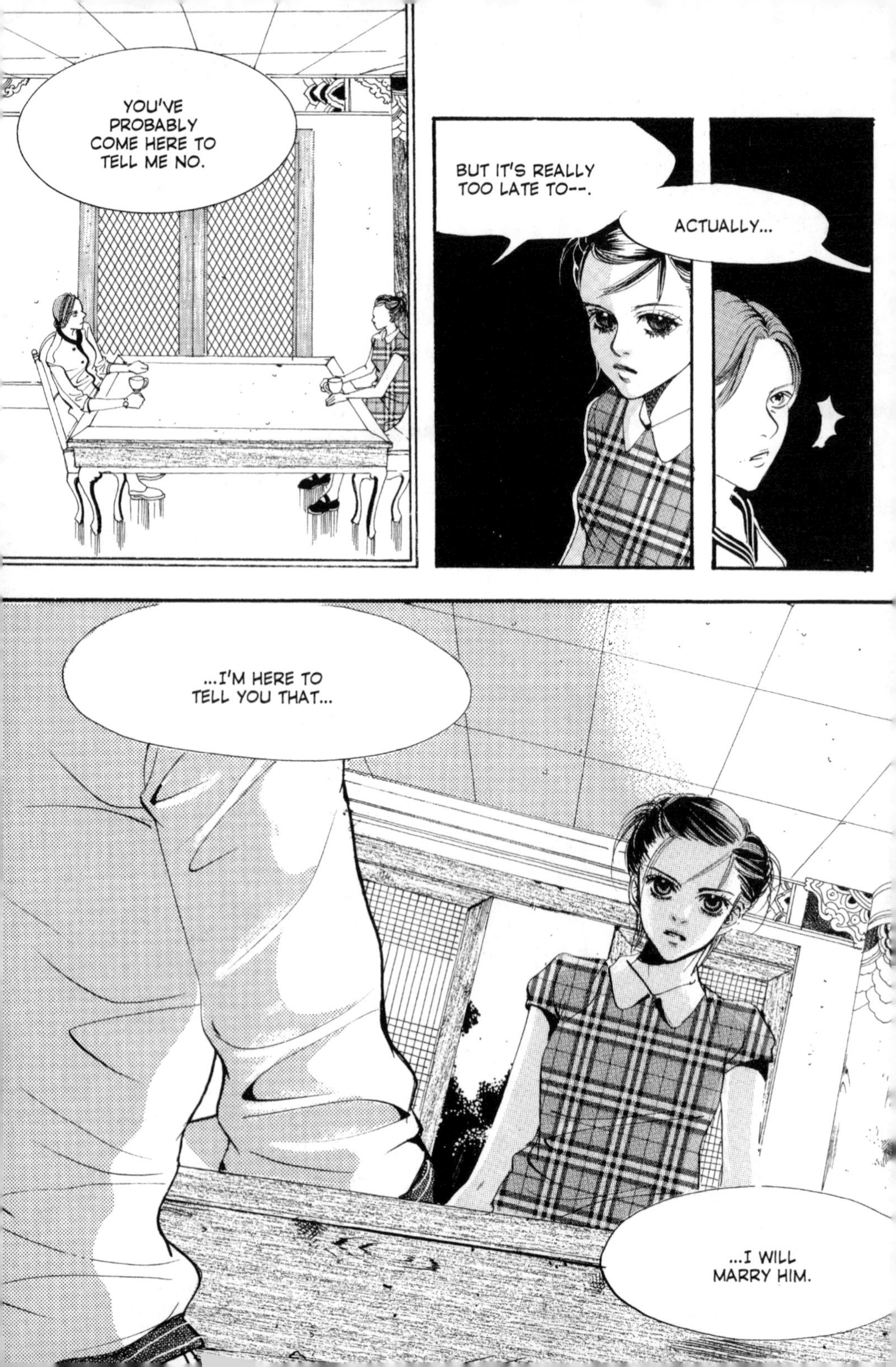
YOU'VE PROBABLY COME HERE TO TELL ME NO.
BUT IT'S REALLY TOO LATE TO--.
ACTUALLY...
...I'M HERE TO TELL YOU THAT...
...I WILL MARRY HIM.

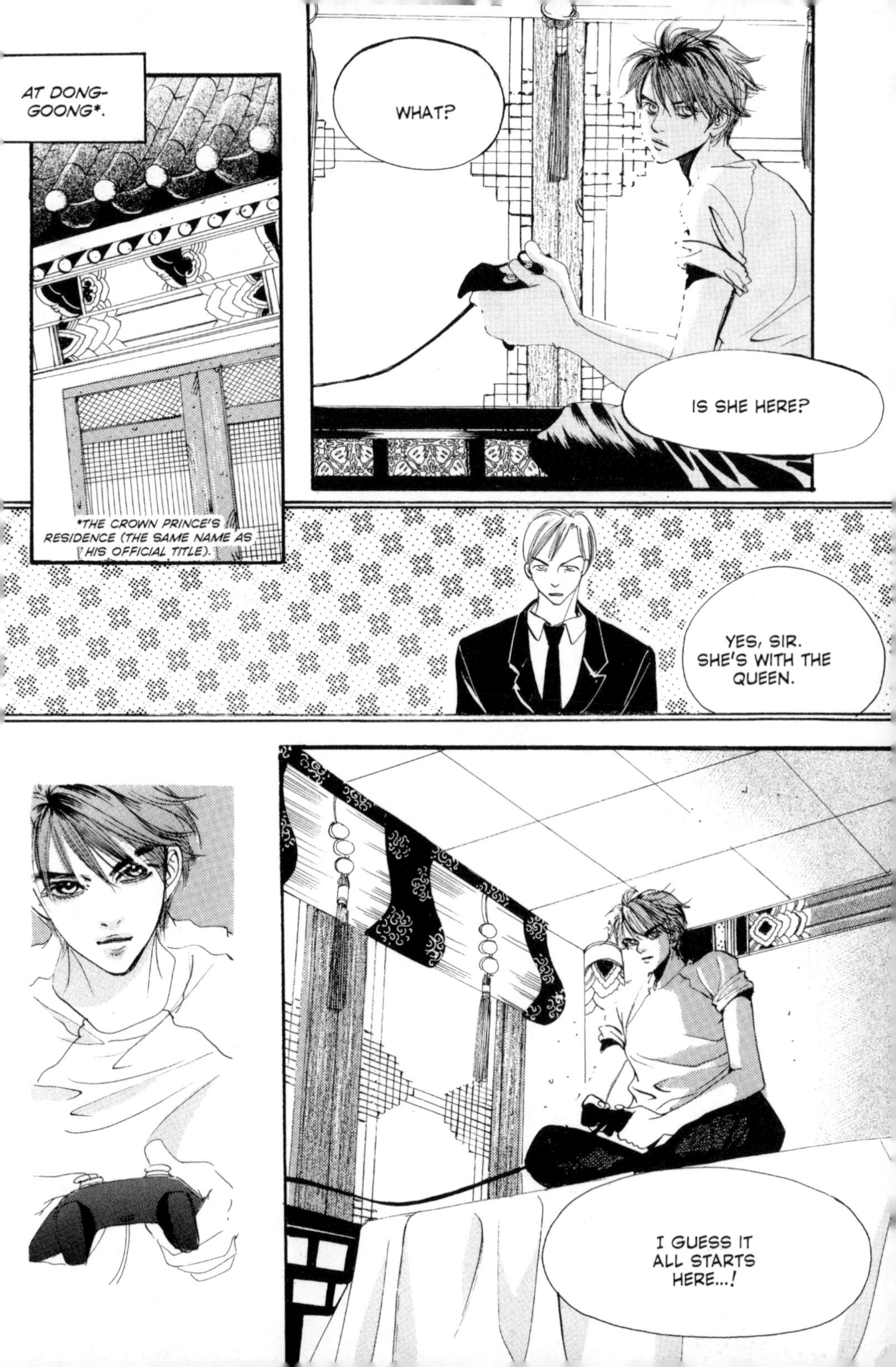
AT DONG-GOONG*.
*THE CROWN PRINCE'S RESIDENCE (THE SAME NAME AS HIS OFFICIAL TITLE).
WHAT?
IS SHE HERE?
YES, SIR. SHE'S WITH THE QUEEN.
I GUESS IT ALL STARTS HERE...!

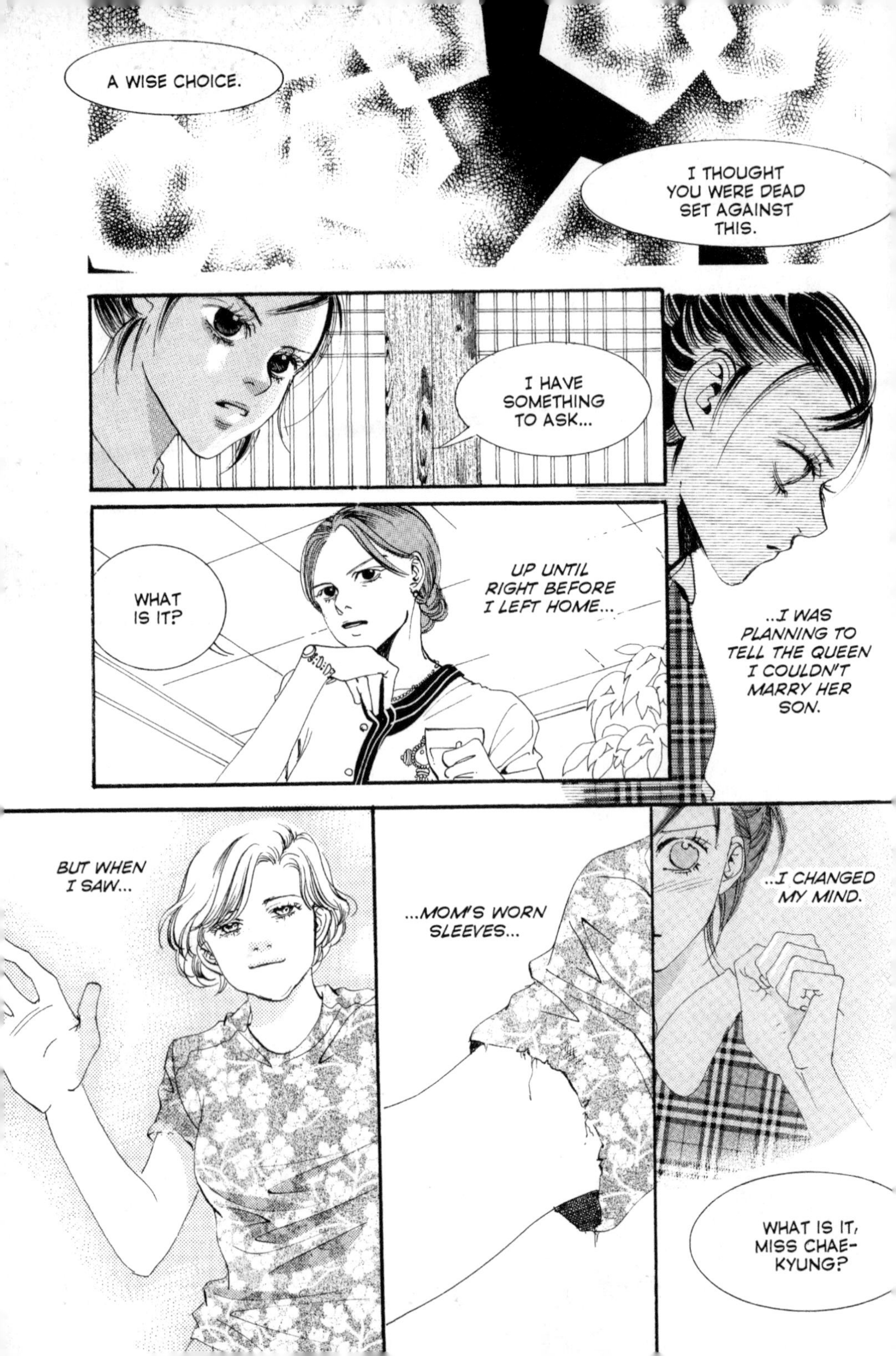
A WISE CHOICE.
I THOUGHT YOU WERE DEAD SET AGAINST THIS.
I HAVE SOMETHING TO ASK...
WHAT IS IT?
UP UNTIL RIGHT BEFORE I LEFT HOME...
...I WAS PLANNING TO TELL THE QUEEN I COULDN'T MARRY HER SON.
BUT WHEN I SAW...
...MOM'S WORN SLEEVES...
...I CHANGED MY MIND.
WHAT IS IT, MISS CHAE-KYUNG?

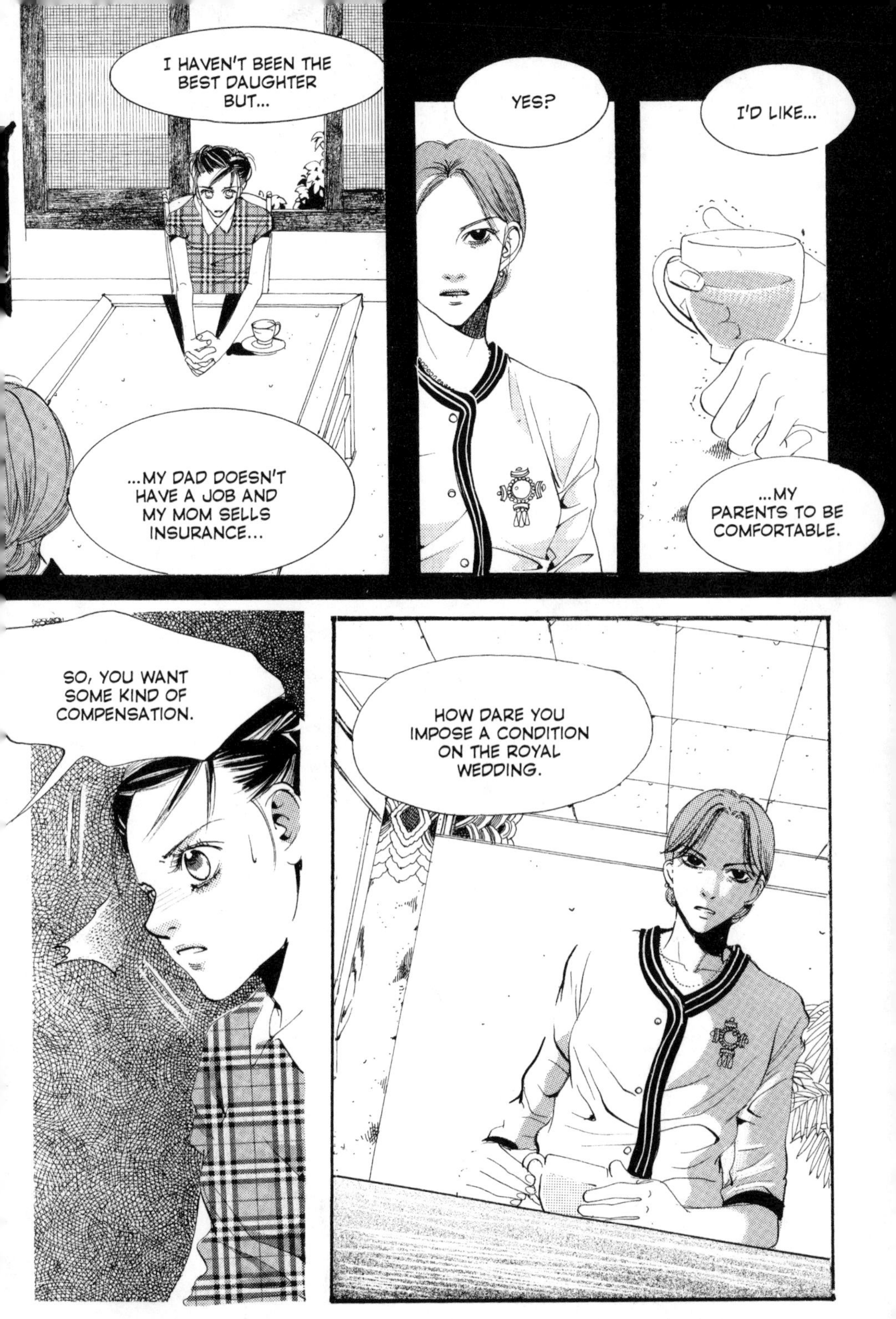
I HAVEN'T BEEN THE BEST DAUGHTER BUT...
...MY DAD DOESN'T HAVE A JOB AND MY MOM SELLS INSURANCE...
YES?
I'D LIKE...
...MY PARENTS TO BE COMFORTABLE.
SO, YOU WANT SOME KIND OF COMPENSATION.
HOW DARE YOU IMPOSE A CONDITION ON THE ROYAL WEDDING.

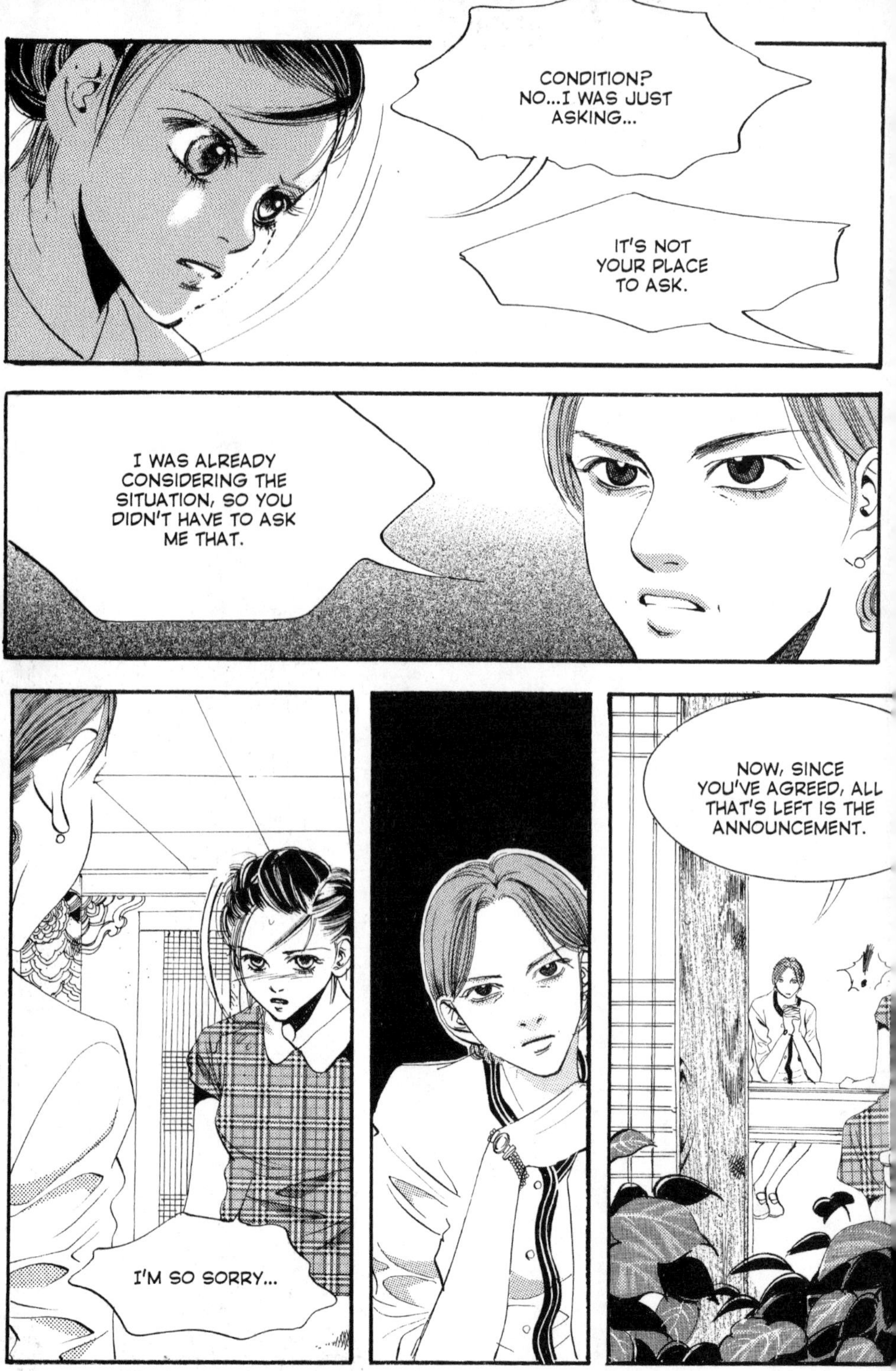
CONDITION? NO...I WAS JUST ASKING...
IT'S NOT YOUR PLACE TO ASK.
I WAS ALREADY CONSIDERING THE SITUATION, SO YOU DIDN'T HAVE TO ASK ME THAT.
I'M SO SORRY...
NOW, SINCE YOU'VE AGREED, ALL THAT'S LEFT IS THE ANNOUNCEMENT.
!

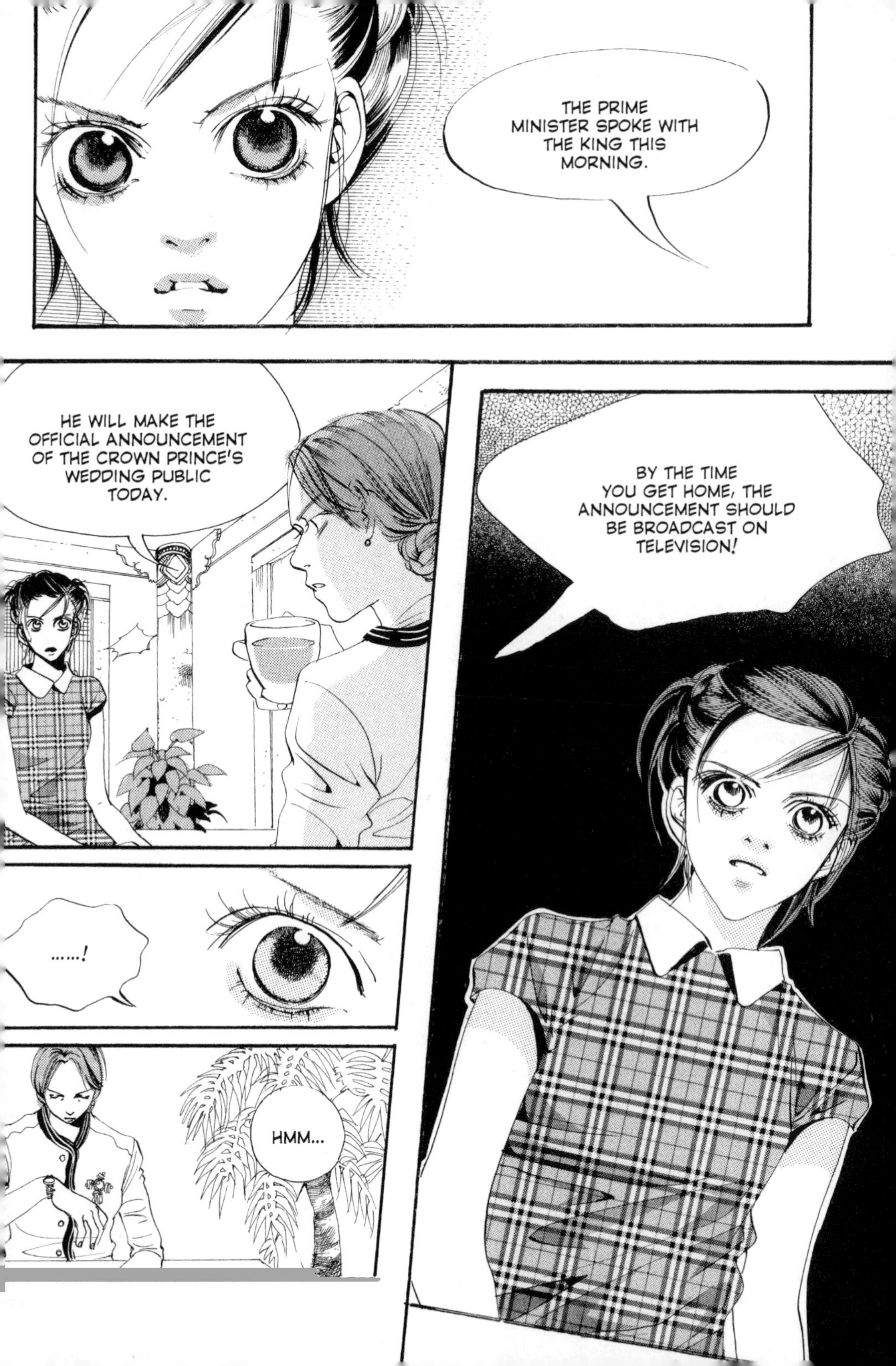
THE PRIME MINISTER SPOKE WITH THE KING THIS MORNING.
HE WILL MAKE THE OFFICIAL ANNOUNCEMENT OF THE CROWN PRINCE'S WEDDING PUBLIC TODAY.
......!
HMM...
BY THE TIME YOU GET HOME, THE ANNOUNCEMENT SHOULD BE BROADCAST ON TELEVISION!

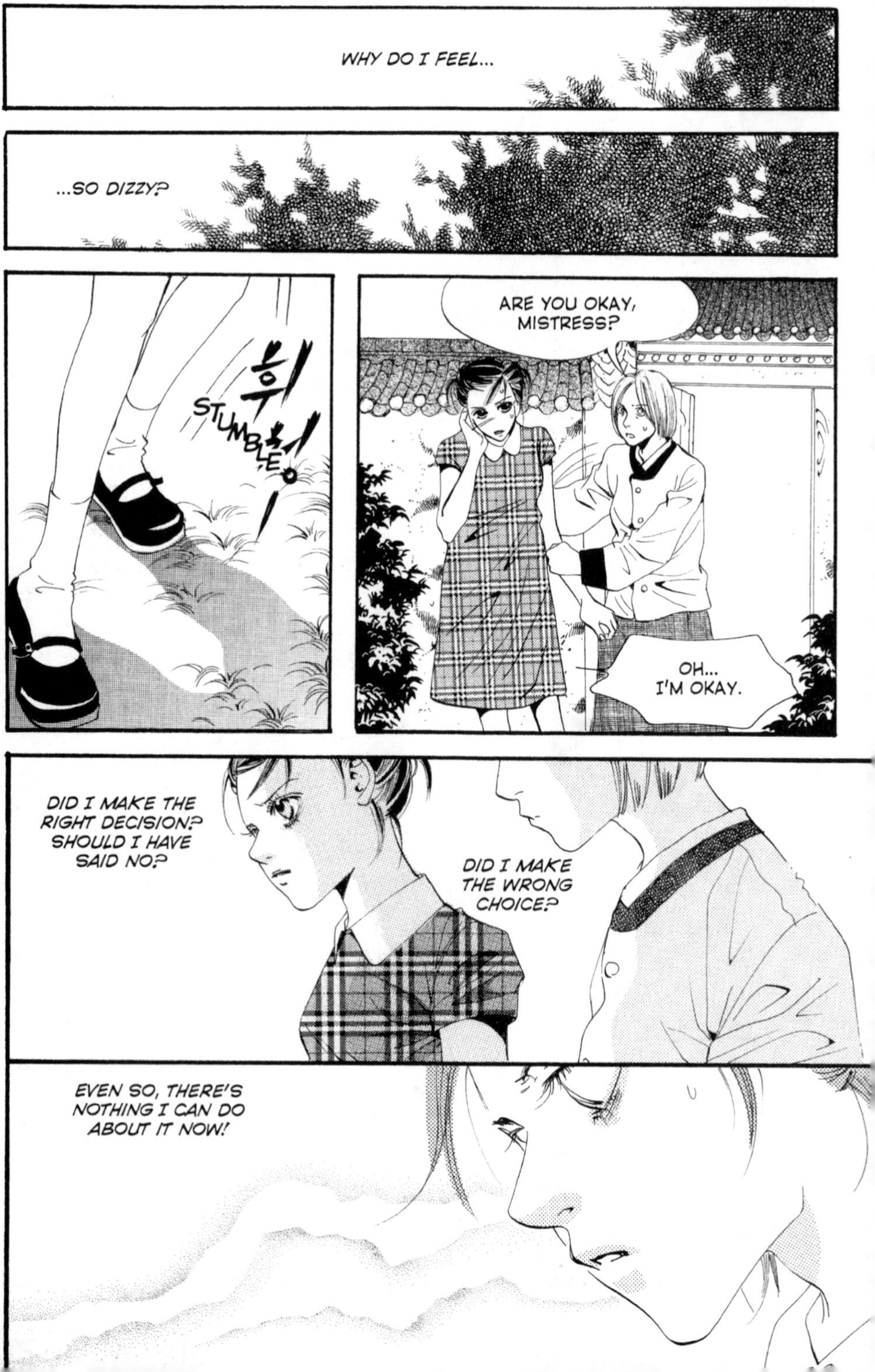
WHY DO I FEEL...
...SO DIZZY?
STUMBLE
휘청
ARE YOU OKAY, MISTRESS?
OH... I'M OKAY.
DID I MAKE THE RIGHT DECISION? SHOULD I HAVE SAID NO?
DID I MAKE THE WRONG CHOICE?
EVEN SO, THERE'S NOTHING I CAN DO ABOUT IT NOW!

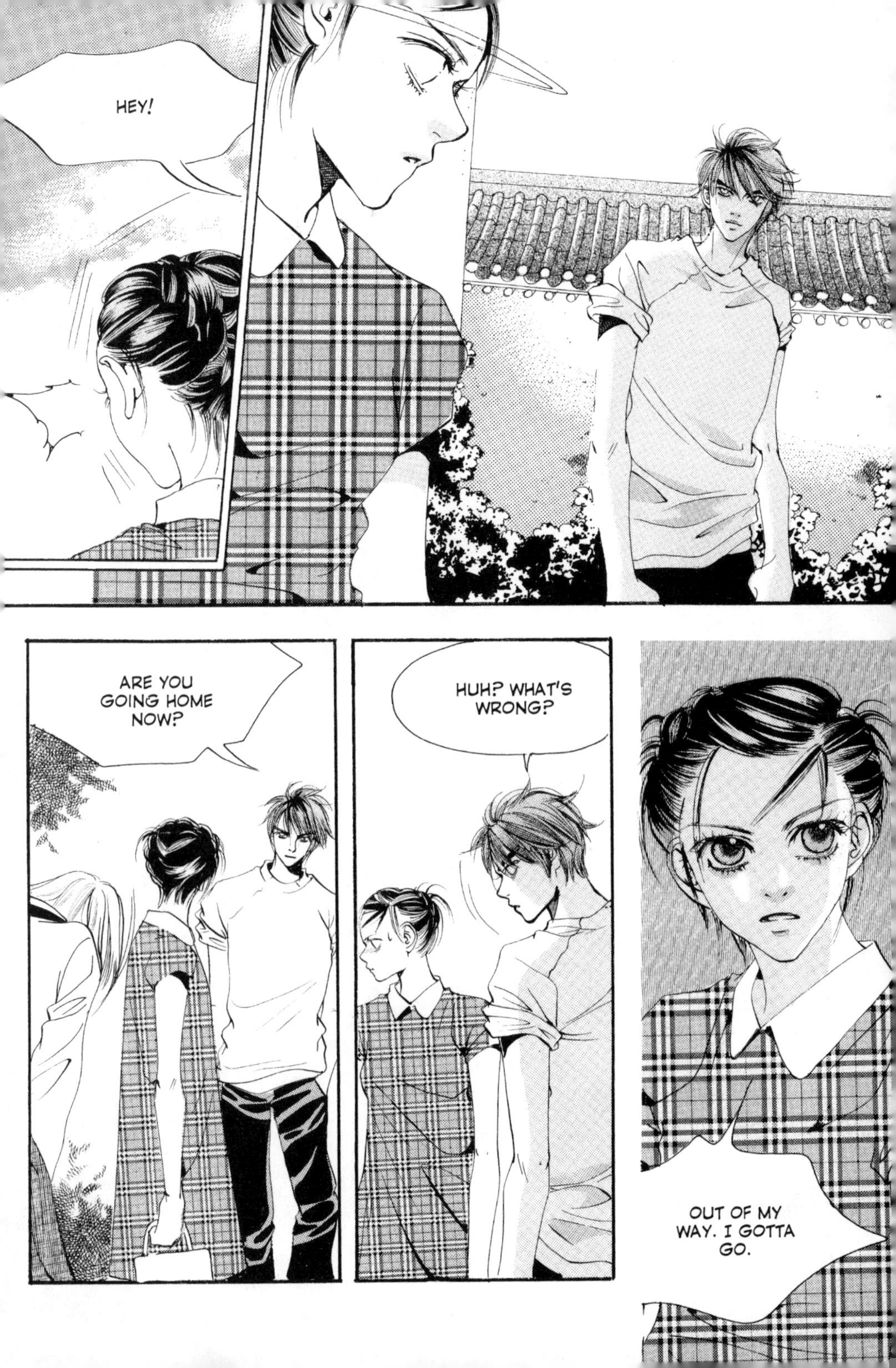
HEY!
ARE YOU GOING HOME NOW?
HUH? WHAT'S WRONG?
OUT OF MY WAY. I GOTTA GO.

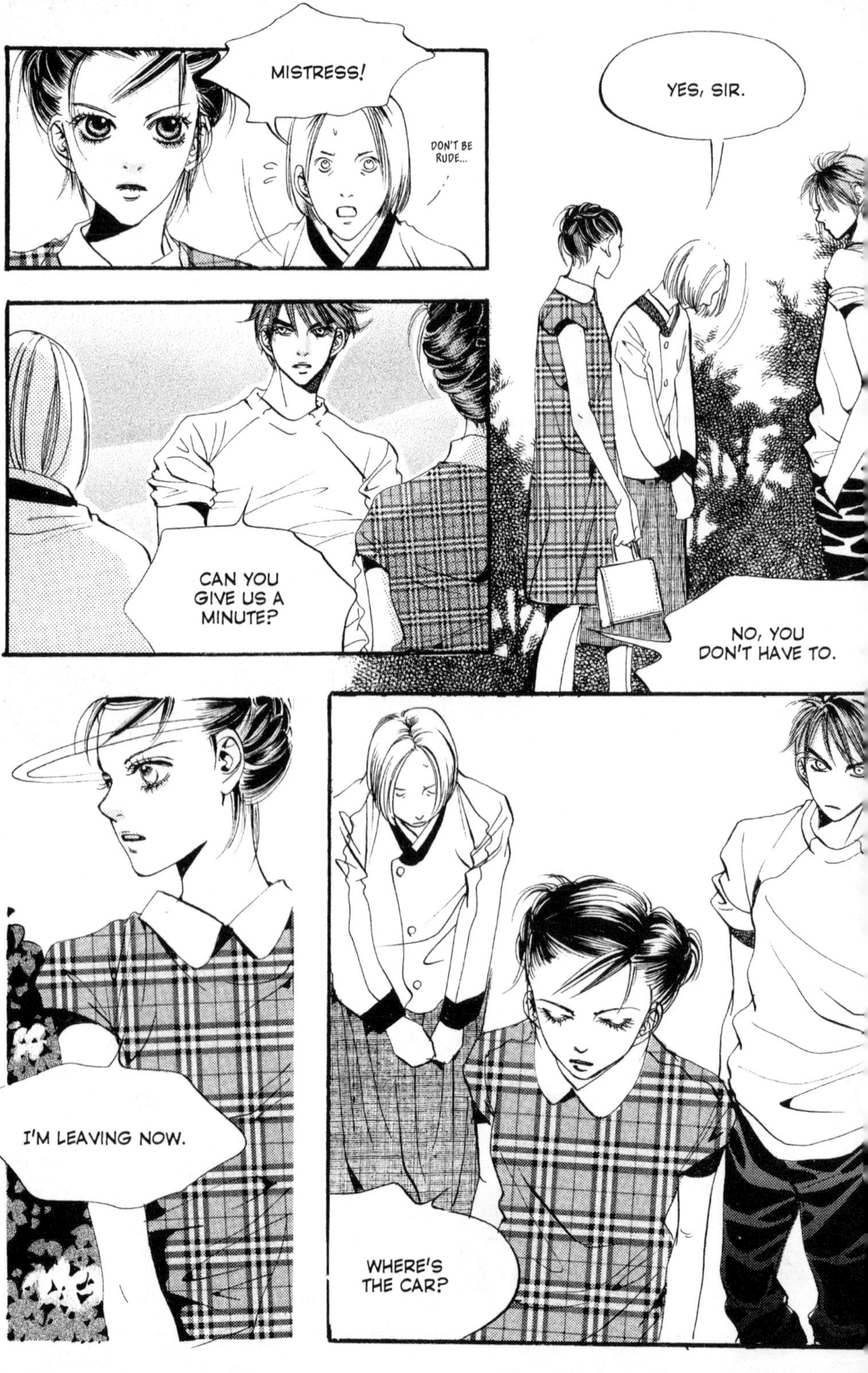
MISTRESS!
DON'T BE RUDE...
CAN YOU GIVE US A MINUTE?
YES, SIR.
NO, YOU DON'T HAVE TO.
I'M LEAVING NOW.
WHERE'S THE CAR?

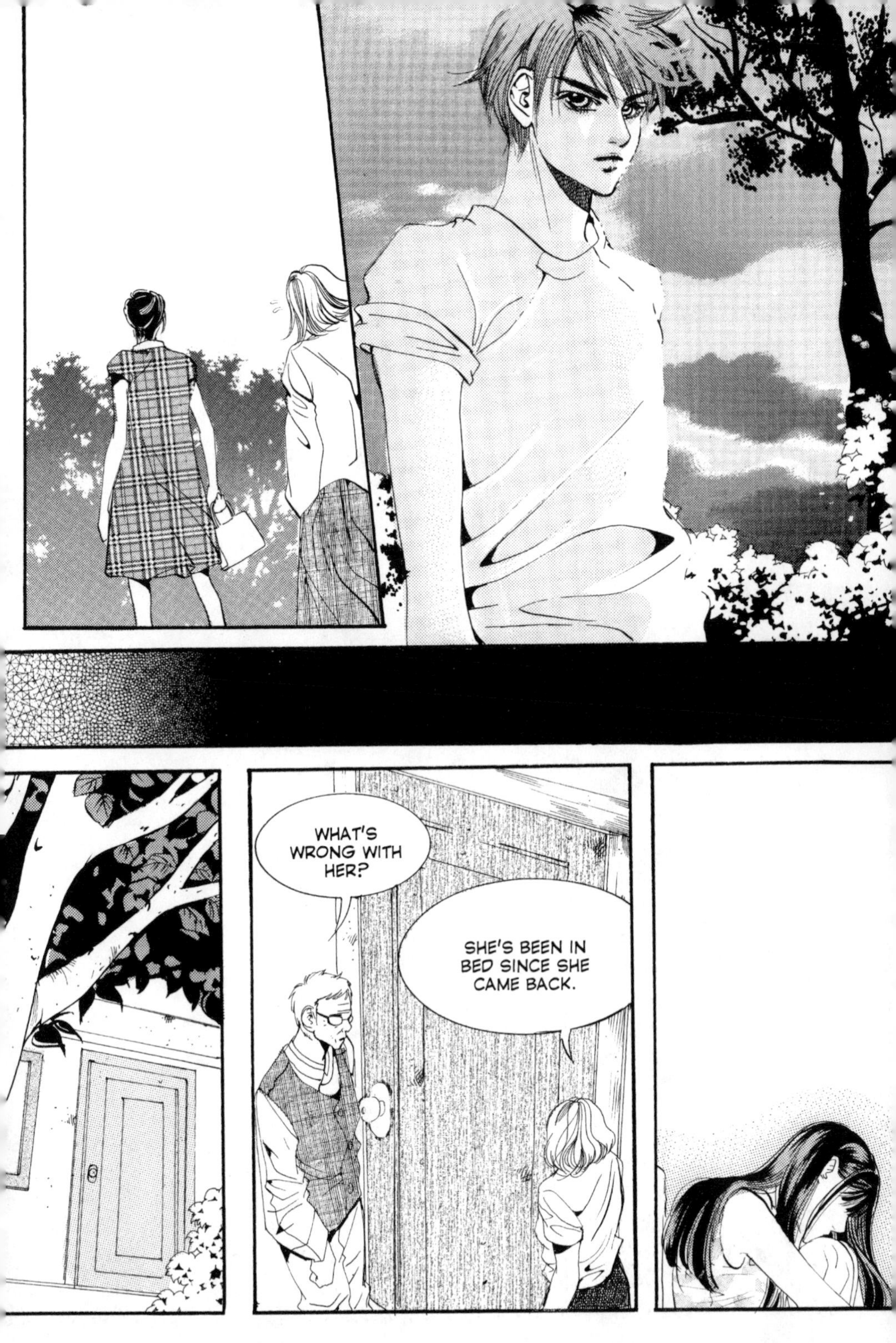
WHAT'S WRONG WITH HER?
SHE'S BEEN IN BED SINCE SHE CAME BACK.

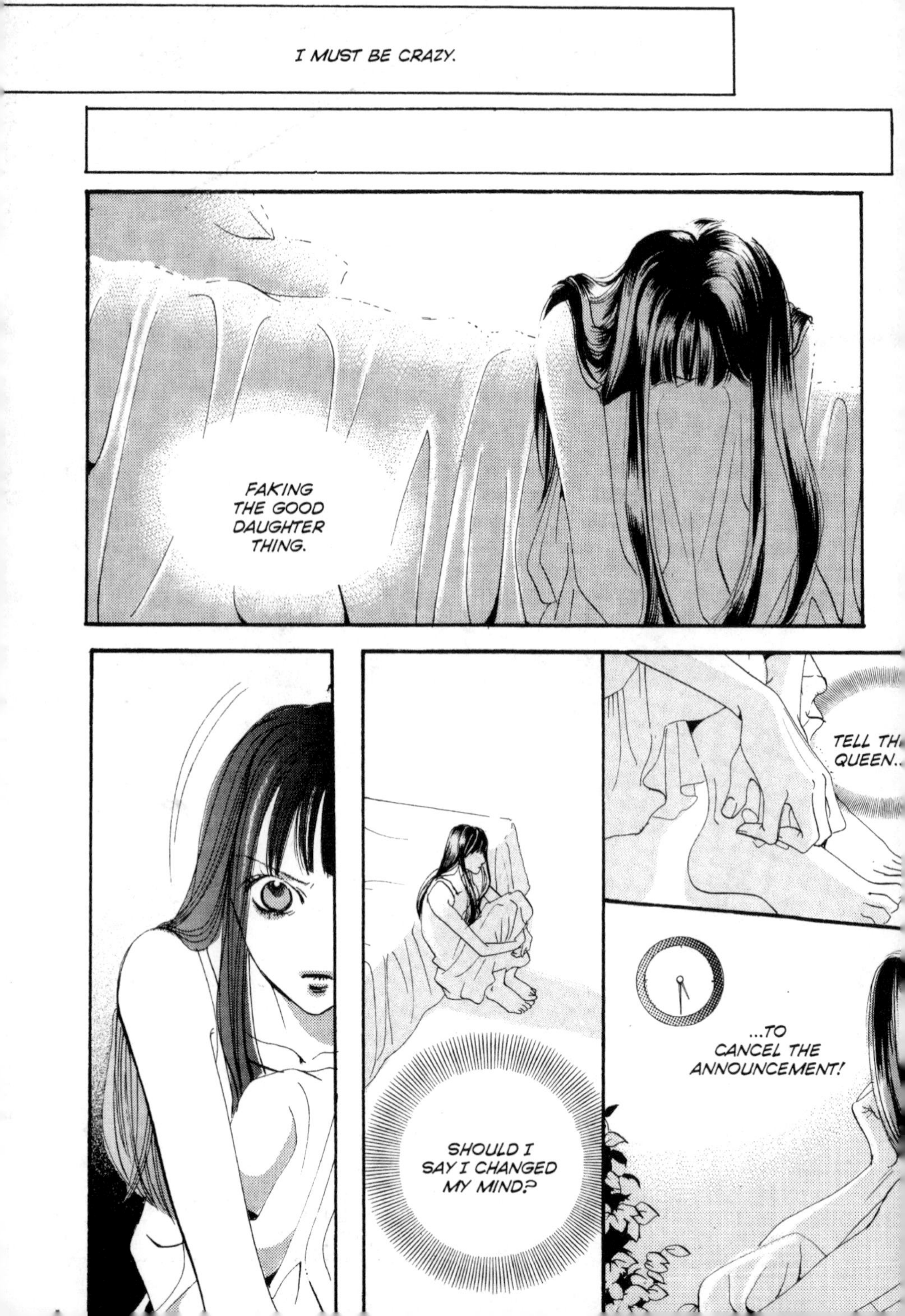
I MUST BE CRAZY.
FAKING THE GOOD DAUGHTER THING.
SHOULD I SAY I CHANGED MY MIND?
TELL TH
QUEEN..
...TO CANCEL THE ANNOUNCEMENT!

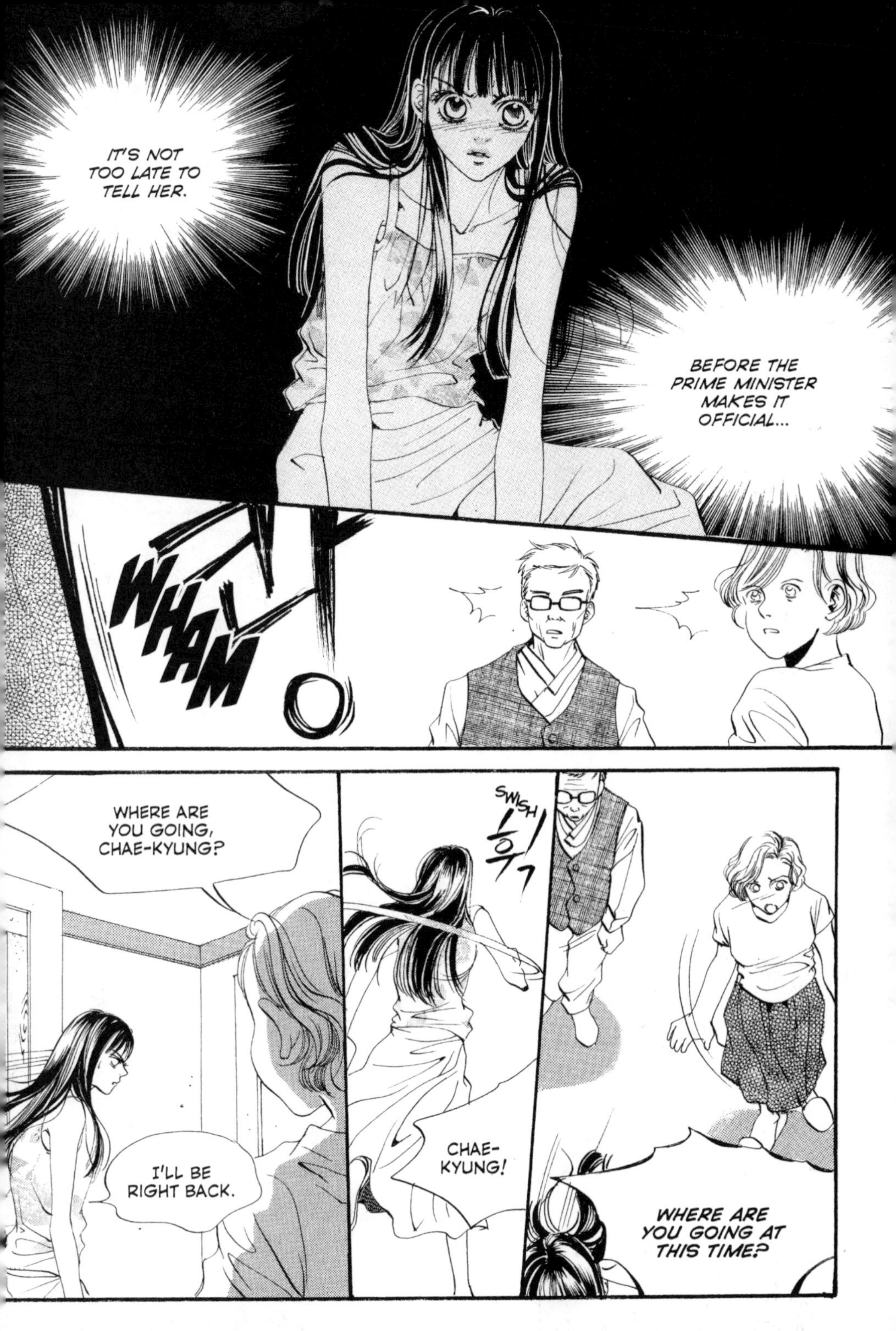
IT'S NOT TOO LATE TO TELL HER.
BEFORE THE PRIME MINISTER MAKES IT OFFICIAL...
WHAM!
WHERE ARE YOU GOING, CHAE-KYUNG?
I'LL BE RIGHT BACK.
SWISH
CHAE-KYUNG!
WHERE ARE YOU GOING AT THIS TIME?

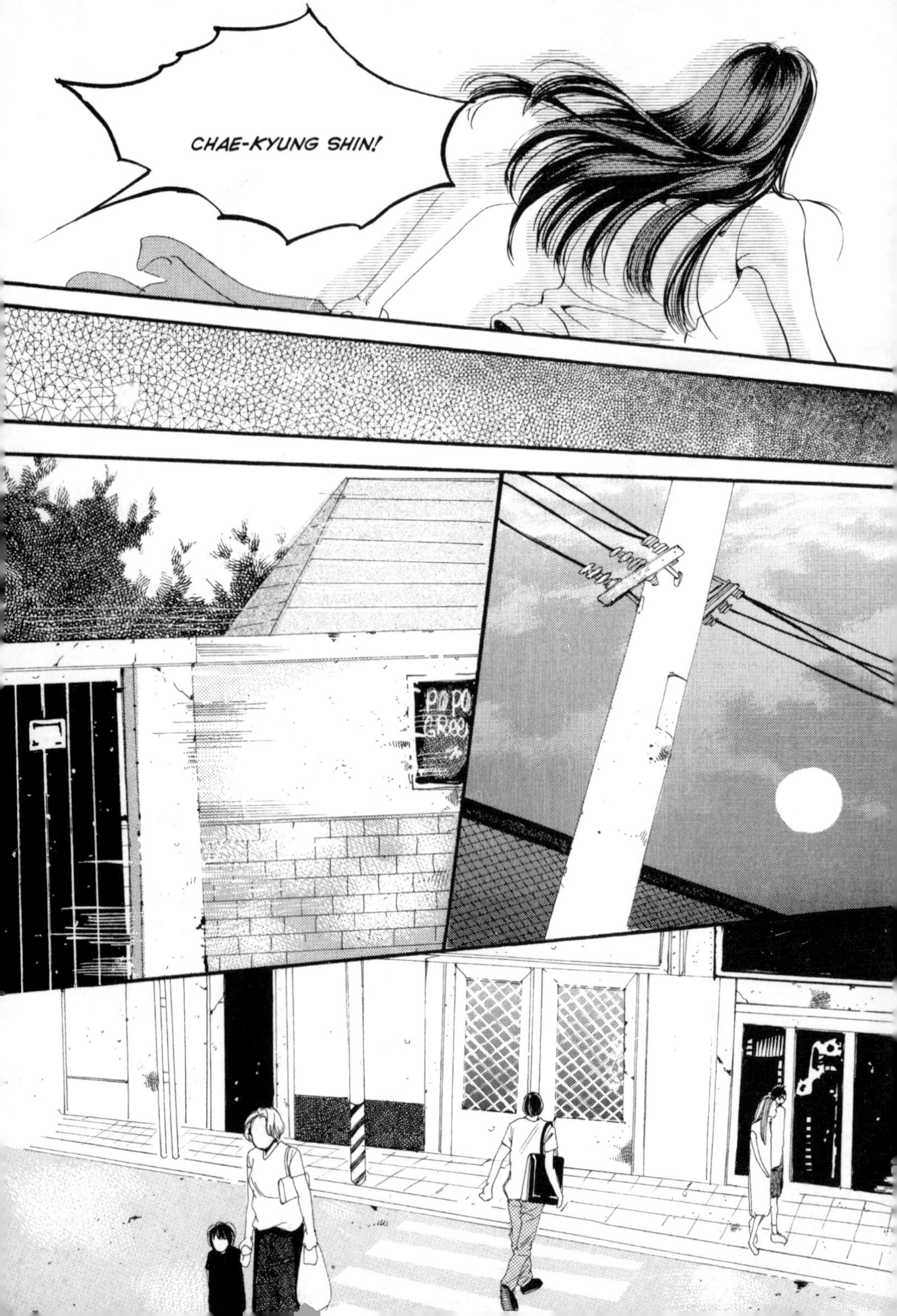
CHAE-KYUNG SHIN!

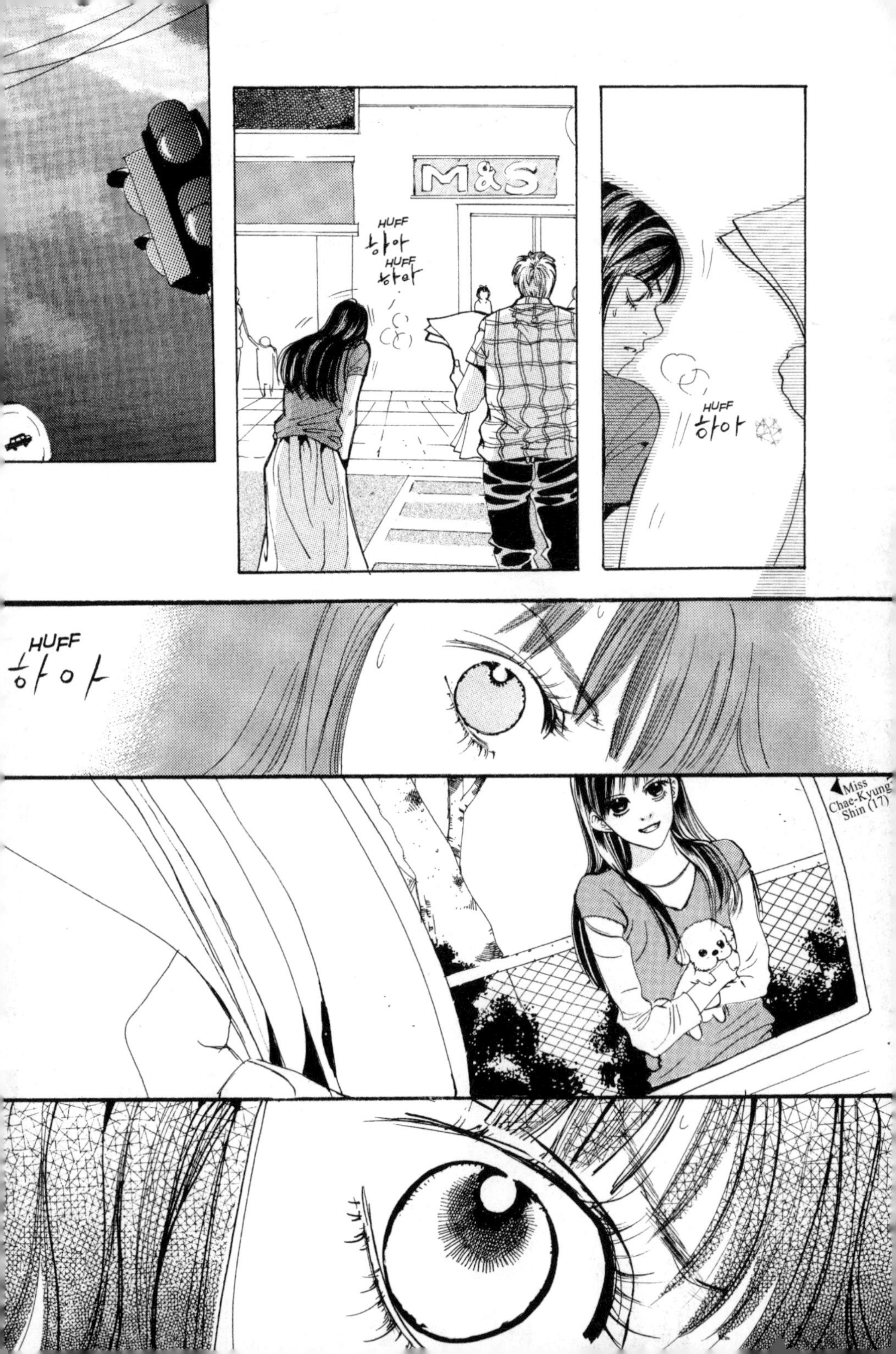
HUFF
하아
HUFF
하아
HUFF
하아
HUFF
하아
Miss Chae-Kyung Shin (17)

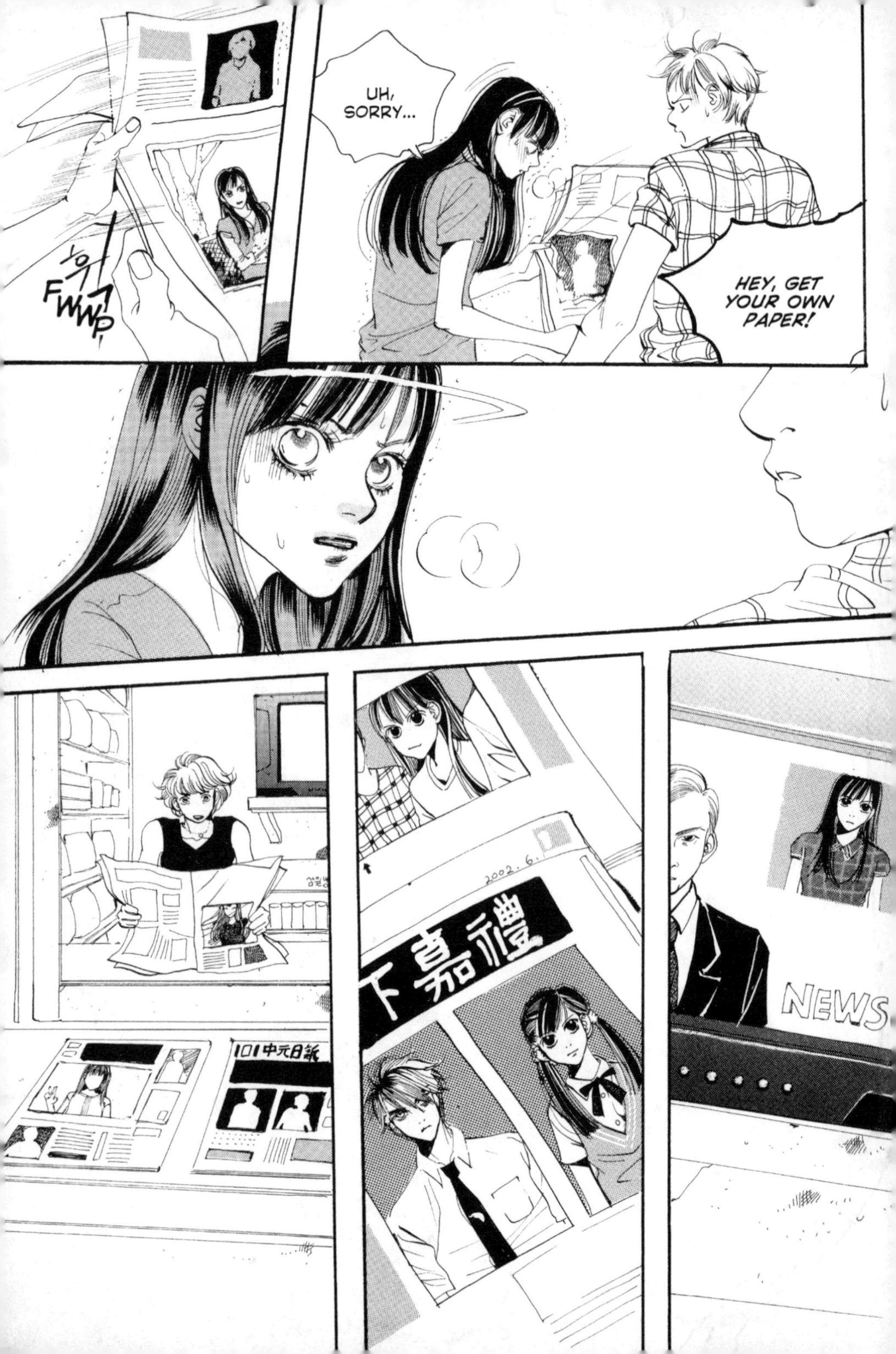
FWWP
UH, SORRY...
HEY, GET YOUR OWN PAPER!
2002. 6.
下嘉禮
NEWS

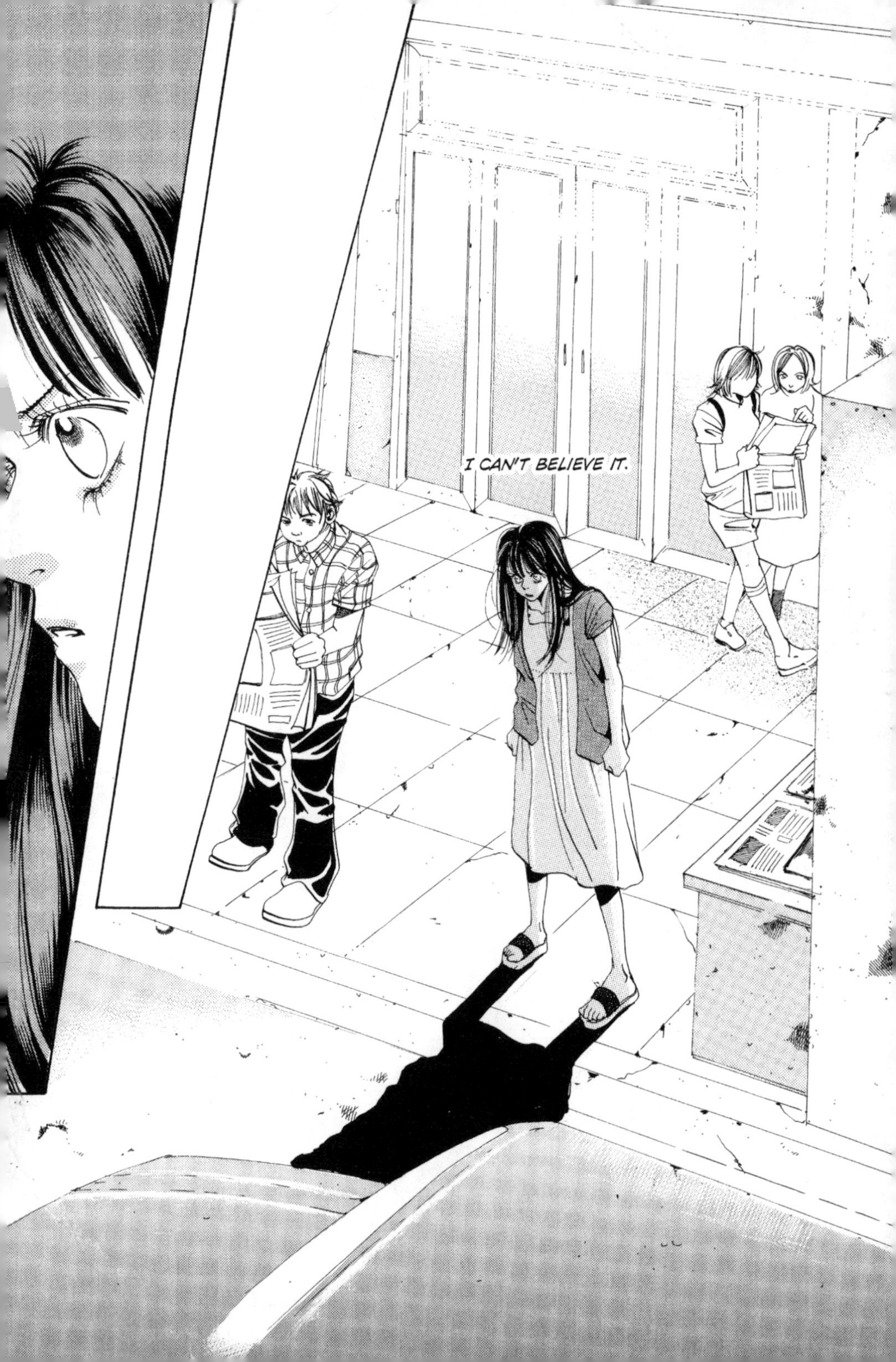
I CAN'T BELIEVE IT.

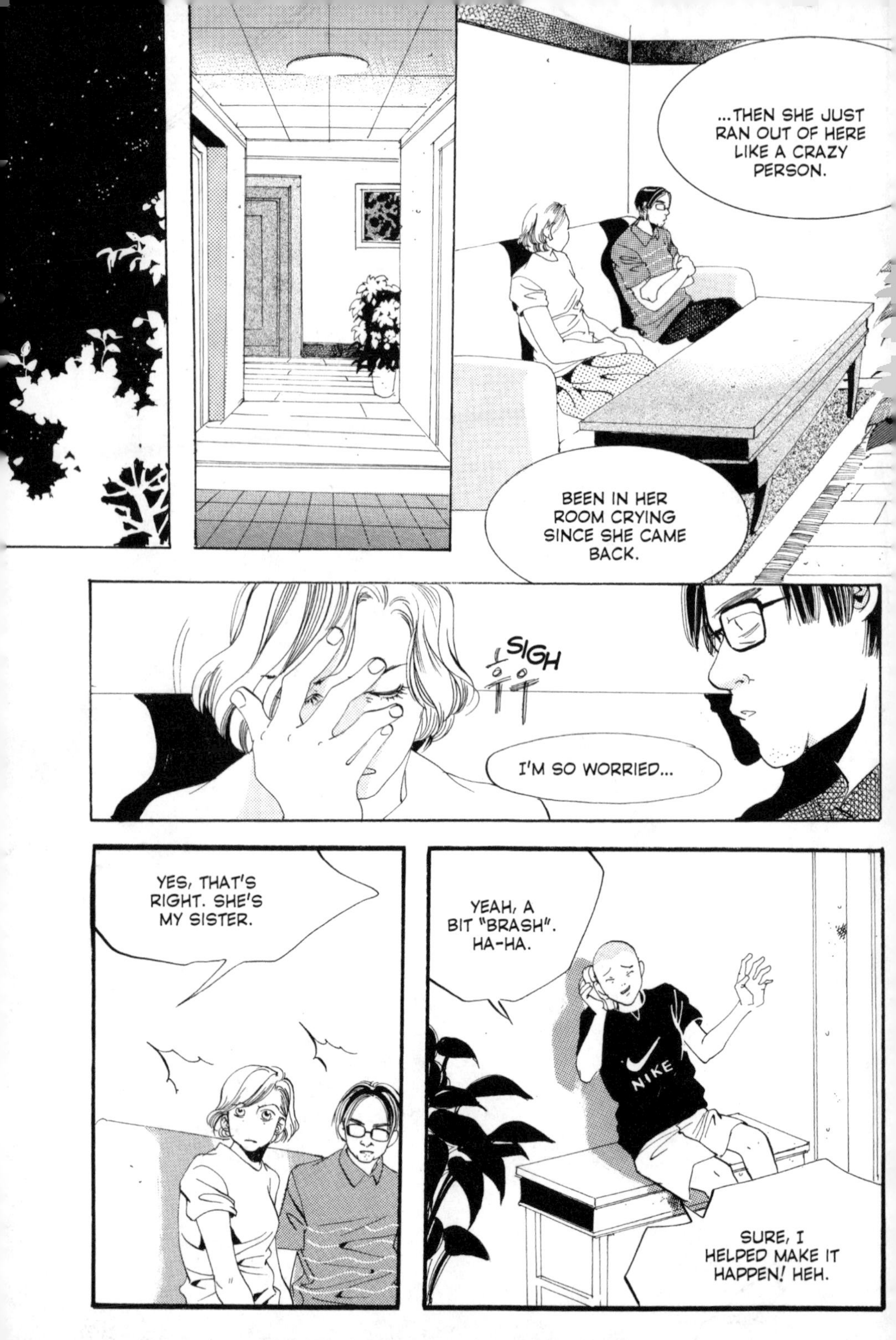
...THEN SHE JUST RAN OUT OF HERE LIKE A CRAZY PERSON.
BEEN IN HER ROOM CRYING SINCE SHE CAME BACK.
SIGH
I'M SO WORRIED...
YES, THAT'S RIGHT. SHE'S MY SISTER.
YEAH, A BIT "BRASH". HA-HA.
NIKE
SURE, I HELPED MAKE IT HAPPEN! HEH.

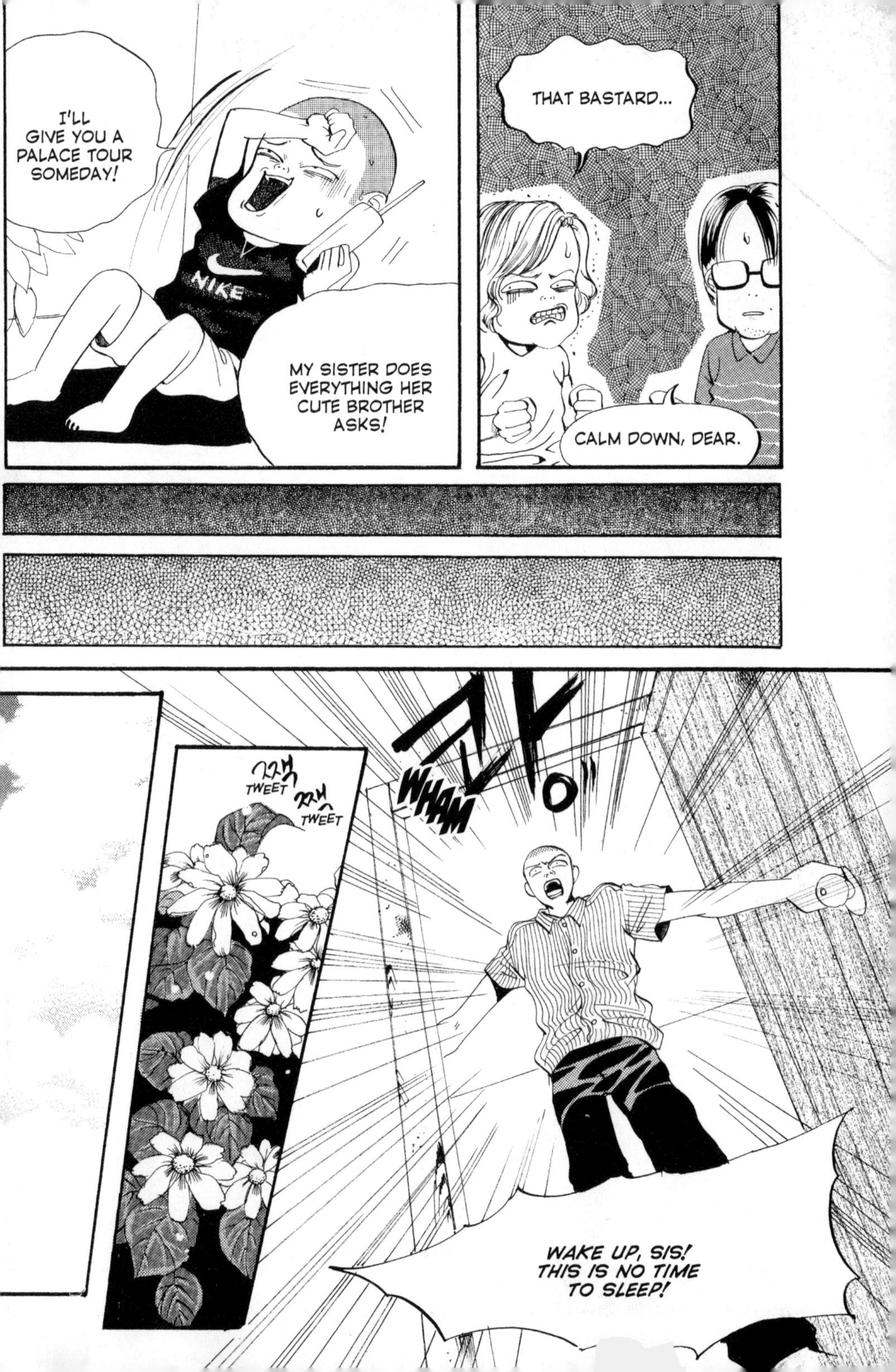
I'LL GIVE YOU A PALACE TOUR SOMEDAY!
MY SISTER DOES EVERYTHING HER CUTE BROTHER ASKS!
THAT BASTARD...
CALM DOWN, DEAR.
TWEET
TWEET
WHAM
WAKE UP, SIS! THIS IS NO TIME TO SLEEP!

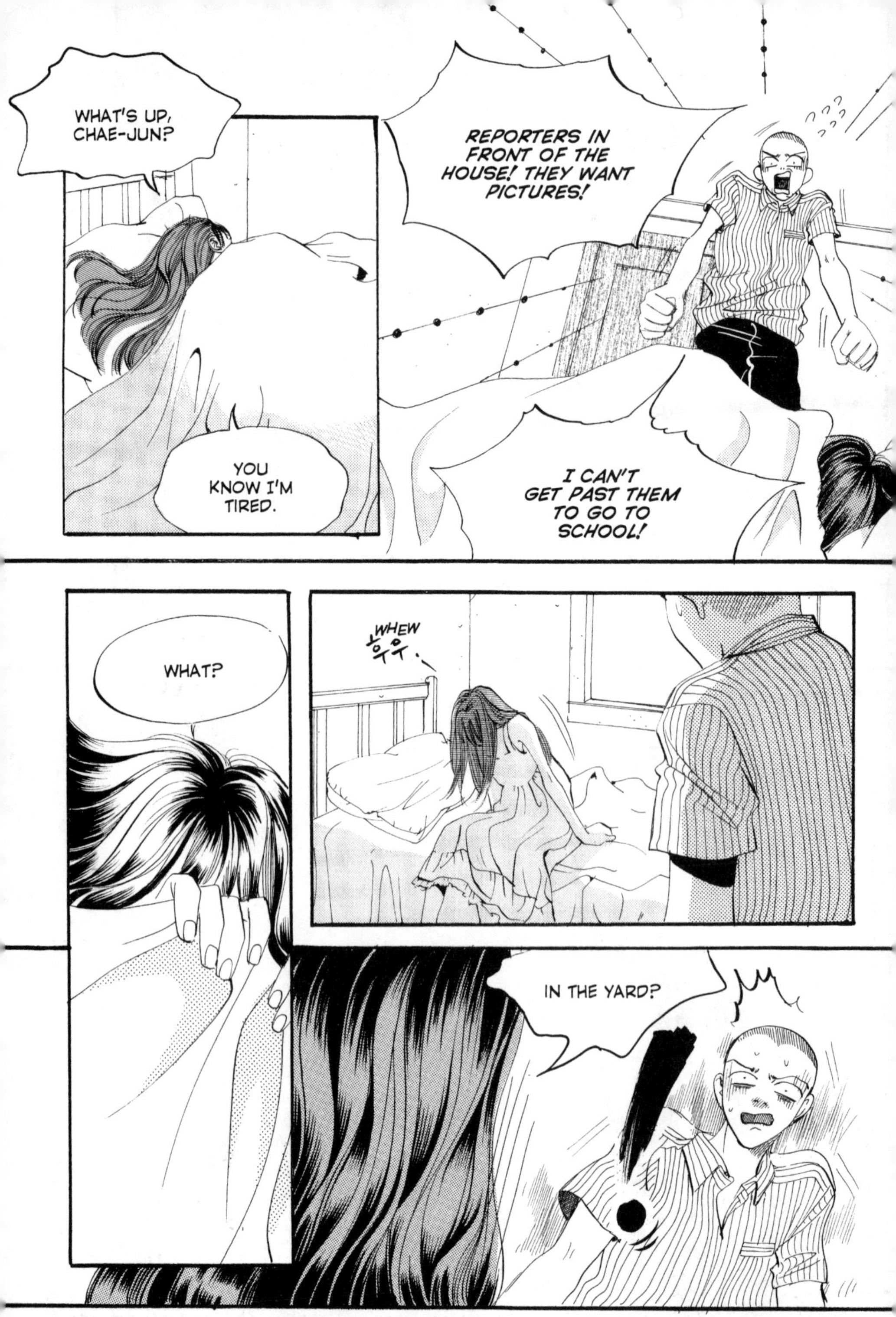
WHAT'S UP, CHAE-JUN?
YOU KNOW I'M TIRED.
REPORTERS IN FRONT OF THE HOUSE! THEY WANT PICTURES!
I CAN'T GET PAST THEM TO GO TO SCHOOL!
WHAT?
WHEW
후우..
IN THE YARD?

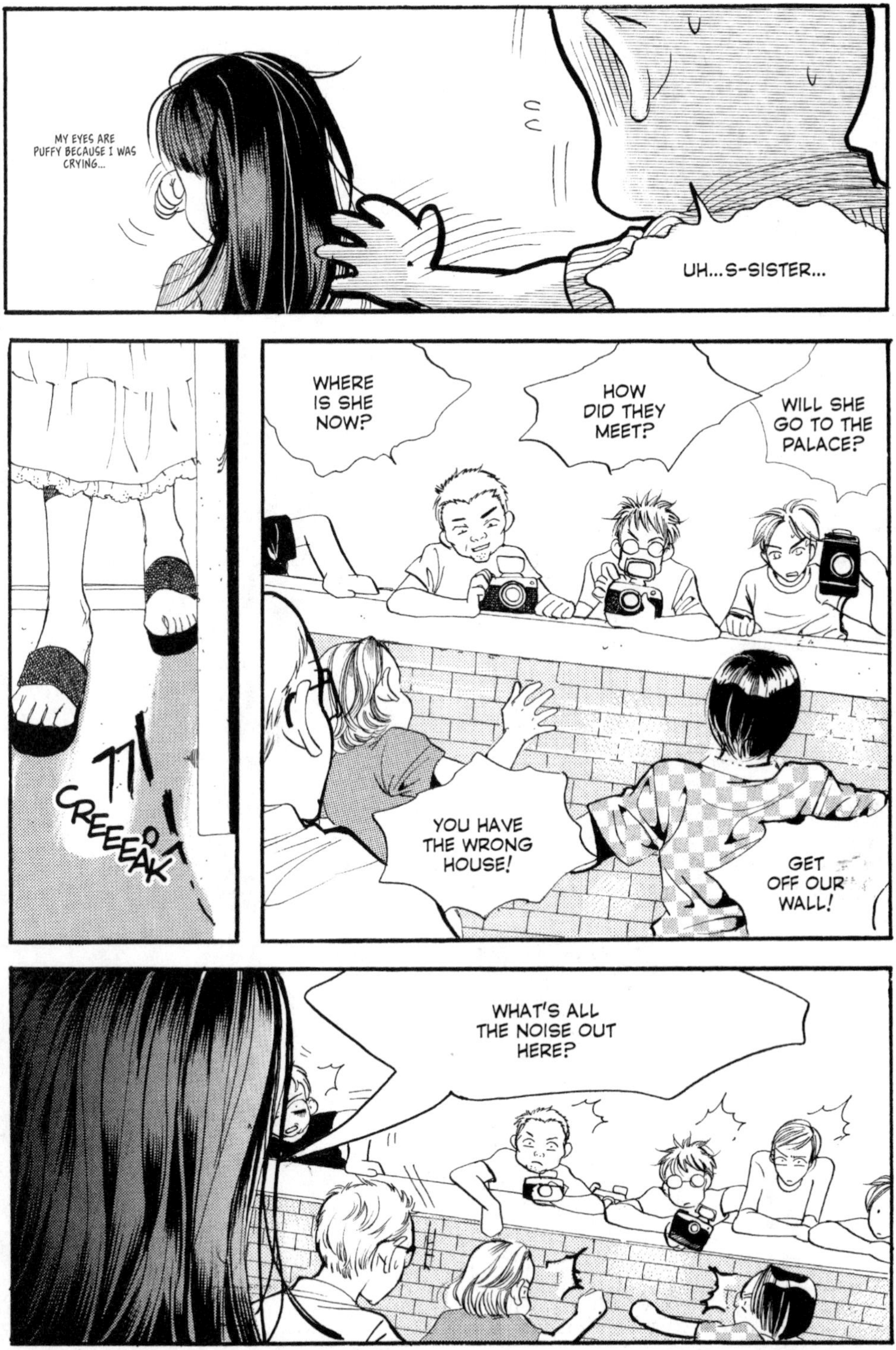
MY EYES ARE PUFFY BECAUSE I WAS CRYING...
UH... S-SISTER...
CREEEEAK
WHERE IS SHE NOW?
HOW DID THEY MEET?
WILL SHE GO TO THE PALACE?
YOU HAVE THE WRONG HOUSE!
GET OFF OUR WALL!
WHAT'S ALL THE NOISE OUT HERE?

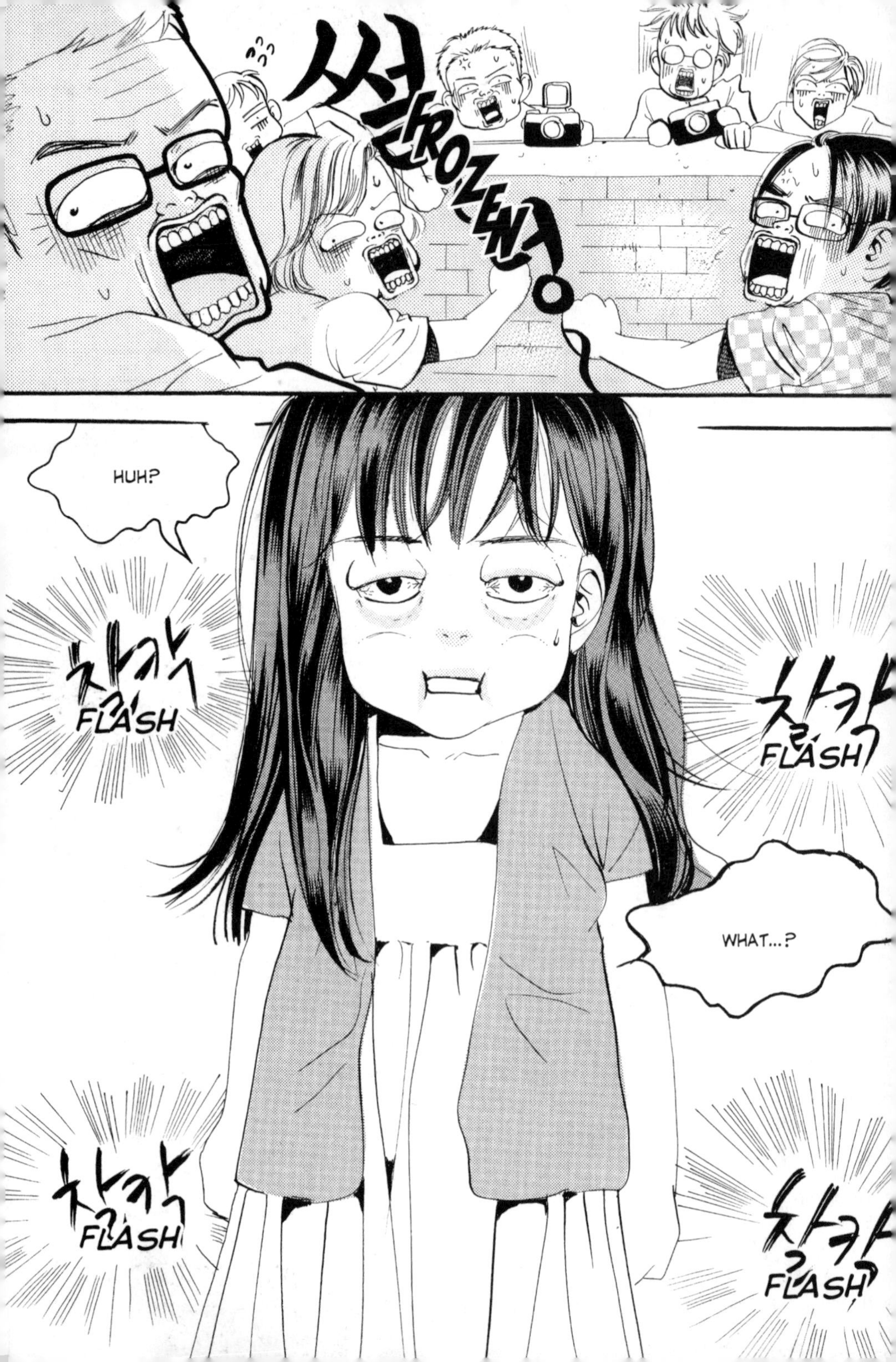
FROZEN
HUH?
FLASH
FLASH
WHAT...?
FLASH
FLASH

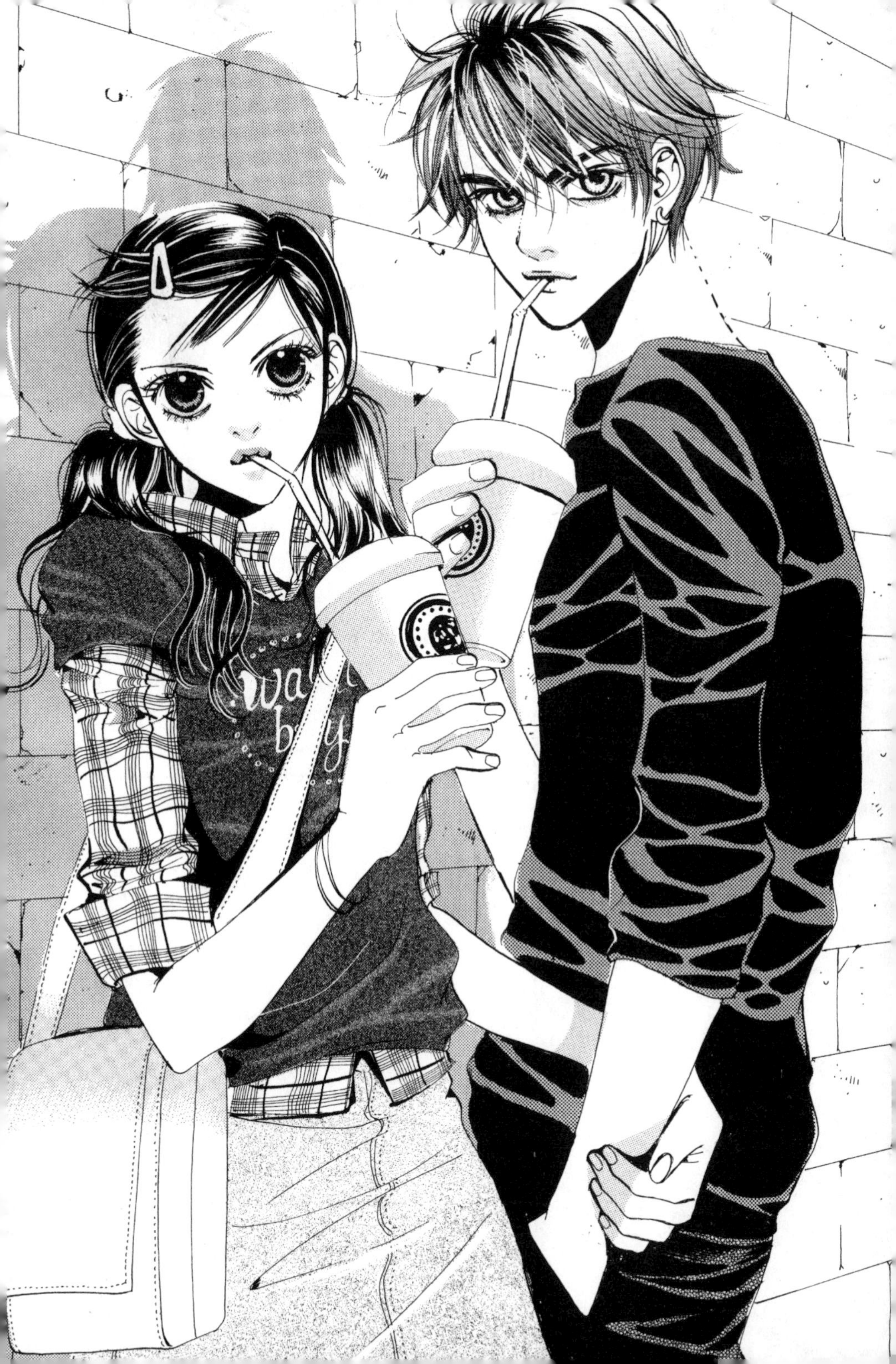

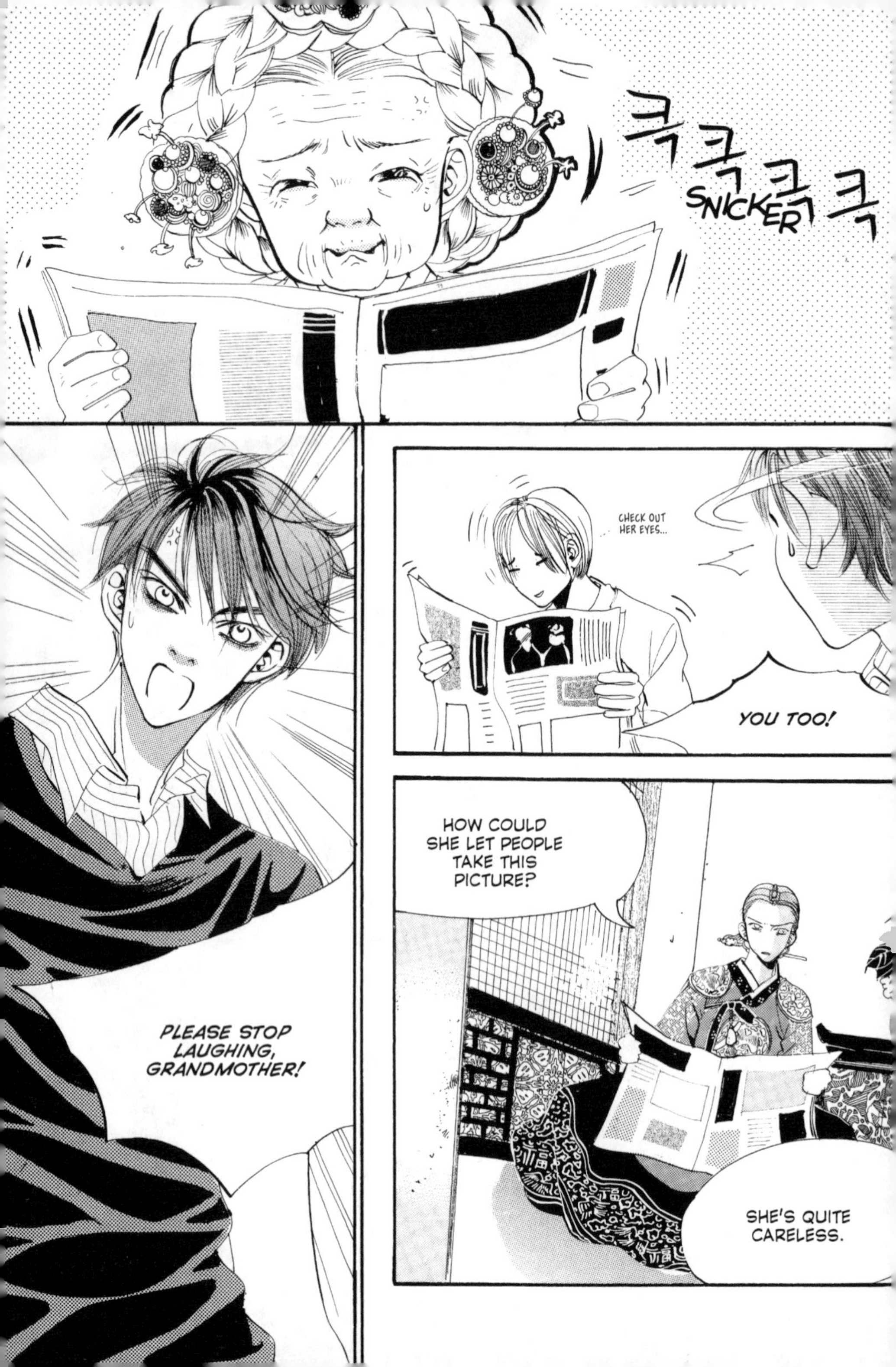
큭큭 큭큭
SNICKER
PLEASE STOP LAUGHING, GRANDMOTHER!
CHECK OUT HER EYES...
YOU TOO!
HOW COULD SHE LET PEOPLE TAKE THIS PICTURE?
SHE'S QUITE CARELESS.

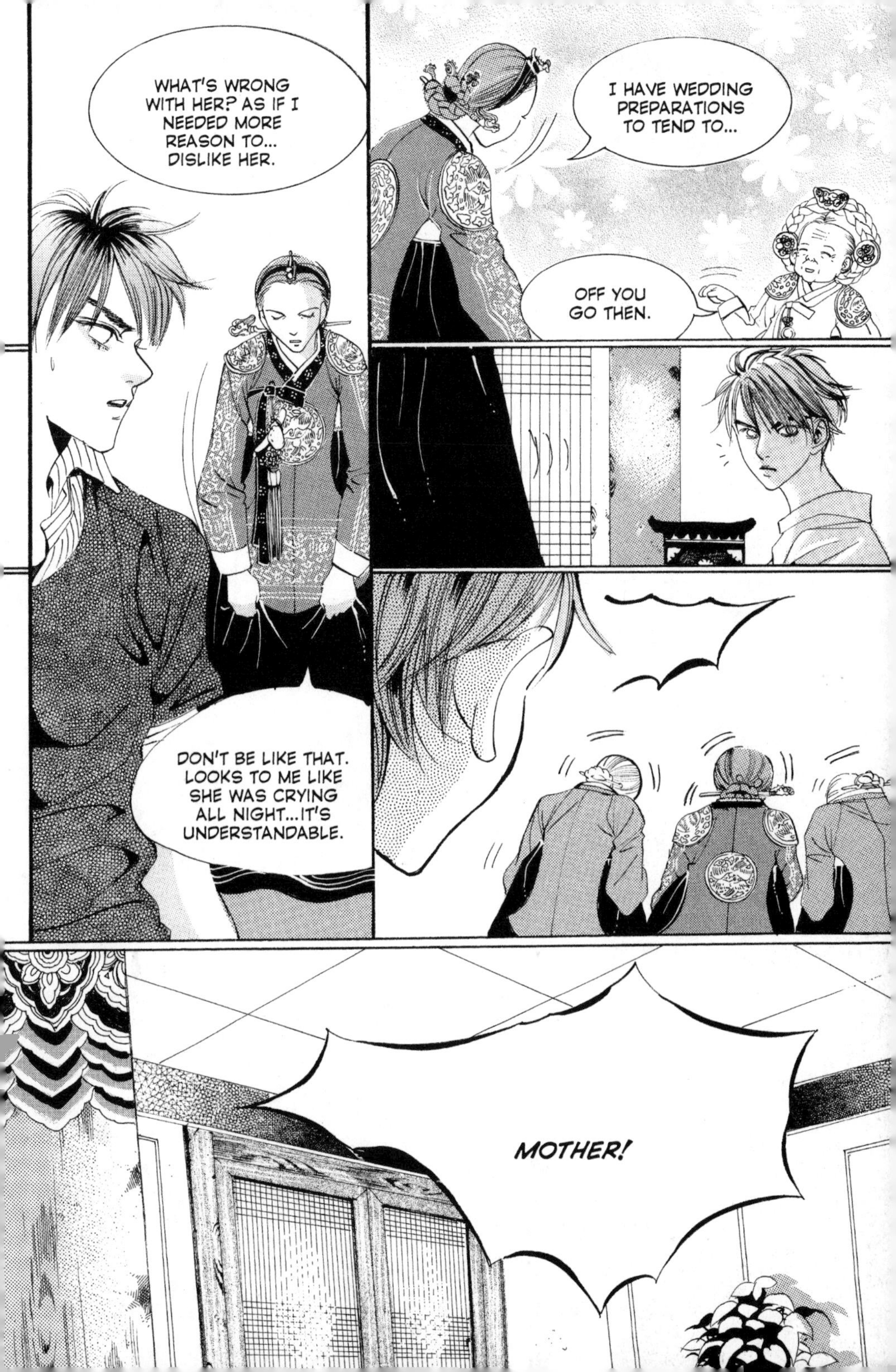
WHAT'S WRONG WITH HER? AS IF I NEEDED MORE REASON TO... DISLIKE HER.
DON'T BE LIKE THAT. LOOKS TO ME LIKE SHE WAS CRYING ALL NIGHT...IT'S UNDERSTANDABLE.
I HAVE WEDDING PREPARATIONS TO TEND TO...
OFF YOU GO THEN.
MOTHER!

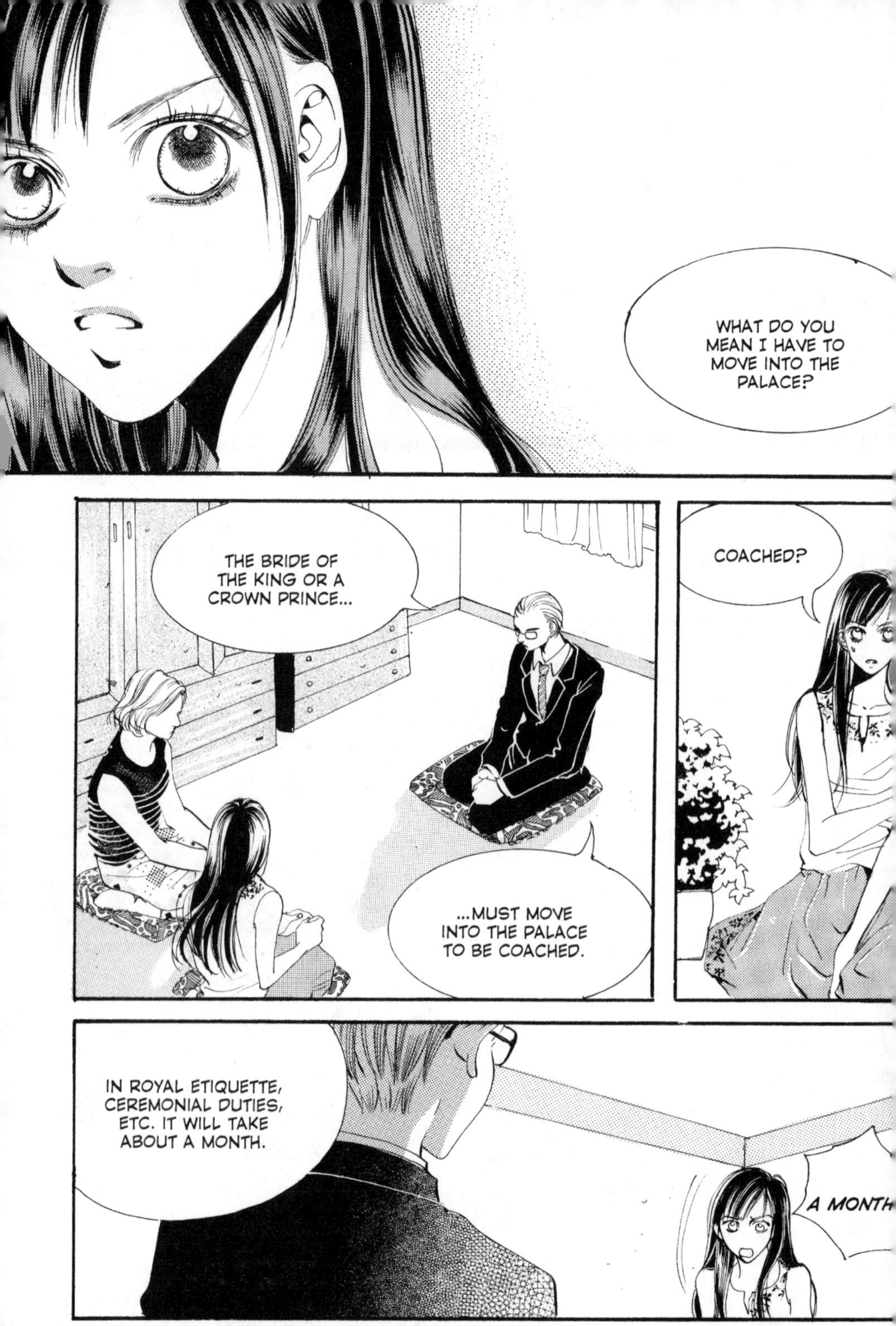
WHAT DO YOU MEAN I HAVE TO MOVE INTO THE PALACE?
THE BRIDE OF THE KING OR A CROWN PRINCE...
...MUST MOVE INTO THE PALACE TO BE COACHED.
COACHED?
IN ROYAL ETIQUETTE, CEREMONIAL DUTIES, ETC. IT WILL TAKE ABOUT A MONTH.
A MONTH

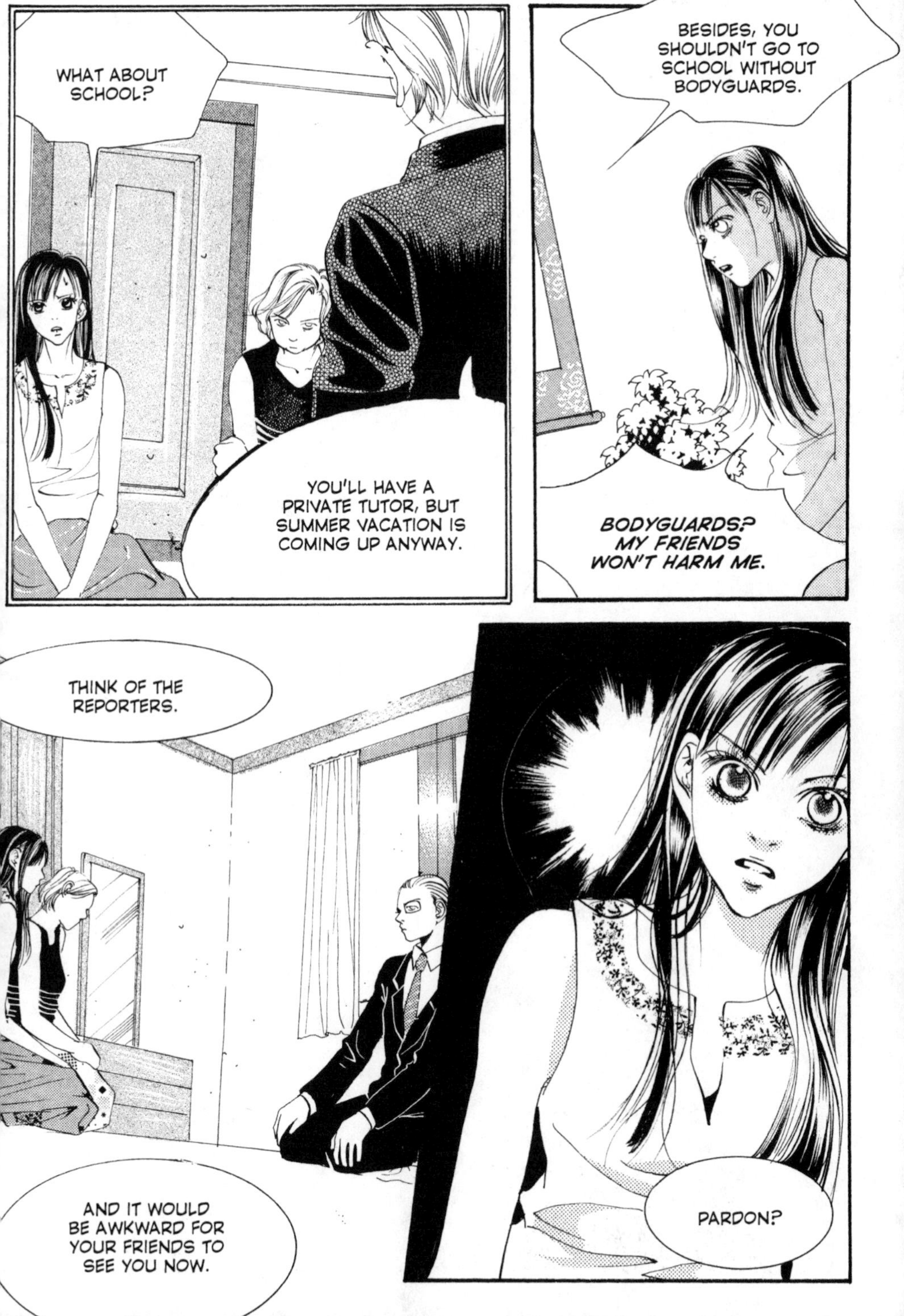
WHAT ABOUT SCHOOL?
YOU'LL HAVE A PRIVATE TUTOR, BUT SUMMER VACATION IS COMING UP ANYWAY.
BESIDES, YOU SHOULDN'T GO TO SCHOOL WITHOUT BODYGUARDS.
BODYGUARDS? MY FRIENDS WON'T HARM ME.
THINK OF THE REPORTERS.
AND IT WOULD BE AWKWARD FOR YOUR FRIENDS TO SEE YOU NOW.
PARDON?

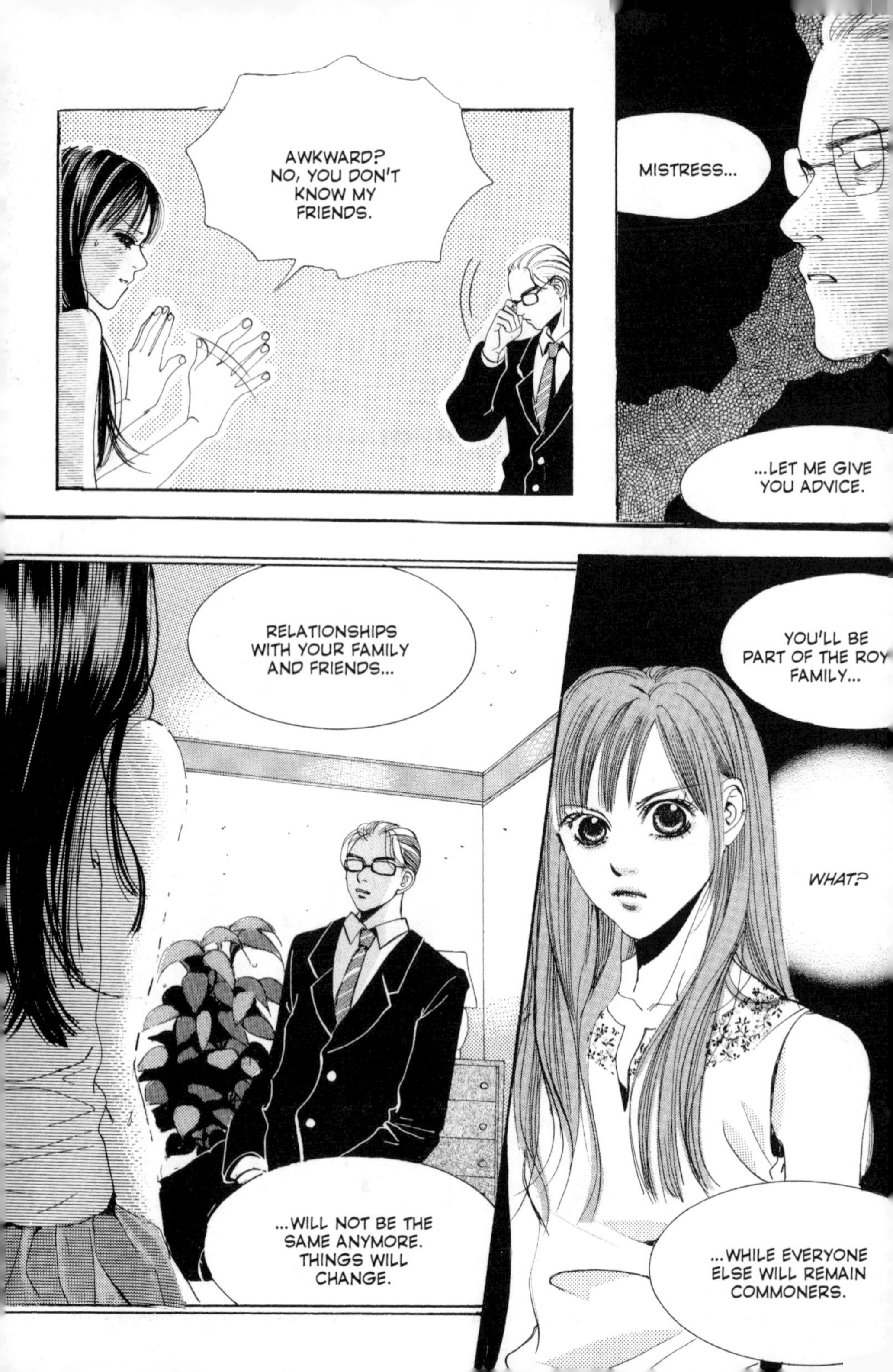
AWKWARD? NO, YOU DON'T KNOW MY FRIENDS.
MISTRESS...
...LET ME GIVE YOU ADVICE.
RELATIONSHIPS WITH YOUR FAMILY AND FRIENDS...
...WILL NOT BE THE SAME ANYMORE. THINGS WILL CHANGE.
YOU'LL BE PART OF THE ROY FAMILY...
WHAT?
...WHILE EVERYONE ELSE WILL REMAIN COMMONERS.

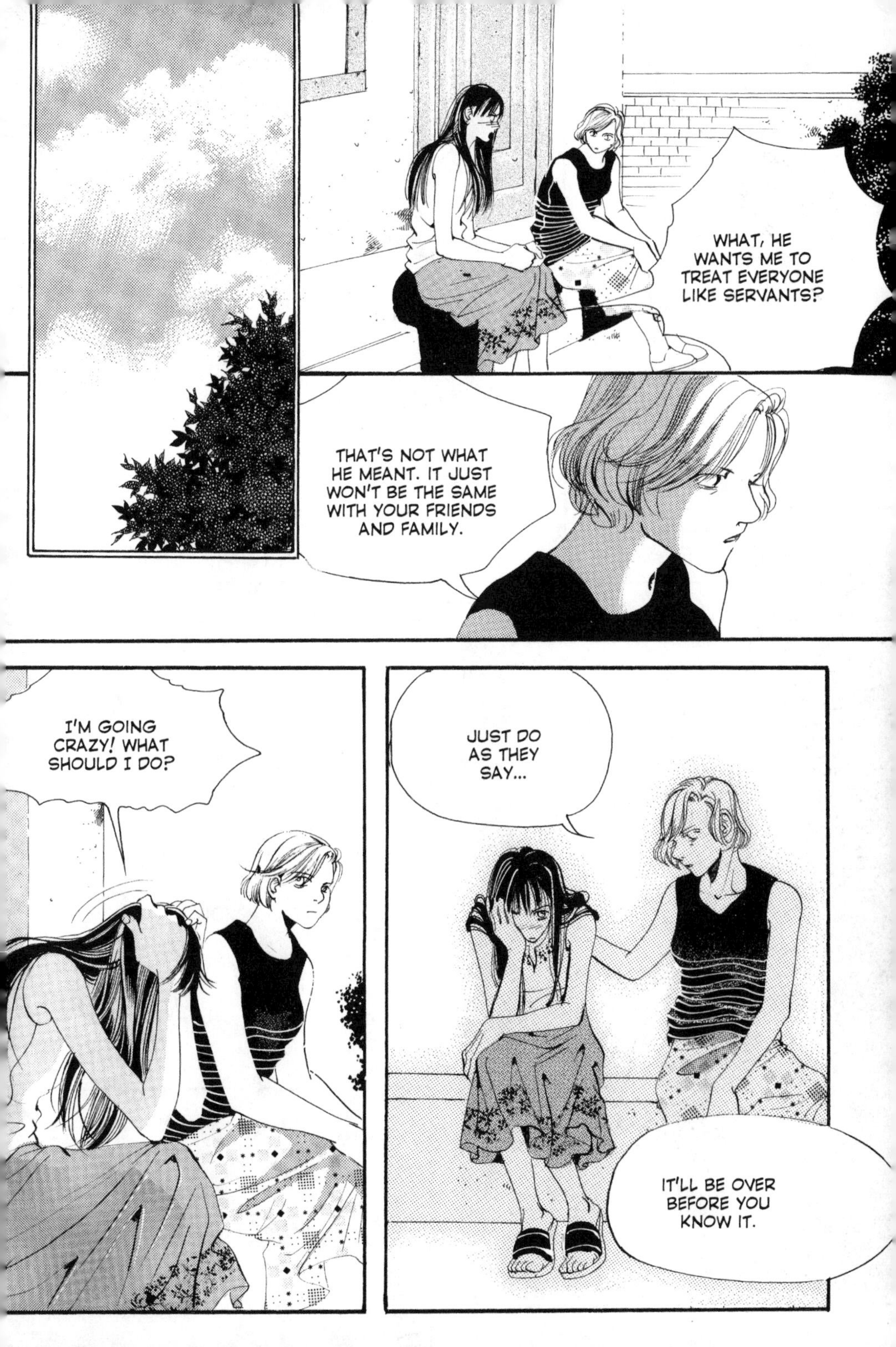
WHAT, HE WANTS ME TO TREAT EVERYONE LIKE SERVANTS?
THAT'S NOT WHAT HE MEANT. IT JUST WON'T BE THE SAME WITH YOUR FRIENDS AND FAMILY.
I'M GOING CRAZY! WHAT SHOULD I DO?
JUST DO AS THEY SAY...
IT'LL BE OVER BEFORE YOU KNOW IT.

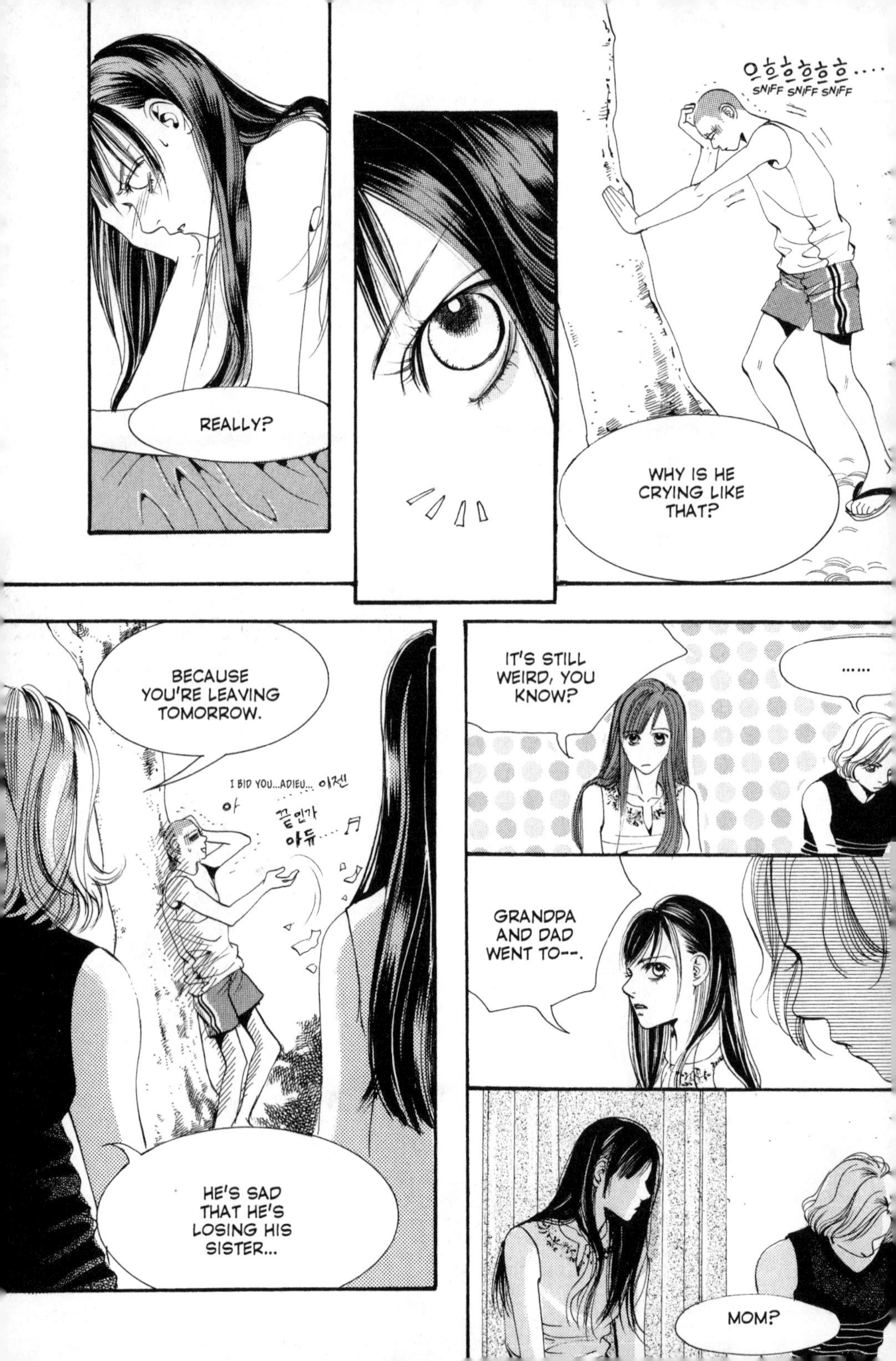
REALLY?
으흐흐흐흐흐....
SNIFF SNIFF SNIFF
WHY IS HE CRYING LIKE THAT?
BECAUSE YOU'RE LEAVING TOMORROW.
I BID YOU...ADIEU... 이젠
아
끝인가
아듀....♪
HE'S SAD THAT HE'S LOSING HIS SISTER...
IT'S STILL WEIRD, YOU KNOW?
......
GRANDPA AND DAD WENT TO--.
MOM?

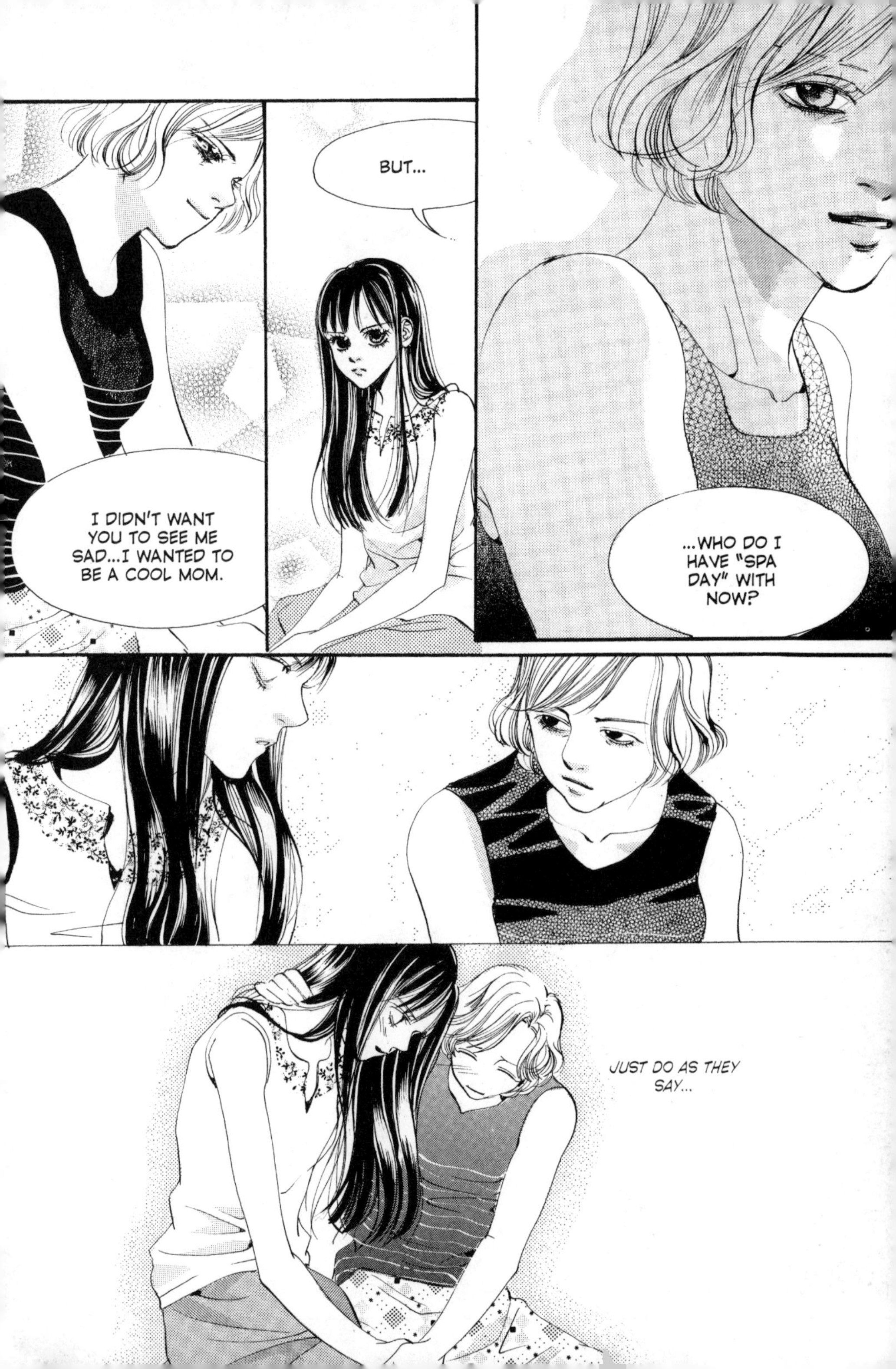
I DIDN'T WANT YOU TO SEE ME SAD...I WANTED TO BE A COOL MOM.
BUT...
...WHO DO I HAVE "SPA DAY" WITH NOW?
JUST DO AS THEY SAY...

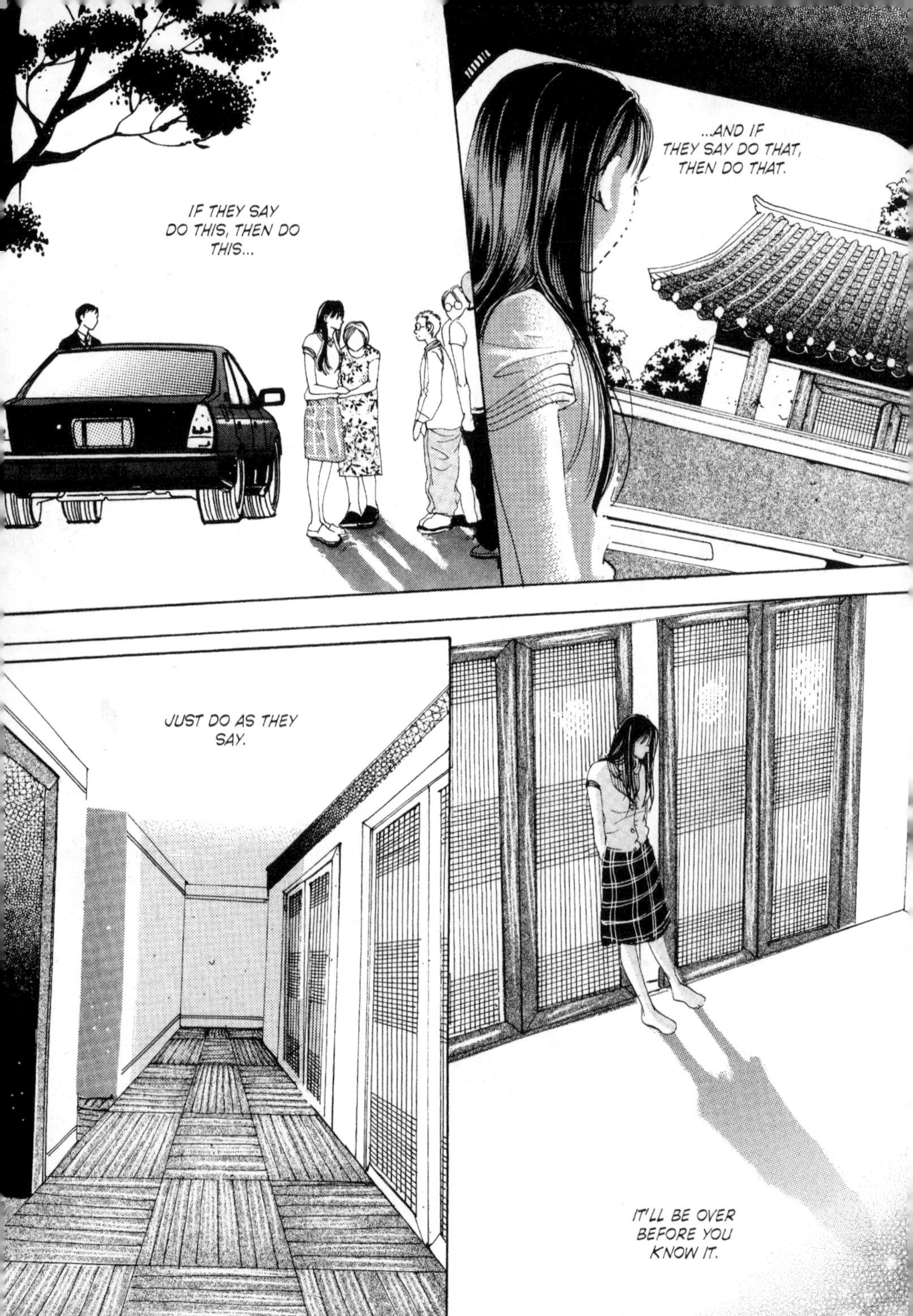
IF THEY SAY DO THIS, THEN DO THIS...
...AND IF THEY SAY DO THAT, THEN DO THAT.
JUST DO AS THEY SAY.
IT'LL BE OVER BEFORE YOU KNOW IT.

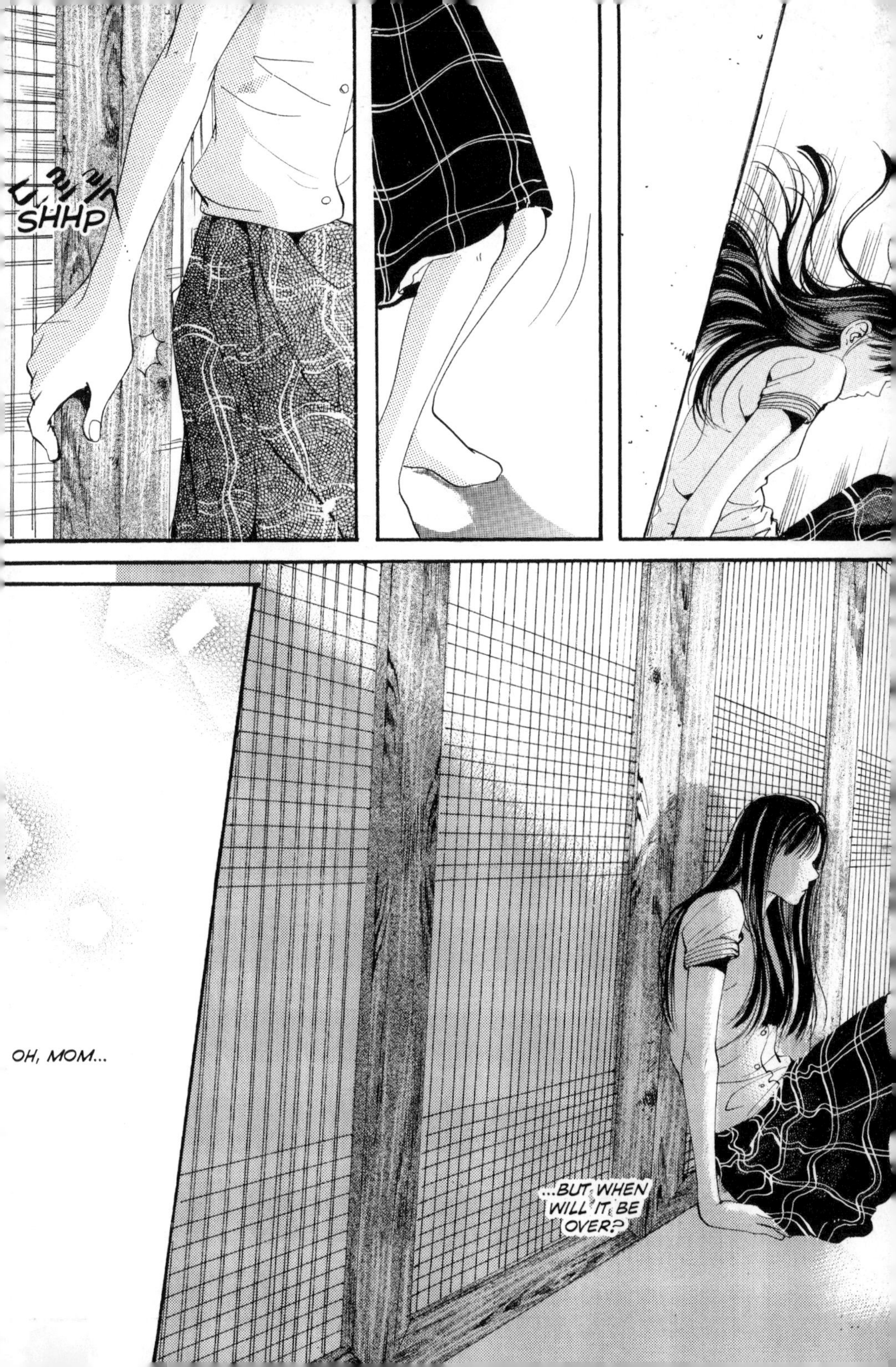
SHHP
OH, MOM...
...BUT WHEN WILL IT BE OVER?

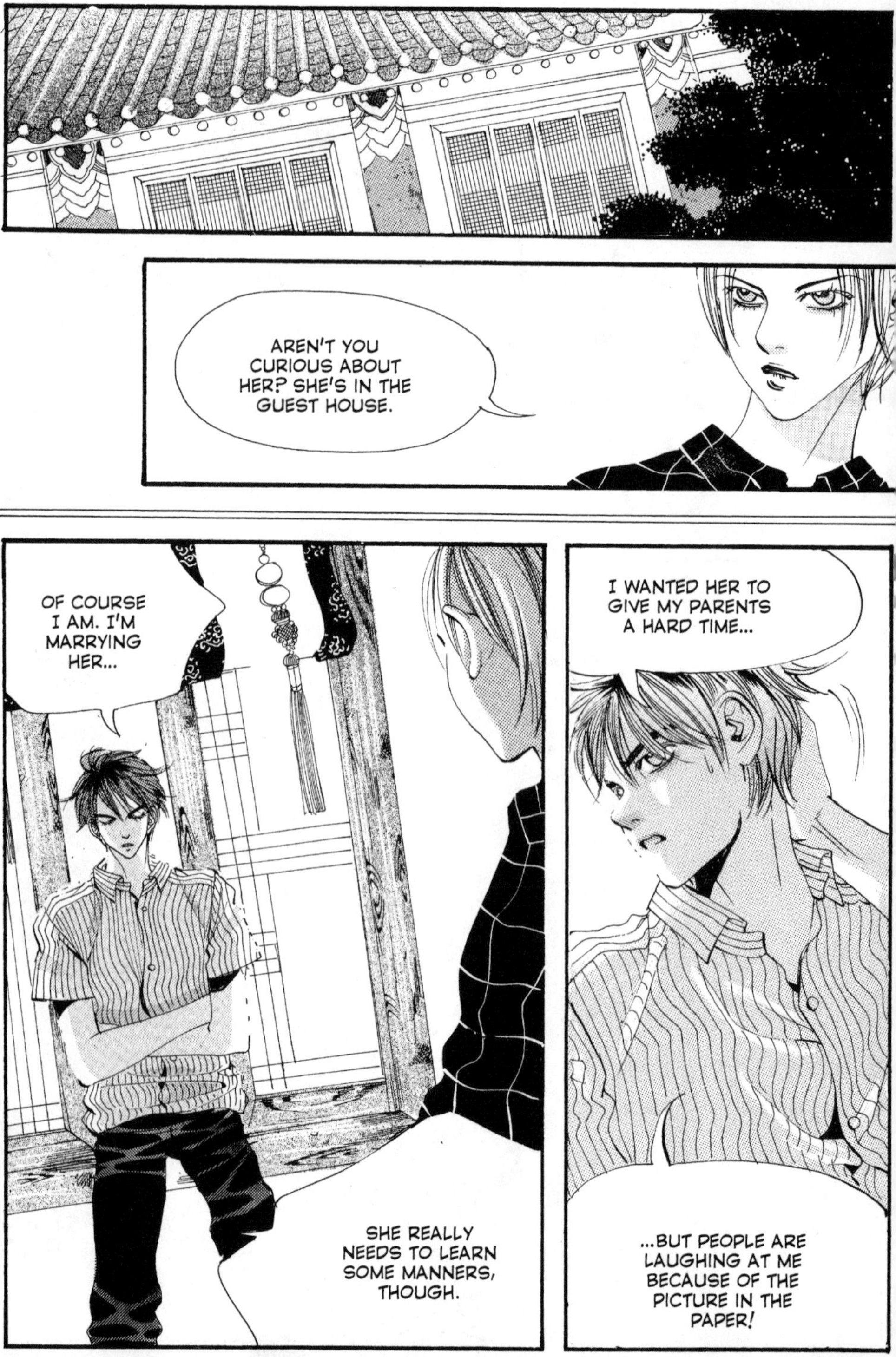
AREN'T YOU CURIOUS ABOUT HER? SHE'S IN THE GUEST HOUSE.
OF COURSE I AM. I'M MARRYING HER...
SHE REALLY NEEDS TO LEARN SOME MANNERS, THOUGH.
I WANTED HER TO GIVE MY PARENTS A HARD TIME...
...BUT PEOPLE ARE LAUGHING AT ME BECAUSE OF THE PICTURE IN THE PAPER!

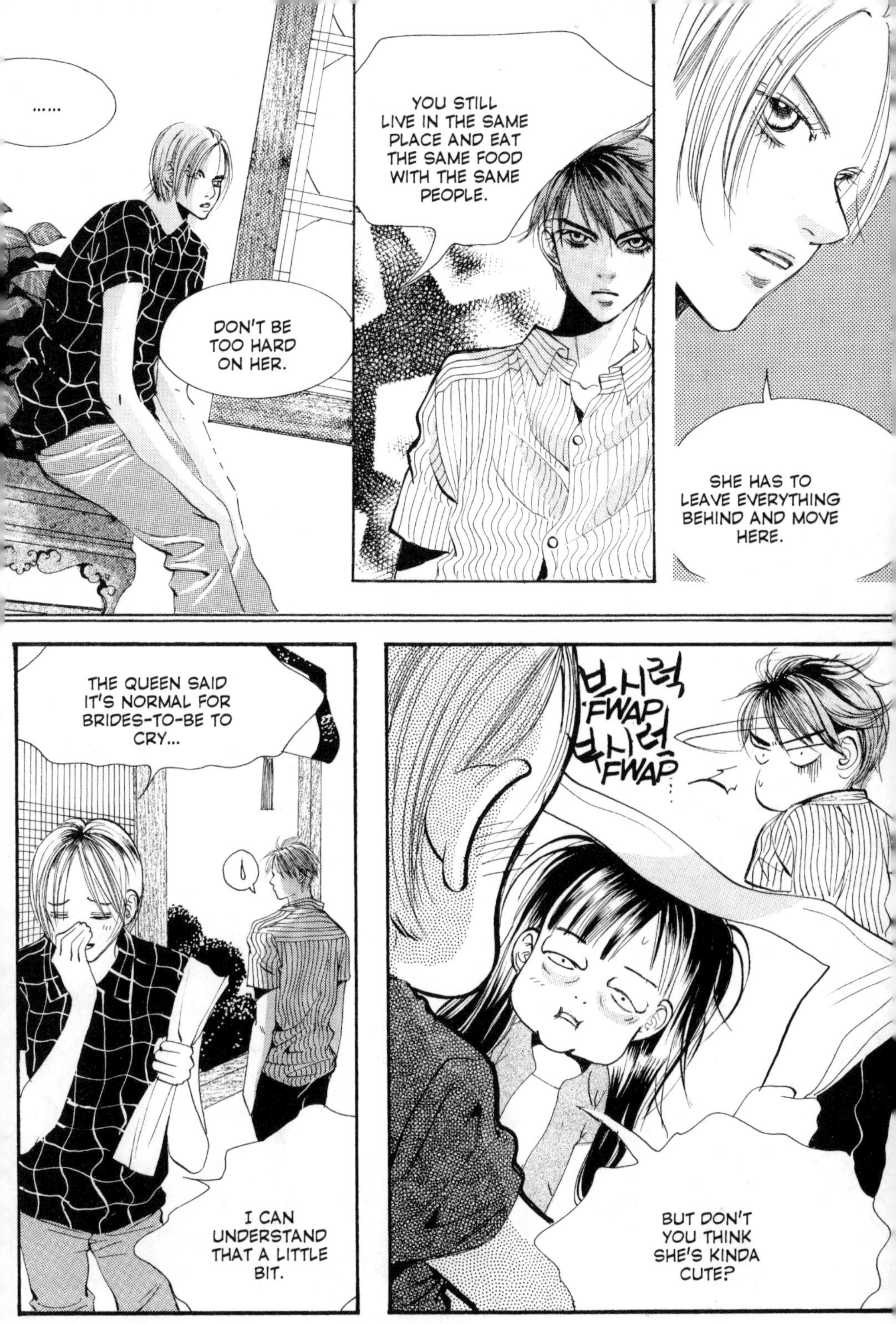
......
DON'T BE TOO HARD ON HER.
YOU STILL LIVE IN THE SAME PLACE AND EAT THE SAME FOOD WITH THE SAME PEOPLE.
SHE HAS TO LEAVE EVERYTHING BEHIND AND MOVE HERE.
THE QUEEN SAID IT'S NORMAL FOR BRIDES-TO-BE TO CRY...
!
I CAN UNDERSTAND THAT A LITTLE BIT.
부시럭
FWAP
부시럭
FWAP
BUT DON'T YOU THINK SHE'S KINDA CUTE?

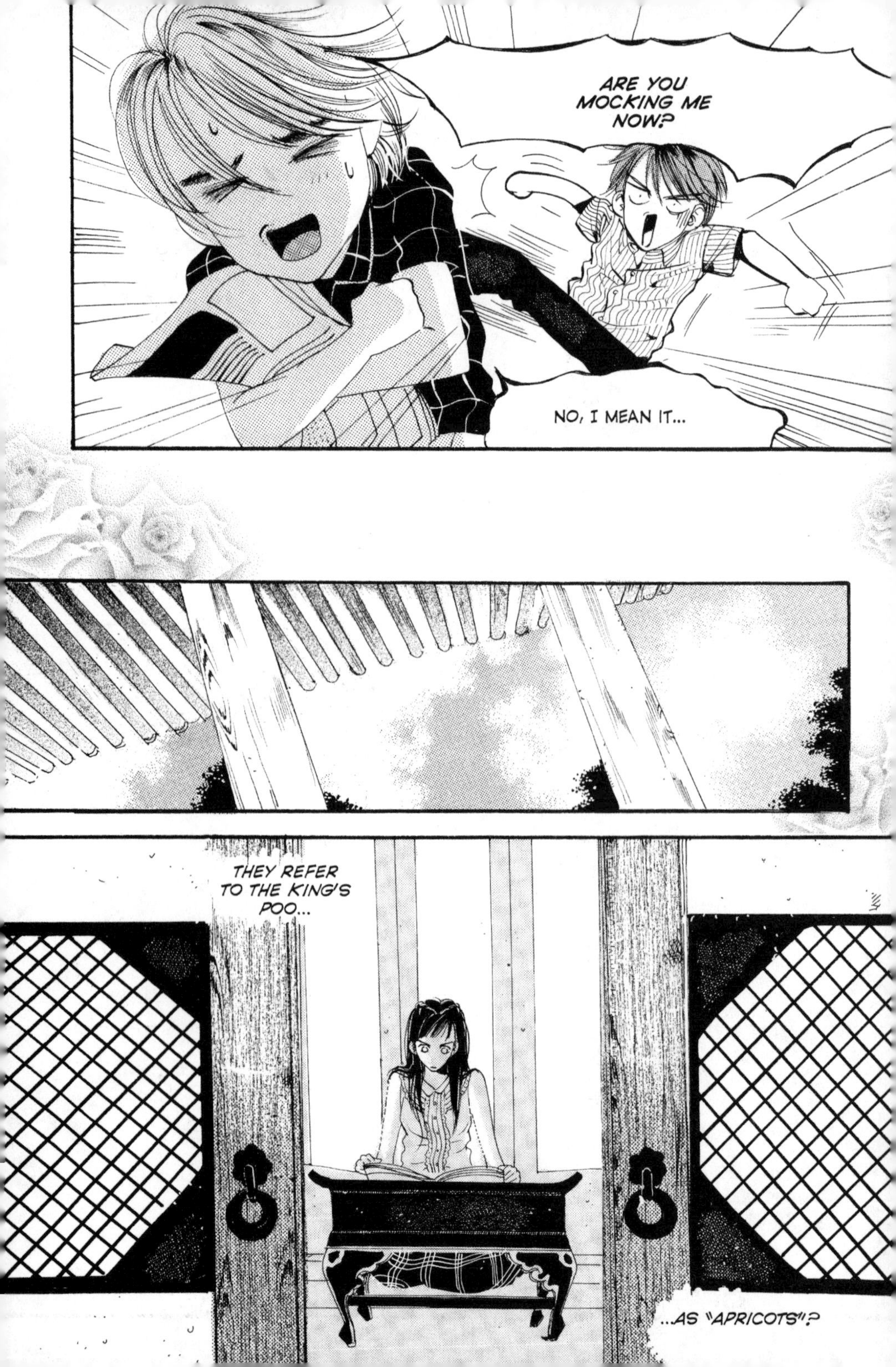
ARE YOU MOCKING ME NOW?
NO, I MEAN IT...
THEY REFER TO THE KING'S POO...
...AS "APRICOTS"?

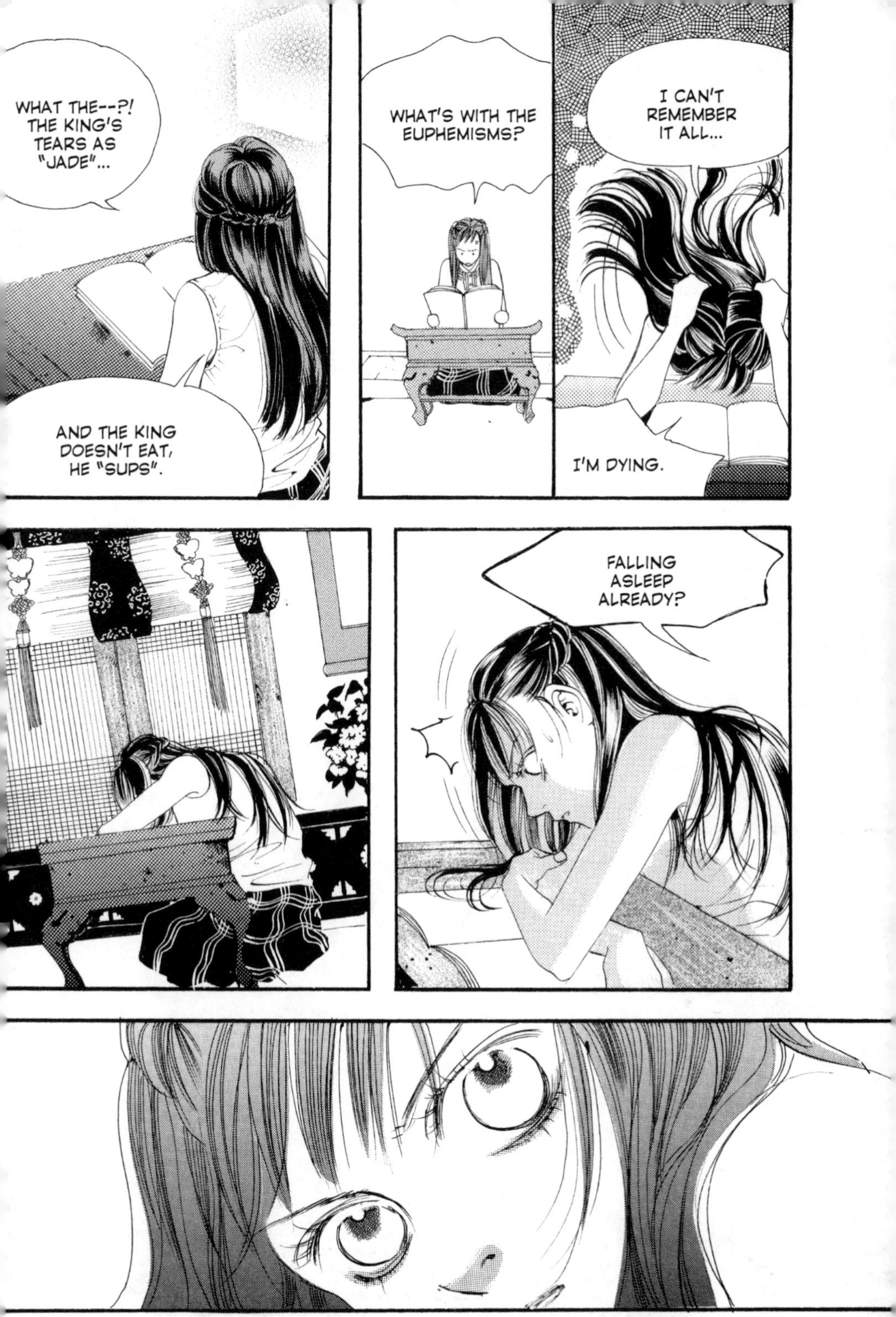
WHAT THE--?! THE KING'S TEARS AS "JADE"...
AND THE KING DOESN'T EAT, HE "SUPS".
WHAT'S WITH THE EUPHEMISMS?
I CAN'T REMEMBER IT ALL...
I'M DYING.
FALLING ASLEEP ALREADY?

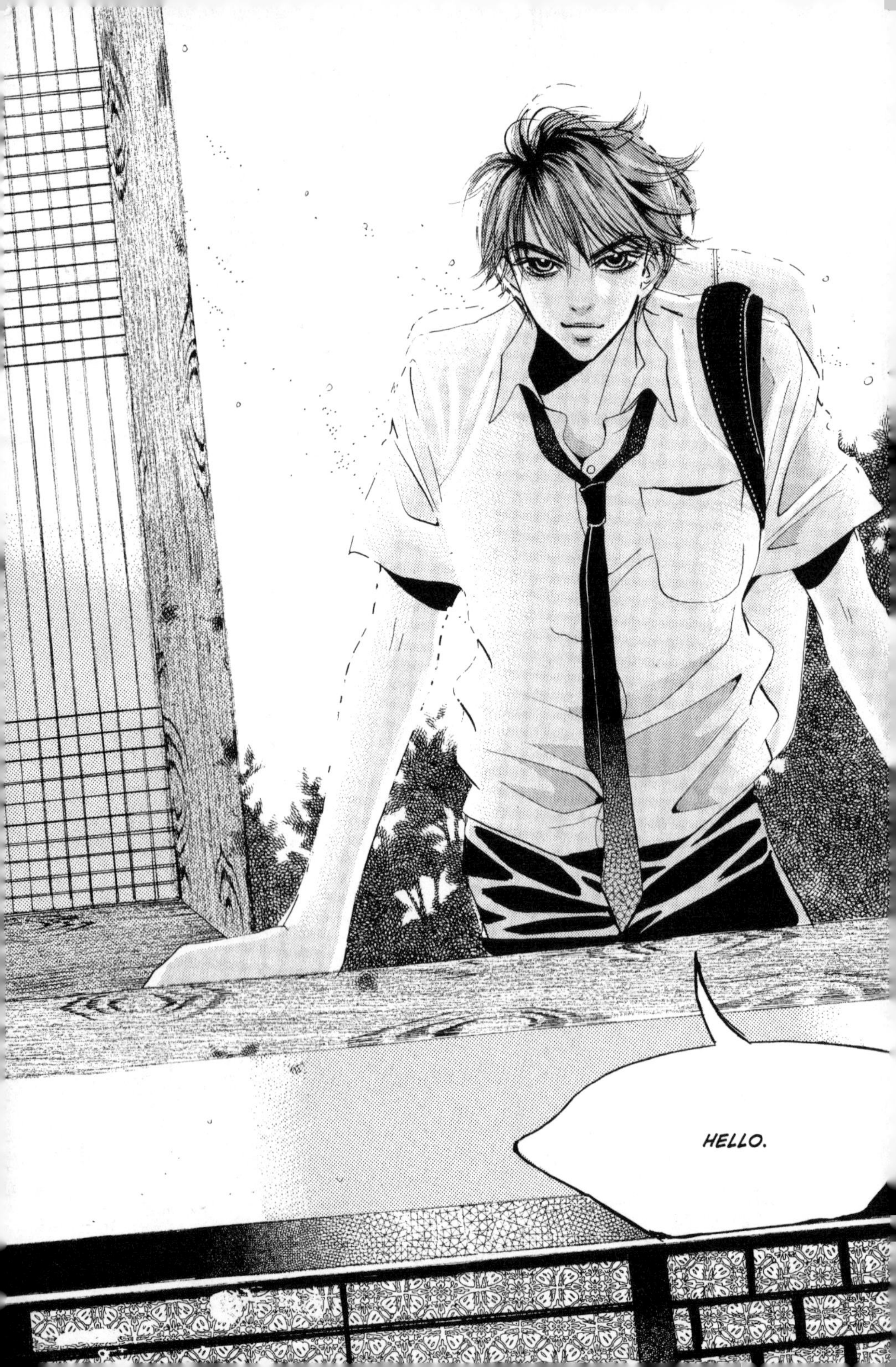
HELLO.

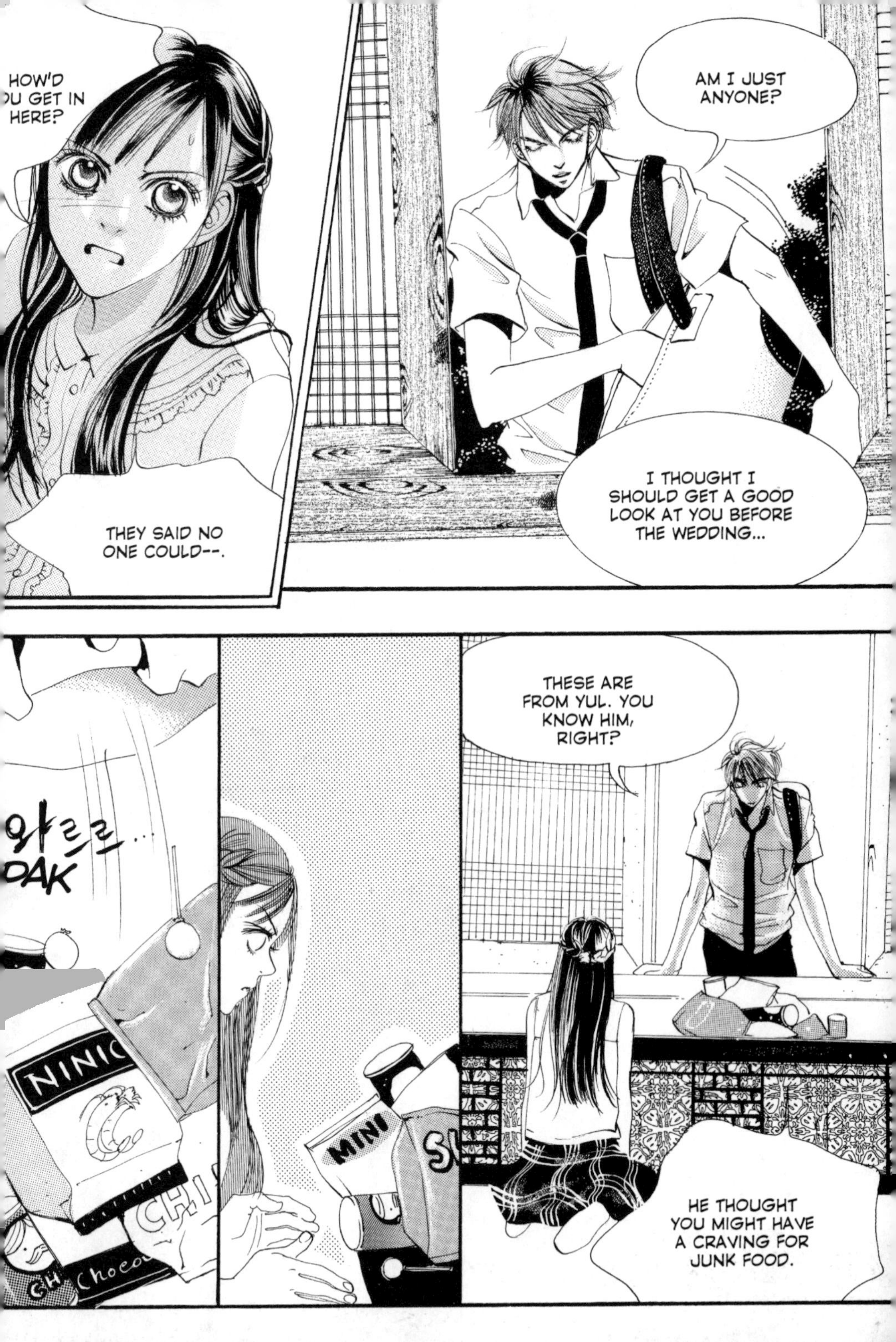
HOW'D OU GET IN HERE?
THEY SAID NO ONE COULD--.
AM I JUST ANYONE?
I THOUGHT I SHOULD GET A GOOD LOOK AT YOU BEFORE THE WEDDING...
와르르...
DAK
THESE ARE FROM YUL. YOU KNOW HIM, RIGHT?
HE THOUGHT YOU MIGHT HAVE A CRAVING FOR JUNK FOOD.

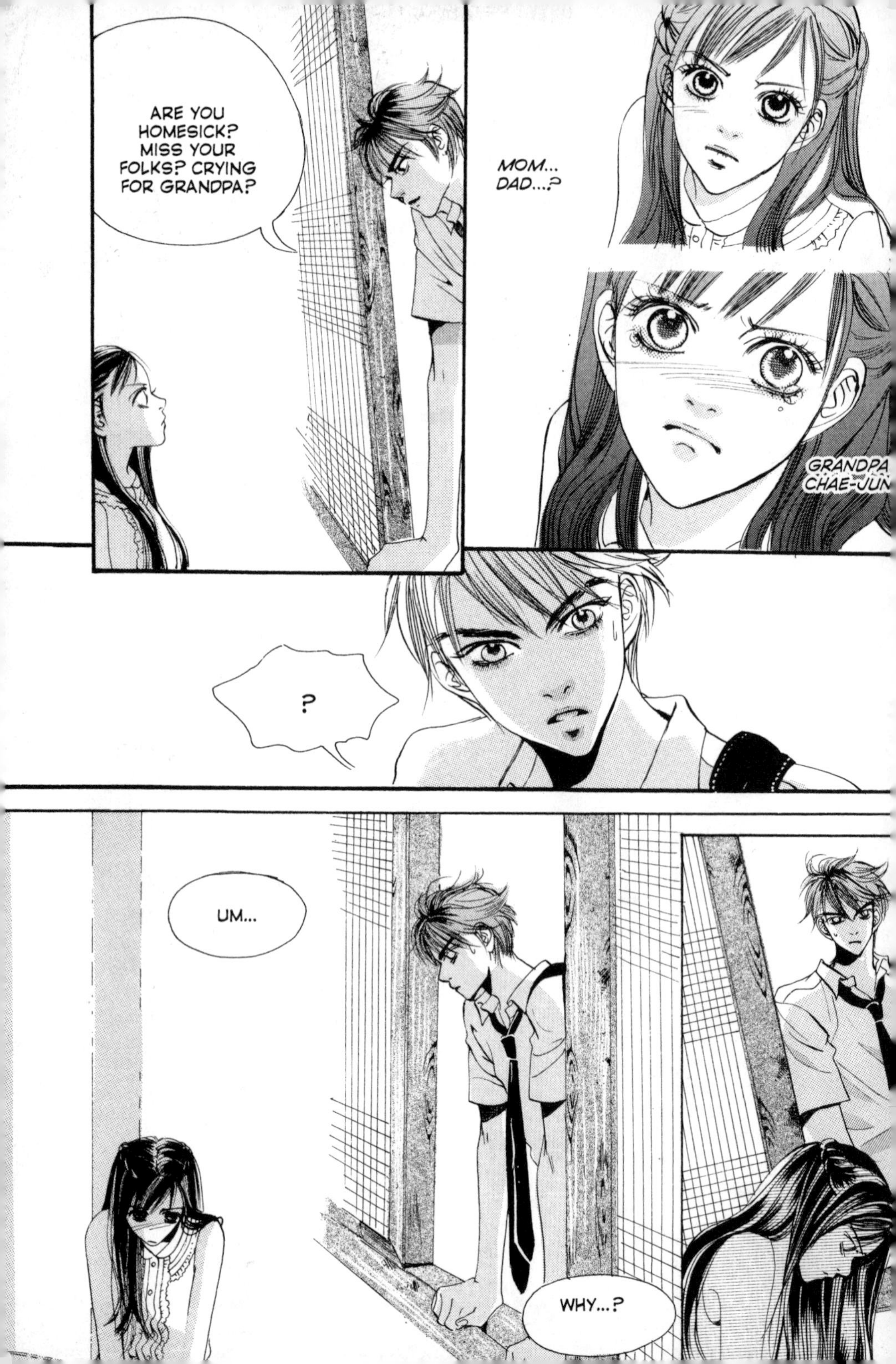
ARE YOU HOMESICK? MISS YOUR FOLKS? CRYING FOR GRANDPA?
MOM... DAD...?
GRANDPA CHAE-JUN
?
UM...
WHY...?

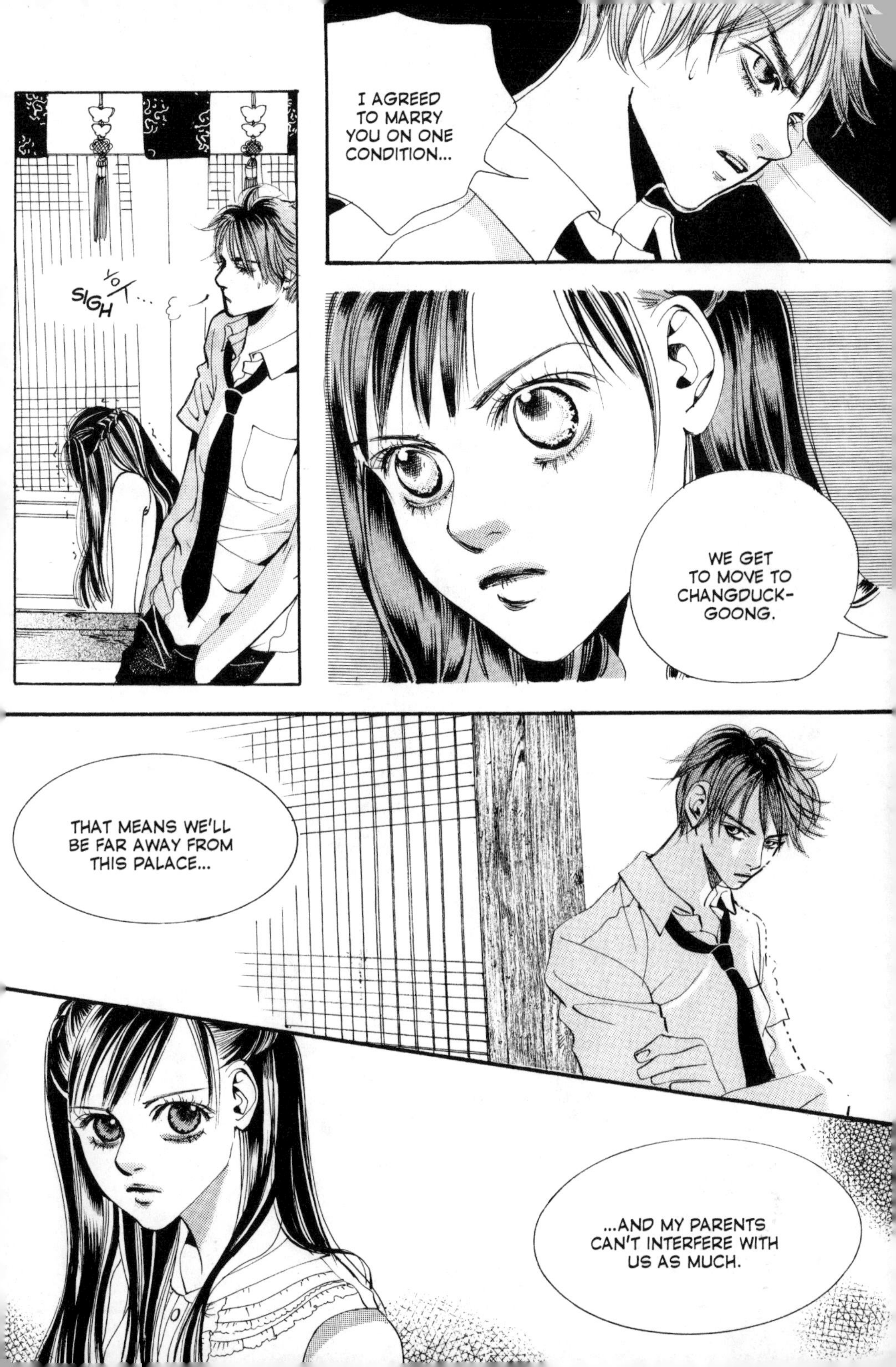
SIGH
I AGREED TO MARRY YOU ON ONE CONDITION...
WE GET TO MOVE TO CHANGDUCK-GOONG.
THAT MEANS WE'LL BE FAR AWAY FROM THIS PALACE...
...AND MY PARENTS CAN'T INTERFERE WITH US AS MUCH.

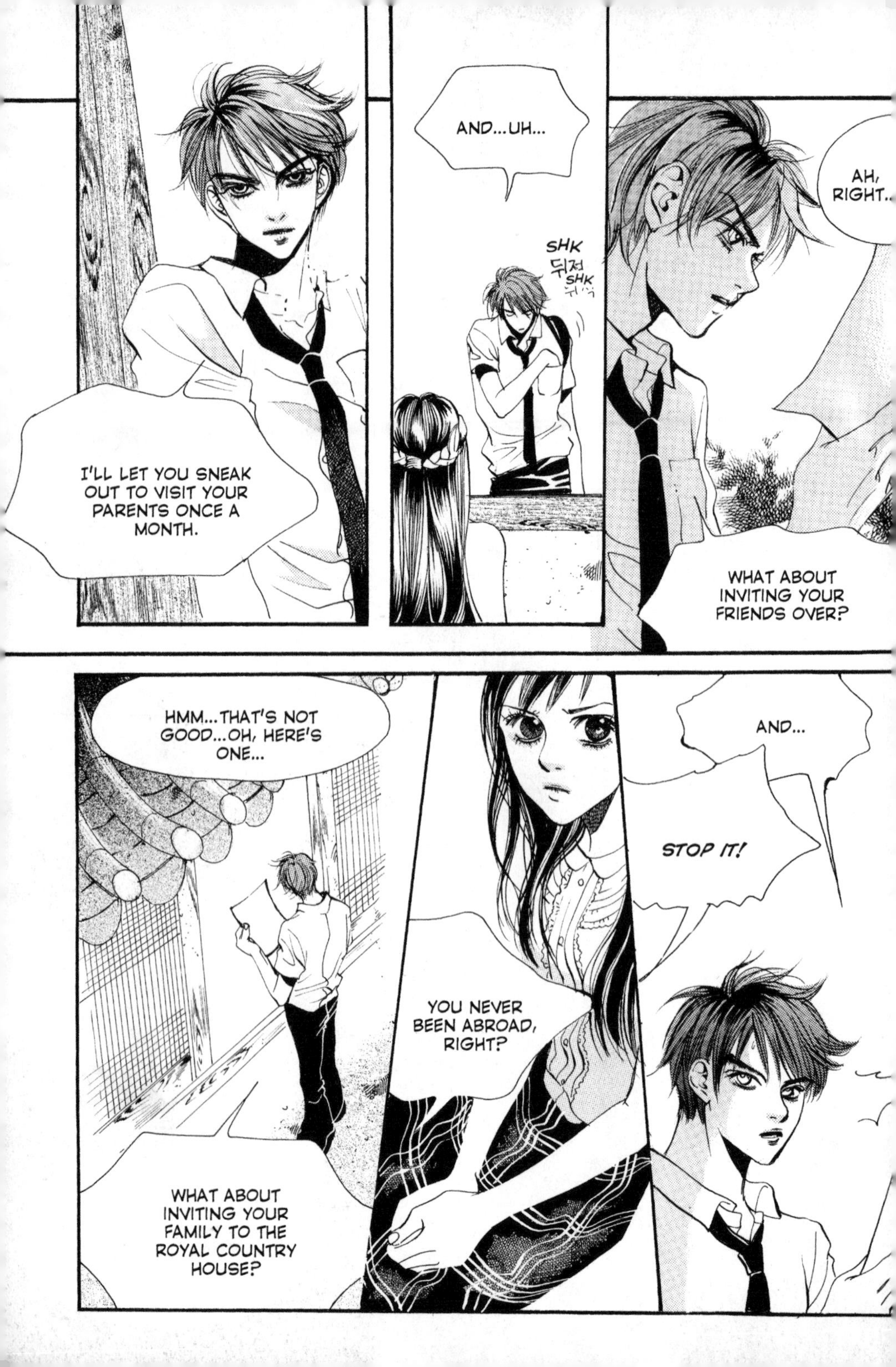
I'LL LET YOU SNEAK OUT TO VISIT YOUR PARENTS ONCE A MONTH.
AND...UH...
SHK
뒤적
SHK
AH, RIGHT..
WHAT ABOUT INVITING YOUR FRIENDS OVER?
HMM...THAT'S NOT GOOD...OH, HERE'S ONE...
WHAT ABOUT INVITING YOUR FAMILY TO THE ROYAL COUNTRY HOUSE?
YOU NEVER BEEN ABROAD, RIGHT?
AND...
STOP IT!

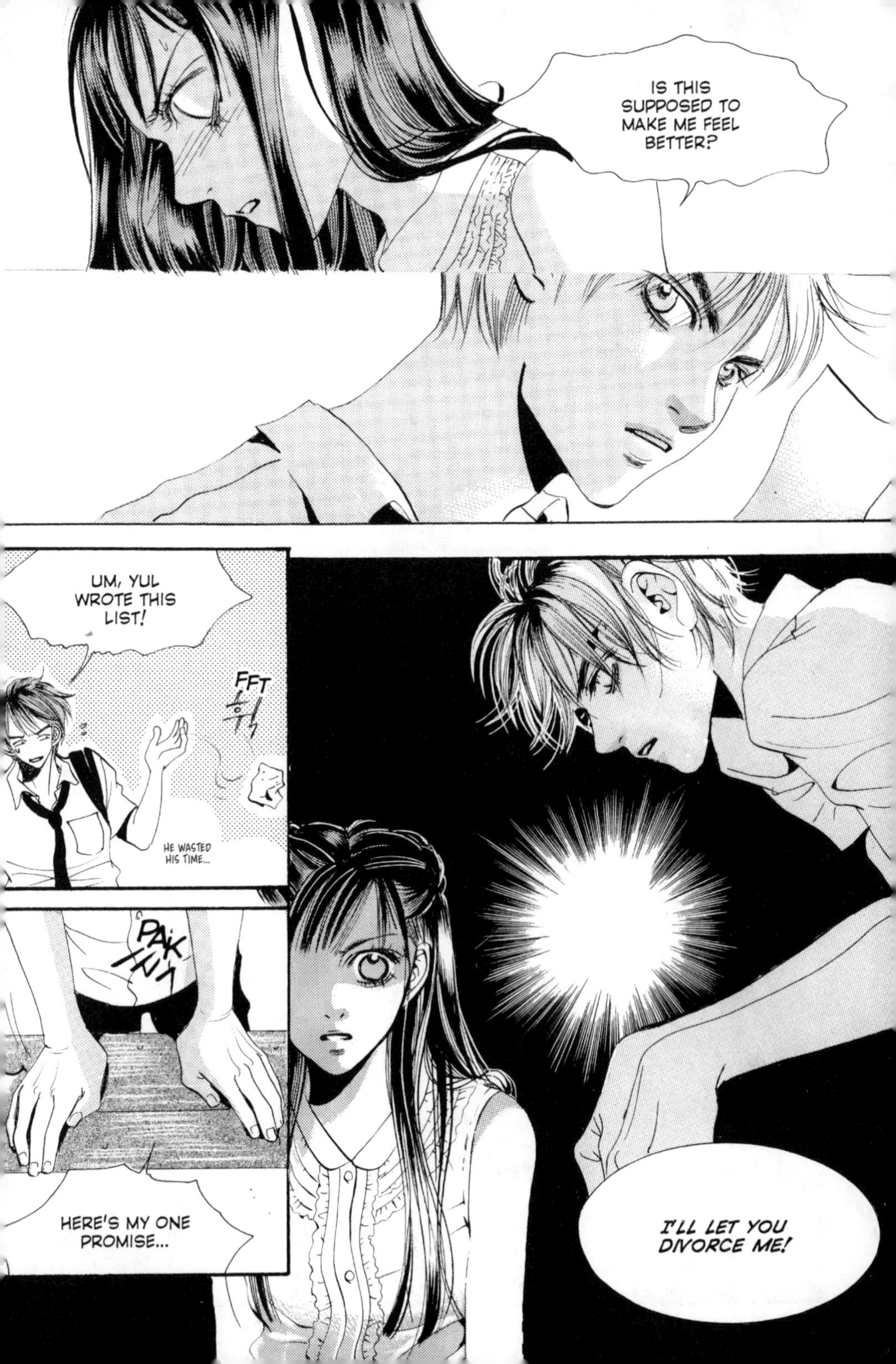
IS THIS SUPPOSED TO MAKE ME FEEL BETTER?
UM, YUL WROTE THIS LIST!
FFT
HE WASTED HIS TIME...
PAK
HERE'S MY ONE PROMISE...
I'LL LET YOU DIVORCE ME!

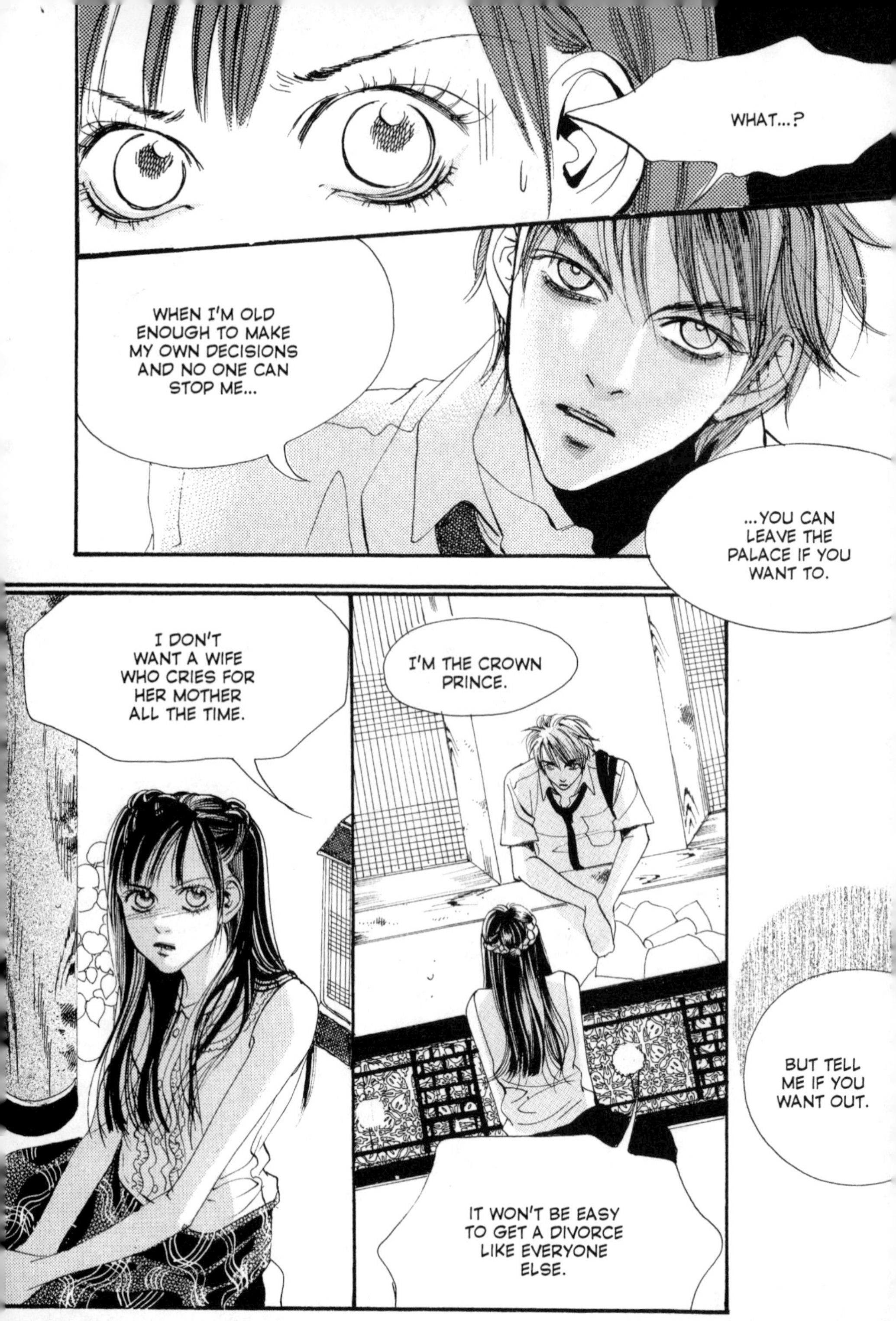
WHAT...?
WHEN I'M OLD ENOUGH TO MAKE MY OWN DECISIONS AND NO ONE CAN STOP ME...
...YOU CAN LEAVE THE PALACE IF YOU WANT TO.
I DON'T WANT A WIFE WHO CRIES FOR HER MOTHER ALL THE TIME.
I'M THE CROWN PRINCE.
IT WON'T BE EASY TO GET A DIVORCE LIKE EVERYONE ELSE.
BUT TELL ME IF YOU WANT OUT.

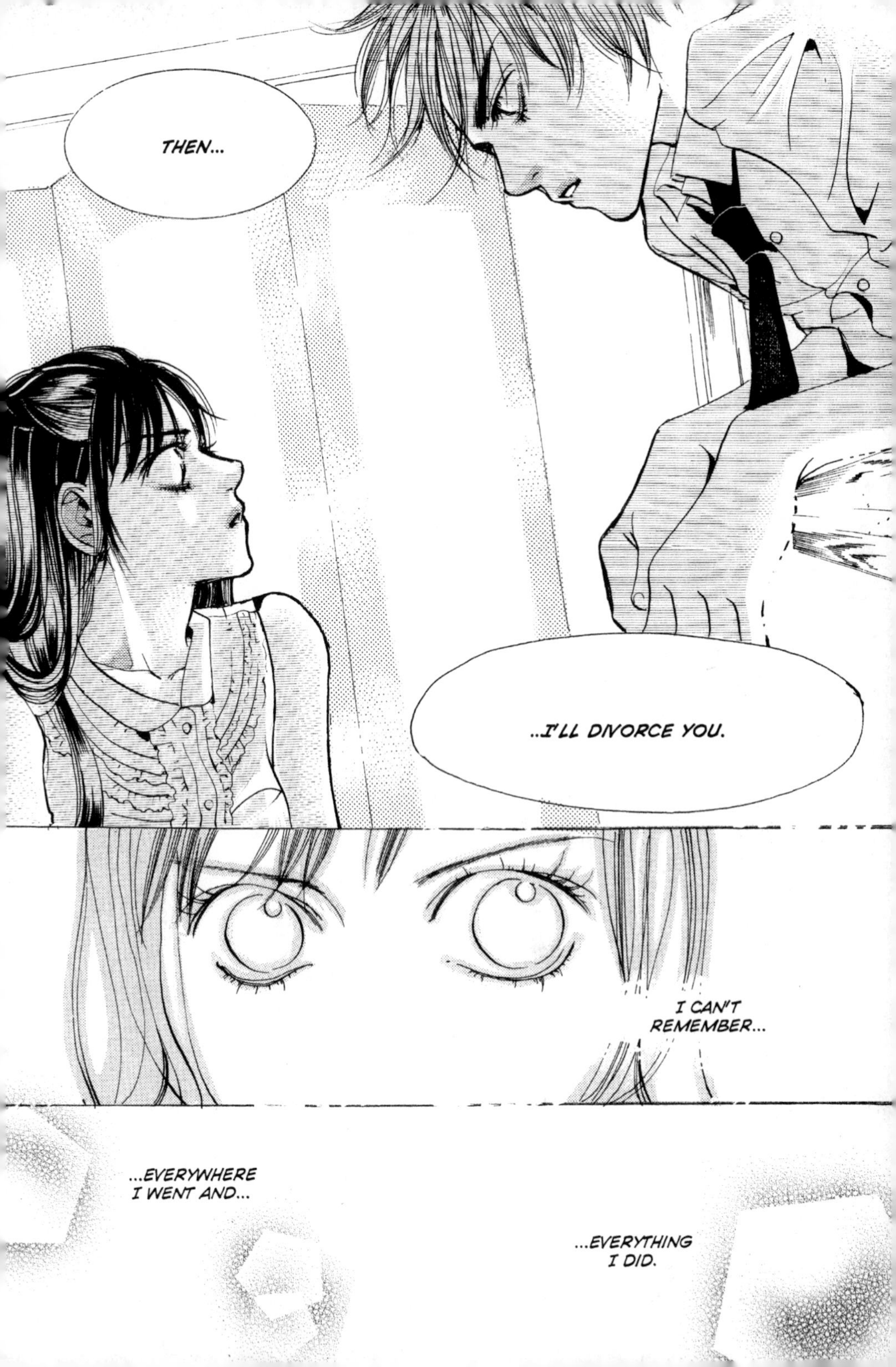
THEN...
..I'LL DIVORCE YOU.
I CAN'T REMEMBER...
...EVERYWHERE I WENT AND...
...EVERYTHING I DID.

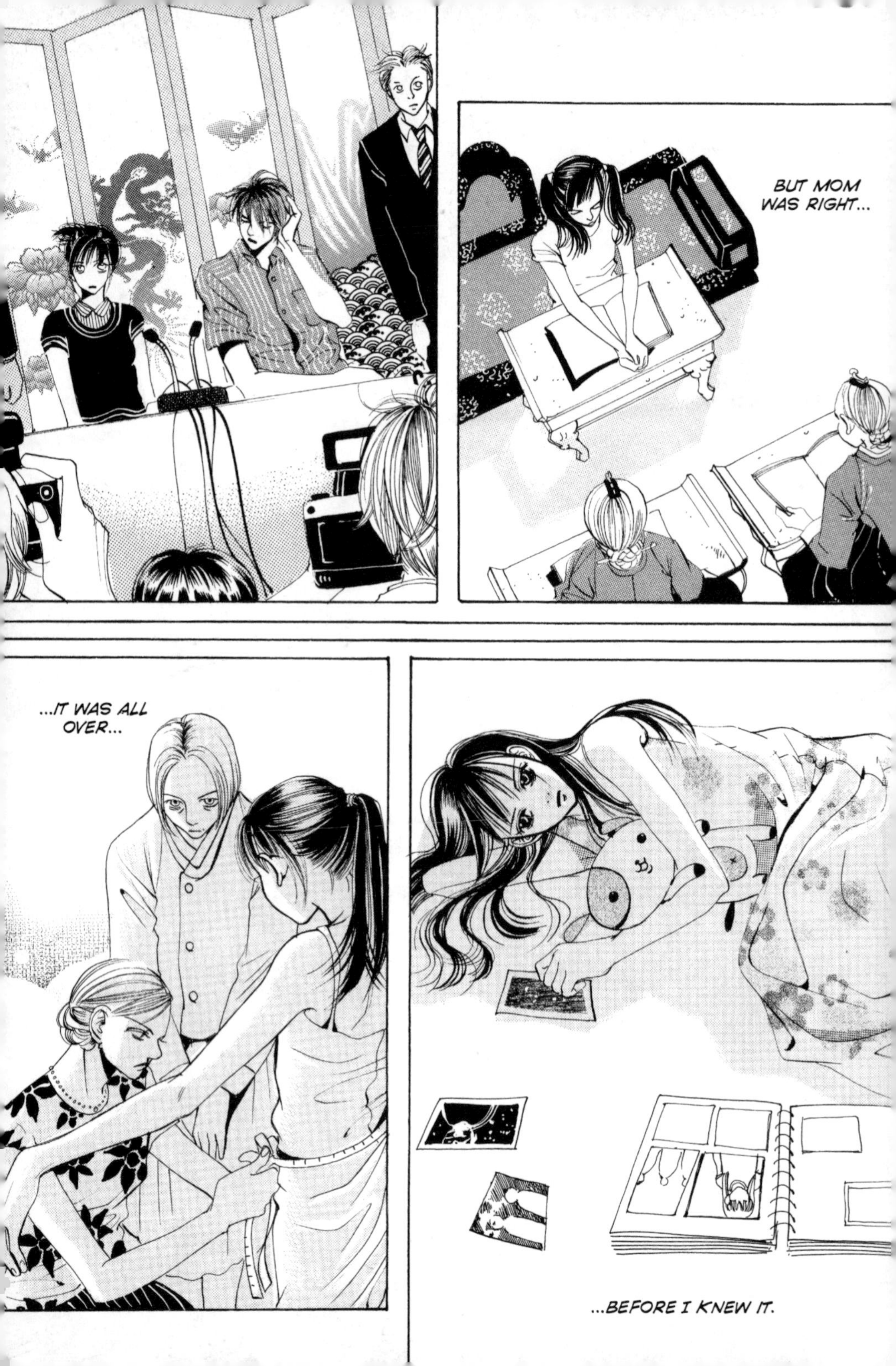
BUT MOM WAS RIGHT...
...IT WAS ALL OVER...
...BEFORE I KNEW IT.

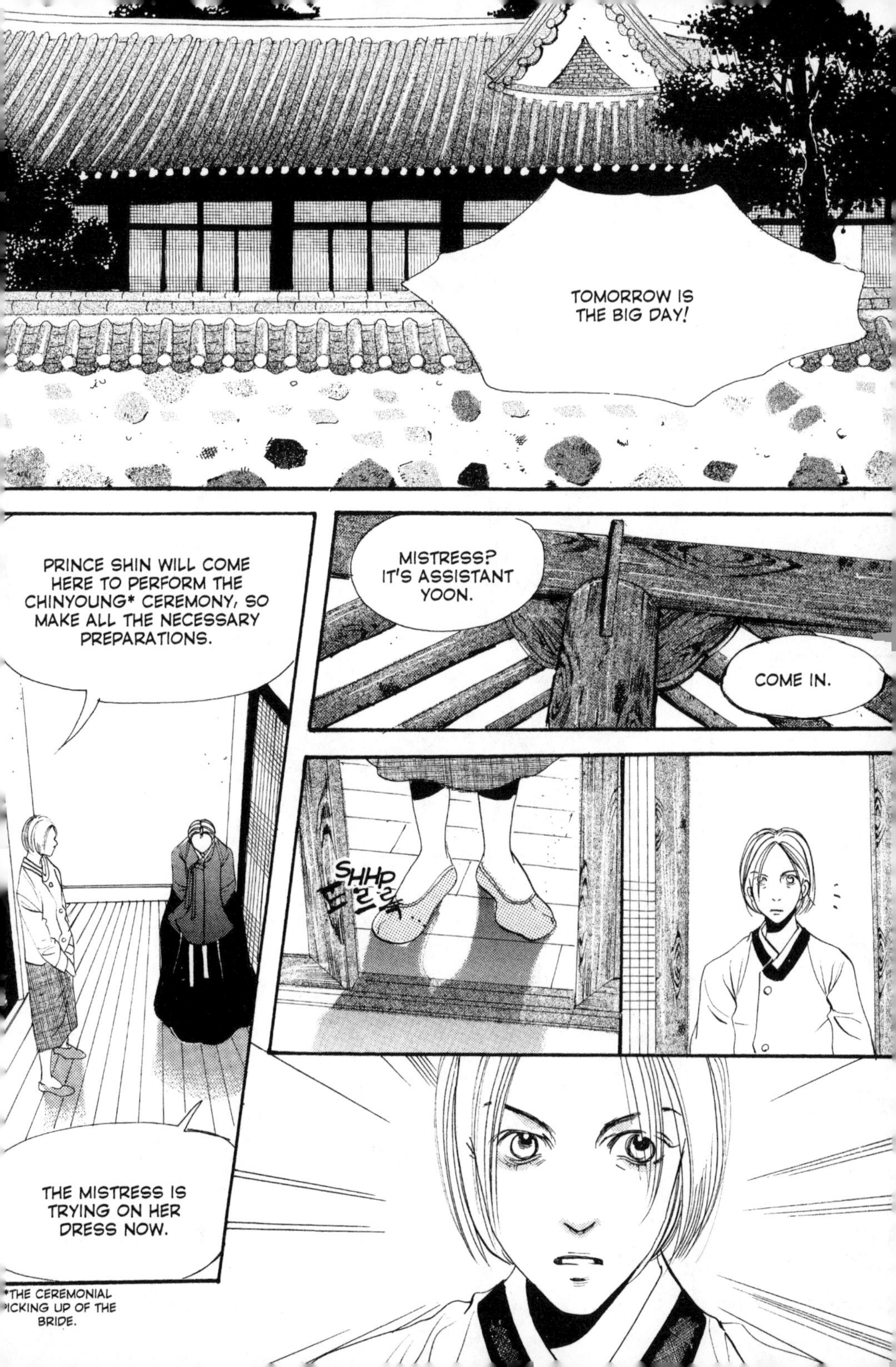
TOMORROW IS THE BIG DAY!
PRINCE SHIN WILL COME HERE TO PERFORM THE CHINYOUNG* CEREMONY, SO MAKE ALL THE NECESSARY PREPARATIONS.
THE MISTRESS IS TRYING ON HER DRESS NOW.
MISTRESS? IT'S ASSISTANT YOON.
COME IN.
SHHP

*THE CEREMONIAL PICKING UP OF THE BRIDE.

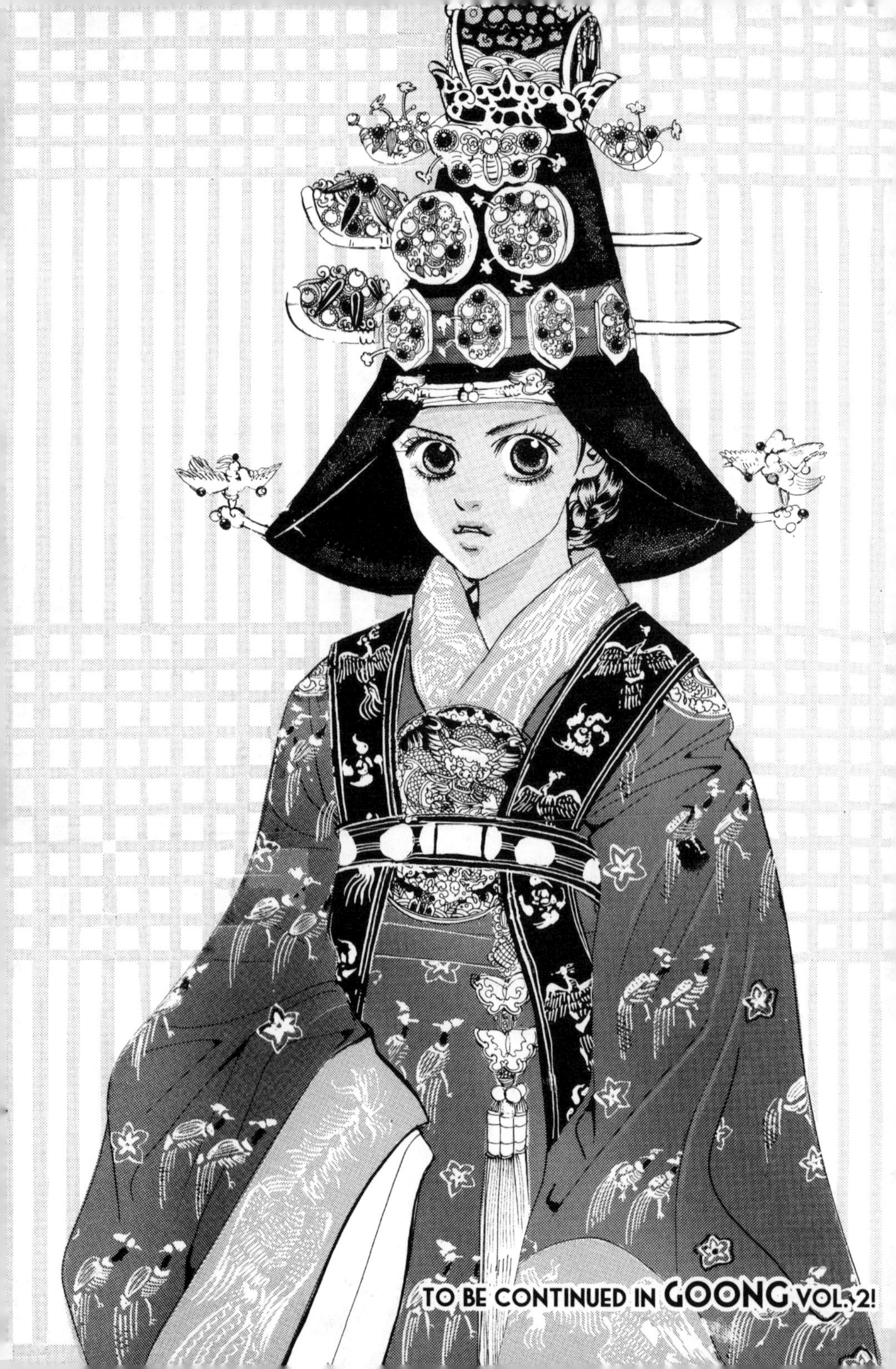
TO BE CONTINUED IN GOONG VOL. 2!

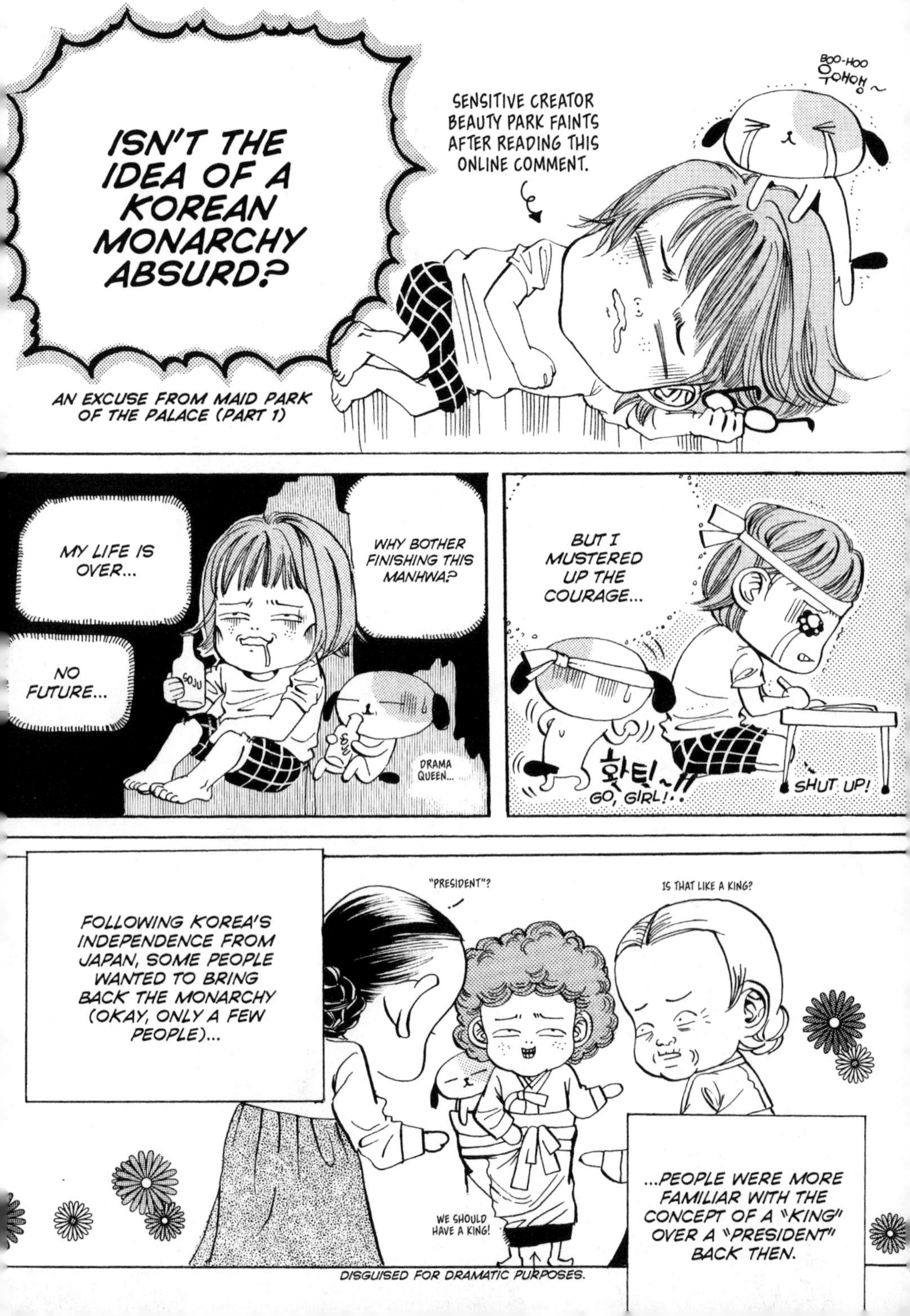
ISN'T THE IDEA OF A KOREAN MONARCHY ABSURD?
AN EXCUSE FROM MAID PARK OF THE PALACE (PART 1)
SENSITIVE CREATOR BEAUTY PARK FAINTS AFTER READING THIS ONLINE COMMENT.
BOO-HOO
MY LIFE IS OVER...
NO FUTURE...
SOJU
WHY BOTHER FINISHING THIS MANHWA?
DRAMA QUEEN...
BUT I MUSTERED UP THE COURAGE...
화팅!~!!
GO, GIRL!
SHUT UP!
FOLLOWING KOREA'S INDEPENDENCE FROM JAPAN, SOME PEOPLE WANTED TO BRING BACK THE MONARCHY (OKAY, ONLY A FEW PEOPLE)...
"PRESIDENT"?
WE SHOULD HAVE A KING!
IS THAT LIKE A KING?
...PEOPLE WERE MORE FAMILIAR WITH THE CONCEPT OF A "KING" OVER A "PRESIDENT" BACK THEN.
DISGUISED FOR DRAMATIC PURPOSES.

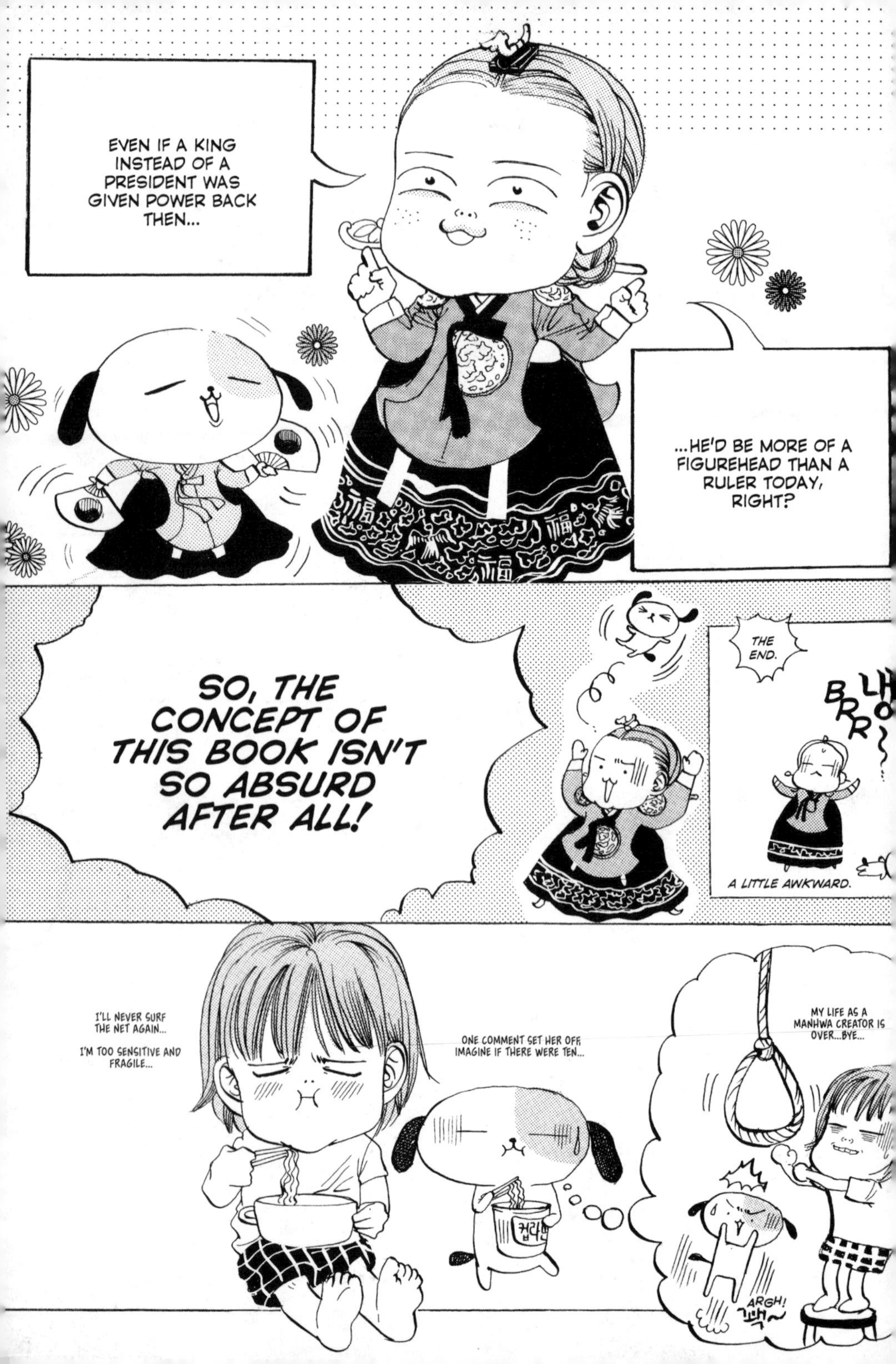
EVEN IF A KING INSTEAD OF A PRESIDENT WAS GIVEN POWER BACK THEN...
...HE'D BE MORE OF A FIGUREHEAD THAN A RULER TODAY, RIGHT?
SO, THE CONCEPT OF THIS BOOK ISN'T SO ABSURD AFTER ALL!
THE END.
BRRR~
A LITTLE AWKWARD.
I'LL NEVER SURF THE NET AGAIN...
I'M TOO SENSITIVE AND FRAGILE...
ONE COMMENT SET HER OFF, IMAGINE IF THERE WERE TEN...
컵라면
MY LIFE AS A MANHWA CREATOR IS OVER...BYE...
ARGH!

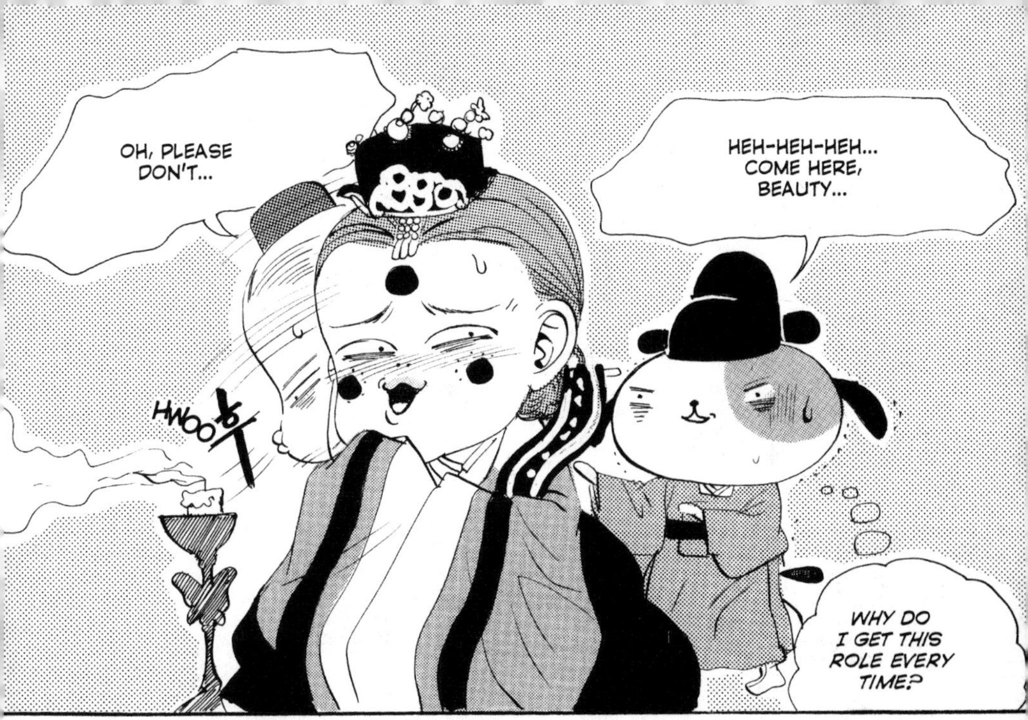
OH, PLEASE DON'T...
HEH-HEH-HEH... COME HERE, BEAUTY...
HWOO
WHY DO I GET THIS ROLE EVERY TIME?

MAID PARK OF THE PALACE REMEMBERS...

AN EXCUSE FROM MAID PARK OF THE PALACE (PART 2)

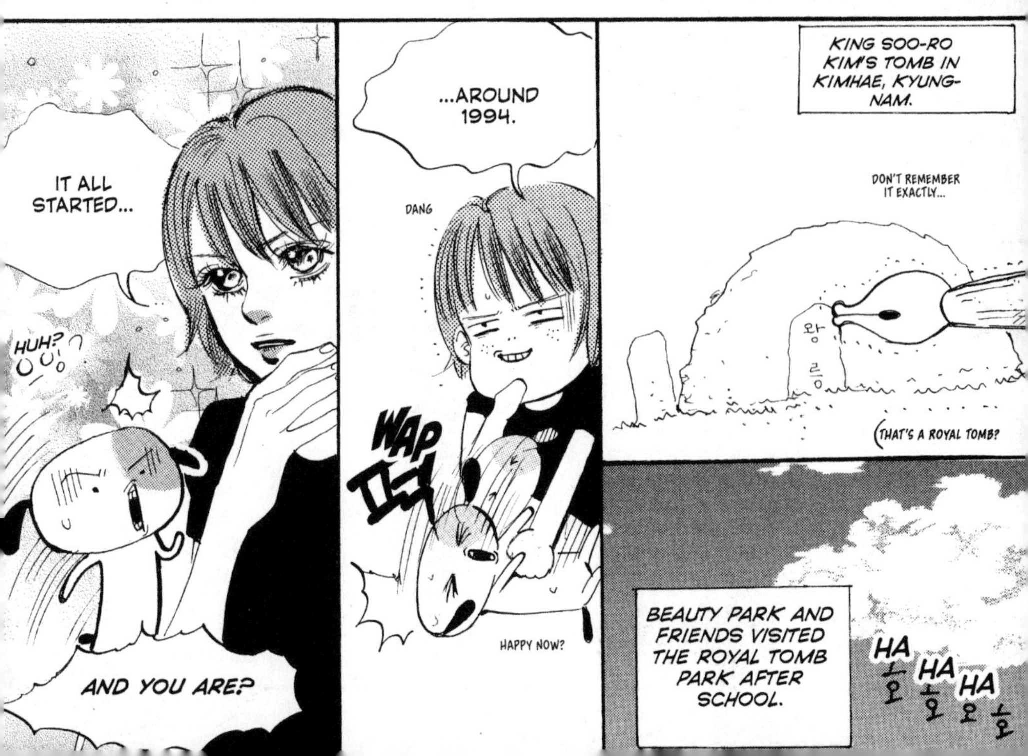
IT ALL STARTED...
HUH?
AND YOU ARE?
...AROUND 1994.
DANG
WAP
HAPPY NOW?
KING SOO-RO KIM'S TOMB IN KIMHAE, KYUNG-NAM.
DON'T REMEMBER IT EXACTLY...
왕릉
(THAT'S A ROYAL TOMB?
BEAUTY PARK AND FRIENDS VISITED THE ROYAL TOMB PARK AFTER SCHOOL.
HA HA HA

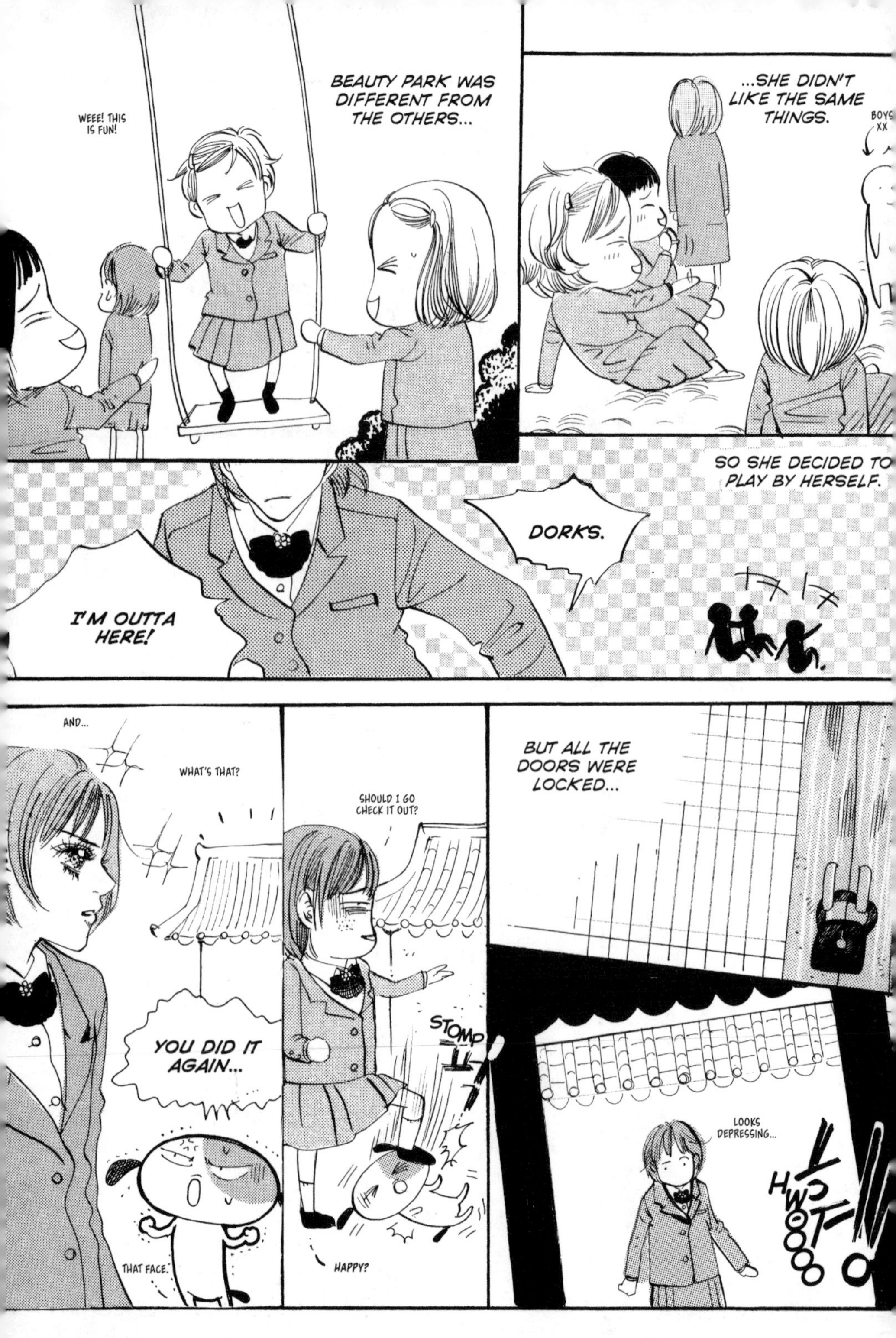
BEAUTY PARK WAS DIFFERENT FROM THE OTHERS...
WEEE! THIS IS FUN!
...SHE DIDN'T LIKE THE SAME THINGS.
BOYS XX
I'M OUTTA HERE!
DORKS.
SO SHE DECIDED TO PLAY BY HERSELF.
AND...
WHAT'S THAT?
YOU DID IT AGAIN...
THAT FACE.
SHOULD I GO CHECK IT OUT?
STOMP
HAPPY?
BUT ALL THE DOORS WERE LOCKED...
LOOKS DEPRESSING...

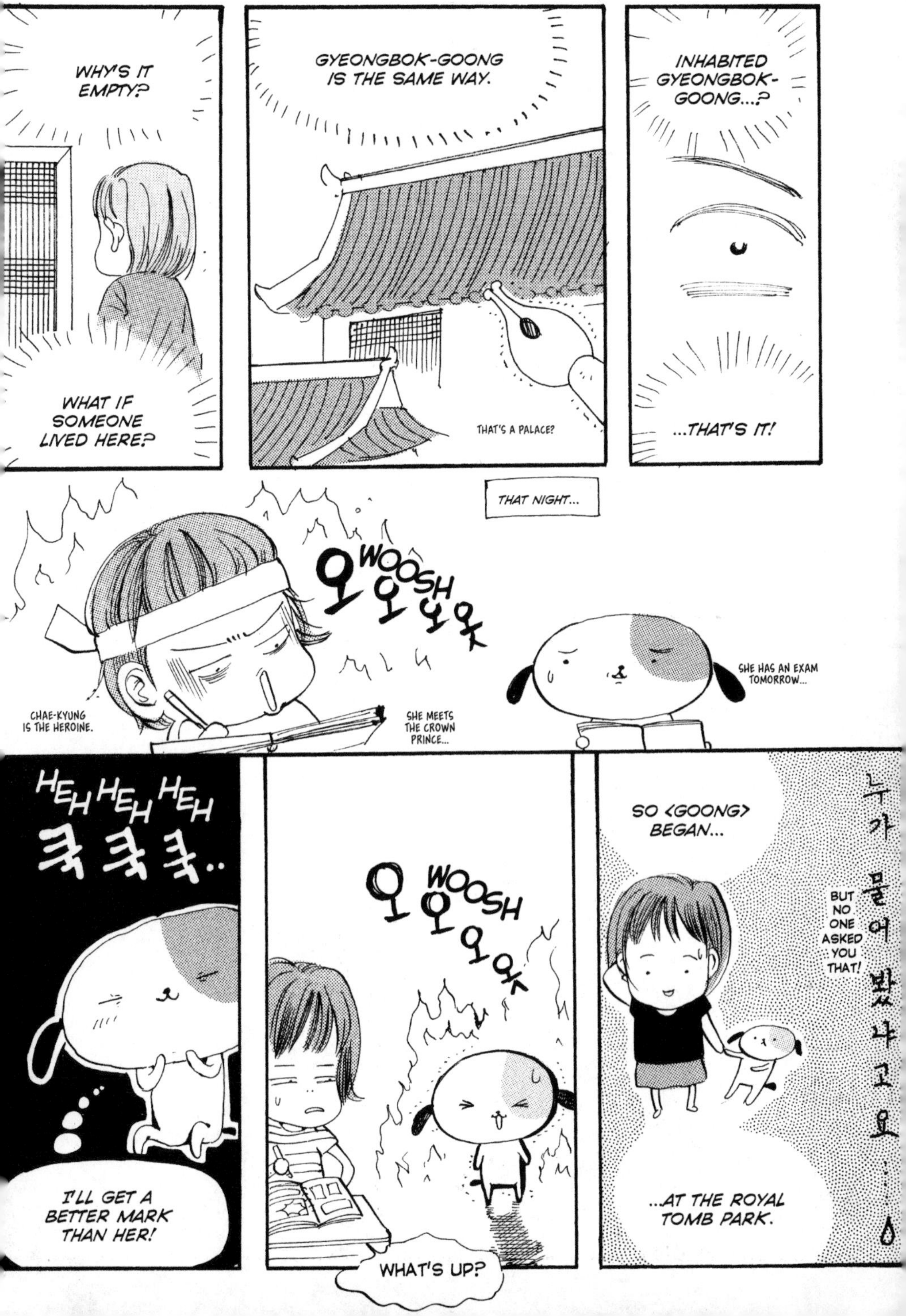
WHY'S IT EMPTY?
WHAT IF SOMEONE LIVED HERE?
GYEONGBOK-GOONG IS THE SAME WAY.
THAT'S A PALACE?
INHABITED GYEONGBOK-GOONG...?
...THAT'S IT!
THAT NIGHT...
CHAE-KYUNG IS THE HEROINE.
오오오옷
WOOSH
SHE MEETS THE CROWN PRINCE...
SHE HAS AN EXAM TOMORROW...
HEH HEH HEH
쿡쿡쿡..
I'LL GET A BETTER MARK THAN HER!
오오오옷
WOOSH
WHAT'S UP?
SO <GOONG> BEGAN...
...AT THE ROYAL TOMB PARK.
BUT NO ONE ASKED YOU THAT!
누가 물어 봤냐고요...

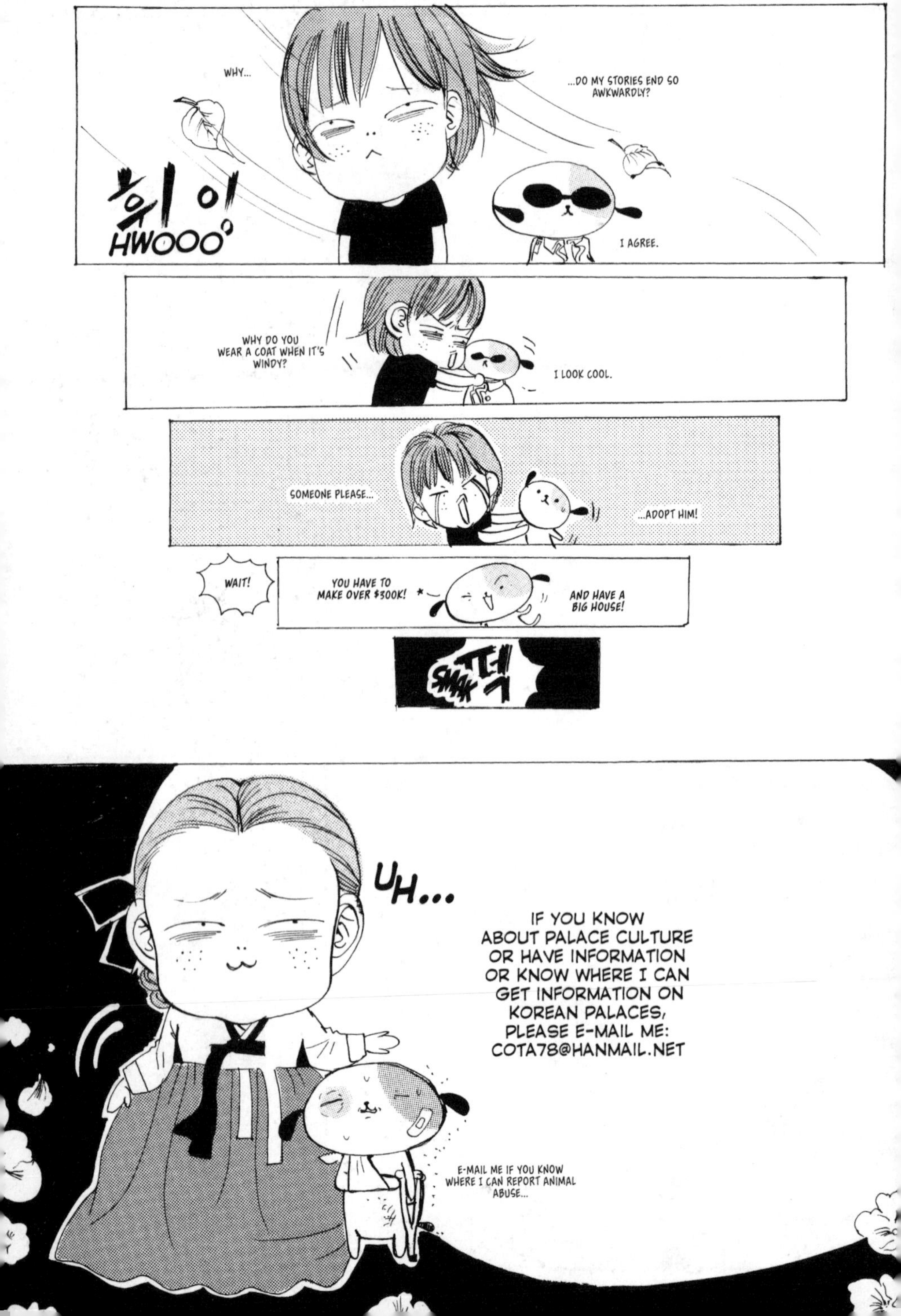
WHY...
...DO MY STORIES END SO AWKWARDLY?
휘이
HWOOO
I AGREE.
WHY DO YOU WEAR A COAT WHEN IT'S WINDY?
I LOOK COOL.
SOMEONE PLEASE...
...ADOPT HIM!
WAIT!
YOU HAVE TO MAKE OVER $300K!
AND HAVE A BIG HOUSE!
SMAK
UH...
IF YOU KNOW ABOUT PALACE CULTURE OR HAVE INFORMATION OR KNOW WHERE I CAN GET INFORMATION ON KOREAN PALACES, PLEASE E-MAIL ME: COTA78@HANMAIL.NET
E-MAIL ME IF YOU KNOW WHERE I CAN REPORT ANIMAL ABUSE...

Getting Personal
Interview with the Creator

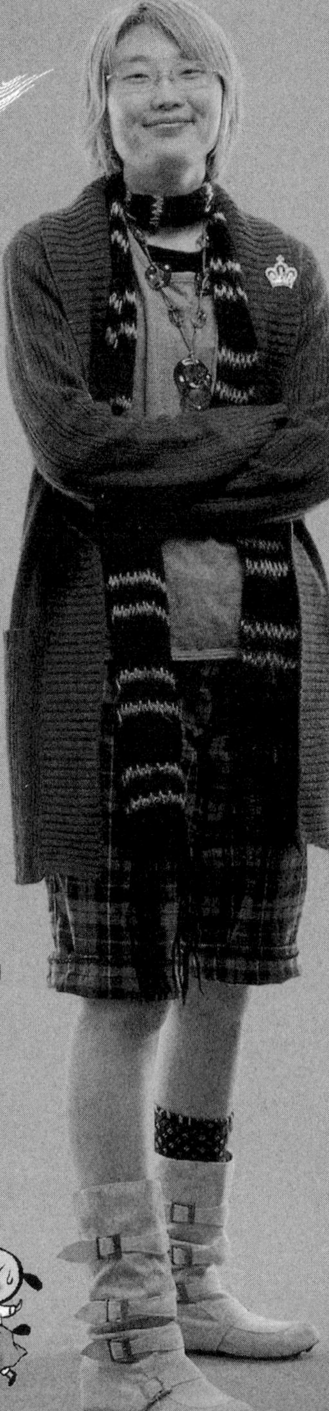

Section 1 *The Creator : So-Hee Park*

How did you become a manhwa creator?
Simple: because I love manhwa. There was no specific reason. It's because my life has been led the way that I can draw and write manhwa as much as I want. My major in college was manhwa and I debuted after winning a new manhwa creator contest.

Does your personal experience influence your work?
I think about half of my experiences influence my work. Not only my experiences but also my thoughts or reactions to certain things influence the main characters in my books.

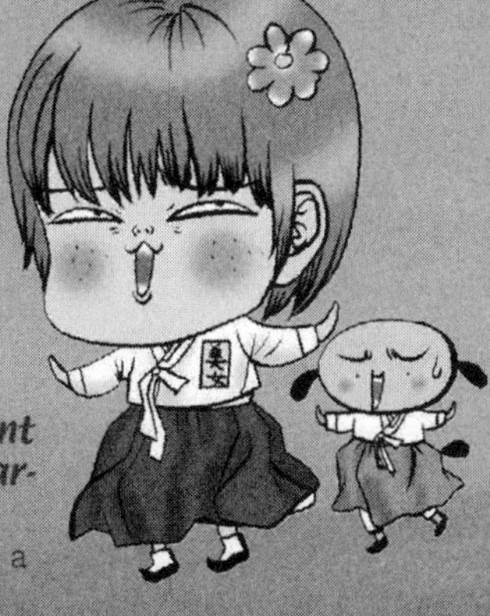

What is the most important thing when you draw a character?
Readers not only read but also see a

comic book, so the drawing has to look good. Like most manhwa creators, I am obsessed with drawing beautiful stuff. I try to draw characters that I think are beautiful. But I also try to write the character's dialogue and make them act realistically in a given situation.

Where do you get ideas from when you create a new manhwa?

My ideas come from different places, including books, TV shows, the Internet, my life and so on. Especially good ideas come to mind while I sleep.

Which of your works are you the most proud of?

I always love the most the one I'm working on now. For that reason, I love ⟨Goong - The Royal Palace⟩ and I hope I can make it as good as possible.

Do you have a specific procedure when you work?

I have no specific order when I work. I do sketches one minute but I do toning and inking the next minute. My working style is all over the place.

What creator do you respect and who

influenced you the most?

I respect all the manhwa creators who came before me. If I have to name one, it's Kyung-Ok Kang. I was so impressed by her art when I was young. And I was so touched by the characters and dialogue in her manhwa and her writing style. Kamizo Astushi from Japan was an influence on me when I became an adult.

What is the meaning of manhwa to you?

Manhwa is rice to me. It is not only my way of making a living but also something that feeds and moves me.

Section 2 *The Book : ⟨Goong - The Royal Palace⟩*

You have been working on ⟨Goong - The Royal Palace⟩ for ⟨Wink⟩ magazine since July 2002. What's the most difficult thing working on one title for a long time?

I'm always tired physically because the magazine is bi-weekly. Sometimes ideas come easily but other times they're harder to come by. But deadlines don't care whether or not I'm having a hard time. Finishing work on time even if I'm having a hard time is the

So-Hee Park

toughest thing.

The background of <Goong> is very unique. What's the reason for the set-up of having Korea still ruled by a king in the story?

I thought it would be very interesting if Korea still had a monarchy. If we had the royal family, we would've watched their lives closely and our traditional culture would've been preserved better. I also thought that the royal family would've helped with the reunification of Korea. Furthermore, Korea would have fared better in the wake of the Japanese occupation. I think a king has a way of bringing a country together.

You started working on <Goong> when you were in 10th grade. What's the story behind the creation of the book?

In 1994, my friends and I skipped a class and went to King Soo-Ro Kim's Tomb in Kimhae, Kyung-Nam. Parts of the old palace near the tomb were empty and looked sad. I thought how wonderful it would be if the place was full with people. I extended my imagination to Gyeongbok Palace and I started to think what if a king, a queen and a prince still lived in the palace. I became obsessed with the idea even though I was in the middle of exams.

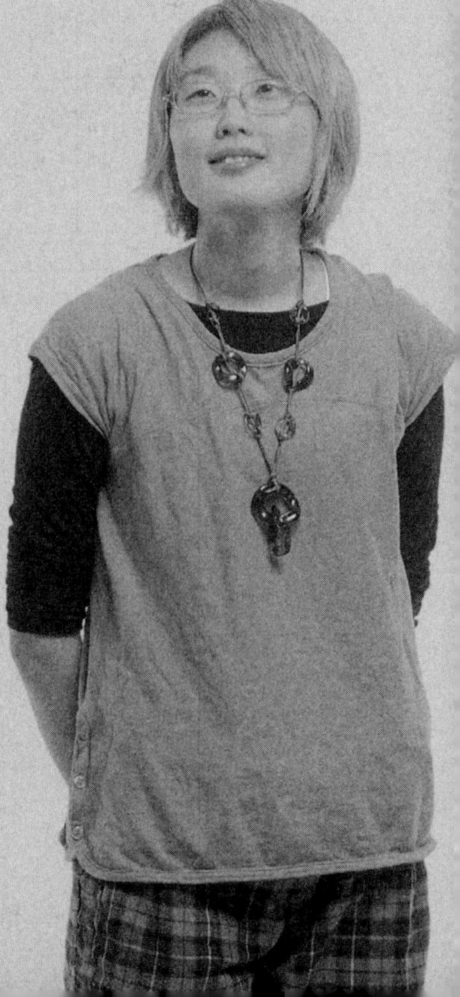

I heard the art for <Goong> that you did in high school is different from now. What are those drawings like and how are they different from your current art?

It's natural that the drawings back then were very different from now since I was just a super beginner. The story is different too. In the old story, Chae-Kyung was going out with Shin not knowing he was a prince. They got married because paparazzi took pictures of them during a school field trip. Also, Shin had younger siblings and the king had a second wife too. I remember rushing the story to a happy ending because my friends told me that I'd get a great treat from them when I finished.

You must have great love towards the characters in the book since you have worked on them since high school.

Of course. They have a great influence on me not only in the book but also in real life. I feel like they are my family because I've been thinking about them for so long. When I see a pretty dress, I think "That would look good on Chae-Kyung." When I go to a nice place, I think "Shin and Chae-Kyung would love this." No matter how much time you work on a book, all characters are like family to the creator. They eat, watch TV, and listen to music, etc. with me all the time. They observe everything I do.

Chae-Kyung is a very lovely character. Is there a model for her? And are there models for Shin and Yul as well?

Before casting was completed for the 〈Goong〉 TV show, I said in an interview that "X might be good as Chae-Kyung." But some people twisted that to "X was the model for Chae-Kyung" and that upset me. That interview was done way before I signed the contract for the TV show and I didn't say anything about models for the characters. I don't have models for the main characters.

You must have thoroughly researched the palaces and the hanbok for <Goong>. How did you do your research?

I visited Gyeongbok Palace but mostly my research is from books. I got a lot of help from 〈The Study of Customs in the Palace〉, 〈The Education of the Crown Prince〉, and 〈The Royal Costumes and Life of the Chosun Dynasty〉. I'd love to visit more palaces

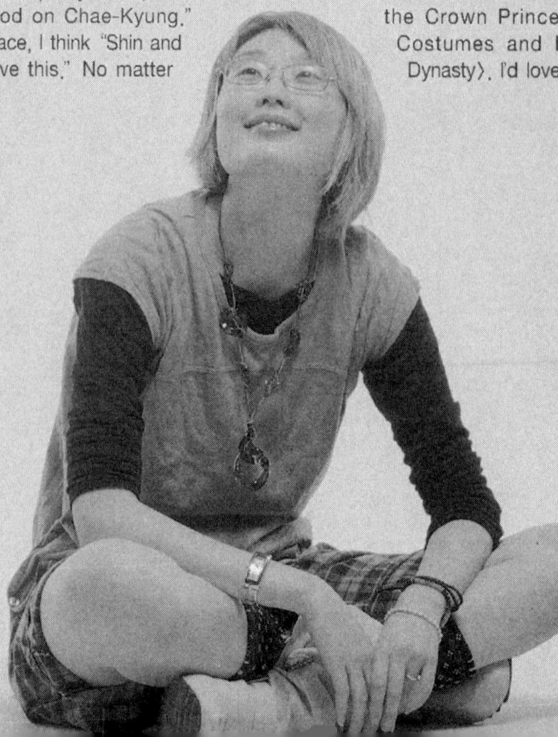

but I have no time.

Did you discover any interesting customs during your research?

When a king sleeps in one of his mistresses' places, she has to go to the queen in the morning. It's like apologizing to the queen. "I'm sorry I served the king instead of you." Another interesting custom was that when a new maid joined the staff, one of the eunuchs would ceremoniously pretend to "burn" her mouth. This was to warn her not to tell other people about what was going on in the palace. I may use this in the book someday.

Could you tell us the most difficult thing you encountered while working on <Goong>?

I found a lot of interesting things while I studied royal customs and history. And I want to use some of that in my book but it's hard to incorporate them smoothly within the story. It's easy when the story slows down, but really hard if the pace is picking up. I feel I have to work more to be a better writer.

The hanbok in <Goong> are very beautiful. Are all those styles hard to draw?

It's not so difficult. I'm happy to draw different styles of hanbok.

I heard that <Goong> is very hot in Japan. How do you feel about your book being published in the country where manga originated?

"Very hot" is a bit of an exaggeration, but the truth is that it's doing better than I thought. I get postcards and letters from Japanese readers and I've noticed the similarities and differences between our two cultures. I hear about many Korean TV shows tailoring themselves for Japanese viewers so they can be exported to Japan. But I think the Korean story style is more fun and interesting to foreigners. The same goes for manhwa too. It's so amazing that Japanese people read and talk about my book, but it puts some pressure on me as well. I'm worried that Japanese readers will think <Goong> is political because it's talking about the monarchy which no longer exists in Korea. Japan still has a king so I'm also worried about how Japanese people think about this book. Anyway, it's bit of a relief that it is doing okay.

What do you consider your best scene and best dialogue from the series?

It's quite embarrassing to talk about the best scene or the best dialogue in my book. But the most memorable scene to me is the one in which Chae-Kyung puts on the traditional wedding dress to get married in volume 1. And the best dialogue line would be "Can I live without you?" from volume 7. That is Shin's line to Chae-Kyung during the school field trip. I like it because that is the first time Shin shows his true feelings.

So-Hee Park

<Goong> is super popular. Does this put pressure on you for the next project?

It's true that I feel a lot of pressure from <Goong> becoming more popular than I expected. But I think working on a new project puts pressure on a creator whether or not the previous work was popular. I'm excited about working on a new book, a new world, and new characters. I'm also worried about how well I do and what readers will think about the new book. But I decided not to scare myself about the worst case scenario before I became a well-known manhwa creator. So, for my next book, I'll just do what I want and not worry. I have so many ideas that I want to work on, from a story set in the Middle Ages, to something set in a school, to some historical fiction, to a story about old people, to a story about animals and so on. I haven't decided when I'll finish <Goong> so I'd like to concentrate on that before deciding on my next book.

You once said <Goong> had to be funny no matter what. What is the most exciting and amusing scene for you?

Chae-Kyung and Shin's first night together. I feel like I'm projecting some of my own desires on Chae-Kyung in that scene. I worried about what readers would think of Chae-Kyung being so aggressive and honest about her sexual desires. But...ha-ha-ha...readers loved the scene. I wonder if they're projecting something too (laugh).

Can you tell us about a proud or happy moment you've had while working on <Goong>?

This may sound too obvious but I feel proud and happy when readers tell me <Goong> is really fun. I'm a human being too so I get hurt by critics and I feel happy when people cheer for me. My reaction is very simple because my brain is simple. So many good things have happened while I worked on <Goong>. Many people have heard about me as a manhwa creator, I've won many awards, and I've had many opportunities to visit foreign countries to talk to different comic book creators. I also feel happy about small things such as sitting and doing nothing after finishing some pages on time, my penciling looking better than the thumbnails, and getting letters from fans.

Section 3 *The TV show : <Goong>*

Many manhwa are made into TV shows, musicals, and movies. What do you think about this trend?

Of course that is a good trend. But I think it's important to respect the creator and the original work with any adaptation. It's important that any changes made to the story are agreeable to the original creator. Because the original story is very closely related to the creator.

Did you hesitate when you first got the offer to make <Goong> as a TV show?

Like other manhwa creators, I sometimes think about how this actress would be good as this character from the book I'm currently working on. It's not because I hope my book becomes a TV show, but it's fun to imagine things and it helps me to humanize the characters. I wasn't hesitant but I was a bit worried about the genre of ⟨Goong⟩ when I got the offer. TV shows are usually divided into two genres: realistic and slice-of-life stories or fantasy stories. I thought it would be hard to make ⟨Goong⟩ because of the complex genre of the book. But I think it will be a positive thing, if my book helps to create some variety in terms of genre in TV shows. I hope to see some good results as the creator and a viewer thanks to hard work of the people involved with the show.

What was your expectation from the director?

I told Mr. Whang that I wanted him to show beautiful hanbok and our traditional culture on the show. I thought it would be great to show them in color on TV because there was that limitation in the black and white manhwa book. It's difficult to express colors or space realistically on the page. This is not only because my skills aren't good enough but also because manhwa books have their limitations. Actually, I wanted him to create his own style of story and characters because TV is a different medium. But I didn't think it was my place to ask this of him.

Did you make any special requests of the writer of the TV show?

I asked her to make sure that she wrote a different ending from the book.

So-Hee Park

People complained about the main characters. What do you think about the casting?
A manhwa book is a totally different medium from a TV show. And they have different systems. The staff, actors, and actresses I met from the 〈Goong〉 TV show perfectly understood the characters of the book. They seemed to have studied hard and were passionate about the characters. I was sad to hear complaints about the casting but I also realized that so many fans cared about Chae-Kyung, Shin, Yul and Hyo-Rin. People who love 〈Goong〉 and people who worry about the casting see the characters as their friends or people they know. I think Chae-Kyung and Shin were reborn as real people who live among the readers. After the TV writer read the book, Chae-Kyung was reborn in her heart like other readers. Chae-Kyung from the book and the TV show will be different and it's the staff's job to cast the right person for the characters of the TV show. I hope readers understand that.

The TV show <Goong> is on air now. You must have different feelings as the creator.
I should feel so happy or something but I don't. It's because I got the original offer quite a long time ago and I'm always too busy working on the deadline for the magazine. I feel quite calm because I always thought that manhwa books were different from TV shows. My friends from high school who witnessed the creation of 〈Goong〉 are more excited and happy about it.

Have you met the actors and the actresses who play the main characters on the TV show?
I met them once. I didn't try to compare them with the characters from my book. I think it's up to the writers and the actors to analyze the characters for the TV show. I won't be surprised even if Chae-Kyung and Shin are different from my book. That would be more fun too.

I personally like the TV show because it tries different things. What do you like most about the show?
I love the art. So many experts are working on the show and I often think "This is so amazing." Every scene is beautiful and artful. I especially love the set. The set was beautiful when I saw it in person but it's more beautiful on TV. I also like Chae-Kyung's character. Of course I love the other actors and actresses but Chae-Kyung, who is played by Eun-Hye Yoon, is so lovable. It's quite refreshing to see her a little bit different from the book.

What is the most impressive scene from the TV show?
I love the wedding scene which is similar to the original but with added color. And I'm impressed by Chae-

Kyung and Shin's tango scene which the book doesn't have. I'm also impressed by Chae-Kyung and Shin's first night together which is very funny with the maids' comic faces.

The TV show's ratings are very high. Did you expect the show to be that popular?

The success of a TV show is only determined by ratings nowadays. I tried not to think about that because it seemed greedy but as the creator I still wanted the show to be loved. I also thought about the people who worked hard to make the show as good as it is. Anyway, I'm happy that the show is popular but I'm embarrassed when people congratulate me for doing nothing. I hope it leaves people with a good impression. (I'm talking very cool but I may pray for ratings later. Mwa-ha-ha.)

Do you feel any pressure because of the show? Does it stress you out?

I'm actually relieved because the TV show is doing well. But I don't know what to do when the TV show does something similar I've been thinking to use in my book. I thought about a scene in which Chae-Kyung and Shin would go to Jeju Island so I took a lot of pictures there last summer. But the TV show already aired a similar scene so I'm wondering what to do. I have other stories but I'll stop here because I don't want to spoil the book...

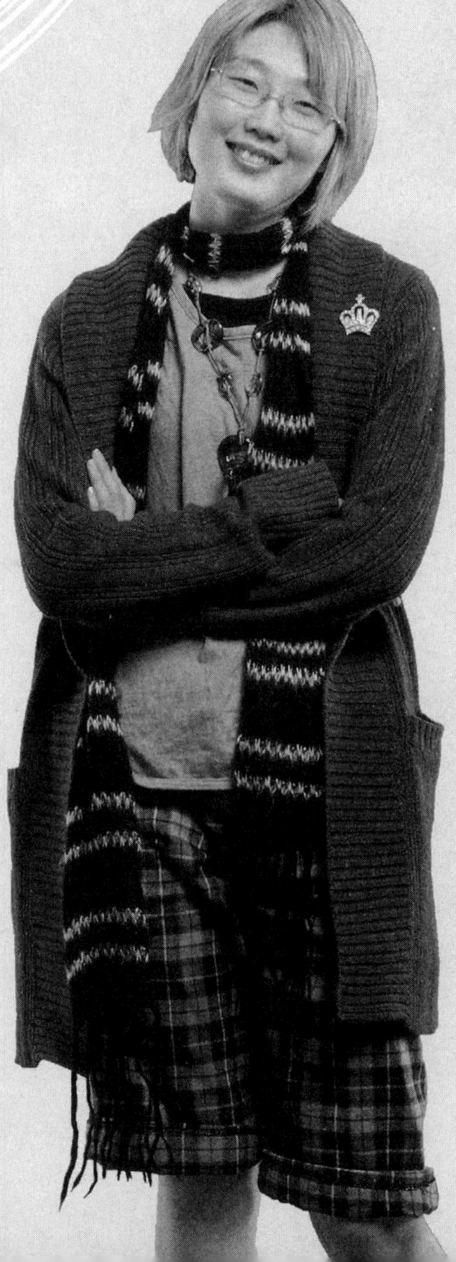

Wonderfully illustrated
modern day crossover
fantasy, available at
your local bookstore
or comic shop!

Apart from the fact her
eyes turn red when the moon
rises, Myung-Ee is your average,
albeit boy-crazy, 5th grader. After
picking a fight with her classmate
Yu-Da Lee, she discovers a startling
secret: the two of them are "earth
rabbits" being hunted by the "fox
tribe" of the moon!
Five years pass and Myung-Ee
transfers to a new school in search of
pretty boys. There, she unexpectedly
reunites with Yu-Da. The problem is
he doesn't remember a thing about
her or their shared past!

Moon Boy 월요일 소년 1~6

Lee YoungYou

Yen Press
www.yenpress.com

Totally new Arabian nights, where Shahrazad is a guy!

Everyone knows the story of Shahrazad and her wonderful tales from the Arabian Nights. For one thousand and one nights, the stories that she created entertained the mad Sultan and eventually saved her life. In this version, Shahrazad is a guy who wanted to save his sister from the mad Sultan by disguising himself as a woman. When he puts his life on the line, what kind of strange and unique stories would he tell? This new twist on one of the greatest classical tales might just keep you awake for another ONE THOUSAND AND ONE NIGHTS.

Yen Press
www.yenpress.com

Available at bookstores near you!

One thousand and one nights 1~7

Han SeungHee · Jeon JinSeok

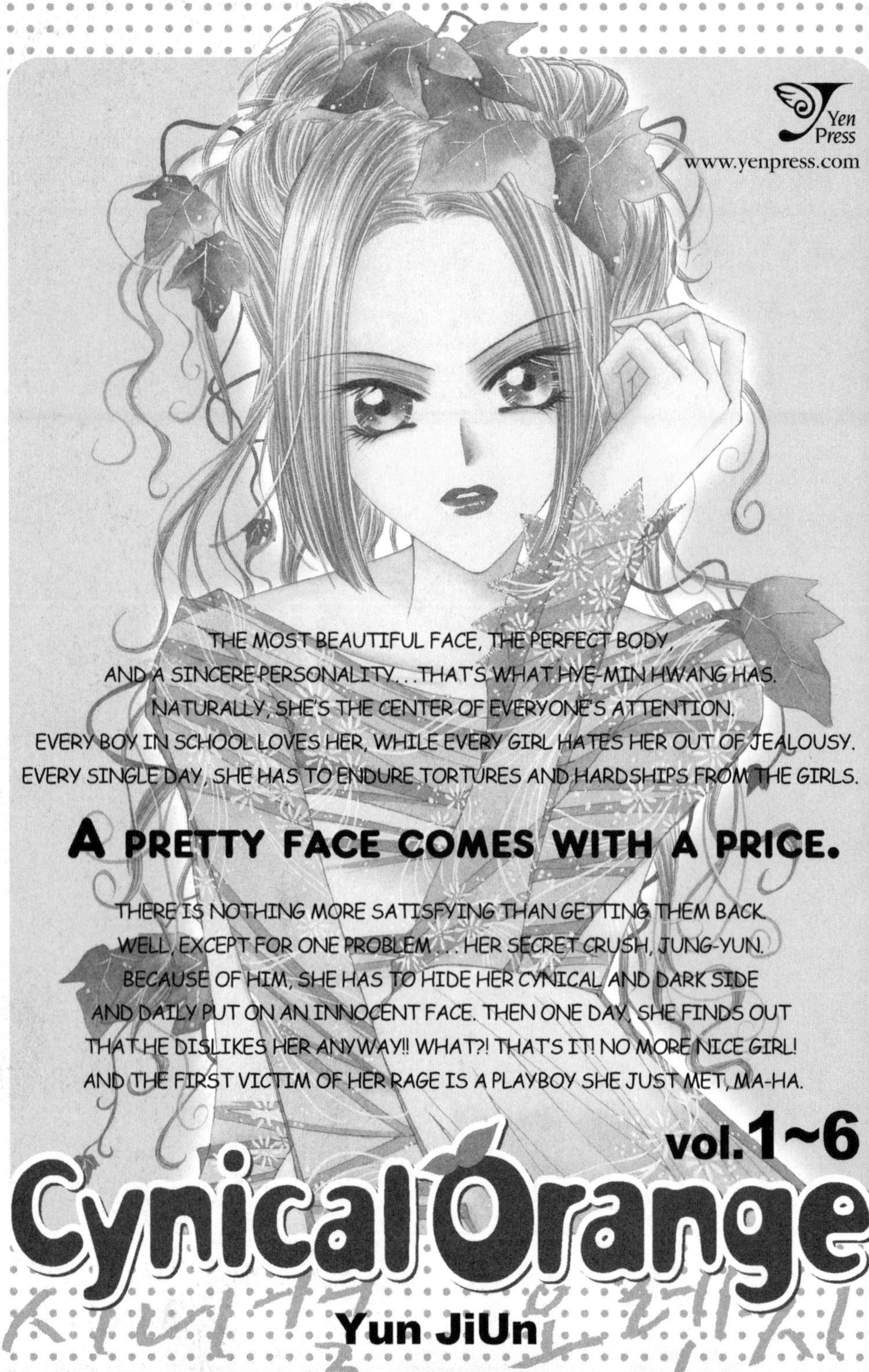
Yen Press
www.yenpress.com
THE MOST BEAUTIFUL FACE, THE PERFECT BODY,
AND A SINCERE PERSONALITY. . .THAT'S WHAT HYE-MIN HWANG HAS.
NATURALLY, SHE'S THE CENTER OF EVERYONE'S ATTENTION.
EVERY BOY IN SCHOOL LOVES HER, WHILE EVERY GIRL HATES HER OUT OF JEALOUSY.
EVERY SINGLE DAY, SHE HAS TO ENDURE TORTURES AND HARDSHIPS FROM THE GIRLS.
A PRETTY FACE COMES WITH A PRICE.
THERE IS NOTHING MORE SATISFYING THAN GETTING THEM BACK.
WELL, EXCEPT FOR ONE PROBLEM . . . HER SECRET CRUSH, JUNG-YUN.
BECAUSE OF HIM, SHE HAS TO HIDE HER CYNICAL AND DARK SIDE
AND DAILY PUT ON AN INNOCENT FACE. THEN ONE DAY, SHE FINDS OUT
THAT HE DISLIKES HER ANYWAY!! WHAT?! THAT'S IT! NO MORE NICE GIRL!
AND THE FIRST VICTIM OF HER RAGE IS A PLAYBOY SHE JUST MET, MA-HA.
vol.1~6
Cynical Orange
Yun JiUn

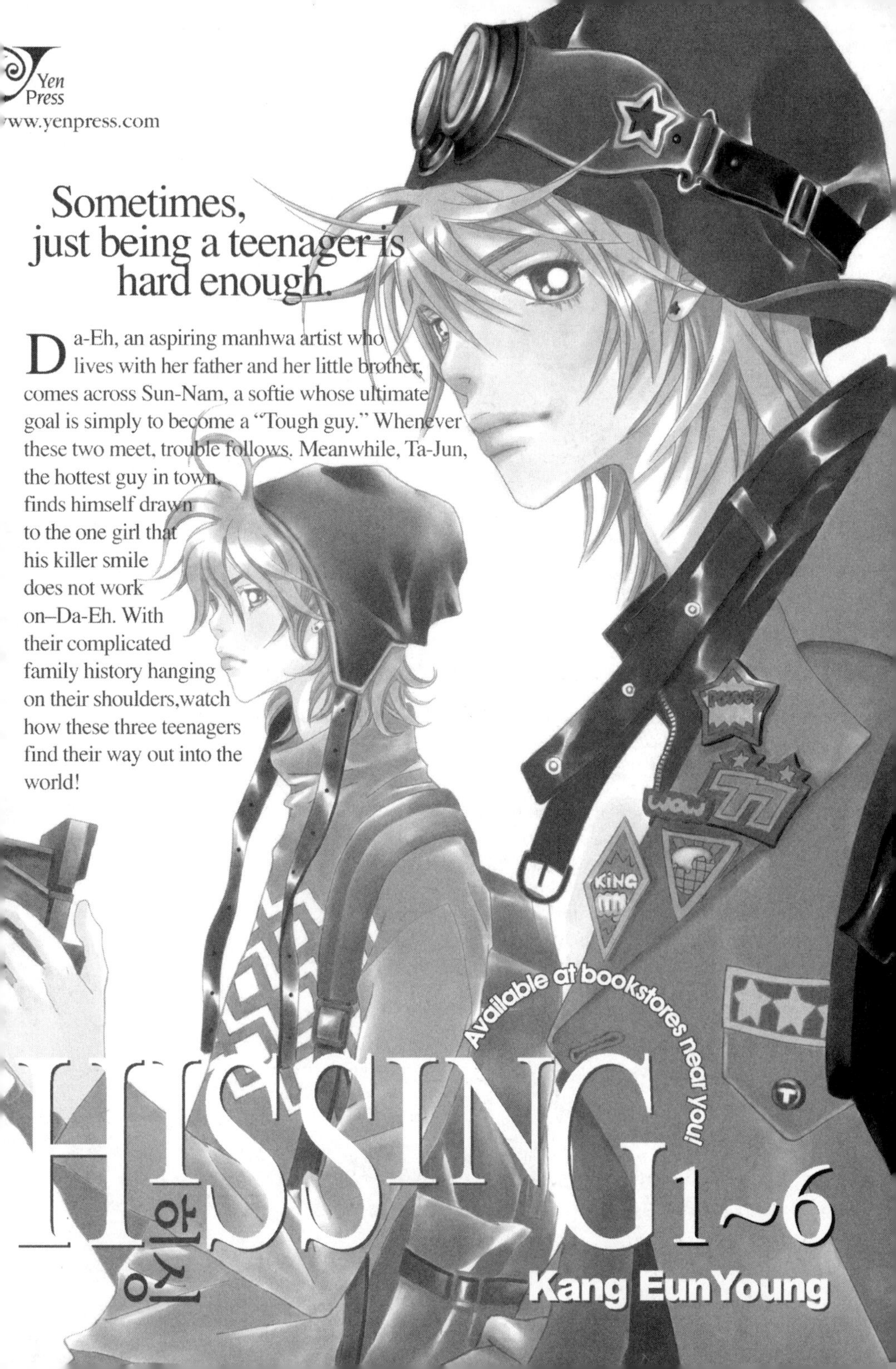
Yen Press
www.yenpress.com
Sometimes, just being a teenager is hard enough.
Da-Eh, an aspiring manhwa artist who lives with her father and her little brother, comes across Sun-Nam, a softie whose ultimate goal is simply to become a "Tough guy." Whenever these two meet, trouble follows. Meanwhile, Ta-Jun, the hottest guy in town, finds himself drawn to the one girl that his killer smile does not work on–Da-Eh. With their complicated family history hanging on their shoulders,watch how these three teenagers find their way out into the world!
Available at bookstores near you!
HISSING 1~6
히싱
Kang EunYoung

The newest title from the creators of <Demon Diary> and <Angel Diary>!

Once upon a time, a selfish king summoned the monstrous Bulkirin into the real world. The monster killed half of all human beings, leaving the rest helpless as to what to do. That is, until one day when a hero appeared and defeated the Bulkirin with the legendary "Seven Blade Sword." But… what does all this have to do with 8th grader Eun-Gyo Sung?! First, she gets suspended from school for fighting. Then, she runs away from home. The last thing she needed was to be kidnapped—and whisked into the past by a mysterious stranger named No-Ah!

Available at bookstores near you!

Legend

1-4

K a r a · W o o S o o J u n g

www.yenpress.com

Available at bookstores near you!

CHOCOLAT

1~7

Shin JiSang · Geo

Kum-ji was a little late getting under the spell
of the chart-topping band, DDL. Unable to
join the DDL fan club, she almost gives up
on meeting her idols, until she develops a
cunning plan–to become a member of a
rival fan club for the brand-new boy band
Yo-I. This way she can act as Yo-I's fan
club member and also be near Yo-I,

How far would you go to meet your favorite boy band?

who always seem to be in the
same shows as DDL. Perfect
plan...except being a fanatic is a lot
more complicated than she
expects. Especially when you're
actually a fan of someone else. This
full-blown love comedy about a fan
club will make you laugh, cry, and
laugh some more.

Yen
Press
www.yenpress.com

THE HIGHLY ANTICIPATED NEW TITLE FROM THE CREATORS OF <DEMON DIARY>!

Dong-Young is a royal daughter of heaven, betrothed to the King of Hell. Determined to escape her fate, she runs away before the wedding. The four Guardians of Heaven are ordered to find the angel princess while she's hiding out on planet Earth – disguised as a boy! Will she be able to escape from her faith?! This is a cute gender-bending tale, a romantic comedy/fantasy book about an angel, the King of Hell, and four super-powered chaperones...

Angel Diary 1~8

Kara · Lee YunHee

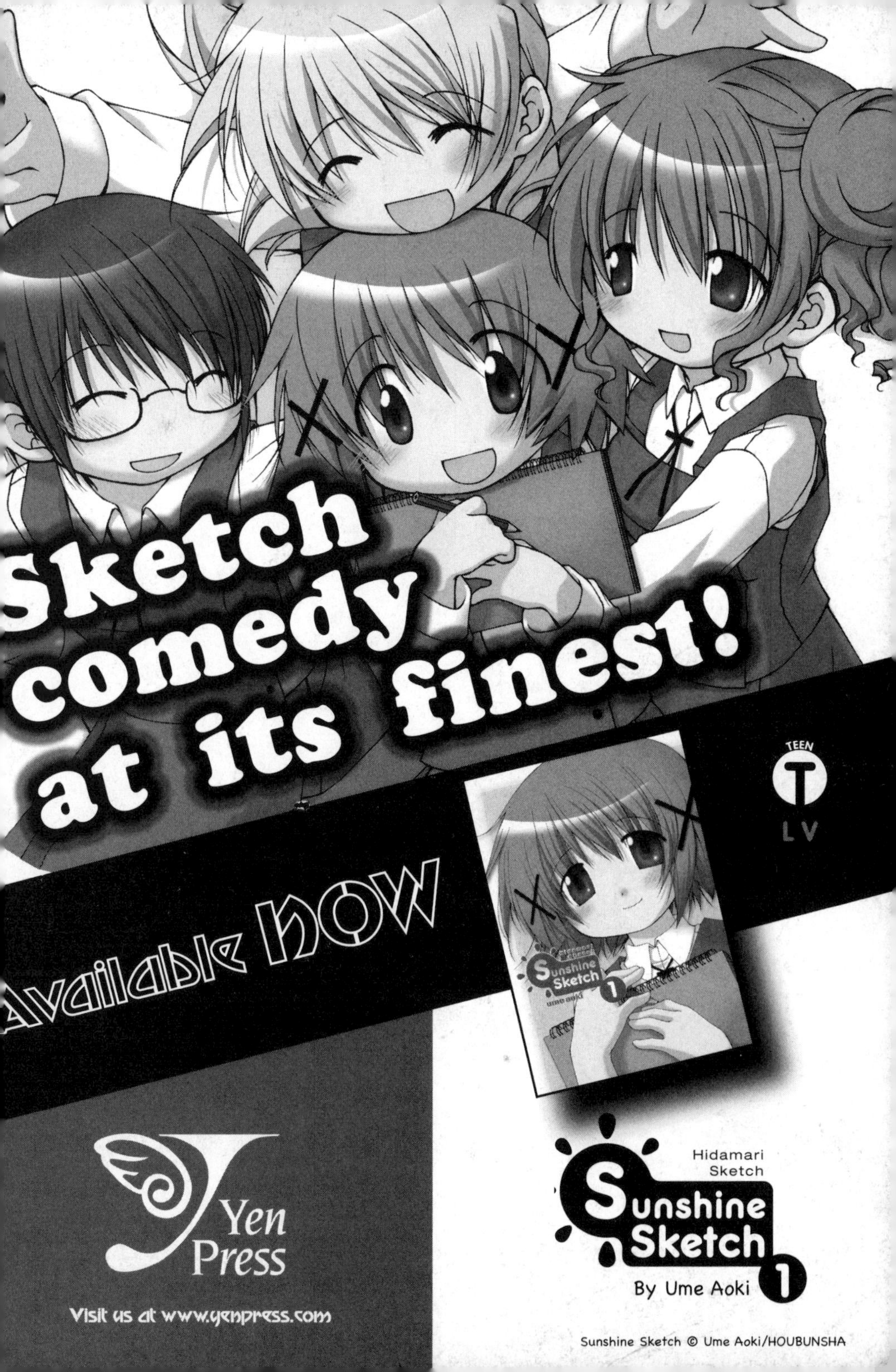
Sketch comedy at its finest!
TEEN
T
LV
Available NOW
Sunshine Sketch 1
ume aoki
Yen Press
Visit us at www.yenpress.com
Hidamari Sketch
Sunshine Sketch 1
By Ume Aoki
Sunshine Sketch © Ume Aoki/HOUBUNSHA

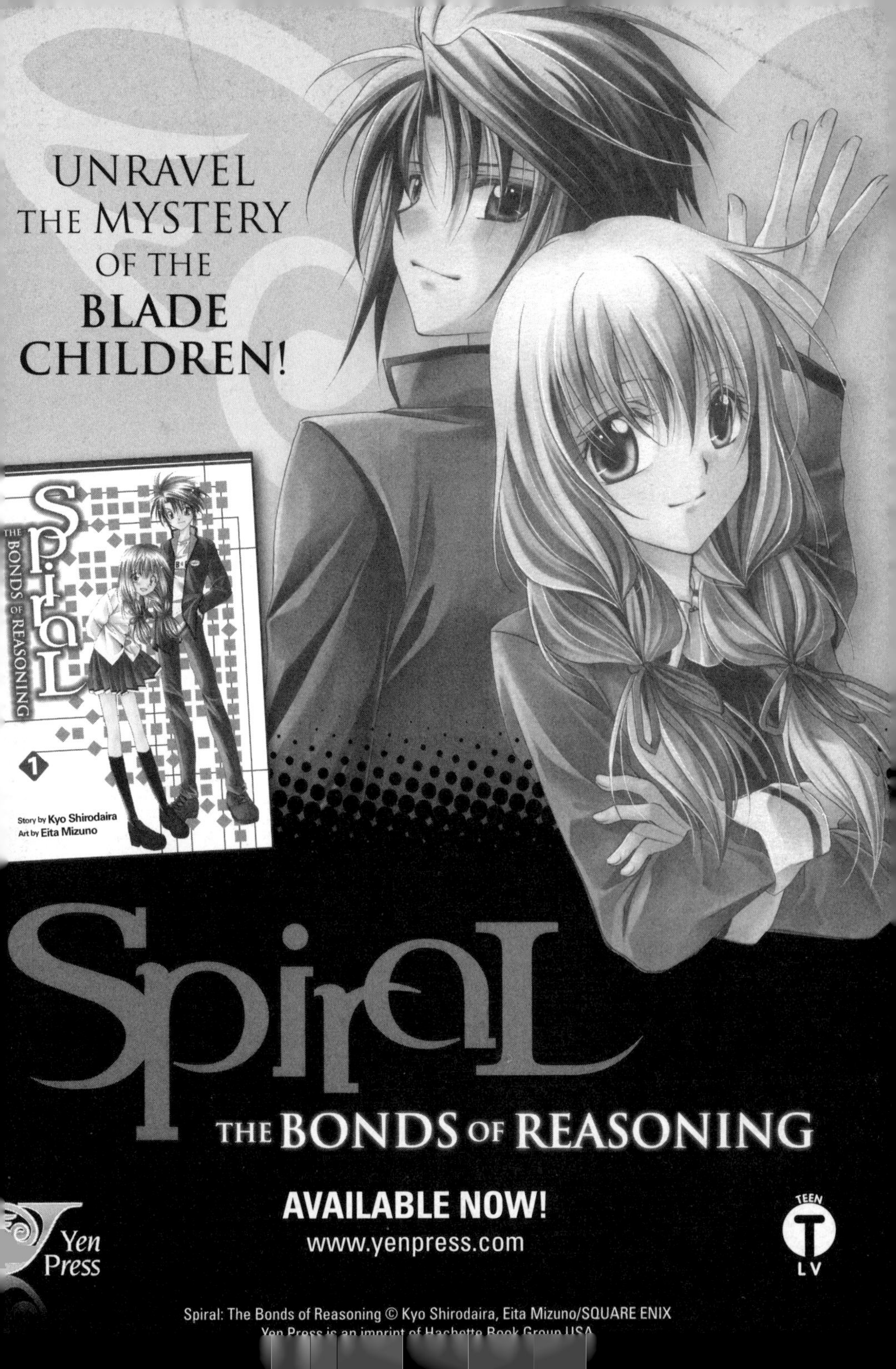
UNRAVEL THE MYSTERY OF THE BLADE CHILDREN!
Spiral
THE BONDS OF REASONING
1
Story by Kyo Shirodaira
Art by Eita Mizuno
Spiral
THE BONDS OF REASONING
AVAILABLE NOW!
www.yenpress.com
Yen Press
TEEN
T
LV
Spiral: The Bonds of Reasoning © Kyo Shirodaira, Eita Mizuno/SQUARE ENIX
Yen Press is an imprint of Hachette Book Group USA

Goong vol. 1

Story and art by SoHee Park

Translation HyeYoung Im
English Adaptation J. Torres
Lettering Terri Delgado · Marshall Dillon

Goong, Vol. 1 © 2002 SoHee Park. All rights reserved. First published in Korea in 2002 by Seoul Cultural Publishers, Inc. English translation rights arranged by Seoul Cultural Publishers, Inc.

The characters and events in this book are fictitious. Any similarity to real persons, living or dead, is coincidental and not intended by the author.

Yen Press
Hachette Book Group
237 Park Avenue, New York, NY 10017

Visit our Web sites at www.HachetteBookGroup.com and www.YenPress.com.

Yen Press is an imprint of Hachette Book Group, Inc. The Yen Press name and logo are trademarks of Hachette Book Group, Inc.

First Printing: December 2006
First Yen Press Edition: February 2009

ISBN: 978-89-527-4487-6

10 9 8 7 6 5 4 3 2

BVG

Printed in the United States of America